THE MAN WHO
SHOCKED THE WORLD

THE MAN WHO
SHOCKED THE WORLD

The Life and Legacy of
Stanley Milgram

THOMAS BLASS, PH.D.

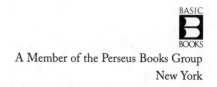

A Member of the Perseus Books Group
New York

Text excerpts throughout. Figures 4 and 6, Experiment 5, from *Obedience to Authority: An Experimental View* by Stanley Milgram. Copyright © 1974 by Stanley Milgram. Reprinted by permission of HarperCollins Publishers Inc.

Books published by Basic Books are available at special discounts for bulk purchases in the United States by corporations, institutions, and other organizations. For more information, please contact the Special Markets Department at the Perseus Books Group, 11 Cambridge Center, Cambridge MA 02142, or call (617) 252-5298, (800) 255-1514 or e-mail special.markets@perseusbooks.com.

Designed by Brent Wilcox
Set in 11-point Adobe Caslon by Perseus Books Group

Library of Congress Cataloging-in-Publication Data
Blass, Thomas.
    The man who shocked the world : the life and legacy of Stanley Milgram / Thomas Blass.—1st ed.
        p.   cm.
    Includes bibliographical references and index
    ISBN 0-7382-0399-8
    1. Milgram, Stanley.   2. Social psychologists—United States—Biography. 3. Authority.   4. Obedience.   5. Social psychology.   6. Social psychology—Experiments.   I. Title.

HM1031.M55B57   2004
302'.092—dc22

                                                                    203023841

First Edition
04 05 06 / 10 9 8 7 6 5 4 3 2 1

To
ANNE

CONTENTS

During the summer of 1944, the Nazis, under the direction of Eichmann and with the assistance of their Hungarian allies, were in the process of rounding up the Jews of Budapest for deportation to the gas chambers of Auschwitz. Budapest is split by the Danube River into two parts: Buda and Pest. One day during the roundups, a Jewish mother and her two-and-a-half-year-old child were taking the trolley from Pest, where they had been visiting relatives, to Buda, where they had recently found an apartment. Unlike most of her fellow Jews, this woman believed the rumors about what "resettlement for work in the east" really meant. So rather than remaining in Pest, she obtained forged Christian identity papers and moved to Buda, which was largely non-Jewish. The trolley was crossing the bridge between the two parts of the city when the rhythmic clatter of the car's wheels was interrupted by the insistent sound of the child's voice: "Mommy," he asked, "why don't I wear a cap like other Jewish boys?" This was within earshot of many of the other passengers, including members of the Nyilas, the Hungarian Nazi militia. With a resourcefulness spawned by desperation, the mother quickly turned to her child and said, "This is our stop," grabbed his hand, and got off the trolley—right in the middle of the bridge, quite a distance from their destination. Miraculously, no one stopped them.

I was that little boy on the bridge. As I grew into adulthood, my mind would occasionally drift back to that precarious moment on the trolley—when time seemed to stand still, enabling my mother to act quickly—and I would ask myself: What was special about that moment? Surely, if I had made the same remark before the war, my mother would not have taken evasive action. So why did she feel so threatened then?

It was only after my training in social psychology broadened my perspective on human behavior that I came to the realization that my question, in a more general form, was one of the primary psychological puzzles underlying the mass destruction of European Jewry: What psychological mechanism transformed the average, and presumably normal, citizens of Germany and its allies into people who would carry out or tolerate unimaginable acts of cruelty against their fellow citizens who were Jewish, resulting in the death of six million of them?

It was during graduate school that I first learned about Stanley Milgram and his remarkable exploration of the human tendency to obey authority, which was to become the most famous social-psychological research of all time. In the opening paragraph of his first journal article about that research, Milgram explicitly embedded it in the Holocaust. This wasn't surprising, given that the question of how apparently normal people could so readily turn into brutal killers is first and foremost a psychological one. Indeed, psychology had been trying to explain the Holocaust since the end of World War II, and by the time Milgram's research appeared in print in 1963, a number of psychological works pertaining to the horrors perpetrated by the Nazis had already been published. What set Milgram's contribution apart was his use of a scientific laboratory experiment to help shed light on the perpetrators' behavior. In adopting an experimental approach, Milgram achieved two goals that at first might seem incompatible. He brought a degree of objectivity—relative to other forms of inquiry—to a topic that did not lend itself easily to dispassionate analysis. At the same time, by bringing the demonstration of destructive obedience closer to home, both in time and place, Milgram made it more difficult for those who learned about the experiments to distance themselves from their baleful implications.

Milgram conducted his obedience studies when he was an assistant professor, fresh out of graduate school. They marked the beginning of one of the most productive, eclectic, and innovative careers in psychology. Milgram would go on to research topics as wide-ranging as the small-world problem (also known as "six degrees of separation"), the lost-letter technique, and mental maps of cities. Several decades ago, I became curious about the human being behind the scientist and, through my research, discovered in Milgram a personality as unusual and multifaceted as his research.

This book is the product of my twenty-year immersion in Milgram's eye-opening and sometimes troubling research. Clearly, my harrowing experiences in Nazi-dominated Hungary gave me a special appreciation of the value of his most widely known work—the obedience experiments. But I wrote this book because I believe that we all stand to gain from Milgram's work, which sheds light on the most basic of human interactions and has the power to change the way we view our very social world.

ACKNOWLEDGMENTS

I met Stanley Milgram only once—at a convention of the American Psychological Association in the early 1970s. We only chatted briefly, but that encounter left a lasting impression on me. He was standing in front of the book exhibit of one of his publishers. I recognized him from photographs I had seen in psychology textbooks and went up to him to introduce myself. He knew my mentor and thesis advisor, Aaron Hershkowitz. Aaron had been in New Haven, running a post-doctoral program in social psychology at the local Veterans Administration Hospital, when Stanley was conducting his obedience experiments at Yale. When I introduced myself to Milgram, I noted my connection to Hershkowitz. He replied, "You know, I learned a lot from Aaron Hershkowitz," which astonished me. He had already achieved a good measure of fame—at the convention, as I recall, he gave a talk that drew about 1,000 people—and still had the humility to acknowledge his intellectual debts.

In the process of researching this book, I came to learn that that personal quality was only one piece—and not even an especially representative one—of a complex and sometimes puzzling personality.

There are many people who helped me, directly or indirectly, to put the pieces of the puzzle together. Although I received help from dozens of people, a few deserve special mention.

First, I want to express my deep appreciation to Sasha Milgram. I first met Sasha in the spring of 1993, spending two enchanting afternoons in her apartment, as she recalled for me the details of her life with Stanley.

Over the next 10 years there would be more visits and countless phone calls during which she gave generously and good naturedly of her time to provide me with further information and insights about Stanley. In addition, she shared with me her personal collection of papers and memorabilia, without which the story of Stanley Milgram would have been incomplete. My deep thanks also to Stanley's siblings, Joel Milgram and Marjorie Marton, who provided me with vital information, especially about Stanley's childhood. The Milgrams' children, Marc Milgram and Michèle Marques, have helped round out the picture of Stanley as father and family man.

Francois Rochat, a Milgram scholar from Switzerland, first informed me of the existence of the Stanley Milgram papers at Yale, and he has been a true friend whose constant encouragement helped to keep me focused whenever I felt overwhelmed. Harold Takooshian, one of Milgram's students, takes genuine pleasure in helping others attain their goals. Beginning with arranging for my invitation to address the American Psychological Association's convention in 1993 about Milgram, his helpfulness has continued to benefit me over the course of the past ten years. When I first began thinking seriously about writing this book, Samuel Vaughan, who was then a senior editor at Random House, provided me with the needed reassurance that it was a worthwhile undertaking and the confidence that I could do it.

Diane Kaplan, archivist at Yale University library, masterfully converted 90 boxes of papers donated by Sasha Milgram into the organized collection of the Stanley Milgram Papers, and I thank her for her helpfulness during my many research trips to New Haven. Thanks also to staff at the Harvard University Archives and the Archives of the History of American Psychology (AHAP) in Akron, Ohio. The visit to AHAP was facilitated by my receiving the J. R. Kantor Fellowship for 1998–1999, an annual award by AHAP.

Closer to home, thanks are due the staff at the UMBC library, especially Michael Romary, for the valuable assistance they have provided for many years. And I want to express my deep appreciation to my department chairman, Carlo DiClemente, for his supportiveness during both the research and writing phases of the biography.

I have been fortunate to have the services of two talented people, my agent Theresa Park and my editor Amanda Cook. Both shared my vision of the biography and helped turn it into reality. Amanda's enthusiasm, combined with her exacting standards, made her the ideal editor for the book. And many thanks to Michael Denneny, who worked tirelessly in helping me with needed revisions to the manuscript.

A vital part of the research for the book was the information and insights provided by dozens of people—Milgram's colleagues, students, and others—during the course of interviews and conversations, in person or by telephone, and in a few cases via e-mail. At the risk of forgetting a few, I want to thank the following individuals: Robert Abelson, Scott Armstrong, George Bellak, Arthur Asa Berger, Sidney Blatt, Norman Bradburn, Joseph Brostek, Roger Brown, Jerome Bruner, Robbie Chafitz, Stephen P. Cohen, Lane Conn, Tom Cottle, Rosamond Dana, Florence Denmark, Alan Elms, Paul Errera, Kenneth Feigenbaum, Roy Feldman, Hilry Fisher, Eva Fogelman, Bernard Fried, Harry From, Sam Gaertner, Joan Gerver, Lt. Col. Dave Grossman, Paul Hollander, Ronna Kabatznick, Irwin Katz, Herb Kelman, James Korn, Nijole Kudirka, Howard Leventhal, Leon Mann, Brendan Maher, Elinor Mannucci, Robert McDonough, Murray Melbin, William Menold, Hedwin Naimark, Robert Palmer, Robert Panzarella, E. L. Pattullo, James Pennebaker, Tom Pettigrew, Sharon Presley, Salomon Rettig, Eleanor Rosch, Robert Rosenthal, John Rothman, Eva Sabena, John Sabini, Ann Saltzman, John Shaffer, Vincent Sherman, Leonard Siger, Maury Silver, Chas Smith, Saul Sternberg, Phil Stone, Hans Toch, Judith Waters, Arthur Weinberger, Rabbi Avi Weiss, Walter Weiss, Herb Winer, David Winter, Ed Zigler, and Philip Zimbardo.

And last but not least, I want to acknowledge the assistance of my wife, Anne. Thanking one's spouse has become almost cliché. But it is literally true that this book would not have happened without Anne's loving and devoted assistance. She was the one who first suggested turning my interest in Milgram's life and work into a biography, and it was her gentle but insistent prodding that finally made me decide to undertake this project. It was her unflagging good cheer and support, both in spirit and substance—which included help with word processing at odd hours of the day and night—on top of her own daytime job and taking care of our children, that made a daunting task immeasurably less so.

PROLOGUE

A substantial proportion of people do what they are told to do, irrespective of the content of the act and without limitations of conscience, so long as they perceive that the command comes from a legitimate authority. . . . This is, perhaps, the most fundamental lesson of our study: ordinary people, simply doing their jobs, and without any particular hostility on their part, can become agents in a terrible destructive process.

—STANLEY MILGRAM, 1974

Stanley Milgram entered the public consciousness—with a jolt—in the fall of 1963. Newspapers around the country were reporting a startling discovery he had made in his psychology laboratory at Yale in conducting what became known as "the obedience experiments." He found that average, presumably normal, groups of residents of New Haven, Connecticut, would readily inflict very painful, and possibly harmful, electric shocks on an innocent victim whose actions did not merit such harsh treatment. As part of an experiment supposedly dealing with the effects of punishment on learning, subjects were required by an experimenter to shock a learner every time he made an error on a verbal learning task, and to increase the intensity of the shock in 15-volt steps, from 15 to 450 volts, on each subsequent error. The results: 65 percent of the subjects continued to obey the experimenter to the end, simply because he commanded them to.

These groundbreaking and controversial experiments have had—and continue to have—enduring significance, because they demonstrated with stunning clarity that ordinary individuals could be induced by an authority figure to act destructively, even in the absence of physical coercion, and that it didn't take evil or aberrant individuals to carry out actions that were immoral and inhumane. More generally, Milgram's findings have sensitized us to our malleability in the face of social pressure, reshaping our conceptions of individual morality. While one might think that when confronted with a moral dilemma we will act as our conscience dictates, Milgram's obedience experiments taught us—dramatically—that, in a concrete situation containing powerful social pressures, our moral sense can readily get trampled underfoot.

...

Social psychology is the branch of psychology that studies the way our thoughts, feelings, and behavior are affected, directly or indirectly, by other people. Since most of our daily activities involve interacting with other people, a typical social psychology course covers a wide range of normal behaviors, such as first impressions, attraction, hostility, group pressure, and helpfulness.

The field has a long past and a short history. It is as old as human beings' attempts to understand and predict others' behaviors. Ancient writings are filled with insights about social behavior that have withstood the test of time. For example, the following statement is found in the *Talmud,* the compendium of Jewish scholarship written thousands of years ago: "Do not look at the container, but at what is in it." This advice was based on a truism, repeatedly verified by modern experimental research: that a person's acceptance of an argument will be affected by the persuader's attractiveness, race, or gender—all irrelevant to the argument.

In spite of its ancient roots, social psychology as an experimental science is very new—just over 100 years old. The first experiment in social psychology is credited to a psychologist named Norman Triplett, whose study appeared in the *American Journal of Psychology* in 1897. Triplett demonstrated by means of a laboratory experiment that subjects performed a manual task (winding fishing reels) faster when they were in direct competition with another person than when they worked alone.

Stanley Milgram began his professional career in the 1960s, when American social psychology was in its ascendancy, a trajectory that had begun after World War II. Social psychologists in the postwar years possessed unbounded self-confidence about their ability to develop theories and methods that would provide new insights about social behavior.

Social psychology's favorable self-image in the early 1960s had two sources. First, many social psychologists had found their skills put to good use during World War II in such areas as morale, propaganda, survey research, and programs of attitude and behavior change—for example, getting consumers to change their dietary habits and eat unpopular but nutritious foods in an effort to conserve scarce resources. Even more important was the influence of Kurt Lewin, a prewar refugee from Nazi Germany, who is generally considered to be the father of experimental social psychology.

During much of the first half of the twentieth century, American academic psychology was dominated by behaviorism, a movement that was pioneered by John Watson, a psychologist at Johns Hopkins University. Watson attempted to create an objective, experimental science of behavior. Dismissing attempts to study inner experience as pseudoscientific, he launched behaviorism in 1913 in an article in the journal *Psychological Review.* The article, which has come to be known as "the behaviorists' manifesto" began as follows:

Psychology as the behaviorist views it is a purely objective experimental branch of natural science. . . . Introspection forms no essential part of its methods, nor is the scientific value of its data dependent upon the readiness with which they lend themselves to interpretation in terms of consciousness.

Watson's manifesto was an attack on the prevailing view of the appropriate subject matter and primary method of experimental psychology, traceable to Wilhelm Wundt, who founded the first psychological laboratory, at the University of Leipzig in 1879. For Wundt, the goal of psychological experimentation was to study the contents of the mind, or consciousness, through the method of introspection. Although becoming an introspectionist required intensive training, the technique turned out to be unreliable, with psychologists in different laboratories obtaining different results even though they used the same methods.

Although Watson's critique was a needed corrective, he went overboard in dismissing subjective experience as beyond the pale of scientific inquiry. The most important heir to Watson's behaviorism was B.F. Skinner, who made reinforcement a central concept of his own radical form of behaviorism. For Skinner, when a behavioral response to a stimulus was followed by reinforcement—a rewarding consequence—a bond was created between the stimulus and the response. For example, if a pigeon in a cage finds that pecking (the response) on a red disc (the stimulus) would deliver food in a tray below it (the reinforcement) but pecking on a green disc would not, it will learn to repeatedly peck on the red disc and ignore the green one.

Behaviorism's grip on American psychology during the first half of the twentieth century encompassed the subdiscipline of social psychology. The first textbook establishing social psychology as a standard course, Floyd Allport's *Social Psychology,* published in 1924, embraced behaviorism. It emphasized the role of learning and conditioning in social behavior.

For the behaviorist, there was nothing distinctively "social" about social behavior. Social psychology was still a psychology of the individual in which other people were merely another class of stimuli—social stimuli—that, in a manner similar to physical stimuli, would produce learned responses. As John Dashiell, an adherent of this approach, wrote in 1935 in a chapter reviewing social-psychological research conducted between 1914 and 1934, "Particularly is it to be borne in mind that in this objective stimulus-response relationship of an individual to his fellows we have to deal with no radically new concepts, no principles essentially additional to those applying to nonsocial situations." His chapter covered experiments that examined the effects of the presence of other people on an individual's performance on mechanical tasks, verbal tests, and puzzles. These kinds of experiments were relatively simplistic and sterile and failed to capture the richness and complexity of real-life social interactions.

It took the ingenuity of Kurt Lewin and his students to apply the experimental method to socially significant behaviors. In doing so, they played a major role in ending the dominance of reinforcement theory in social psychology.

Lewin was a Jewish psychologist who emigrated to the United States from Germany in 1933. After Hitler became chancellor of Germany in January 1933 and restrictive laws against Jews began to escalate, Lewin foresaw that no Jew could continue to live in Nazi Germany. He resigned his faculty position at the University of Berlin, preempting his imminent dismissal by the Nazis, and left Germany. After spending two years on the faculty of Cornell University, in 1935 he took a position at the University of Iowa, where he spent the next nine years.

Lewin had already been recognized as an innovator in both theory and research during his tenure at the University of Berlin and had attracted students from abroad, including the United States. When he moved to Iowa, a new crop of students came to study with him, some of whom were to become leading figures in social psychology. At Berlin, Lewin's research had dealt with such topics as motivation, memory, personality, and child development. After his move to Iowa, his interests shifted to social psychology. This shift came in the form of a series of experiments on leadership styles, first reported in 1939, which one historian of social psychology has described as "path-breaking in their procedural audacity." As a refugee who had experienced the contrasting social climates in Germany and the United States, Lewin was acutely sensitive to the effects that different kinds of leaders could have on the people they govern. Along with his students Ronald Lippitt and Ralph K. White, he created an experiment to study the effects of three leadership styles: democratic, authoritarian, and laissez-faire.

The three researchers created clubs of eleven-year-old boys who met once a week to engage in various activities, such as making masks. The groups were led by adults who role-played the different styles of leadership. The authoritarian leader always made decisions unilaterally, without input from the group. He generally remained aloof from the members of the club, and he praised or criticized them without explaining his actions. In contrast, under democratic leadership, all decisions were made by the group, with the leader, who was always friendly, providing encouragement and guidance. He always gave reasons for his evaluations of the boys. The laissez-faire leader provided no active guidance. Although friendly, he was a passive resource person who provided information only when the boys requested it. Leaders were rotated so that each club experienced all three styles of leadership. Continuous, systematic observations were made of the boys' behavior. Among other things, Lewin's team found that although productivity was roughly equal in the democratic and authoritarian groups and higher than in the laissez-faire groups, club members showed the greatest preference for democratic leaders, and they were most aggressive under an authoritarian leader.

Lewin introduced several pivotal ideas that became, through the influence of his students and his own contagious enthusiasm, defining elements of contemporary social psychology. First, it was possible to concretize even apparently intangible features of social interaction (such as leadership style) and thereby examine their effects in the laboratory. Second, questions of social importance could be answered via the application of the experimental method. One of the most important social psychologists to emerge from Lewin's circle of students was Leon Festinger, who introduced the theory of cognitive dissonance in 1957—a theory based on the idea that holding inconsistent beliefs is an unpleasant state from which a person will seek relief, much like hunger or thirst. Festinger and his students developed high-impact laboratory experiments to test various predictions derived from the theory. Milgram and many other social psychologists of his generation were also influenced by Lewin and his students, absorbing the sense of limitless possibilities of social-psychological inquiry and the use of powerful experimental manipulations.

A third idea introduced by Lewin led to the defining theoretical stance of contemporary social psychology—situationism. According to Lewin, behavior was a function of what he called the "life space." The life space consists of all the potential forces operating on an individual in a concrete situation in the "here and now." Edward E. Jones, an important social-psychological theorist and experimenter, highlighted an important implication of Lewin's emphasis on contemporaneous, situational determinants, as expressed in his concept of the "life space":

[Lewin] conceived of a person as a point in psychological space, constrained to move in certain directions by the field of forces operating in that space. . . . A view of a human being as the product of long developmental history emphasizes the uniqueness and the distinctiveness of his or her responses to a common environment. On the other hand, a view of a human being as a point at the intersection of environmental forces emphasizes the contemporaneous perceptions and related actions he or she shares with others in that same position. Through experimentation, one hopes that such common action patterns can be determined.

Like most social psychologists, Milgram was a situationist—a strong believer in the power of the immediate situation in affecting a person's behavior. But what made him stand out as one of the most important social scientists of the twentieth century and made his research so original was his ability to go beyond the visible situational forces and demonstrate the unexpected power of certain *invisible* features of situations. A unifying theme of Milgram's research—and of this book—is that the intangibles of situations, the unverbalized social rules and norms operating within them, have a more powerful effect on our behavior than we might expect. We will see how he made those unseen and unverbalized norms visible in original experiments ranging from having a young man asking an older passenger on a New York subway train for her seat to studying the temptation to steal from a charity box after observing a similar act on a specially produced TV program. He invented new, sometimes playful, methods—such as the lost-letter technique and the small-world method—to unearth those rules and norms, revealing in often startling ways that our intuitions are not always reliable predictors of our own and others' actions.

Milgram was a complex individual whose personality and actions were sometimes enigmatic, resulting in polarized reactions of either affection or disdain from others. But the traits that made him one of the outstanding scientists of his generation and worthy of our attention were a voracious curiosity and the creativity that enabled him to satisfy it.

Milgram's curiosity led him to expand the boundaries of social psychology by exploring uncharted territory such as mental maps of cities and the "familiar stranger." It also resulted in a rare achievement: the discovery of two universals of behavior, transcending both time and place—people's extreme readiness to obey authority, and the parsimonious interconnectedness of points in very large networks via only "six degrees of separation."

Milgram's relentless curiosity made him willing to live on the edge scientifically and to take risks, especially with his groundbreaking and controversial research on obedience. As the reader will see in this book, not only have those experiments hopped the usual disciplinary fences—they have been discussed in fields as wide-ranging as law, business ethics, and medicine—but they have stirred the dramatic imagination as well, resulting in several movies and plays, and their influence on contemporary life can be seen in the head-spinning variety of writings that have drawn on Milgram's work in one way or another.

This is the story of Stanley Milgram: his life, his inventive brand of science, and its far-reaching impact on public life.

THE NEIGHBORHOOD
WITH NO NAME

STANLEY MILGRAM WAS born in the Bronx on August 15, 1933, to Samuel and Adele Milgram, both Jewish immigrants from Eastern Europe. They met in the United States and were married in February 1931. Like so many thousands of Jews before and after them, their families had undoubtedly been drawn to America by its idealized reputation as the *Goldene Medina*—the land of golden opportunity. Samuel, an expert baker and cake decorator, emigrated from Hungary in 1921 after World War I and returned briefly to Europe a few years later to apprentice in Germany. Stanley recalled that his father seemed "especially sturdy, his heavy-boned arms strengthened by years of kneading dough in the shops, his face reflecting both Jewish warmth and, in his high chiseled cheekbones, traces of his Magyar birthland." He was 5'8", and Stanley thought he looked a bit like Marshall Tito of Yugoslavia. Adele was born in Romania in 1908 and came to the United States at age five with her mother. She was petite, short, and gentle. She radiated cheerfulness, and it was easy to make her laugh. Adele was everyone's favorite aunt, the family sage to whom all turned for advice and for arbitration in family disputes.

Samuel and Adele moved frequently. During the Depression, landlords engaged in a competition to draw and retain tenants. They offered various "concessions" or inducements, such as free gas and electricity or a month's rent. Concessions could save tenants a lot of money, and when their lease was up, they could often find a better offer from another landlord. The

Milgrams, like so many others, found themselves packing up their belongings every few years, sometimes to move just a block or two away.

When Stanley was born, the family was living in a small apartment building at 1020 Boynton Avenue, in a section of the South Bronx, bounded on the west by the Bronx River, where it starts its meandering curve eastward, and on the south by Bruckner Boulevard. As late as 1925, the area still contained some farmland. This section of the Bronx did not have an agreed-upon name, but it did possess a cohesive neighborhood feeling, and the streets pulsated with the energy and drive of people who were trying to improve their situation.

Years later, Stanley would describe it this way:

> The neighborhood was always abuzz with people: plump, animated women, in patterned cotton dresses and aprons, sunning themselves on bridge chairs in front of the apartment houses, knitting in splendid self-containment or exchanging gossip while distractedly rocking their baby carriages. There were plenty of children running around, and always a mother shouting through an open window for "Sey . . . mour" or "Ir . . . ving" in that long drawn out sing-song that was their maternal call. It was a mixed neighborhood of immigrants—but not greenhorns—who came mostly from Jewish Eastern Europe. Many of them worked in small shops or owned them. A few clerks, secretaries, and school teachers lived here too, elevating the prestige of the neighborhood. . . . These bakers, printers, clerks, and housewives were fueled by aspirations, if not for themselves then for their progeny, who played stick ball in the streets, and thought of the local candy store as the outer limit of their world.

Stanley was Sam and Adele's second child. His sister Marjorie was born a year and a half earlier. Stanley was named after a deceased grandfather named Simcha—Hebrew for joy, a feeling apparently lost on his sister, who, sensing that she would now have to vie with the new baby for her parents' attention, demanded: "Throw him into the incinerator." She was constantly tossing things into Stanley's crib, forcing Adele to spread a screen over it to protect him. And Marjorie was constantly being reprimanded for hitting the baby.

A younger brother, Joel, was born five years later. Stanley's first recollection of the imminent arrival of his new brother was sitting with his sister on the marble steps in the vestibule of their apartment house on Boynton Avenue, speculating about the new baby: "We knew that Mom would be going to the hospital to get the baby. Margie insisted that it be a baby girl; I wanted a baby brother. We argued, but we knew the matter was not up to us; it would depend on whatever the hospital decided to give out."

When Joel was old enough, he became a willing accomplice in his brother's pranks, which continued well into their teens. This shared mischief not only enlivened those years, but helped cement the bonds of brotherhood, which held fast for life, no matter how far apart they lived.

In one such incident, Stanley and his buddies decided to try to convince another friend, named Wex (short for Wexelbaum), that he had telepathic powers. To prove it, Stanley brought Wex to his own room in the apartment and told him that he was thinking of a number, which he had written on a slip of paper and put in a lockbox under his bed. Wex should read his mind and say what the number was. After Wex said a number, Joel, hiding under the bed, quickly wrote the number on a piece of paper and slipped it into the lockbox.

In another incident, Stanley and Joel were having a friendly tussle on the living room floor. Among the room's furnishings was a round, ornate French provincial coffee table with four curving, baroque legs. It was recessed in the middle and covered by a clear glass disc, about 30 inches across. They bumped the coffee table, breaking the glass top. To hide their misdeed from their parents, the brothers spread a piece of cellophane tightly across the top. The substitution went undetected for a few weeks, until one day a guest placed a cup and saucer on the table that quickly sank toward the floor.

For the children of the Neighborhood With No Name, the center of their lives was the local elementary school, PS 77, on Ward Avenue. Its main entrance was flanked on both sides by two white columns, their stateliness serving to forewarn those about to enter the building of the supreme importance of what went on inside. The building's symbolic import was abetted by a dress code: Boys had to wear white shirts and ties. Through the third grade, it was a red tie; after third grade, it was a blue tie. There was a similar school "uniform" requirement for girls, who had to wear some type of white blouse and a red—then blue—sash, bow, or ribbon around the neck. The uniforms served as a simple but effective social and economic leveler. The school's principal believed that wearing them would make all children feel equal. Adele loved the dress code, because it took the daily decision about what the children should wear and the hassles associated with it out of her hands. A pretty flower garden separated the school building and the sidewalk. Adele once told little Stanley that babies came from tulips. After that, he would periodically inspect the tulips in the school's garden, waiting for tiny life forms to emerge.

It was at PS 77 that Stanley's superior intelligence became visible to those outside his immediate family. When Stanley was in kindergarten, he would often stand next to his mother at night as she helped his sister with her homework. One evening, the discussion focused on Abraham Lincoln. The following day, when Stanley's kindergarten teacher asked her class to tell what they knew about the great president, little Stanley raised his hand and proceeded to repeat what he had overheard from his mother the night before. His teacher was so impressed that she had the principal take him around from class to class to recite his speech about President Lincoln.

Indeed, Stanley was remembered by his elementary school teachers as an outstanding student. Although as an adult Joel would be proud of his brother's achievements, during their childhood years Stanley's school performance made Joel, a disinterested student who got marginal grades, look even worse. Joel's third-grade teacher, Mrs. Stiller, had been Stanley's third-grade teacher five years earlier. Once, expressing her disappointment while returning a paper to Joel with a low grade, she made it a point to tell him how much better his brother had done in her class.

Most of the boys in the neighborhood spent much of their free time playing ball in the schoolyard and in the streets. Stanley was not very adept at sports, so he did not participate much in those activities. Instead, he developed an early interest in science. An older cousin gave him a chemistry set, and he found himself tinkering with it in his spare time. Occasionally he got some of his buddies to participate in his experiments, one of which involved lowering a large flask containing sodium into the Bronx River. When the "sodium bomb" exploded, fire engines and worried mothers rushed to the site. He was always doing experiments. "It was as natural as breathing," he once told an interviewer, "and I tried to understand how everything worked."

Among Stanley's childhood experiences, two are especially noteworthy, because they turned out to be harbingers of concerns that would later dominate his professional life. The first involved the power of groups. In Stanley's own words:

On [a] summer day, after a child had been knocked down by a passing car, the neighborhood demanded that Boynton Avenue be turned into a one-way street. A crowd of protesters gathered on the sidewalk with crudely fabricated signs. The crowd started to chant, "Sit down strike! Sit down strike!" A barricade of milk crates was formed across the width of the street and protesters sat on the crates preventing traffic from moving through. Police arrived, some words were exchanged and the incident came to an end. . . . I suppose if I had grown up in a more genteel place this kind of thing would not happen. But this was the Bronx in the thirties. It was not a neighborhood of patsies. We got our one-way street.

The second incident occurred when Stanley was four or five years old. His cousin, Stanley Norden, a year and a half older, who lived in the same neighborhood, had come over to play. (The two Stanleys were named after the same grandfather.) They were playing in the bedroom, with cousin Stanley sitting on the floor between two beds. According to Milgram: "I decided to 'measure' the distance between the beds by stretching a belt from one bedpost to the other. The belt slipped, and the buckle, with its sharp spindle, fell on Stanley's head causing a small flow of blood. Stanley began to cry and ran to Aunt Mary [his mother] who was chatting with Mom in the kitchen."

Milgram was soundly scolded by his mother, making him cry. He felt miserable about his misdeed, even though it was an accident and he hadn't meant to hurt his cousin. "Still, to be blamed for such things was a burden. But whether I learned my lesson remains unclear. For many years later, was I not again to become an object of criticism for my efforts to measure something without due regard to the risks it entailed for others?"

Samuel Milgram was a proud father. His children were the smartest and the most beautiful. He always referred to them as his "treasures." Marjorie was his Hungarian princess, and he often boasted about his four-year-old son, Stanley, who could recite the Pledge of Allegiance and Mother Goose rhymes by heart. Stanley identified strongly with his father, even idolized him:

> To any child, who views things from two feet off the ground, all fathers must look big and strong, but Sam seemed especially sturdy. . . . What intense joy we experienced jumping on Dad's chest as he lay on the rug of our apartment, sliding down his knees. . . . When, many years later, I had children of my own, I recall how on Sunday mornings, they would jump all over me in bed, balance themselves on my forked knees, enact little circus performances in which my legs became the stable platforms from which they giggled through their antics and I thought of my father and the delicious joy of jumping on his accommodating chest.

It was a special source of pride to Stanley that everyone said he looked like Sam. Later, Stanley's wife would comment:

> He resembled his father very much physically. . . . His nose looked like it was flattened at the tip, and I never said anything when I first met Stanley. But when I saw the photo of Stanley's father, I thought, Oh! He resembled his father so much that the story goes when Stanley was a little boy playing in the park, and some family members on his father's side came from Europe, and were looking for where the house was, they saw Stanley and recognized him as Sam's son.

One of Stanley's fondest and most vivid childhood memories was accompanying his father as the family moved to a new apartment on Ward Avenue, on the other side of the elevated train tracks running along Westchester Avenue:

> After most of the furniture had been packed into a moving truck, Dad wanted to take over some clothing and small items to the new apart-

ment. . . . He filled [a] cart with clothing, lamps and other household para-phernalia and probably against Mom's objection—she had a stronger sense of decorum—was going to transport the items three or four blocks to the new house. To my great joy I was invited to get into the cart and go along for the ride. . . . It was not a pushcart type of neighborhood: black Chevys and Buick sedans lined the streets. Perhaps the sight of Dad pushing the wagon up Boynton Avenue struck onlookers as eccentric. But I had just turned five. No captain of a frigate could have surveyed the passing chan-nels with greater pride, as I sat atop the bundles of clothing, moving north-ward on Boynton Avenue toward our new place, the vessel powered by my very own father, strong as Hercules.

...

When the United States entered World War II after the attack on Pearl Harbor on December 7, 1941, the Milgrams lived at 1239 Ward Avenue, only two blocks from their previous home on Boynton Avenue. One side of the block was made up of virtually identical brick two-family houses with postage-stamp-sized front lawns. The Milgrams occupied the upstairs apartment of one such house. It was larger than their previous apartment, and they had moved there soon after Joel was born to accommodate the needs of a growing family.

As the country mobilized for war, Sam felt the need to take steps to en-sure that he would not be drafted. He was now forty-three, which made conscription unlikely. But he had fought in World War I—had even been a POW—and he did not relish the thought of having to repeat the expe-rience. So in late 1942 he moved his family temporarily to Camden, New Jersey, to train and work as a welder in the shipyards. Having a job that was crucial to the war effort would protect him from the draft. Although he undoubtedly could have found a war-related job closer to home, he be-lieved that if the Germans were ever to attack the U.S. mainland, New York would be a prime target. He was knowledgeable enough—he thought—about the advanced state of German war technology to believe they had the ability to launch long-range rockets that could reach the

United States. Stanley was very much aware of his family's worries about Nazi Germany. His father had family living in Europe, and he and Adele followed developments there closely on the radio.

The Milgrams were not religiously observant, although their cultural identification was strong and their home resounded with the melodic cadences of Yiddish whenever uncles and aunts came to visit. The religious holidays—such as Passover and Rosh Hashanah—were observed, but more as an occasion for family gatherings than for their religious significance. Stanley attended afternoon Hebrew school for a few years until his Bar Mitzvah.

When it came time for thirteen-year-old Stanley to give a little speech at his Bar Mitzvah celebration, which took place the year after the war ended, he showed a concern over recent events:

> As I come of age and find happiness in joining the ranks of Israel, the knowledge of the tragic suffering of my fellow Jews throughout war-torn Europe makes this also a solemn event and an occasion to reflect upon the heritage of my people—which now becomes mine. I do not know whether I shall be able to cherish this heritage in the same way as my parents did throughout their lives. But I shall try to understand my people and do my best to share the responsibilities which history has placed upon all of us. This is a period of transition—when the whole world undergoes tremendous changes. Perhaps this 13th year of my life will be even more significant as marking the beginning of a new era for the Jewish people, an era of justice and liberty and a homeland Eretz Yisroel. . . . May there be an end to persecution, suffering and war and may Israel be established in Zion bimhareh beyomanu [speedily in our day]. Amen.

In early 1945, as the end of the war drew near, the family returned to their Bronx neighborhood and rented a five-room apartment at 1214 Wheeler Avenue. Sam resumed working in a nearby bakery that he had bought with his brother-in-law, and the children resumed their schooling at PS 77.

In the fall of 1947, Stanley entered James Monroe High School, located a couple of blocks from his home. Bernard Fried, a classmate and one of Milgram's closest boyhood friends, remembers the school as a beautiful but functional building, with excellent facilities and laboratory equipment. It had been constructed in 1925 as a model school, and everything about it was huge and impressive. In Milgram's time its student body numbered between 3,500 and 4,000, and it was reported to have the largest stage of any school in New York, second only to Radio City Music Hall. William Pitt's maxim, "Where law ends, tyranny begins," was chiseled into a marble sign above the entrance.

The school used a tracking system in which the students with the highest IQ and grades were placed in honors classes. Milgram, with an IQ of 158, the highest of all his classmates, was placed in such a class. He finished high school in three years, accelerating his progress by taking summer courses and an extra class or two each semester.

Among the students who graduated the same year as Stanley was Philip Zimbardo, another future social psychologist and a future president of the American Psychological Association, who would become famous for conducting the Stanford Prison Experiment, in which ordinary college students would undergo dramatic behavioral changes after being randomly assigned to the role of prisoner or guard in a mock prison. Zimbardo remembers Milgram as one of the smartest students in his year—the kind of kid who read the *New York Times,* while most others would be reading the *Daily News.*

At Monroe, Stanley was a member of Arista, the honor society. He became editor of the *Science Observer,* a school newspaper, and worked on stagecraft for theatrical productions. He was also on the staff of his graduating class's yearbook, charged with writing the rhyming couplets that appeared below each graduate's photograph. He wrote the following about Phil Zimbardo, who had been one of the most popular students in the class:

> *Phil's our vice president tall and thin,*
> *With his blue eyes all the girls he'll win.*

And he wrote this whimsical couplet about himself:

> *The strangest event of our time,*
> *I'm writing my own little yearbook rhyme.*

He did not date at Monroe—nor did his clique of fellow honors students, virtually all of whom went on to successful careers in professions such as law, medicine, and academia. Milgram's buddy, Bernard Fried—who is now Professor Emeritus at Lafayette College, capping a career as a world-renowned parasitologist—explained:

> If you were going to go on to college and if you were going to make something of yourself, if you were going to be a professional, your best bet [was] to stay away from women until [you were] ready to manage that sort of thing. . . . You didn't get that involved with the other sex. . . . It would distract from what your purpose in life would be.

The bakery Sam and his brother-in-law bought was highly successful but short-lived, because a dispute broke out between them, ending the partnership. In 1947 Sam bought his own bakery, in the Richmond Hill section of Queens. It took three trains and an hour and a half to get there, so Sam stayed at a boarding house during the week and came home only on the weekends. Adele also worked there, but she took the train there every day, coming home late at night. Joel would sometimes wait for her, waiflike, by the subway station.

This proved to be an extremely difficult arrangement, and in 1949 the family moved to 109th Street in Richmond Hill, only a few blocks from the bakery. Stanley did not change schools, instead commuting daily from Queens until he graduated from James Monroe High School.

The move to Queens had also been motivated by a second factor. As Joel approached adolescence, he was becoming a street kid and started hanging out with friends who would occasionally get into trouble. At one point, Joel got into trouble with them, breaking some car windows and getting picked up by the police. Adele feared that if they remained in the neighborhood, she would end up with a juvenile delinquent on her hands.

But the family's troubles continued after the move. Soon after Sam bought the bakery, the business collapsed, because of some duplicity on the part of the former owner. The sales agreement had included a provision that the previous owner could not open another bakery within a twenty-block area, but he managed to circumvent that agreement by opening one in the neighborhood under his wife's name—effectively depriving Sam of the customers he was counting on. The family's financial situation was further worsened by a bad investment. One of Sam's brothers had told him to invest in sugar, because its price would soon rise. Adele had managed, with great difficulty, to save up $8,000 to enable them to buy a house of their own. Sam, confident that his brother's prediction would materialize, asked Adele for the money. She gave it to him reluctantly, but without a word. The price of sugar plummeted, wiping out Sam's investment.

In the fall of 1950 Stanley enrolled at Queens College, a choice dictated largely by the fact that it was close to home and that, like all the other colleges in the City University of New York system, it was tuition free. When Stanley attended, it was a relatively small school, consisting primarily of six compact buildings—previously a reform school—surrounding a grassy quad. There was only one new building, Remsen Hall, which had been built specifically for the college. Marjorie, who also attended the school, remembers it as "the closest thing to going to a city college and feeling that you did have a campus." But convenience aside, Queens College was a good choice academically. In 1953, the Ford Foundation had ranked it second in the nation in the humanities and tenth in the social sciences. People called it the Harvard of the City University system.

During Stanley's precollege years, the hard sciences—mainly chemistry and biology—had dominated his interests and preoccupations. At Queens College, however, the "softer" side of his intellect came to the fore. He majored in political science but also took courses in English literature, music, and art—and, in fact, minored in the latter. He excelled academically: He received the School Award in Political Science and the Certificate of Excellence in Forensics, qualified for membership in the National Political Science Honors Society, and graduated Phi Beta Kappa. He was active in extracurricular activities, becoming president of the International Relations Club and vice president of the Debating Society. He tried his hand at music, collaborating with a classmate on Broadway-type musicals, and he attempted to write poetry.

In the summer of 1953, after his junior year, Stanley toured France, Spain, and Italy on a motorized bicycle. In early September, he wound up at the American Consulate in Genoa with only two dollars in his pocket.

Pleading poverty, he received a little financial help from the maternally minded vice-consul, a kindly woman in her late forties. To return home, he approached the crew of a German ship bound for the United States, hoping they would allow him to come aboard. At first they refused, but he was persistent—an attribute that would serve him well later in life. They finally agreed to let him come on board—putting him to work as a radio communicator—and even provided him with a comfortable room.

Of the three countries he visited that summer, he spent the most time in France. From July 15 to August 14, he enrolled in a French language course at the Sorbonne, which helped him master the language. He eventually attained such fluency that after he became a well-known figure and would periodically appear on French television, people thought he was French. That summer he fell in love with a French girl, Francine, his first love. He also fell in love with the country, and he would return to France many times during his lifetime.

Later that year, on the night of December 11, 1953, Sam Milgram died in his sleep from a coronary thrombosis. He had been sharing a bed with Joel: Sam would sleep in it during the day and get up late at night to go to work in the bakery, and Joel would then use it during the night. On the night of December 11, Joel heard his father's alarm go off, but Sam did not come out.

Adele and the family suffered terribly. Aside from the emotional blow, Sam's death left them virtually penniless: He had taken out a life insurance policy but had depleted it to enable him to buy the bakery. But Adele was a resourceful and resilient person who did not let adversity overwhelm her. With her past experience helping Sam in the bakery, she found a job before long working in another bakery.

For Stanley, the financial impact of his father's death was softened by the fact that his schooling was free and that he had received a New York State Regents Scholarship amounting to $1,400 for the four years he was in college. Marjorie had recently begun teaching in an elementary school and was able to help her mother briefly, until her own marriage the following year.

One effect Sam's death had on Stanley was to give him a resolve to protect his own future family from financial disaster in the event of his own death, which he worried would also be premature. In fact, during their first year of marriage, Stanley told his wife that he expected to die by age fifty-five—a prediction completely at odds with his perfect state of health at the time. She recalled:

> He kept saying he would live to be fifty-five, and I just looked at him. Stanley was one of the healthiest persons I knew, physically and emotionally. . . . If he had a cold, he'd just keep going and it would go away. So when he would say he'd live to be fifty-five, I'd say, 'Your father was a different person than you.'

Milgram graduated from Queens College, receiving a B.A. with honors. His studies in political science had led to an interest in a career in the Foreign Service. In the spring of 1952, his sophomore year, he corresponded with the Board of Examiners at the State Department, asking about the educational qualifications needed by a candidate for the Foreign Service and requesting their booklet of sample questions from their entrance examination. During his senior year he applied to, and was accepted by, the graduate program at Columbia University's School of International Affairs.

But then a number of events came together that would result in a major shift in Milgram's life. Stanley's boyhood friend, Bernard Fried, had entered New York University the same year that Stanley began at Queens College. Bernard was majoring in biology, but, as he was still considering the possibility of graduate studies in psychology, he also took a minor concentration in psychology, which gave him a strong background in the field. Fried has a distinct memory of "spending a full day with Stanley" during their senior year, "basically giving him lectures on . . . what I knew about psychology." He believes that this meeting influenced Milgram's decision to switch to psychology.

By this time Milgram had also become increasingly disenchanted with political science. Being as much a doer as a thinker, he was dissatisfied with the largely philosophical approach that characterized political science at the time. One day, early in the spring semester of 1954, a dean overheard him giving a speech in a senior Social Science seminar, was very much impressed, and asked Milgram if he had considered graduate studies in the Department of Social Relations at Harvard. Milgram had never heard about the program, and he sent for the catalogue. Reading the catalogue was an enlightening experience. He learned, for the first time, that it was possible to take an empirical, scientific approach to many of the group phenomena that political scientists were interested in—for example, leadership styles and mass persuasion—and that it was social psychologists who were at the forefront of this approach. He sent off an application to their Ph.D. program in Social Psychology.

During the 1950s, the Behavioral Sciences Division of the Ford Foundation had a fellowship program to encourage young people who had majored in other fields as undergraduates to move into the behavioral sciences. The fellowships provided stipends of $1,800 for one year of graduate school. Stanley applied, and in April 1954 he received a telegram notifying him that he had been selected as one of the recipients. That year the fellowship program had received applications from 103 students at fifty-seven different schools. Milgram was one of twenty-two award winners, and among them, one of eight students who elected to go into Harvard's Social Relations program.

Adele was bursting with pride about what she saw as a special, groundbreaking achievement. He was the first Jew to win a Ford Foundation fellowship, she told the family. This would have been especially noteworthy, since Henry Ford, the founder of the Ford Motor Company, had been a vocal anti-Semite. Both Joel and Marjorie recall her making such a remark, but, as it turns out, she was wrong: The list of twenty-two fellowship recipients for 1954–1955 contains a number of students with typically Jewish names, some from schools in the Eastern United States. Most likely the basis for her statement was an actual "first" that had been transformed through the lens of Adele's ethnic pride: Milgram was the first student at Queens College to win a Ford Foundation fellowship.

Milgram's success with the Ford Foundation was not matched at Harvard. His application was rejected because he lacked adequate preparation—he had not taken a single psychology course as an undergraduate at Queens. In a letter to the Social Relations Department dated May 30, 1954, he expressed his great disappointment at being rejected and noted the inherent contradiction involved in this action: If he had had the relevant background preparation in psychology, he would not have qualified for the Ford fellowship, which was specifically created for students whose undergraduate education was in fields other than the behavioral sciences. He indicated that he planned to remedy his "defective preparation" over the summer by taking a five-day-a-week psychology course at Columbia University that was equivalent to a full-year course in general psychology, as well as an intensive regimen of reading, directed by the chairman of the Department of Anthropology and Sociology at Queens College.

He received a reply from Gordon Allport, chairman of the Social Relations Department's Committee on Higher Degrees—in effect, the head of the graduate program. Allport doubted that the summer preparation Milgram planned would be sufficient for admission as a regular full-time student in the department in the fall. He suggested that Milgram apply to Harvard's Office of Special Students, to be admitted as a special student for the coming year to make up his deficiencies, and that he tell them "that this Department has advised you to apply." In the fall, Allport would direct him in the selection of courses. Then he "might apply for regular standing for the year following. . . . Meanwhile your summer plans are certainly all to the good." Milgram followed Allport's advice and was admitted by Harvard's Office of Special Students on June 30.

Although Allport's letter was unambiguously encouraging about the prospects of Milgram's admission as a regular student after a year of preparation, it implied that Milgram's preparatory year would need to consist of undergraduate courses. But Milgram had another plan. If he could take graduate courses in the fall that were required of regular students in the Ph.D. program in social psychology, even as a special student, he would not be losing a year. If he did well that first year and achieved regular standing the next year, he could probably petition to have his first-year courses used to fulfill program requirements retroactively.

So he drastically altered his summer plans. He enrolled in *six* undergraduate courses—five in psychology and one in sociology—at three different colleges in the New York area: Brooklyn, Hunter, and New York University. He took two courses at each school. At Brooklyn College he signed up for Psychology of Personality and a course titled An Eclectic Approach to Social Psychology; at Hunter he enrolled in General Psychology and Gestalt Approach to Social Psychology; at New York University he audited two courses—Child Psychology and Language and Society, a sociology course. He completed each of the four graded courses with As.

During their correspondence, Milgram concluded one of his letters to Allport by offering "his sincerest expression of appreciation for the generous consideration and advice which I received from you and the Department. I look forward to a pleasant and profitable association with both." And Allport ended one of his letters to Milgram by telling him to come to see him when he arrived in Cambridge in the fall and then "we can discuss a plan for the year that will best advance your interests."

This initial exchange of letters set the tone for their future relationship as student and mentor. Allport was to become the most important person in Milgram's academic life and a constant source of encouragement. He had a bemused admiration for Milgram's limitless drive and persistence in the face of obstacles. And when Allport felt that Stanley needed prodding, he knew how much pressure to apply without provoking resistance. Stanley, in turn, was always deferential enough to Allport to get his way without seeming to be too pushy.

Later, several years after Allport's death, Milgram reflected on him with fondness and appreciation: "Gordon Allport was my longtime mentor and friend. He was a modest man with a pink face; you felt an intense loving quality about him. . . . He gave me a strong sense of my own potential. Allport was my spiritual and emotional support. He cared for people deeply."

Milgram's move to Harvard was a pivotal juncture in his development. It would help him extract a particular career path from among his many interests. He would form close friendships, some of which lasted a lifetime. Although he had been interested in a number of women at Queens, they had remained largely infatuations. The greater self-confidence he would develop at Harvard would lead to more mature relationships with women.

But he couldn't predict any of this in the summer of 1954. For the moment, he was just happy to leave behind a lonely existence in Richmond Hill. He found the other young men in his neighborhood dull, ignorant, and boorish, and he was hungry for intellectual companions. Pursuing further studies would also allow him to extend his student deferment and avoid the draft. He was more than ready for Harvard. But was Harvard ready for him?

CHAPTER 2

MAKING THE
GRADE AT HARVARD

WHEN MILGRAM ARRIVED at Harvard in the fall of 1954 to begin his graduate studies, the Department of Social Relations was a thriving, burgeoning enterprise. The program had been established in 1946 with the aim of integrating the four disciplines of social psychology, clinical psychology, social anthropology, and sociology. Its founding fathers were four outstanding individuals in those fields, respectively: Gordon Allport, Henry Murray, Clyde Kluckhohn, and Talcott Parsons. They all shared the grand vision of uniting these disciplines under one intellectual and administrative roof, but it was Parsons, the sociologist, who was the most vigorous and unswerving proponent of the fusion.

Their vision was no mere mirage; it was an accurate reflection of the productive teamwork that had taken place during World War II among members of different behavioral and social disciplines under the sponsorship of various federal agencies to help with the war effort. For example, social psychologist Kurt Lewin had worked with anthropologist Margaret Mead on a government project to change the public's food consumption habits, helping to conserve scarce resources, and on another that set up a training school for the Office of Strategic Services (OSS), the forerunner of the Central Intelligence Agency.

Gordon Allport was a pioneer in social psychology as well as in the study of personality. Early on, in 1935, he had identified the concept of "attitude" as central to social psychology, and most contemporary textbook definitions of attitude are based on his. He made original contributions to the study of prejudice and of religious belief, introducing a measurable distinction between intrinsic and extrinsic religious orientations—between those with a deep attachment to the core values of their faith and those who use their religion to attain other goals such as status and the approval of others. Henry Murray, who made seminal contributions to personality psychology, is best known for creating the Thematic Apperception Test (the TAT), one of the projective tests that clinical psychologists still use today as a diagnostic tool. Clyde Kluckhohn had studied and written extensively about the culture of the Navajo Indians for more than forty years, drawing on that research for insights about human behavior in general. Talcott Parsons's life goal was to unify the social sciences, and in his writings and teaching he tried to provide an overarching theory and a common language to facilitate the task. Although not without his critics, he achieved wide recognition as a leader in his field and was elected president of the American Sociological Society in 1949.

The rationale behind the founding of the Social Relations Department was spelled out in an article in the April 1946 issue of the *American Psychologist* announcing the establishment of the program:

> While [academic] departmental lines have remained rigid, there has been developing during the last decade, a synthesis of socio-cultural and psychological sciences which is widely recognized within the academic world in spite of the fact that there is no commonly accepted name to designate the synthesis. We propose that Harvard adopt, and thus help establish, the term *Social Relations* to characterize the emerging discipline which deals not only with the body of fact and theory traditionally recognized as the subject matter of sociology, but also with that portion of psychological science that treats the individual within the social system, and that portion of anthropological science that is particularly relevant to the social and cultural patterns of literate societies.

The interdisciplinary aims of the department were to be fostered by two means. First, a Laboratory of Social Relations would be created to facilitate research collaboration among the members of the four different disciplines. Second, specific course requirements were written into the curriculum to ensure that all students, regardless of their specialization, would be knowledgeable about the content and methods of each of the four social sciences constituting the department. During their first year of graduate study, all students took four "qualifying" or core courses, one in each of the department's subdisciplines. To demonstrate concretely the interdisciplinary possibilities provided by the field of social relations, some of the classes in two different qualifying courses would meet jointly. So, for example, during Milgram's first semester more than one-third of the lectures in the two core courses, Problems and Concepts of Social Anthropology and Problems and Concepts of Clinical Psychology, were conducted as joint sessions. To verify their competence in each of the four core areas, students had to take and pass a qualifying exam in each. Another course in the curriculum that was meant to facilitate cross-fertilization was Social Relations 201, in which different lecturers, in turn, would convey their perspectives on each of their disciplines.

Their guiding vision notwithstanding, the program's founders were not blind to the realities of the job market, which operated in terms of the traditional academic and professional distinctions that were still the norm in the world beyond Harvard Yard. Although the program offered an undergraduate concentration and degree in social relations, this was not the case for graduate studies. Despite the integrative philosophy of the program, graduate students would specialize in, and end up with a Ph.D. degree in, social anthropology, clinical psychology, social psychology, or sociology.

This bold experiment in interdisciplinary cooperation ultimately failed. It ended in 1970, when the sociologists walked out. But the seeds of its eventual demise were planted at the program's conception by a potentially problematic feature of its organizational structure. While sociology moved intact into the Department of Social Relations in 1946 and ceased to exist as an autonomous department, the creation of the new program resulted in a drastic change in the Psychology Department. It split into two, with the social-science-oriented psychologists—social psychologists, personologists, and clinicians—migrating to Social Relations and leaving their colleagues from the natural science side of psychology behind—that is, those special-izing in learning theory, sensation and perception, and physiological psy-chology. This was an immediate source of instability for the newly created Social Relations Department, because it made for ambivalence and luke-warm commitments among younger social psychologists, such as Roger Brown and Jerome Bruner, whose broad and varied interests defied pigeon-holing and who had some research interests in common with the psycholo-gists who remained in the Psychology Department.

But Stanley arrived during Social Relations' "golden age," when individ-ual misgivings were overshadowed by a pervasive atmosphere of optimism. The program received hundreds of applications each year, many more than the number of students it could accept. In Milgram's entering year, he was part of a group of about 110 students in the program. This degree of pop-ularity was especially noteworthy for a graduate program that was still in its infancy—less than ten years old. It had received votes of confidence from evaluating committees commissioned by the Ford Foundation in 1954. And, as the founding fathers of the department had envisioned, its mem-bers were actively involved in interdisciplinary collaborations. A prime ex-ample was the book *Personality in Nature, Society, and Culture,* which was obligatory reading for generations of students in psychology and other so-cial sciences. One of its chapters contains the following memorable epi-gram, which despite its bare bones simplicity, conveys a deep truth about human nature.

> Every man is in certain respects:
> (a) Like all other men;
> (b) Like some other men;
> (c) Like no other man.

During his subsequent years at Harvard, Stanley would thrive on the rich intellectual stimulation provided by its diverse faculty, and the social relations program helped develop in him a wide-ranging interest in the so-cial sciences. He, in turn, left his imprint on the program. Roger Brown, one of Milgram's mentors and a lifelong friend, recalled:

When Stanley Milgram was a graduate student at Harvard, I was an assistant professor, and we had several seminars and reading courses together. The only thing I can now recall from a term-long seminar in psycholinguistics is Stanley's presentation. Instead of leading yet another bookish discussion, he brought in an audio tape he had made of many kinds of psycholinguistic phenomena: slips of the tongue, rhetorical flourishes, a child's first few words, a stretch of psychotic speech, all wittily edited and assembled and presented to us as things to be appreciated first and then, perhaps, explained. And the only reading course I remember was the one with Stanley on crowd behavior in which he did no reading at all for some time, but, instead, went all over Boston joining crowds of every kind and bringing back snapshots of curious group formations.

During his first year at Harvard, Milgram lived in Perkins Hall, a graduate dormitory. At that time, students did not have their own telephones in their rooms. There was a pay phone in the hallway, which was used by the residents on that floor both for making and receiving calls. Often the phone would ring endlessly before someone would drag himself out of his room to answer it and then find the person the caller was looking for. Answering the phone was a chore, because the call could be for anybody on the floor and it wasn't clear who should answer it. What was needed was some sort of rule, and Milgram came up with one. He wrote it on an index card that he posted next to the phone:

> To share equitably the burden of answering this phone, students should answer the phone two times for each call they receive. (This is to take account of those occasions when a call is received for you, and you are not in.)

He had created a norm, a guideline for appropriate conduct, in what previously had been a behavioral vacuum. Five years later, in 1959, he was back at Harvard after spending two years abroad in Norway and France conducting his doctoral research. One day he had occasion to use a pay phone in another dormitory and, as he picked up the receiver, he noticed an index card next to the telephone: "To share in the burden of answering this telephone, it is traditional for students to answer the phone two times for each call he receives . . ." etc. He found that the notices had spread throughout the campus.

...

The Social Relations Department was headquartered in Emerson Hall, in the northeast corner of Harvard Yard. Its rectangular shape and terra-cotta ornamentation projected subdued elegance; its only pretensions of architectural grandeur were the giant brick columns flanking its entrances. The Biblical verse, from the Psalms, "What is man that Thou art mindful of him?" inscribed in stone across the top of the north entrance was a silent reminder of the building's beginnings as the headquarters of Harvard's social gospelers.

During its early years, brilliant philosophers such as George Santayana and Alfred North Whitehead taught in its classrooms, as did William James, one of the founding fathers of American psychology. In the late 1800s James had founded the Psychological Laboratory within Harvard's philosophy department and produced the first Ph.D.'s in psychology in America. When Gertrude Stein was at Radcliffe, she took an introductory philosophy course with James in Emerson Hall. According to Harvard lore, during the final exam she wrote on her test booklet, "I don't want to take this exam; it's too nice out," and she picked herself up and left. Supposedly, when William James returned the exam book, he had written on it, "Miss Stein, you truly understand the meaning of philosophy, 'A'."

Allport's office was located in Emerson Hall, along with the other administrative offices of the department. On September 27, soon after Milgram arrived in Cambridge for the fall 1954 semester, he met with Allport for advisement about which courses to take. The program of study that emerged from this initial conference and subsequent consultations with Allport would put Milgram on an equal footing with regular first-year students by the end of that academic year. While the curriculum for Ph.D. students allowed for some individual variations, all students, no matter what their area of specialization, were required to take the four qualifying courses during their first year. Passing the final exams—which served as the qualifying exams—in each of those courses was a requirement for the Ph.D. degree. Milgram was able to take the qualifying courses in social anthropology and clinical psychology in the fall semester and in sociology and social psychology in the spring semester. A letter from Gordon Allport dated June 9, 1955, informed Milgram that "the Department had voted you have passed the Qualifying requirements for the Ph.D. degree in Social Psychology" and that his grades in the four courses were B+, A, A–, and A, respectively. He also attained A's in three other courses he completed that first year. Given the fact that the first-year curriculum was especially grueling, this was a noteworthy accomplishment.

As a result of his outstanding performance, he was allowed to become a regular full-time student in the department, beginning with the 1955–1956 academic year. All vestiges of his special student status in 1954–1955 were eradicated in the fall of 1956 when the graduate school gave him credit for the courses he had taken that first year—in effect retroactively applying them to meet the requirements for his Ph.D. degree, as he had anticipated.

One of the courses Milgram took during his first semester was Cognitive Processes. The course was taught by Jerome Bruner, who—along with Gordon Allport and Roger Brown—was to become one of his important advisers and lifelong friends. Bruner's work in the 1940s and 1950s helped launch the "cognitive revolution" in psychology, effectively displacing the dominant influence of a mechanistic behaviorism in American academic psychology. Bruner had sent a progress report on the eight Behavioral Sciences Fellows who chose to go to Harvard in 1954–1955 to Robert Knapp, the administrator of the program. Bruner reported that Milgram was "doing outstanding work" and that, in fact, he was his best student in his Cognitive Processes course and an "excellent logician."

The objective indices of Milgram's achievement were matched by his feeling of immense satisfaction. By the end of that first year, he had taken courses with the likes of Gordon Allport, Roger Brown, Talcott Parsons, and Jerome Bruner. For Milgram, they opened a new window on the world, framed by the guiding message that social reality—not just physical reality—had an underlying structure and that there were tools with which to grasp it, such as the controlled experiment, survey research methods, and self-report measures of personality and attitudes. His courses not only exposed Milgram to new ideas, they also stimulated him to create his own. By the end of that first year, he was bubbling over with a dozen or so different lines of research he was ready to pursue. More important, he set his sights on a career in social psychology. Robert Knapp had sent a questionnaire to all the recipients of the Behavioral Sciences Fellowships. One of the questions in it was: "Do you have any long-range plans involving a career in the behavioral sciences?" Milgram wrote: "Yes. This year I really fell in love with the discipline and, if possible, will continue working in it. I hope to follow through to a Ph.D. in Social Psychology and then, probably, secure a position with a psychology faculty of a fair sized university, where I would teach and engage in research."

However, for a stretch of time, there was a real possibility that Milgram's newfound love might remain unrequited. In the spring of 1955, Milgram applied to the Ford Foundation for an extension of his fellowship for a second year. Much to his dismay, he was informed by Robert Knapp that, although Ford was very pleased with his outstanding academic performance, as a matter of policy, the Behavioral Sciences Fellowships were one-year, nonrenewable awards. Toward the end of the semester, the Social Relations Department recommended him for a full scholarship, based on his excellent track record for the year, but Harvard's Central Scholarship Committee did not accept that recommendation.

Without financial assistance, Milgram could not continue his graduate studies, and if he left school he would lose his student deferment from military service, and there was a strong possibility that he would be drafted the following year. Military service would not help advance his academic career, since the GI Bill of Rights—and the educational benefits it provided—had been discontinued after the end of the Korean War, in July 1953.

This was not the first time Milgram had confronted the prospect of entering the armed forces. In the fall of 1951, an Air Force Reserve Officers' Training Corps (ROTC) program was established at Queens College, and Milgram joined it. When the Korean War began in the spring of 1950, the U.S. government reinstated the draft as well as the GI Bill of Rights, both of which had been discontinued at the end of World War II. Although there are no records to tell us—and no one in the Milgram family knows—why he joined, most likely it was a way of making the best of the inevitable. With the country in the midst of a war, Milgram would be eligible for the draft once he graduated. With the completion of the ROTC program, he would have the advantage of doing his military service as a commissioned officer, not as just another draftee. Completion of ROTC training required taking an ROTC course every semester until graduation. As it turns out, Milgram never completed the requirements. After completing the equivalent of six semesters of ROTC courses by the end of his junior year in 1953, he only had two courses left to take in his senior year. Although he did sign up for the ROTC course, Aviation Science 13, in the fall of 1953, the first semester of his senior year, he withdrew from the course on November 16 without completing it. Two main factors, undoubtedly, led to this decision: The Korean War had ended the previous spring, diminishing the odds that he would be drafted, and by this time he had decided to go to graduate school.

At the beginning of the summer of 1955, Milgram was still without any financial support for the upcoming academic year. Desperation clouded his thinking, because on June 6 he sent off another letter to the Behavioral Sciences Fellowship office, reiterating his earlier request for an extension of his fellowship—despite the fact that he had already been told that it was a "firm policy" that the fellowships were not renewable. This time, Knapp's negative, though empathetic, reply had even greater finality: The Directors of the Ford Foundation had decided to discontinue the fellowship program altogether.

He had survived—and bested—the rigors of the first-year curriculum and the chronic state of anxiety engendered by impossibly long reading lists and terrorizing three-hour qualifying exams. Now, all that work appeared for naught. Despite the successes of the past year, self-doubt began to envelop him. Who was he? Where was he heading? He found himself in a no-man's land of self-definition. He took a summer job at the Commodore Hotel in Manhattan, although it would not pay nearly enough to cover his school expenses for the next semester. It was more a reenactment of a summer ritual, a way of grounding himself in uncertain times. He had worked almost every summer, including the previous summer, when he had worked at the Commodore as a night clerk, which had enabled him to study for his six college courses on the job. When he wasn't working, he was at home in Queens, reading psychology books and doing sleep-learning experiments on himself. This was patently aimless busy work, but it did prevent him from hearing despair knocking at his door.

It wasn't until the middle of the summer that Milgram had cause for optimism about the coming year. On July 21, he received a reassuring letter at home from Mrs. Eleanor Sprague, Allport's highly knowledgeable secretary. She wrote that Milgram was high on the list of applicants for financial assistance, and the chances of his receiving it looked very good. "We are almost certain to need more assistance in psychology courses," she wrote, "where you could fit in easily. I wouldn't worry too much about work for the fall—either teaching or research should be available."

As she had predicted, Milgram received a graduate assistantship for the fall as well as the spring semester. (The following year he was again awarded assistantships for both semesters.) But Milgram's appointments in 1955–1956 did much more than solve his financial problems of the moment. They had an immeasurable long-term significance, one that more than adequately compensated for the stressful summer of uncertainty. The faculty member he was assigned to that fall—Solomon E. Asch—was to become Milgram's most important scientific influence.

...

Solomon Asch was widely admired for his ability to combine a deep concern about philosophical issues with an inventive, uncluttered experimental style that enabled clear-cut conclusions to be drawn from his research. He was on the faculty at Swarthmore College and came to Harvard's Social Relations Department as an invited visiting lecturer in the 1955–1956 academic year to take the place of Jerome Bruner, who would be spending the fall semester on sabbatical in Cambridge, England. Both

Bruner and Allport agreed that this would be a good opportunity to bring in Asch.

Allport assigned Milgram to be Asch's assistant for the year. In the fall, Milgram served as Asch's teaching assistant for Social Relations 107, Psychological Foundations of Social Behavior, and in the spring he continued as Asch's research assistant. Asch was very pleased with Stanley's work and said so in a letter to department chairman Talcott Parsons. An important consequence of the letter was that it assured Milgram that he would be provided with assistantships for the rest of his stay at Harvard.

One of the things that had made Asch famous was the invention of an elegantly simple but powerful experimental paradigm to study conformity. Asch's interest in conducting research on conformity was stimulated by his dissatisfaction—and vigorous disagreement—with a prevailing view of human beings that had "almost exclusively stressed the slavish submission of individuals to group forces [and] has neglected to inquire into their possibilities for independence and for productive relations with the human environment." Asch had a more optimistic view of human nature: Rather than a passive reaction to social pressures, a person's social behavior, he argued, was typically a more rational process, the end product of an active and reasoned weighing of the behavioral alternatives available. This view represented a drastic departure from the prevailing mechanical approach to the social influence process, which was grounded in behaviorism. For behaviorists, reinforcement or reward played a central role in the learning and maintenance of new behaviors. We yield to social pressures, they argued, because in the past whenever we conformed to other people's opinions some rewarding consequence would typically follow. In the stimulus-response language of behaviorism, because of past reinforcements, another person's opinion serves as a stimulus that automatically evokes a conforming response. Asch's more rational perspective on social interaction supplemented the role played by Kurt Lewin and his students in freeing social psychology from the grip of behaviorism.

The essence of Asch's experimental procedure to study conformity was to put an individual into a group situation in which he discovers his judgments to be in direct conflict with those of everyone else. Roger Brown referred to this experimental paradigm as an "epistemological nightmare" for the experimental subject. Specifically, in Asch's classic experiment on independence and conformity, when a participant arrived at the laboratory for his scheduled appointment, he would be directed to join seven other participants who were already seated at a table. Asch explained that the purpose of the experiment was to study perceptual judgment. On each of eighteen trials, Asch would present different sets of four vertical lines to the group. On each trial, the subject's task was the same: to match the length of one line with one of three other lines of varying lengths. Each member of the group, in turn, was to announce his judgment publicly. Although the experiment seemed absurdly simple at the beginning, one subject would very quickly find himself saddled with a dilemma. His predicament was made possible by the fact that he was the only naïve subject: The other seven participants were secretly in cahoots with Asch. These "confederates," as they are called, were trained to announce incorrect matches on twelve of the eighteen trials (these twelve are referred to as the "critical" trials).

On the first two trials, things generally proceed smoothly, with all members of the group announcing the same correct matching line. On the third trial, the third line is the correct match, and the naïve subject waits for his turn to say so. The first "subject" announces "line 1." Then the second person says "line 1." *Something's terribly wrong here*, the real subject might think to himself as each of the other participants in turn gives "line 1" as his answer. By the time it is his turn, the puzzled subject finds himself trapped in a conflict that demands immediate resolution: Should he trust his own judgment or should he go along with the unanimous majority? Asch found, to his surprise, that subjects went along with the bogus majority's answers about a third of the time.

Asch went on to conduct a number of variations on this basic procedure, in order to identify the factors that lead to lesser or greater amounts of conformity. For example, in different experiments he examined the effects of the size of the bogus majority, the difficulty of the perceptual task (by varying the length differences among the three possible matching lines), and the importance of a non-unanimous majority (where a member of the false majority was instructed to deviate from the others and also give correct answers).

...

No longer shackled by financial worries and buoyed by a renewed self-confidence, Milgram felt freer to be himself in his second year at Harvard. He unveiled an unbuttoned persona, marked by spontaneity, imaginative whimsy, an uninhibited sociability, a wry sense of humor, and sometimes cockiness. Contrary to Harvard norms, he conversed on a first-name basis with younger faculty such as Richard Solomon and George Mandler, with whom he took the Pro-seminar in Social and Clinical Psychology in the fall of 1955. He would get his friend John Shaffer to join him in little improvisational skits and parodies. He would readily start conversations with strangers in the street. Sometimes he sat in his dorm room for an hour or two, eyes closed, creating and watching richly textured movies in his head. He used peyote with a small group of classmates. One of these was Robert Palmer, who went on to become a clinical psychologist. Palmer remembers the accentuated sensory experience that peyote created. He recalls driving through the streets of Cambridge with colored lights becoming extremely bright and vivid, and walking through a room and seeing the colors red and green float onto the surface of a white linoleum floor.

In the spring semester of 1956, while working as a research assistant to Asch, Milgram signed up for four courses. On February 21, three weeks into the semester, he received a note from Mrs. Sprague informing him that he had exceeded the maximum number of courses (three) that students could take when they had assistantships. He wrote back to her, contesting her interpretation of the rules and telling her that, if she was correct, he planned to petition the dean, adding dryly: "In anticipation of the correctness of your view, I am already looking for a scribe to write out my petition in the form of an illuminated manuscript—and in Latin—that will certainly have its effect." Eleanor Sprague—who was a walking repository of departmental rules, both written and not, was right, of course. Milgram's appeal to the dean was turned down, and he had to drop one of the courses.

When he wrote to Frederick Mosteller, the acting dean of the Committee of Higher Degrees, about taking two summer courses, the letter was tinged with chutzpah: He ended his letter by saying that "since it appears to me unlikely that your office will object to my program, I shall regard it as considered satisfactory by the Department unless I am informed otherwise." Despite his cockiness—or perhaps because of it—he must have been "informed otherwise," because his transcript shows that he took only one course that summer.

CHAPTER 3

NORWAY AND FRANCE

T HE TOPIC MILGRAM chose for his doctoral dissertation was "national character"—those traits that distinguish one culture from another. Milgram first became fascinated with cross-cultural differences during the summer of 1953, when he traveled through France, Spain, and Italy. When he came to Harvard, this interest took on a more disciplined and systematic guise. He did an analysis of national stereotypes for Allport's social psychology qualifying course in the spring of 1955. A year later, he took a reading course on national character with Roger Brown in which he covered about a hundred articles and books related to the topic. Milgram's exposure to Asch's group pressure experiments when he served as his teaching and research assistant during the 1955–1956 academic year gave him the experimental tools to extract a specific researchable question from the sprawling, unruly domain of cross-cultural inquiry: How did two or more nationalities compare in their degree of conformity?

He wanted Allport to be his dissertation supervisor, since they had already established a warm relationship and the study of cultural differences and intergroup relations was one of Allport's diverse research interests. Perhaps most important was Allport's mentoring style, which would give Milgram a good deal of latitude in the development and implementation of his research ideas. As Tom Pettigrew, another Allport student, put it, "A firm believer in the uniqueness of personality, Gordon practiced what he preached with his doctoral students. He let us follow our own pursuits and methods. . . ."

Milgram's plan was to complete virtually all of his course requirements for his Ph.D. degree in social psychology during the 1956–1957 academic year and then conduct research for his doctoral dissertation in 1957–1958. He needed to obtain financial support for it—especially since the research he had in mind would need to be done abroad. In the fall of 1956, he made some inquiries and found that a research training fellowship offered by the Social Science Research Council (SSRC) seemed a like a good fit for his needs and qualifications.

Allport had been out of the country since the spring of 1956. Milgram was reluctant to bother him during his travels, but SSRC's deadline for fellowship applications was January 7, 1957, and Allport wasn't scheduled to return to the United States until the beginning of December. So, on October 17, Milgram sent a lengthy letter to Allport—who was then in Italy—asking him to be chairman of his dissertation committee and describing his research idea:

> I am very sorry to impose on your stay in Europe with matters that ordinarily should be confined to Emerson Hall, but time has a bearing on the matter I would like to discuss. . . . I would like to write my thesis in 1957–58, on the subject of national character, and with you as my thesis director. . . . There is no other person in the Harvard community I would prefer to work with. I know of other staff members for whom national character is a more central interest than it appears to be for you, but I see my approach as far more congruent to your sympathies—as expressed, say, in chapter six of [Allport's book] *The Nature of Prejudice*, titled "The Scientific Study of Group Differences." I anticipate differing views here and there but within a clear context of extensive accord.

He told Allport that in his immersion in the writings on national differences, he found them largely speculative and impressionistic, with very little grounded in objective, scientific research involving the direct, systematic observations of concrete behavior. The specific experimental technique he had in mind was one he had become intimately familiar with when he served as Asch's assistant. He would conduct a cross-cultural replication of

Asch's conformity experiment in three countries—England, France, and Germany. It would be a variation of the original procedure in which the task of distinguishing between a pair of acoustic tones would be substituted for judgments of length of lines. This modification would make the procedure more economical, since he could prerecord the "pressure group's" incorrect responses, eliminating the need to use confederates.

In concluding his letter to Allport, he noted that although his own enthusiasm for the project "has been enduring and high . . . I do not presume it to be contagious. Still, you may not think it too bad an idea, and perhaps you will consent to be my thesis director."

In his letter of reply from Rome, Allport expressed his general approval of the proposed area of research and its value for the reasons Milgram stated. He was glad that Milgram was interested in the topic of national character and that he had already done intensive reading on it. And he agreed to be Milgram's thesis supervisor, provided that the project they would work out would be mutually satisfactory. But the experiment itself concerned him: "The design you outline is not feasible, I fear. Chiefly, the difficulty is your overly optimistic view of facilities, availability of subjects, European collaboration. These are serious problems and you would experience endless frustration." Allport told Milgram to "hold the problem over" until his return to Cambridge in early December when they could have a conference to pursue it further in person.

The meeting with Allport after his return to Harvard resulted in a streamlining of Milgram's research plans into a more realistic and workable project. From a three-way comparison of conformity, it was modified to a two-country comparison between the United States and Norway. Allport had suggested Norway because the Institute for Social Research in Oslo seemed ideally suited for cross-cultural research. It had served as the initiator and central office of one of the few cross-cultural studies conducted up to that point that had used experimental methods—a multination study of the consequences of deviation from group norms, conducted by a short-lived group, the Organization for Comparative Social Research (OCSR). The institute had staff members who had interests in cross-cultural investigations, such as Ragnar Rommetveit and Stein Rokkan. It seemed likely

that the institute and its staff would be hospitable to Milgram and his intended research.

Allport wrote Rommetveit and Rokkan, with a copy of the proposal
Milgram was sending to the SSRC, asking whether it was feasible for Milgram to do the research at the institute and whether they would be able to
provide any necessary help once he was there. Allport added that "Milgram
himself is a young and zealous fellow, full of drive, responsive and friendly,
about 23 years of age. I think you would like him." In their replies to Allport, both men expressed a genuine interest in Milgram's project. They referred Milgram to the appropriate personnel who would help him work out
the technical details, both at the Institute for Social Research and at its af-
filiate, the Psychological Institute (the Department of Psychology) at the
University of Oslo.

Milgram's application to the SSRC for the Research Training Fellowship
went out during the last week of 1956. On March 26, 1957, he was informed by a letter from the SSRC that his name was placed on a short list
of alternates; the possibility of his being awarded a fellowship was contin-
gent on some awardees turning down their offers. Apparently that did in
fact happen, because only two weeks later, on April 10, he was awarded a
fellowship—a sum of $3,200 for a twelve-month period.

Unfortunately, two months later, Milgram received a letter from Allport
informing him that "at its meeting on June 6th, this Department voted that
you fail [sic] the examination in Statistics." As a requirement for the Ph.D.
degree, students had to pass several special exams demonstrating their com-
petencies in various areas, one of which was statistics. It was given only
once a year, in the spring, so Milgram could retake it the following year at
the earliest.

When Allport informed Elbridge Sibley, the executive director of the
SSRC, about this unexpected development, Sibley was "considerably distressed," since mastery of statistical techniques was necessary to enable
Milgram to do the data analyses involved in his dissertation research. Milgram wrote Sibley that despite the fact that he managed to bungle the statistics exam, he felt—and he had been told—that his level of competence in
statistics, attained in part by an honors course in statistics in the summer of

1956—was more than adequate to meet the needs of his research project. But if Sibley was not satisfied by this affirmation, Milgram proposed to prepare a detailed "statistical monograph" containing a precise description of the data-analytic techniques he would use in his research—and he would do this before his departure for Norway. After receiving assurances about Milgram's competence from Allport and Fred Mosteller, Sibley told Milgram that he could move ahead with his research plans without additional statistical preparation. The reassurance from Mosteller was especially compelling, since he was a leading expert in the field of statistical techniques.

Milgram started receiving the monthly installments of his fellowship stipend in July, which he used to carry out pretesting of his research procedure with Harvard students over the summer.

One final hurdle had to be cleared before Milgram could sail for Norway. He needed to get formal approval of his thesis proposal from his thesis committee at a meeting convened for that purpose. Since most of the committee members were away during the summer, that meeting could not take place before September 23, the first day of the fall semester, when all of the faculty would be back in Cambridge.

Milgram's meeting with his thesis committee took place on September 24. Although the committee offered some suggestions and criticisms that they wanted Milgram to take into account—not an uncommon feature of thesis proposal conferences at most universities—they approved the proposal. In a follow-up letter, Allport summarized the points raised by the committee at the thesis meeting and concluded with what amounted to a vote of confidence in the soundness of Milgram's judgments:

Let me repeat that we know change will be needed in the design and we hope you will prove flexible in handling the new situation and the advice of your Norwegian colleagues. At the same time don't change your subject to the "Norwegian Herring Market" without consulting us!

You have our best wishes for a very fine year.

Cordially yours,
Gordon W. Allport

On October 5, Milgram departed from New York aboard the Oslo-bound ocean liner *Bergensfjord*, a sleek new acquisition of the Norwegian-American Line. The ship docked in Oslo on an uncharacteristically sunny day. The autumn air was brisk and the city was suffused by the light of the mellow October sun. People were bustling about energetically engaged in their everyday business. In a letter to a female friend a few days after his arrival, Milgram joked that his hosts at the Institute for Social Research had sent a cute blonde secretary to meet him, but they had missed each other. He observed that Oslo was much more like an American city than Paris, Rome, or Madrid, with big cars plying the streets and people dressing much like in Minneapolis or Podunk. The girls were very attractive and very tall, most of them "tower[ing] over little Stanley." Still, he noticed that there were enough of his size, and he was looking forward to getting to know them. He noted that Oslo "clearly lacks the charm of Copenhagen. In fact, it more or less lacks charm." Over the course of the year, that glib judgment would be displaced by a more nuanced view that included a greater fondness for the city and its people. In fact, about a month later, he wrote to Allport: "I have great respect for what the Norwegians have created from a land none too generous in its natural offerings. On the other hand, someone might tactfully suggest to some of our modern Vikings that Grieg does not exactly rank with Bach, nor Ibsen with Shakespeare."

Although Milgram's host organization was the Institute for Social Research, it turned out that the institute did not have a room available that would be suitable for Milgram's experiment. But his hosts were able to help him get one in the basement of the Department of Psychology of the University of Oslo, with which they had a close working relationship. In fact, his primary mentor and adviser in Norway, the social psychologist Ragnar Rommetveit, had a joint appointment at both places. In addition to the help provided by the faculty and staff at the institute and the department, Milgram could seek out the advice of two prominent American social psychologists—Irving Janis, of Yale University, and Daniel Katz, from the University of Michigan—who happened to be there as visiting Fulbright scholars.

Milgram's first month in Oslo was devoted to the intricate technical details of setting up his experimental procedure—from drilling holes and hooking up electrical connections to tape-recording instructions, pairs of tones, and the voices of the persons who would serve as the pressure group. A final preparatory step was to do a dry run with some pretest subjects. In order to conduct the experiment in the subjects' native language, Milgram had hired Guttorm Langaard, a doctoral student in psychology. His was the voice of the Norwegian experimenter, and he helped with the recruitment of subjects and other details.

By the middle of November, Milgram had a well-oiled experimental setting and routine in place, ready to receive subjects. To enhance the generalizability of his findings, he made sure all the regions of Norway would be represented among his sample of student subjects. This would be easy, because the University of Oslo was the only full-fledged university in the country at the time, and its student body came from all over—from the Oslo area in the South to the Nord-Norge region beyond the Arctic Circle in the North.

Whenever an appointment was made with a subject, the importance of promptness was stressed, since he would be one of six people participating at the same time, and the session could not begin until everyone was present. When a subject arrived at the lab, he was asked to put his coat on a bench, which was already piled high with other outer garments. A series of six numbered doors lined the laboratory, and the subject was taken to the one marked "Subject 6" in Norwegian. These and other details were meant to create the impression that all the other subjects were already there. The door was opened, revealing a small booth. The subject was seated in the booth, earphones were fitted over his head, and he was handed a microphone.

The experimental task involved judging which of a pair of short acoustic tones was longer, the first or the second. There were thirty trials. On each, a different pair of sounds would be heard through the headphones. The subject would be the last to give his judgment, after hearing the voices of the other five subjects, one after the other, giving their judgments. The other five voices, of course, were the voices of Milgram's confederates. On sixteen of the thirty trials, interspersed throughout the series, the confederates unanimously gave the wrong answer. On those sixteen critical trials, Milgram's subjects confronted a troubling conflict, similar to the one Asch's subjects had faced: Should they maintain their independence of judgment or yield to group pressure and announce the same incorrect answer?

The subject also did not know that the others constituted a "synthetic group" that was not physically present in the lab. Each subject heard only the voices of the group, which Milgram had prerecorded on tape and deftly synchronized—so deftly, in fact, that Milgram had a hard time convincing many a subject, after the experiment was over, that he had been the only "live" subject in the lab.

Milgram had an irrepressible sense of humor—with almost a life of its own—that refused to be tethered by common conventions of appropriateness, such as that dissertations should be written with a straight-ahead, and sometimes unintendedly soporific, seriousness. So, in his dissertation, he explained one of the practical benefits of an imaginary pressure group as follows: "The group is always willing to perform in the laboratory at the experimenter's convenience, and personalities on tape demand no replay royalties."

In the first experiment, subjects conformed to the bogus majority—that is, gave the wrong answer—on 62 percent of the critical trials. After each experimental session, Milgram conducted individual interviews with the participants to gather qualitative information, after which he revealed to them the true purposes and details of the experiment. Almost all subjects completely denied or underestimated the majority's influence on their own answers. Although Milgram gradually attained a serviceable mastery of Norwegian over the course of his year in Oslo, during the early experiments he worried that he did not know the language well enough to conduct the interviews in the subjects' native language. He quickly discovered that this was a needless worry because he could conduct the interviews in English. "It is hard to convey," he wrote with a palpable sense of wonder, "how uniformly competent these subjects were in expressing themselves in English." Not a single one of the 150 university student participants had to exclude himself from the interview because of insufficient knowledge of English.

In a second experiment, Milgram wanted to see if putting a premium on answering correctly, by suggesting the students' behavior would have serious consequences, would make the students less conforming. He did this by telling them (as well as the subjects in subsequent variations) that information gleaned from the experiments would be applied to the design of safety signals on airplanes. This information did reduce the level of conformity to 56 percent, but the difference between this figure and the 62 percent conformity rate in the first experiment, referred to as the *Baseline condition,* was not statistically significant.

Even though Milgram had jacked up the consequences of responding inaccurately in this second experiment—the *Aircraft condition*—people were still yielding to peer pressure more than 50 percent of the time. While the Baseline and Aircraft conditions differed in how motivated subjects were (or should have been) to answer accurately, both required a public response that could be heard, or so the subjects thought, by the others. Milgram wondered: Would eliminating this feature free the subjects to act more independently, or was their propensity to conform so deeply ingrained that even if their answer would not be heard by others, they would yield to group pressure?

In the next experiment, another group of subjects was given the same test as the subjects in the Aircraft experiment, with one important difference: After hearing the answers of the other "subjects" over the intercom, they were asked to write their answers on paper rather than announce them publicly for the group to hear. In this *Private condition,* the rate of conformity dropped further, but not as precipitously as one might have expected. Subjects still conformed to the majority almost 50 percent of the time.

Milgram's initial dissertation research proposal called for a Norway-U.S. comparison. He planned to return to the United States after he completed the Norwegian data collection phase and put a comparable group of American college students through the same experimental procedures, completing both parts of the research in one year. In the research proposal accompanying his application to SSRC, he had hypothesized that Americans would conform more than Norwegians. This expectation was based largely on impressionistic reports—it was more an educated guess than a deeply held conviction. Milgram's main goal was to harness the enlightening power of the experimental method to provide objective evidence of behavioral differences between cultures. He was more interested in *whether or not* such differences could be identified than the specific direction those differences would take.

This approach was a departure from the prevailing view among postwar social psychologists, who believed that theory-based research aimed at testing directional hypotheses was the royal road to scientific purity, a legacy inherited from the "harder" sciences. There was also an unspoken and largely unconscious motivation: To develop a hypothesis and then have it verified in an experiment would be evidence of one's scientific acumen and prescience.

Although Milgram identified solidly with social psychology, he disagreed with its heavy emphasis on hypothesis-testing:

> It is a common fallacy of social psychology that the most important function of experimentation is to verify hypotheses. Sometimes there is a good reason to guess the outcome of an experiment, but often such a guess is neither warranted nor desirable. In this study, the group pressure experiment was conceived as a tool for controlled observation and measurement. At this stage of cross-national research, when even simple, objective descriptions of national groups have not been attained, an experiment is no more in need of an hypothesis than is a thermometer. The utility of a measuring instrument does not depend on the guess we make about its reading.

It did not take Milgram long to discover—through the high conformity rates he was seeing in his lab, discussions with his subjects and others, and his own direct observation of life in Oslo—that his hypothesis about Norwegian individualism crashed head-on with the realities of Norwegian behavior and values. He observed a society pervaded by an egalitarian ethos where group solidarity and cohesiveness were valued and where standing out from the crowd, being conspicuous, and drawing too much attention to oneself were frowned upon. Milgram's Norwegian colleagues introduced him to the *Janteloven,* or the "Jante Laws," whose ten "commandments" embody, and perhaps help maintain, the norms of group solidarity found in Norway and other parts of Scandinavia. Three of these commandments are:

Thou shalt not believe thyself better than us.
Thou shalt not believe thou knowest more than us.
Thou shalt not think thou art wiser than us.

Milgram had sent Allport a detailed progress report after the completion of the first three experiments. He noted that the general pattern of scores he found among his Norwegian subjects was very similar to those of his American subjects in his pretests at Harvard, effectively invalidating his hypothesis regarding Norwegian-U.S. differences: "My guess that Norwegians would be impressively more independent than Americans appears to be contradicted by the experimental results." Furthermore, he concluded that "one need not live here too long before being convinced that Norwegians more closely resemble Americans in temperament, outlook, and way of life than any other European people. The problem of finding experimental differences between national groups is imposing enough without jeopardizing the outcome by choosing an unpromising comparison nation."

This development forced Milgram to think about which country might in fact be a promising substitute for the United States as a comparison to Norway. France came immediately to mind. His experience living in Paris during the summer of 1953 suggested that France was a country marked by far less social consensus than Norway, a country with a tradition that seemed to prize critical judgment and diversity of opinion. "France seems to me to be a very good bet," he wrote Allport. "It takes me from the Nordic to Latin system; Norwegians and Frenchmen regard themselves as very different (and probably inter-sterile) breeds of men."

The intriguing and unexpected findings of the first few conditions convinced Milgram of the need for additional experimental variations, beyond the few planned originally, to test the limits of Norwegian conformity. There was also the gnawing question of generalizability. No matter how many additional experiments he conducted with his sample of university students, he could not be sure his findings were representative of the population at large. Even though his subjects came from all over Norway, at that time only one out of 1,000 Norwegians attended the University of Oslo. Thus, Milgram felt it would be important to repeat at least a couple of the conditions with a non-university sample.

Allport was delighted with Milgram's progress. He found the rationale for his modified plans reasonable and convincing, and he gave them his blessing. The change of plans meant that Milgram would have to extend his stay in Norway. It was now mid-February. He estimated that he could complete the additional Norwegian experiments by the end of May, a month before his fellowship year was up and the monthly stipends would end. It was clear that, regardless of which comparison country he and Allport agreed on, he would need funding for another year. As he was mulling over this problem, he received, "with the expediency of a Biblical miracle," a letter from Elbridge Sibley informing him that the SSRC had just begun a Completion of Doctoral Dissertation fellowship program that would provide him with the financial support to continue his doctoral research into a second year. Besides completing an application form spelling out his research plans, he needed a confidential evaluation from someone familiar with his work so far. In a letter to Sibley, Allport readily provided a strong recommendation: "Since Milgram is a very bright person and making such excellent progress, I hope you will find it possible to back him an additional year." Milgram was notified that he had been awarded the one-year extension on March 20, 1958.

He then went about designing some additional experiments with Norwegian college students. In one, Milgram wanted to test his subjects' sensitivity to audible criticisms. So he taped comments from his confederates— such as "Trying to show off?"—which, by means of a separate tape recorder, Milgram would inject immediately after a subject gave a correct response that contradicted the majority's erroneous responses. This kind of censure from peers—the *Censure condition*—caused the conformity rate to jump to 75 percent.

The last experiment with his student population was aimed at ruling out an alternative explanation for the findings in the previous experiments. In postexperimental interviews, some subjects claimed that they matched the majority's judgments because they were unsure of their own accuracy. But if they had been able to overcome their doubts, they would have remained more independent. To explore the validity of this claim, Milgram modified the laboratory procedure to enable subjects to request—by ringing a bell that would be heard by the experimenter and, supposedly, by the other "subjects"—that a pair of tones be presented again so they could reexamine them before giving their answers. The rate of conformity dropped somewhat to 69 percent. Even more telling was the fact that only five out of the twenty subjects in this *Bell condition* requested a repetition. The fact that a majority of the subjects did not avail themselves of the opportunity to hear the tones again provided strong verification that the subjects' yielding responses were indeed indicators of their conforming tendencies and not merely their doubts about the accuracy of their answers.

To verify that the levels of conformity he had obtained so far were not aberrations, limited for some reason to college students, Milgram tested a group of factory workers at the Elektrisk Bureau, the Norwegian equivalent of General Electric or Westinghouse. With the meticulous attention to detail that made his experimental dramas so credible, Milgram made a new set of tapes of this phony majority, using employees from the same factory so that the naïve subjects would hear genuine working-class accents similar to theirs. Milgram replicated two experiments—the Aircraft and Censure conditions—with this group.

He found that the workers were more independent than the students. In the Aircraft condition, their conformity rate was 49 percent, compared with the student rate of 56 percent. In the Censure condition, they yielded to the majority on 68 percent of the critical trials, compared with the students' yielding rate of 75 percent. These differences were not statistically significant, however; that is, they were within the range that could be due to chance. For all practical purposes, then, the level of conformity among both groups was about the same, enabling Milgram to conclude that, in their totality, his results were broadly indicative of an important Norwegian behavioral characteristic.

To obtain subjects' reactions to the ethical issues pertaining to the experiment, Milgram distributed a questionnaire to his Norwegian student subjects about two months after their participation. One question asked subjects how they felt immediately after the experiment. Most of them expressed annoyance with themselves because they hadn't figured out what was really going on.

A second question asked, "Do you feel now that the experiment was ethical or unethical?" with four response options: Very unethical, unethical, ethical, and neither ethical nor unethical. Of the 91 subjects who responded to this question, no one rated it very unethical, 8 judged it unethical, 14 as ethical, and the majority—69 subjects—rated it neither ethical nor unethical.

A third question asked: "How do you feel now about having been in the experiment?" There were five response options, anchored by "I'm very glad to have been in the experiment" at one end and "I'm very sorry to have been in the experiment" at the other. No one selected this last option. Only one out of 93 respondents said he was sorry, and a majority—70 subjects—said they were glad or very glad to have been in the experiment. This is a question Milgram would employ again in later years as his experiments grew increasingly controversial.

Milgram ended his presentation of the postexperimental results with some observations about them:

> It appears that most subjects were glad to have participated, despite the trickery involved. The reasons for this seem to be: First they understood that any deception used was not primarily for personal gain, but for the advancement of knowledge. They appreciated that they were informed of the true character of the experiment as soon as possible. They understood that whatever their performance may have been, we placed them in a position of trust by revealing the true purpose and methods of the experiment, and they knew that the success of the experimental project depended on their willingness to support this trust. If for twenty minutes, we abused their dignity, we reaffirmed it by extending to them our confidence.... Most subjects accept the necessity of deception in this experiment and do not

condemn it morally. That is not to say they should have the last word on the matter. No action is divested of its unethical properties by the expedient of a public-opinion poll; nor is the outcome of such an inquiry irrelevant to the issue.

This degree of attention to the ethics of experimentation was unusual at the time among psychological researchers. A notable exception was Asch, who in his various reports about his conformity experiments addressed the ethical issues connected with his research. For example, in one of his reports he noted that "the circumstances [of the experiment] place a special responsibility on the experimenter and obligate him to surround the procedure with proper safeguards. It has been the writer's experience that far more important than the momentary pain or discomfort of the procedure is the way in which the experimenter deals with the subject." Milgram had read those reports, but in describing his ethics questionnaire to Allport, he did not reference Asch. Rather, he credited discussions by another social psychologist, Richard Crutchfield, and unspecified others about the ethical problems associated with conformity experiments as sources for the idea. However, it seems reasonable to assume that contact with Asch, through his writings and as his assistant at Harvard, played an important role in the development of Milgram's ethical sensitivities.

...

Although the experiments absorbed most of Milgram's time and attention during his stay in Norway, and then later in France, he found time to develop a social life, cultivate friendships, become part of the local student culture, maintain an active correspondence with family and friends back in the United States, and take trips to other European countries during vacation breaks.

In a letter to a friend in New York, he bragged that word had reached him from Harvard that his doctoral research was being lauded as one of the most important studies being conducted by a member of the department. But he admitted that this was not as impressive as it might sound, because *he* was the one who had circulated the rumor in the first place. In addition to sending letters to his mother, Joel, and Marjorie, he would sometimes send them souvenirs. Once, after sending some carved wooden Norwegian figurines for Joel, he confided that they were actually carvings of *himself*: "It's amazing how a change in climate and diet affects alteration in appearance and character." He would keep his mother informed about the progress he was making in his work. She would, in turn, write chatty letters expressing her pride in his accomplishments and about her new little car, the movies she had seen, and the like. And she was the caring Jewish mother, in the best sense, asking him to be especially careful driving in his Volkswagen; gently suggesting that he buy a good suit or two for a planned trip to England, "but only what you will be proud to wear back home"; wishing before a subsequent trip to England that he wouldn't go because of a flu epidemic; admonishing him for overdrawing his checking account; and wondering if he ever met any nice Jewish girls.

But Milgram's letters home could also be somber. One, written to his Harvard schoolmate, John Shaffer, has a prophetic poignancy, in light of his later preoccupations:

> My true spiritual home is Central Europe, not France, the Mediterranean countries, England, Scandinavia, or Northern Germany, but that area which is bounded by the cities of Munich, Vienna, and Prague. . . . I should have been born into the German-speaking Jewish community of Prague in 1922 and died in a gas chamber some twenty years later. How I came to be born in the Bronx Hospital I'll never quite understand.

Among Milgram's most memorable activities in Norway was skiing, which became one of his true joys. He found himself drawn irresistibly to the sport by the glistening beauty of the snow-covered hills of Nordmarka surrounding Oslo, and he was glad to have succumbed. As he wrote Mrs. Sprague, "I did not know how to ski when I arrived in Oslo; I did not exactly know how to ski when I deserted from Oslo, but somewhere in the middle

I remember gliding down long, quiet mountain trails in the early evening, and the sun lighting up a cloud of snow powder thrown up by flying skis."

What made his Norwegian experience even more pleasurable was finding some female companionship. In January 1958, he met a British girl, Rosalind, who became his steady girlfriend for the next three months until she had to return home. On Saturdays they would go skiing together and then cook dinner in his apartment. Although Stanley didn't fall in love with her, he was very fond of her, and her constant company made him happy and contented.

During his stay in Oslo, Milgram shared an apartment with a group of Norwegian students in the *Studentbyen*, the student residences on the hills surrounding Oslo. One of his apartment-mates was Arne Olav Brundtland, who was engaged to a future prime minister of Norway, Gro Harlem Brundtland. Stanley had never seen five people living in such close quarters getting along so well. A sense of camaraderie and community developed within the group, which made parting at the end of the school year a genuinely sad experience.

Milgram's warm feelings about the Norwegians he came to know were in stark contrast with his reactions to the physical surroundings. Writing to a Norwegian friend after he had left the country, he recalled that this was "the damp season in Oslo, when the skies pour down their waters on the urine colored walls of the older parts of the town. It is the season for pneumonia, sinusitis and despondency. The season of mud. But when the sun does shine, it has an agreeably thick quality to it, and the sunlight washes everything in its amber fluidity."

Milgram ended up staying in Norway longer than he had planned. Although he had completed the experiments with the student population in late March, locating a non-university subject population for the last part of his research proved difficult. It took till the middle of May to line up the workers at the Elektrisk Bureau, and it was the middle of July by the time he had completed the two experimental conditions with them. He stayed in Oslo for another month to use the computing facilities at the institute— punching his data onto IBM cards—and to analyze them and draft a preliminary write-up of his results. He then traveled to Paris, arriving there in mid-August.

Stanley's acclimation to life in Paris occurred more quickly and more easily than in Oslo. Things didn't appear to have changed much over the five years since the summer of 1953. He was captivated by the city's physical beauty:

> Paris is the city I like best in the world. It is especially beautiful . . . in the autumn, when the tan and gold maple leaves float by the classical marble statuary in the Jardin du Luxembourg, when the air is fragrant with autumn smoke, and the Seine captures the tan, crimson, and orange colors of the season. Oslo is a town, Copenhagen a city, New York a metropolis, and Paris a civilization. . . .

He had mixed feelings about the people of France, however. Not long after his arrival he expressed his pessimism in a letter to a Harvard classmate, Saul Sternberg, about the prospects of getting the kind of cooperation he had received in Oslo: "There is so much selfishness, dishonesty and pettiness in this country. These damned alcoholic frogs are about as cooperative as megalomaniacal mules."

On the other hand, in a letter to another friend a couple of months later, he wrote that he felt constantly attuned to the city of Paris: "If I am feeling depressed here, I need only walk through the crowded marketplace or the bustling narrow streets or noisy squares and before I know it I am aglow with the feeling of being part of humanity. There is something about the French that is poignantly human. They laugh, they shout, they scowl, joke, cheat, cry, sing, bargain, argue, smile, explode, repent in a way that lets me know they are my species. . . ."

Milgram's acclimation to Paris included becoming informed about its temptations. Recalling his Paris experience in a letter to a close friend in the United States, he wrote:

> When my girl 'friend' left Paris I started appraising the price of French meat. Very high. The girls must be unionized. 1500 francs buys you a fair to mediocre 'companion' in Paris. If you're willing to spend 5,000 francs ($12.50

at the then current exchange rate, black market of course) we American boys, who spoke good French could arrange with a stunning French slut on the Champs Elysees. Of course I was in no position to throw away 5,000 francs (Ye gads, I lived on that for my last three weeks). In Seville, the situation is much less agonizing and a piece of choice Spanish meat could be had for $1.10 (44 pesetas). Kosher meat can't be had anywhere. . . .

As in Oslo, he immersed himself in the local student scene. He had found living accommodations in one of the many university student residences associated with the University of Paris, Fondation Victor Lyon, located on Boulevard Jourdan. He paid $20 a month for a private modern room with a charming floor-to-ceiling window providing a panoramic view of a classical garden. He was able to obtain a French government meal subsidy that kept him well fed for less than sixty cents a day. He confided in a letter to an American friend that his entry into the Victor Lyon residence was gained fraudulently. While the letter contains no further explanation, most likely living in one of the student residences as well as qualifying for the meal subsidy required being a university student in Paris, and he passed himself off as one.

His stay at Victor Lyon was almost cut short by the dictatorial director of the residence. In December 1958, she threatened to evict him for staying up until all hours typing and getting up late in the morning, which she deemed dissolute behavior inconsistent with the rather rigid rules of conduct she expected the students to follow. He managed to stay on, but his troubles with "La directrice" came to a head when he wrote an article, in perfect idiomatic French, for *Le Journal de Victor Lyon*, a newsletter put out by the student residents of Victor Lyon—a biting criticism of the director for creating an oppressive atmosphere:

To Madame the Director, the most important thing in our Fondation is neither a book of science, nor a sketchbook filled by an art student, nor the writings of a resident, but the little notebook that the night guard keeps with jealousy, and in which he reports the name of every student who comes back after 1:00 A.M. . . . This notebook . . . , secretly looked at, is for me a symbol of what is wrong at Victor Lyon.

Although other writers expressed similar sentiments in the newsletter, she was so enraged by his article that she sent a complaint to his department at Harvard. The matter ended up a mere tempest in a carafe after some local administrators came to Milgram's defense. The Committee on Higher Degrees of the Social Relations department took up the matter at a meeting but decided to take no action given the supportive letters Talcott Parsons had received from a couple of administrators of the student residences. One wrote: "Thanks to the newsletter, the students have gotten most of the requests that they were asking for. All of the facts cited in the various articles are completely true. By his [Milgram's] frankness, his good humor and general friendliness he has the appreciation of all his fellow students. . . . In all matters he has behaved in a responsible manner." The letters laid the matter to rest for good, although a brief notation on the discussion about him in the meeting of the Committee on Higher Degrees remained in his graduate record.

...

Milgram's pessimism about getting assistance in France—a pessimism shared by Allport—turned out to have some basis. It wasn't until mid-October, about two months after his arrival in Paris, that he found an appropriate location to set up his lab to conduct his experiments. Jerome Bruner had contacted Professors Robert Pagès and Daniel Lagache of the Social Psychology Laboratory at the Sorbonne on his behalf. As a result of their help, he obtained the use of two rooms within a large student housing complex located in Antony, a small town four miles south of Paris. An important advantage of this setting was the ready availability of a large pool of potential subjects residing within the housing complex who could be approached by door-to-door solicitation.

Since the residence housed students from all parts of France, his subjects represented a broad geographic distribution, as in Norway. Other than the fact that the experiments were conducted in French, Milgram made sure that they were as similar as possible to those conducted in Norway. As an example of Milgram's meticulous attention to detail, he used the same stimulus tapes he had used in Norway—spliced into the French recordings—played on the same tape recorder, "and as it worked on 50 cycle synchronized operation both in France and Norway, we have every assurance that very close tolerances in tape speed were maintained."

As in Norway, Milgram carried out five experiments: Baseline, Airplane, Private, Censure, and Bell conditions. Some readers might wonder: If Milgram's main purpose was to provide a direct behavioral comparison of conformity and independence in Norway and France, why did he do so many variations in each country? Wouldn't repeating the same single experiment in both countries be sufficiently informative? Here is how Milgram explained the rationale for multiple experiments in both countries:

> It would have been superficial to conduct a single experiment in Norway, one in France, and then draw conclusions. . . . If we are concerned with studying national differences, we should be less interested in the simple incidence of conformity in two nations than in a comparison of the patterns of measures stemming from the several experiments. Various uncontrolled factors may raise or lower the absolute level of conformity from one country to the next, but within a nation these factors are likely to affect measures in a uniform way and not upset the relationships among them.

So, how did the French students compare with the Norwegians? On average, the French subjects yielded to the majority less often—about 50 percent of the time—than their Norwegian counterparts, who conformed on 62 percent of the critical trials, and the difference was statistically significant. Moreover, there was a remarkable consistency underlying this overall difference: The French subjects conformed less than the Norwegians in each of the five experimental conditions (see Table 3.1).

Furthermore, while conformity levels were higher among the Norwegian than among the French subjects, the pattern of fluctuations among the conditions was similar in both countries (see Figure 3.1). For example, both groups of students conformed less in the Aircraft condition than in the Baseline condition; in both countries, censure from peers resulted in a greater tendency to yield to them, and so on.

TABLE 3.1   Percentage of Critical Trials That Were Pro-Majority for Five
Experimental Conditions in Norway and France

| | Percentage of Critical Errors | |
| | Norwegian Students | French Students |
Condition		
Baseline	62	50
Aircraft	56	48
Private	50	34
Censure	75	59
Bell	69	58
Average Percentage	62	50

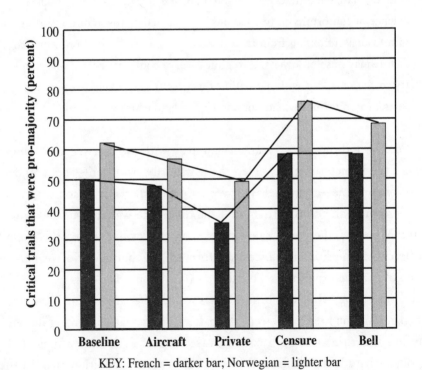

KEY: French = darker bar; Norwegian = lighter bar

FIGURE 3.1   Differences in Levels of Conformity Among the Five
Conditions in Norway and France.

Some additional findings point up the pervasiveness of French-Norwegian differences in their tendency to yield to group pressure: In the Bell condition, in which the subjects were given an opportunity to listen to the tones again before giving their judgment, only five of the twenty in the Norwegian group reexamined the tones, whereas a majority of the French students, fourteen out of twenty, did so. Also, all but one of the French subjects resisted the group at least once, whereas among the Norwegian subjects, 12 percent yielded to the majority on all the critical trials. The French students also expressed their stronger individualism by being more reactive, and sometimes temperamental, in the experimental situation. In the Censure condition, more than half of them made some kind of retaliatory comment in response to the other "subjects'" criticisms—in two cases quite explosively. In Norway, however, this rarely happened.

Milgram had also contemplated testing French workers for comparison with his Norwegian workers. However, he needed adequate time to prepare for the statistics exam in May, and he was concerned that adding a factory sample would unduly prolong his research and interfere with his studying.

Milgram's cross-cultural experiment had broad, groundbreaking significance. It represents a major milestone in the transformation of the topic of national characteristics from armchair speculation to an object of scientific inquiry. In reflecting back on his experiments, Milgram was struck by the compatibility of his findings with features of each country's culture observable in daily life outside of the laboratory, providing additional validation of his results. Norwegians, he noted, have a strong feeling of group identity and social responsibility. "It would not be surprising," he observed, "to find that social cohesiveness of this sort goes hand in hand with a high degree of conformity."

French society, in contrast, is marked by much less unity and a greater diversity of opinions, which could help immunize the individual against social pressures. France, he also noted, has a tradition of dissent. Its citizens place a high value on critical judgment, a tendency that, in Milgram's opinion, "often seems to go beyond reasonable bounds." This in itself, Milgram argued, could help explain the relatively low degree of conformity he found among his French subjects.

Milgram completed the conformity experiments with his French student subjects in late February and planned to return by ship to the United States in March, but his return trip was delayed a few weeks as he waited to find out whether his French girlfriend was pregnant. "Each time something like this happens," he wrote to a Norwegian friend, "I resolve to abandon the irresponsible practice of sharing my pillow, but alas!"

An influential chapter in Milgram's life had ended. Milgram's year-and-a-half sojourn in Europe no doubt played an important role in his becoming a man of unusually broad and eclectic interests. One of his graduate students, Leon Mann, recalled:

> Stanley was quite international and European in his interests and sensibilities—cities, cinema, theater, literature, philosophy, history, social and political movements. There was a very cultured European style about Stanley: Softly spoken, inquisitive, curious about a wide range of . . . topics, gesturing with his hands. He was both a scholar and intellectual.

But even more important was the professional growth he experienced. His conformity study was pioneering research. It was the first time an objective technique was used to study cross-cultural differences in behavior. He now knew that he was capable of doing original research that would provide new insights about human behavior. It was an accomplishment that made him aim high and not settle for the mundane in his future career as a scientific researcher. Those experiments also had more specific carryover effects. The benign responses he received from his Norwegian subjects in the postexperimental questionnaire he had given them unquestionably lifted some of the ethical doubts that might later have prevented him from pursuing controversial research using deception. Indeed, the idea for Milgram's obedience experiments, which grew out of his conformity work, would begin to take shape soon after his return to the States.

CHAPTER 4

FROM THE
"PRINCETITUTE" TO YALE

AFTER RETURNING FROM Europe, Milgram was brimming with self-confidence. He had single-handedly created and carried out a highly ambitious piece of research that broke new ground in cross-cultural studies. He even passed (with "distinction") the statistics exam he had failed before leaving for Europe. His success on the exam was due in part to his experiences applying statistical techniques to the data produced in Norway and France. As a result of his European research and three intellectually stimulating years with some of the best minds in the social sciences at Harvard, he was now sure of what he wanted to do with his life—to have an academic career that would enable him to do original research.

It felt good to be back in Cambridge after an absence of two years. He spent a lazy summer enjoying its delights and reconnecting with classmates and old girlfriends, but making only minimal headway working on his dissertation. After an exhausting search, he found a beautiful apartment and planned to spend "a final, beatific year in Cambridge" completing his dissertation.

He also spent some of his summer at home in Queens. It was during such a visit, toward the end of the summer, that he received a letter from Asch, then at the Institute for Advanced Study in Princeton, that resulted in a drastic change of plans for him.

Since 1947, Asch had been on the faculty at Swarthmore College, but he was spending 1958–1960 at the Institute for Advanced Study as a Visiting

Member. Located on an idyllic campus adjacent to a large nature preserve, the institute was founded in 1930 by philanthropists Louis Bamberger and Caroline Bamberger Field as a setting for pure intellectual inquiry. The choice of a tranquil and remote spot was deliberate, to facilitate scholarly activity without distractions.

Asch had contacted Milgram to invite him to help edit a book Asch was writing on conformity. The job would run through June 1960 and came with a salary of $4,200. Milgram agonized over the pros and cons of accepting Asch's invitation. On the one hand, he felt it would be folly to turn down an invitation from someone of Asch's stature and potential clout as a job reference. Besides, the money would certainly come in handy. On the other hand, having already worked for a year for Asch at Harvard, he could see no further intellectual benefit from any additional apprenticeship with him.

Milgram finally accepted Asch's offer. He decided that perhaps the quietude of Princeton—as compared with Cambridge—would make it easier to concentrate on his own dissertation writing. In addition, he successfully petitioned his department to accept his work with Asch as a substitute for a Topical Seminar in Social Psychology, a requirement for the Ph.D. that he had not yet fulfilled.

While still in high school, on March 1, 1949, Milgram had begun a diary notebook he titled "Thoughts." Over the next eleven years, he would use it sporadically for introspective musings. Milgram's entry for October 2, 1959, provides a blurry snapshot of his state of mind as he was preparing to leave for Princeton:

> Tomorrow I shall abandon my full breasted mistress, Cambridge, for the glitter of the Princetitute. I don't know what's happening, but I trust the deep sources of instinct that guide me in such decisions. Is it too soon to say that a great growth has occurred? Europe was its seedbed, but the fruits are appearing now. . . . The summer was generally unproductive, yet pleasant. There was satisfactory contact with women, and deep sexual satisfaction from renewed episodes with Enid [a girl he first met in the summer of 1956. She was then a math major at Barnard, attending Harvard summer

school]. I have yet to find the woman of my life, and a stable routine of productive labor is far from established; nor is the way to an integration of artistic and academic needs in sight. But new strains of confidence say it is all possible. The mood may pass in an hour, but it is pleasant to support at the moment. Perhaps the hot chocolate of several hours ago is at the root of it.

He had accepted the job with Asch with the expectation that he would be permitted to spend part of his time writing his dissertation, that housing near the institute would be arranged for him, and that he would have some kind of formal affiliation with the institute that he could put on his résumé—although it is not clear how many of these things were made explicit.

As it turned out, not only was the latter expectation not fulfilled, but Milgram was never made to feel at home at the institute—even the use of a sheet of paper or an ink blotter was apt to become a major issue. No housing arrangements were made for him, and he had to settle for a cramped rented room in a private rooming house on Wiggins Street in Princeton. Bureaucratically, Milgram was an invisible man: his name does not appear in any of Asch's correspondence with the administration of the institute. Milgram *was* able to work on his dissertation, but Asch begrudged him the time it took away from assisting him with the book. Milgram ended up having to do his own writing in the evenings and on weekends. At one point, the conflicting pressures became so unbearable that Milgram wrote a letter of resignation to Asch and placed it in his mailbox—only to retrieve it at the last minute.

It turned out to be a very stressful and demoralizing year for Milgram. The dissertation did get completed on time, and so did Asch's book, but on a sour note. Milgram felt that because of the quality of his editorial work, he deserved some citation on the title page of Asch's book—not a coauthorship, but something that would have been of more professional value than a mere "thank you" in the preface. He met some resistance from Asch on this matter and, out of frustration, came up with the following suggested wording in a letter to Asch (which he also ended up not sending):

INDEPENDENCE AGAINST CONFORMITY
by
SOLOMON E. ASCH
In spite of
S. MILGRAM

There were a few bright spots, however. There were stimulating meal-time conversations with some of the most outstanding people in their fields, such as Louis Fischer, an expert on foreign policy, George F. Kennan, the historian and diplomat, and J. Robert Oppenheimer, the atomic scientist and, at the time, the director of the institute. Gazing out at the beautiful milewide expanse of grass in front of the institute's main building provided Milgram an occasional respite from brooding over his situation.

But the more prevailing mood was one of despondency, which he expressed in pitiful letters to friends:

> My only pleasure is to sit on a curbstone and watch the sky for an occasional bird flying south for the winter. I am not used to being so very much alone, and I can think of a few sweet faces with whom I wouldn't mind sharing my pillow when the hour for sleep comes around. . . . I'm listless, uneasy, dissatisfied, bored and fed up. I suffer from status insecurity, incipient mononucleosis, and sexual privation. I'm the little man looking around for some totalitarian movement I can join.

One night, to break up the monotony of his isolated existence, he impulsively drove into New York and ended up in a coffeehouse in Greenwich Village. He struck up a conversation with a stranger sitting nearby, unburdening himself about his work. That stranger turned out to be the singer and actor Theodore Bikel.

Meanwhile, life went on for the other members of his family. Adele continued working in a bakery and maintaining an apartment in Queens, now by herself, since all the children had moved away from home. Milgram's sister, Marjorie, had earned a teacher's degree from Queens College and taught first grade only briefly before marrying a Long Island businessman in 1954, the year Stanley entered Harvard. Now, she kept busy as a housewife raising a family. In 1956, his brother Joel entered the Coast Guard to prove his manhood, but hated it almost from the first moment, leaving after just six months. In 1957, with Stanley's encouragement, he began college at the State University of New York (SUNY) in New Paltz. He got married in 1960, a year before he graduated.

One of the few things that helped keep Milgram emotionally afloat during that difficult year was Allport's constant support and confidence in his judgments as he began writing his dissertation.

On November 4, 1959, Milgram wrote Allport: "I have dropped all pretensions to writing a classic and am deep into the writing of my thesis. . . . I am not satisfied with my level of writing. Given the time I can turn felicitous sentences, but at the present rate of advance there is just enough time to make sure that all sentences contain the required parts of speech." Allport replied: "Your progress report really pleases me. The Table of Contents seem to be efficiently designed, and to promise a work of high quality. . . . No one ever writes a classic by setting out to do so. One says what's on one's mind as well as one can; and, lo, sometimes a classic results. But locally we'll settle for a sound and solid regulation-type thesis."

On January 16, 1960, Milgram reported to Allport that "the dissertation has been pushed forward since my last letter, though not to the point advertised therein. I had planned to have the first draft completed by early January, but this has not been accomplished. I am sending you the outline and have checked off what has been done. As you can see, all fourteen experiments have been written up." Allport wrote back: "Your progress reports are always masterpieces of conviction. (The fact remains that I haven't seen a single word of your thesis!) But I can see that you are well occupied. I am hoping that I can see the thesis or most of it before the final submission [deadline of] April 1. But even this matter I leave to your convenience."

On February 29, 1960, Milgram sent Allport a draft of a chapter, noting that it was "an intermediate version of one of the experimental chapters. . . . How enviable a position you have as thesis advisor. It's like working as night editor for the *New York Times, Christian Science Monitor* and *Manchester Guardian* all at once." Allport: "Perhaps I'm slipping but I cannot find any nasty editorial remarks to make about Experiment five. It is clearly written, pointed, economical."

Milgram completed his dissertation and sent it to Allport during the last week of March, making the April 1 deadline. On May 3, he received a letter from Leonard Doob, a social psychologist and one of the senior members of the Yale Psychology Department, informing him of an opening for an assistant professor of social psychology and inviting him to visit the department to discuss it if he was interested in the position.

Milgram wrote back promptly, telling Doob that the position he described was "of definite interest" but that he had already been offered an excellent position at Harvard for the coming year, and he would have to deal with that situation before he could consider himself free to weigh alternatives. He told Doob that he would get back to him the next week to arrange for a meeting. Milgram was not playing hard-to-get. He *did* have a position lined up for the fall—as a Research Fellow in Cognitive Studies in the newly formed Center for Cognitive Studies, headed by Jerome Bruner and George Miller, another highly respected cognitive psychologist.

The meeting with Doob resulted in an offer from Yale, which—after some indecision and consultation with friends—Milgram accepted. He would be an assistant professor with a starting annual salary of $6,500. Describing to Allport how and why he decided in favor of Yale, Milgram wrote:

> It was a very hard decision that no one seemed willing to make for me, so I let the mist swirl round and round until a vague imbalance inclined my step toward Yale. . . . I conducted a public opinion poll among my eminent friends—Mike Wallach, Asch, Roger Brown, Dick Crutchfield, and the polls favored Harvard. Then I realized how useless such a procedure was, and tried to feel my way through to a preference. The thread of a motive must have latched on to something that Yale offered. What was it?—status, challenge, a chance to leave 'home' and work up a good set of credentials on my own?

Allport had been trying to help Milgram find an academic position since the spring, even before he had completed his dissertation, so he was delighted that his protégé had landed a position at Yale. Milgram would be joining three other Harvard graduates on the psychology faculty there. Allport told Milgram that he felt like "a proud rooster" because all of them were his former students.

After Allport received Milgram's completed dissertation, he asked two members of the department to serve as readers, which was the department procedure. They read and critiqued the thesis and suggested some changes.

One of the readers was Herbert Kelman, a social psychologist who had received his graduate training at Yale. He had worked closely with Carl Hovland, a pioneer in the study of persuasion and attitude change, who had chaired his doctoral dissertation. He joined the Social Relations Department in 1957 as a lecturer in social psychology, moved to the University of Michigan in 1962, and then returned to the department in 1969 as Richard Clarke Cabot Professor of Social Ethics, a chair first held by Gordon Allport. Although he has made a variety of contributions to social psychology, he is best known for his writings on research ethics. Through his criticism of the widespread use of deception in experimentation, he sensitized his fellow social psychologists to the ethical dilemmas their work sometimes poses. Although he made extensive comments and criticisms of Milgram's dissertation, Kelman judged it to be "an excellent study both in its conception and execution . . . [and] of great potential significance."

On June 1, Milgram sent Allport a revised version of his thesis in which the readers' criticisms had been addressed. Allport replied with a letter letting him know that he had received the revision by the required deadline, and he concluded with the following comment:

If I did not previously tell you so, my judgment is that your thesis is very good indeed, and written with an elegant professional touch that augurs well for your career. And for this career you have all my warm wishes—even at Yale.

Cordially yours,
Gordon W. Allport

Milgram knew that to succeed in academic life he would have to come up with an important and distinctive program of research with which to make his mark. He told Roger Brown that he hoped to find a phenomenon of great consequence, such as Asch had done, then "worry it to death." By the end of his year in Princeton, he knew what that program of research would be: the study of obedience to authority.

Milgram's interest in obedience was rooted in his early identification with the Jewish people and his determination to fathom the Holocaust. He made the connection between the Holocaust and his obedience research explicit in his book *Individual in a Social world:*

> [My] laboratory paradigm . . . gave scientific expression to a more general concern about authority, a concern forced upon members of my generation, in particular upon Jews such as myself, by the atrocities of World War II. . . . The impact of the Holocaust on my own psyche energized my interest in obedience and shaped the particular form in which it was examined.

The idea for the specific experimental technique—which enabled him to transform his broad concerns about authority into concrete plans to study it—came to him during the spring or early summer of 1960, during his last few months in Princeton working for Asch. The idea was grounded in Asch's conformity experiments. Here is how Milgram described the connection between the Asch experiments and the invention of his experimental technique for studying obedience:

> I was trying to think of a way to make Asch's conformity experiment more humanly significant. I was dissatisfied that the test of conformity was judgments about *lines*. I wondered whether groups could pressure a person into performing an act whose human import was more readily apparent, perhaps behaving aggressively toward another person, say by administering increasingly severe shocks to him. But to study the group effect . . . you'd have to know how the subject performed without any group pressure. At that instant, my thought shifted, zeroing in on this experimental control. Just how far *would* a person go under the experimenter's orders? It was an incandescent moment. . . .

When exactly that "incandescent moment" took place cannot be pinpointed, but it can be narrowed down to a period of time between March 2 and the end of June 1960. In a letter to Allport dated March 2, Milgram listed a number of research projects that he would be interested in pursuing, and the study of obedience was not among them. Milgram worked for Asch until near the end of June. Asch told an interviewer that he first learned about Milgram's plans to study obedience when they parted. Interestingly, on May 11, Israeli agents abducted the former Nazi official Adolf Eichmann from his home in a suburb of Buenos Aires, Argentina, and flew him to Israel to stand trial for his role in the murder of six million Jews. It's certainly possible that this was the event that crystallized the obedience research in Milgram's mind.

...

Milgram arrived in New Haven in early September 1960. Classes would not begin until late in the month, and he used the time to plan his courses and to ruminate about designing the boldest and most significant research possible. He had heard that New Haven was a dreary place, so he was pleasantly surprised to find the city in the midst of a vigorous program of urban renewal and beautification.

However, Yale's architecture did not fare particularly well in his eyes, especially since his yardstick of beauty was Harvard's expansive campus with its lawn and trees. He regarded Yale's neo-Gothic (or pseudo-Gothic, as he called it) aesthetic ponderous and confining, an alien import out of kilter with the mainstream of American architectural history. Still, he found some consolation in the exquisite courtyards hidden behind some of the heavy brick walls. His favorite of these, where he often loved to sit, was a beautiful classical garden decorated in high Romanesque style right in the middle of the cathedral-like Sterling Memorial Library.

When the semester began, Milgram's responsibilities included teaching a Tuesday afternoon seminar on the psychology of the small group and advising ten students who were writing their senior honors theses. After the pressure-cooker year at the Institute for Advanced Study, he luxuriated in the freedom of academic life: He could do as he pleased six days a week; he could conduct his seminar in whatever manner he chose, and the research he conducted could be guided solely by his own interests. Yet Harvard still was and would continue to be the embodiment of academic Eden for him. As he wrote to Allport early in the semester:

> The transition from Cambridge to New Haven has been exceedingly smooth, and life at Yale is very nice. It is true that here one is sometimes confronted with the question: "Are you a psychologist or are you doing human research?" But deep down you know that all is tempered by the tolerance befitting a great university. Harvard, it goes without saying, is just noticeably greater.

Milgram was renting a three-room furnished apartment on the second floor of a brownstone on York Square Place. It had the twin advantages of being affordable, since he had rented it from the university, and in close proximity to both the main campus and the Yale New Haven Hospital on Cedar Street, where the Psychology Department's offices and some of its labs were located.

Whatever its advantages, Milgram thought it was a dump. The color of the apartment's walls was a nameless, dreary refugee from the color spectrum, and he was ready to trash its contents from the moment he moved in. It had clumsy furniture that he told a friend he would have submitted to a public burning had it not belonged to the university. One day, when he could no longer look at the shabby living room carpet, he rolled it up, dropped it into a rental car he was using, and left it there when he returned the car to the rental agency.

Although Milgram already had plans to study obedience as he was leaving Princeton, the first research he set out to conduct at Yale was altogether different and reflected a fusion of his artistic sensibilities and his scientific interests. It also allowed him to continue his occasional dabbling in drugs—such as when he and a small group of friends sampled peyote as graduate students at Harvard—but now under the cloak of academic legitimacy.

On October 7, 1960—less than two weeks into the semester—Milgram submitted a small grant proposal to the American Council of Learned Societies requesting $2,000 to test the effects of mescaline on aesthetic judgments of art. This was merely a side interest, he assured Allport when he wrote to him for a letter of support, and he was not abandoning social psychology. Besides his own experience with drugs at Harvard, his interest had been stimulated by reading Aldous Huxley's *Doors of Perception* as well as the definitive text on the subject, Heinrich Klüver's *Mescal*. Perhaps not surprisingly, his request was turned down. However, his interest in testing mescaline's behavioral effects persisted, so he did some self-experimentation with the drug. And in February 1963, with a colleague and a graduate student, he conducted an informal experiment demonstrating that ingesting mescaline could improve one's accuracy in a dart-throwing game.

Over the years, he occasionally used other drugs—marijuana socially, and amphetamines and cocaine to help him overcome writer's block. He claimed that he could tell by looking at a piece of his writing which drug he had used when he wrote it. Different drugs had distinct effects on him, which he felt he could recognize in the way he expressed himself.

Even as he applied for a grant for the mescaline research, however, his main focus was on obedience. As he told Allport in a letter dated October 10:

> Next year I . . . plan to undertake a long series of experiments on obedience. While this series will stand by itself as an independent study, it is also preparation for the project on German character—in which comparative experimental measures of "obedience to authority" will play an important part.

In October and November, Milgram sent preliminary letters of inquiry to three governmental agencies about the prospects for grant support for his planned research on obedience. The first went out on October 14 to Luigi Petrullo, the head of the Group Psychology Branch of the Office of Naval Research, which was then in the forefront of supporting group-related social-psychological research. For a preliminary inquiry, the letter was quite long, and in fact portions of it ended up in the formal proposal he submitted a few months later. In its six pages, Milgram made a case for the importance of studying obedience and outlined the experimental procedure he planned to use.

> Obedience is as basic an element in the structure of social life as one can point to. Every power system implies a structure of command and action in response to the command.
>
> The question is not so much the limits of obedience. We know that given certain general circumstances, such as the situation of an army in war, men can be commanded to kill other men and will obey; they may even be commanded to destroy their own lives and will comply. Thus it is by no means the purpose of the study to try to set the absolute limits of obedience. Within a laboratory situation we cannot create the conditions for maximum obedience; only the circumstances of real life will extract the highest measure of compliance from men.
>
> We can, however, approach the question from a somewhat different viewpoint. Given that a person is confronted with a particular set of commands "more or less" appropriate to a laboratory situation, we may ask which conditions increase his compliance, and which make him less likely to comply.
>
> Ideally, the experimental situation should be one in which a subject is commanded to perform a specific set of acts. The acts should bear on important themes in human relations and should be of personal significance to the subject. . . .
>
> Subjects [in the planned experiments] believe they are performing in an experiment in human learning. . . . [The subject] operates a control panel, consisting of a series of switches set in a line. The switch at the left is labelled "1-Very Light Shock"; . . . the switch at the extreme right is labelled "15-Extreme Shock: Danger." This control panel allows subject A [the naïve subject] to administer a graded series of shocks to subject B [the victim]. . . . It goes without saying that subject B, the victim, does not in reality suffer, but is a confederate of the experimenter. Subject A is unaware of this and believes that he is actually administering shocks to subject B. . . .
>
> As the learning experiment proceeds the subject is commanded to deliver increasingly more potent shocks. Internal resistances become stronger,

and at a certain point he refuses to go on with the experiment. Behavior prior to this rupture we shall consider as obedience, in that the subject complies with the commands of the experimenter. The point of rupture is the act of disobedience.

Milgram also described several possible variations on this experiment, but he added that "it would be foolish" to make a firm commitment to a specific set of experiments at this time. That was a prudent qualification: Of the four possible experimental variations he described in the letter, only one—a condition in which the naïve subject is part of a team of "teachers"—bore any resemblance to those he later conducted. Milgram concluded his letter with a brief biographical sketch, which included his work with Asch. He expressed his intellectual debt to Asch, but at the same time he noted a fundamental difference in their concerns: "[Asch's] influence is certainly apparent in my work. I particularly admire his technique of systematic experimental variation. We differ in that he is concerned with judgments, cognitions, and the realm of thought. My own interests center on the social act as the crucial observational focus."

Appended to Milgram's letter to Petrullo was a rough sketch of a rudimentary version of the shock box that was to be used in the experiments. This sketch turned out to acquire special importance the following year, when an aggression researcher, Arnold Buss, came out with his own shock machine. The sketch helped Milgram substantiate his priority in creating such a machine, or at least their independence. Milgram suspected that Buss had copied his machine, and while an exchange of correspondence between them allayed Milgram's suspicions, it did not completely eliminate them.

In mid-November, Milgram sent out letters of inquiry to two other grant prospects, the National Institute of Mental Health and the National Science Foundation (NSF). By now he was immersed in preparations for his pilot studies, which he referred to in these letters. He planned to include his results in the formal grant proposal to strengthen it.

These pilot experiments were carried out by members of his Psychology of Small Groups class. Having gone through the research literature on small groups with his students, Milgram wanted them to get some hands-on experience conducting research. After discussing various possibilities with them, the choices were whittled down to two: One was a pilot version of the obedience experiment; the other was a study of communication patterns in groups. Milgram left the ultimate choice up to them, removing himself from the classroom so they could take a private vote. When he returned, the students told him that the obedience experiment had won—by a small margin.

Milgram gave his students a drawing of the shock generator that would be needed, and within a week the students capably turned the conception into the real thing. The pilot studies were conducted in the elegant Interaction Laboratory located on the first floor of Linsly-Chittenden Hall. The Sociology Department, which owned the laboratory, allowed Milgram and his class to use it. The class conducted the experiment during five different sessions in the lab in late November and early December. Although Milgram gave a condensed description of the procedure in his written report of the pilot research, the basic laboratory techniques seem to have been very similar to the one he outlined in his letter to the Office of Naval Research. Milgram described the results as follows.

> Before an experiment is carried out it is often hard to visualize exactly what its flavor would be. Thus, there was a certain amount of excitement and anticipation as we awaited the first subject. The study, as carried out by my small groups class under my supervision, was not very well controlled. But even under these uncontrolled conditions, the behavior of the subjects astonished the undergraduates, and me as well. Audiences who view films of the obedience experiment sometimes find themselves laughing nervously. This occurred in amplified form among the undergraduates who were observing the experiment behind the one-way [mirror] rooms. This may seem an unseemly response but it happened and I report it as such. I do not believe that the students could fully appreciate the significance of what they were viewing, but there was a general sense that something extraordinary had happened. And they expressed their feelings by taking me to Mory's Tavern when we had finished with our work, a locale then off limits to mere faculty.

The replies Milgram received from all three agencies indicated that each of them was receptive to considering the kind of research he had in mind. But the prospects at the National Science Foundation seemed most promising. So on January 27, 1961, he sent the NSF a formal application, "Dynamics of Obedience: Experiments in Social Psychology," requesting $30,348 for a two-year period from June 1, 1961, to May 31, 1963.

The grant proposal included a description of the pilot research and its findings, accompanied by some photographs depicting some of the subjects' behavior. The small sample size—twenty Yale undergraduate subjects—precluded a quantitative presentation, so Milgram gave a qualitative description of the results. This was sufficiently effective, for not only did the pilot studies demonstrate that Milgram had a laboratory procedure in place to study obedience, but also they uncovered some unexpected and troubling behavior. In essence, Milgram found that people would obey commands even when those commands were contrary to their deeply rooted standards of behavior. Equally important, the subjects readily accepted the reality of the experiments; they believed they were giving extremely painful electric shocks to another person (who acted as if he was receiving shocks but in reality was in cahoots with Milgram and his students and received no actual shocks). The subjects also showed signs of tension. One subject nervously pulled his hair, gripped his chair, and repeatedly rubbed his face. Another wiped his sweating palms numerous times and shook his head in dismay, as if trying to communicate to the "learner" that he regretted what he was doing. Many subjects were willing to administer the most extreme shocks in response to the experimenter's commands. But when they were asked if they would be willing to sample the shock they had just given, they refused.

Milgram's main, grant-funded series of experiments built on the pilot studies but differed from them in a number of ways. First, the shock machine used in the main experiments was a more refined version of the shock box used in the pilot studies. The control panel of the first consisted of two rows of six voltage switches labeled in 30-volt increments. To enhance the experiment's credibility, the second one had a more professional look. It consisted of a single row of thirty switches, with each switch marked 15 volts higher then the previous one. Second, in the pilot studies the "learner"—the person supposedly being shocked—was on the other side of a silvered glass window, through which the "teacher" (the subject) could dimly see him. In the main experiments, in most conditions the two people were separated by a wall, permitting the learner to be heard, but not seen. In a few of the conditions, the learner was seated near the teacher in the same room.

Third—and this was an important difference—whereas the naïve subjects in the pilot studies were Yale undergraduates (and in Milgram's grant proposal he indicated that he would use Yale students), in the main series he ended up using adult volunteers between the ages of twenty and fifty from New Haven, Bridgeport, and surrounding areas. Looking back after the main body of experiments was completed, Milgram was glad he had made this change, because it strengthened his argument that his findings were generalizable to normal, everyday people. But the original impetus for a change in the subject population was based on two factors. The first was a colleague's criticism, which Milgram took to heart. After hearing Milgram describe his pilot studies and its findings, the colleague dismissed it as having no relevance to the ordinary man in the street. Yale students, he asserted, were so aggressive and competitive that they would step on each other's necks with little provocation.

The second factor had to do with timing. Milgram's grant proposal to NSF was approved on May 3, 1961. As soon as he received notification, he was eager to get started. But the 1960–1961 academic year was almost over, and students would not return to campus until September 20. So, in order to start in the summer, he began recruiting adult community residents with a display ad in the June 18 issue of the *New Haven Register* and by direct mail solicitations. By the end of the month he had a pool of 300 potential subjects. Throughout the summer he would add to this pool with mailings to people selected randomly from the telephone book. By the time the fall semester started, he had completed the first four experiments.

An unusual feature of Milgram's grant proposal was a section titled "Responsibility to Subjects." When Milgram was planning and conducting his obedience studies, he was operating in an ethical vacuum. There were no formal ethical guidelines for the protection of the human subjects in experiments. Researchers tended to use their own judgment about whether their research posed an ethical problem. At most, they might ask for their colleagues' informal opinions. In deciding whether or not to conduct a study, ethical questions—if they were considered at all—took a back seat to scientific value.

Here is what Milgram wrote in that section of the grant proposal:

> A final but important note must be added concerning the investigator's responsibility to persons who serve in the experiment. There is no question that the subject is placed in a difficult predicament and that strong feelings are aroused. Under these circumstances it is highly important that measures be taken to insure the subject's well-being before he is discharged from the laboratory. Every effort will be made to set the subject at ease and to assure him of the adequacy of his performance. . . .

Milgram's expression of concern for his subjects' well-being in the grant proposal did not diminish the extreme stress many of them experienced during the experiment. Nor did it lead, in practice, to a uniformly thorough "debriefing" for all subjects—although at a minimum, subjects left the lab knowing that the "victim" was not hurt. Nonetheless, Milgram was, generally speaking, ahead of his time in giving this kind of explicit attention to the subjects' welfare in the planning of an experiment.

The NSF review process included a site visit to Yale on April 13, 1961, by Henry Riecken, head of the NSF Office of Social Sciences, accompanied by Richard Christie, a social psychologist, and James Coleman, a sociologist. In the "Diary Note" of that visit, Riecken observed somewhat critically that it was "clear that Dr. Milgram neither has nor plans to have an elaborate a priori theory."

A site visit is not always part of a grant review process. Riecken's committee came to New Haven out of concern for the subjects. Milgram's answers to their questions relieved the committee's anxiety. Nonetheless, the committee raised the question with their general counsel of who would be responsible—the National Science Foundation or Yale—for any negative effects on the subjects. The lawyer thought that Yale would be legally responsible.

The NSF final panel rating was "Meritorious." In the panel discussion notes, the proposal is described as "a bold experiment on an important and fundamental social phenomenon." Although panel opinion on the merits of the proposal had been divided, the final judgment was to recommend support. Milgram was notified of approval on May 3, 1961, for a sum of $24,700 for a two-year period beginning June 1. This was about $5,600 less than Milgram had requested. The reduction was based on the committee's belief that Milgram had been too cavalier about the problem of "subject contamination"—especially if he used community residents. Information about the details of the experiment would quickly spread, and Milgram's potential pool of subjects would be exhausted faster than he thought. The committee therefore recommended reduced funding to reflect a lower cost of payment for fewer subjects. (Paying subjects for their participation was, and still is, a common practice in psychological research.)

Awaiting a funding agency's decision on a grant proposal can make even the most seasoned of scientists anxious. Foundations invariably receive more applications than the amount of money available, so the outcome can never be assumed. For Stanley, something happened around the time he submitted his grant proposal that undoubtedly helped divert his attention. At the end of January 1961, he met Alexandra (Sasha) Menkin at a party in the Inwood section of Manhattan. There were some similarities in their backgrounds. Sasha was also a child of European Jewish immigrants. Neither set of parents was religiously observant, though they spoke to each other in Yiddish, especially when they didn't want the children to understand what was being said. Sasha's father was born in Geneva, Switzerland, her grandmother having moved there from Russia to study at a university, since higher education was virtually out of the question for a Jewish woman in pre–World War I Russia. Eventually, Sasha's father and his family emigrated to the United States, where he went on to become an engineer. Sasha didn't remember her father, though, because he died when she was very young. Her mother had emigrated from Russia to the United States, where she had met and married her husband. Like Stanley, Sasha was born in the Bronx. Her mother was a dancer, performing professionally and teaching.

Sasha had graduated from Hunter College in Manhattan and—taking after her mother—had an interest and training in dance, but at the time she met Stanley she was doing office work. She was 5'5", petite (Stanley was only 5'7") and vivacious, and she was easy to talk to. They discovered that they had a mutual interest in art and travel, and Stanley hardly left her side that night. From her perspective, the chemistry was all there, and by the end of that first evening, she knew that he was the one for her. As he drove Sasha home to her Greenwich Village apartment the night they met, he blurted out something that suggested he was already thinking about a future together. Turning to her, he said, "You know, I'd make such a terrible husband." Sasha looked at him, surprised at such candor, and asked, "Well, why?" He replied, "Well, sometimes I work late at night. It's terrible; I get involved and I can't stop." To which Sasha answered, "Whoever would marry you would love you for the way you are." Despite the mutual attraction, it took Stanley a couple of weeks to call her for a date.

In wasn't long before he was driving down to see her virtually every weekend. Howard Leventhal, his closest colleague at Yale, provided an intriguing and insightful perspective on their courtship:

> He was very impressed with Sasha, because she was a dancer as I recall, and appealed to him as she would appeal to anyone, because she was attractive as a person, a warm person. And I think a very strong appeal to Stanley was her aesthetic quality. She was statuesque in a way—in many ways she appealed to him like a piece of art. . . . She brought a kind of aesthetic quality to life. . . . People who are able to do that are rare, and I think that was a very powerful factor in the attraction in that relationship. . . . She lent a certain grace to everyday activities.

Their mothers had opposite reactions to the match—rooted, at least partially, in the same reason: Sasha was four and a half years older than Stanley. Stanley's mother was initially concerned about this (although she came to like Sasha), although Sasha's mother was ecstatic about Stanley. At age thirty-two, Sasha had finally found the right man—someone who was bright and well educated and had a clear sense of direction.

David Sears, who was then a graduate student in the Yale Psychology Department, and who Stanley thought was more experienced in such matters, told him, "It's impossible to maintain such a relationship from New Haven. Eventually, you either have to drop it or marry her." Stanley decided to marry her. They were married in a small ceremony on December 10, 1961, at the Brotherhood Synagogue in Greenwich Village, attended primarily by their immediate families. Ever the keen observer, Stanley would recall that the cantor wore his galoshes during the ceremony.

Milgram's life was changing in more ways than one. He was about to enter one of the most productive—and challenging—periods of his academic career. The obedience experiments would draw on everything he had learned at Harvard and Princeton, as well as his European experiments, and would catapult him into the limelight. The reverberations would be felt for decades to come.

CHAPTER 5

OBEDIENCE:
THE EXPERIENCE

As SOON AS the National Science Foundation notified Milgram that his grant was approved in May 1961, he sprang into action, turning his attention to the many details that needed to be worked out in preparation for the experiment. It took him two full months, June and July, to fine-tune them to his exacting specifications. Subjects were recruited, a false shock machine was built, laboratory procedures were worked out, scripts were written and practiced, and a research team was assembled. Pretest subjects were "run" through the procedure until all the kinks were worked out. Finally, on August 7, the laboratory doors opened.

Subjects were scheduled at hourly intervals, Monday through Friday from 6:00 P.M. to 11:00 P.M. and the whole day on Saturdays and Sundays. When a subject arrived for his scheduled appointment at Linsly-Chittenden Hall, located on High Street on Yale's Old Campus, he would first enter a remarkably ordinary building, easily overshadowed by the magnificent clockarch nearby, straddling High Street at Chapel Street. The only thing noteworthy about Linsly-Chittenden Hall was its dubious architectural pedigree, an improbable combination of Gothic and Romanesque styles.

Milgram began recruiting potential volunteers for his experiment with a display ad in the June 18 issue of the *New Haven Register*. He solicited volunteers for what was ostensibly a study of memory. They would be paid $4.00 plus 50 cents for carfare. In the early 1960s, $4.00 per hour was well above minimum wage and 50 cents was sufficient for round-trip bus fare to and from most parts of New Haven. Before placing the ad, he first cleared it with the department chairman Claude Buxton to make sure there wasn't anything objectionable in it.

The subjects ranged in age from twenty to fifty years of age. In all conditions but one, they were males. To ensure the generalizability of his results, Milgram made sure that all occupational levels, from unskilled workers to professionals, were represented. People had volunteered for Milgram's experiment for a variety of reasons. Some came out of curiosity about psychology experiments, others to learn something about themselves, and some because they had a special interest in the subject of memory. Still others were simply drawn by the opportunity to earn $4.50 for an hour's work.

At the door of the lab, the subject would be met by the experimenter, a short, somewhat stern-looking, gaunt-faced man in a gray lab coat, who introduced himself as Mr. Williams. Milgram had the experimenter wear a gray—rather than white—lab coat, because he didn't want subjects to think that Williams was a medical doctor and thereby limit the implications of his findings to the power of a medical authority. The subject would then be introduced to a Mr. Wallace (actually a man named James McDonough), another participant in the memory experiment, who smiled broadly, but seemed somewhat nervous.

Milgram's primary assistants remained with him from the beginning of August 1961 to the end of May 1962. They were John Williams, who played the role of the experimenter, and James McDonough, who served as the learner. Neither was a professional actor, but they had some natural talents that, with the help of repeated rehearsals, enabled them to play their roles with chilling realism. Both had regular day jobs. Williams was a thirty-one-year-old high school biology teacher, and as the experimenter, he projected a stern aura of technical efficiency. The role of learner, or victim, was played by McDonough, a somewhat pudgy forty-seven-year-old Irish-American with a pleasant, unassuming manner, who was the head payroll auditor of the New York, New Haven & Hartford Railroad. His employers were not very happy about one of their executives working a second job, but as a father of nine children, he needed the extra income. In addition, those extra evening hours, and more on weekends, actually seemed to energize him. The experiment was an interesting diversion from his daytime job, and Milgram seemed pleased with the work he did. In his interview notes, Milgram wrote: "This man would be perfect as a victim—he is so mild mannered and submissive; not at all academic . . . Easy to get along with."

Williams made out the promised check for $4.50 to each of them, which they were told was theirs to keep no matter what transpired in the experiment. The purpose of this unconditional prepayment was to short-circuit the possibility that the money might make subjects feel obligated to comply with the experimenter's wishes.

Williams (hereafter referred to as the Experimenter) then continued: "I'd like to explain to both of you now about our Memory Project. Psychologists have developed several theories to explain how people learn various types of material." Then, pointing to a book on a table nearby, he said, "Some of the better-known theories are in that book, *The Teaching-Learning Process*, by Cantor. One theory is that people learn things correctly whenever they get punished for making a mistake. One kind of application of the theory would be when a parent spanked a child for doing something wrong. The expectation being that the form of punishment will teach the child to remember better, teach him to learn more effectively. But actually we know very little about the effect of punishment on learning because almost no truly scientific studies have been made of human beings. For instance, we don't know how much punishment is best for learning, and we don't how much difference it makes who is giving the punishment, whether an adult learns best from an older or younger person than themselves, or many other things of this sort. So what we're doing in this project is bringing together a number of different occupations and ages. We're asking some to be teachers and some to be learners. We want to find out just what effect different people have on each other as teachers and learners, and also what effect punishment will have on learning in this situation. Next, I'm going to ask one of you to be the teacher and the other to be the learner. And the way we usually decide is to let you draw one of two pieces of paper here. . . ." He then placed two pieces of folded paper in the palm of his hand and had the subject and "Mr. Wallace" (James McDonough, hereafter referred to as the Learner) each take one.

He then continued: "Could you open them and tell me which of you is which please?" "Teacher," said the subject. "Learner," said McDonough.

...

Social psychologists in the 1960s practiced a sleight-of-hand science, which earned them both the envy and scorn of other social scientists. A well-executed social psychology experiment often owed as much to dramaturgy and stagecraft as to the tenets of the scientific method. Specifically, within the first few minutes of entering the "Memory Project" lab, a subject would be led to believe several things which were not, in fact, true: First, the experiment was not about punishment and learning. Second, as noted earlier, Mr. Wallace was not a volunteer participant as the subject was, but actually James McDonough, the mild-mannered accountant playing the role of the learner. Third, the drawing was rigged—both slips of paper said "teacher"— to ensure that the subject would always land the role of teacher and the confederate, McDonough, would always end up the learner. Fourth, the shock machine, which had a central role in the laboratory proceedings, was an authentic-looking, well-crafted prop, but it did not actually deliver shocks to the learner.

The first thing Milgram attended to after being notified of the NSF grant approval was the construction of an improved shock machine. Commercial sources he contacted told him that such an instrument could not be built before December. So he pushed ahead on his own. He had a clear conception of the kind of instrument he wanted and had a good working knowledge of electrical circuitry, enabling him to order the necessary components from various suppliers. However, the actual construction of the machine involved several others. For example, the final wiring was done by a technician employed by Yale, and the front panel was produced by professional industrial engravers to ensure that the shock machine would appear genuine. He was reassured on this point when two electrical engineers examined the instrument and did not detect that it was merely a prop.

The new, improved simulated shock generator was a box-shaped instrument, 3 feet long, 15½ inches high, and 16 inches deep. A label in the

FIGURE 5.1   Simulated Shock Generator. (From the film *Obedience*
© 1965 Stanley Milgram; © renewal 1993 Alexandra Milgram.)

upper left-hand corner of the box read, "SHOCK GENERATOR, TYPE
ZLB, DYSON INSTRUMENT COMPANY, WALTHAM, MASS.
OUTPUT 15 VOLTS – 450 VOLTS." The box had a metallic front panel
whose main feature was a series of thirty lever switches set in a single row.
Above each switch was a voltage label, beginning with 15 volts and contin-
uing in 15-volt increments to 450 volts (see Figure 5.1). In addition, below
groups of four switches were the following labels, from left to right:
SLIGHT SHOCK, MODERATE SHOCK, STRONG SHOCK, VERY
STRONG SHOCK, INTENSE SHOCK, EXTREME INTENSITY
SHOCK, DANGER: SEVERE SHOCK. The last two switches were simply and ominously labeled XXX (see Figure 5.2).

When a switch was pressed, the box emitted an electric buzzing sound,
a small circular light above the switch turned bright red, a blue light labeled
"voltage energizer" flashed, various relay clicks could be heard, and the dial
on the "voltage meter," located in the upper right-hand corner, swung to the
right. Connected to the shock machine was an apparatus that automatically

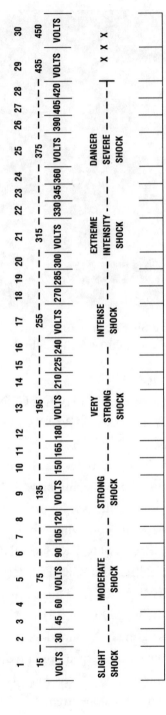

FIGURE 5.2   Schematic Diagram of Control Panel. (SOURCE: Milgram, S. [1974]. *Obedience to Authority: An Experimental View*. New York: Harper and Row.)

recorded not only the shock levels, but also the duration and latency of each shock to 1/100th of a second.

Careful attention was also given to other details to maximize the appearance of authenticity and, more generally, to create the intended effects and perceptions. For example, at the beginning of each experimental session, the subject (teacher) was given a sample shock of 45 volts via electrodes attached to the machine.

And finally, the learner's pitiful screams and insistent demands to be let out were prerecorded on tape and coordinated with specific voltages, and his responses followed a preset pattern of right and wrong answers.

...

"OK, now we are going to set the learner up so he can get some punishment. Learner, could you please come with me? Teacher, you can also come and look on," said the experimenter. Williams now led Wallace to a smaller room, partitioned off from the main part of the lab. It was furnished with a straight-backed metal armchair, facing a counter with a set of four switches sitting on it. Williams asked the learner (Wallace) to sit down and to roll up his right shirtsleeve. Williams then strapped his arms down on the armrests "to prevent excessive movement during the experiment" and attached an electrode to his right wrist. Williams then methodically applied some electrode paste, explaining that it would provide a good contact "to prevent blisters or burns." Williams added that the electrode was connected to the shock generator in the adjacent room.

This was the first time during the procedure that the experimenter stated explicitly that the punishment he had referred to earlier would be in the form of electric shock. The full implication of this connection would become distressingly clear once the subject began the teaching task. Undoubtedly many a subject already found the prospect of using electric shocks troubling, but not a single subject ever refused to at least begin the shock procedure. Glued in place by the commitment he had made, he would continue to watch and listen as Williams explained the procedure to "Wallace."

Experimenter Now, Learner, let me explain exactly what's going to happen, what you're supposed to do. The teacher will read a list of word pairs to you like these: "STRONG arm, BLACK curtain . . ." and so forth. You are to try to remember these pairs. The next time through, the teacher will read only the first word of the pair. For example, he would say: "STRONG." And then he will read four other words, such as "back, arm, branch, push." Now, your job is to remember which one of these four other words was originally paired with STRONG. Now you indicate your answer by pressing one of these four switches. Can you reach them? That's fine. Now if the first word I read, "back," had been paired with STRONG, you would press lever number 1 to indicate to the teacher that you thought it was the first word. If you thought it was the second word, "arm," you press the second lever, and so forth for the third and fourth words. Okay, now remember originally the teacher will read you the correct pair "STRONG arm." So he later reads to you "STRONG: back, arm, branch, push." You would press this one—

Learner The second lever.

Experimenter Right.

Learner Press the lever for "arm."

Experimenter Right. Now you will follow the same procedure for each of the phrases the teacher reads to you. . . . Now if you get it correct, fine. If you make an error, however, you will be punished with an electric shock. So, of course, it is to your advantage to learn all the word pairs as quickly as possible. Now do you have any questions before we begin?

The learner paused for a moment to look apprehensively at the electrode attached to his wrist, turned slowly to Williams and replied:

Well, I think I should say this. When I was in West Haven V.A. Hospital a few years ago, they detected a slight heart condition. Nothing serious—but as long as I'm getting these shocks—how strong are they, how dangerous are they?

Williams quickly replied in a confident, slightly dismissive tone that while the shocks may be painful, they're not dangerous.

Williams now takes the subject back into the larger room and tells him to sit down in front of the shock generator. The learner, seated in the smaller room, is not visible to the subject.

Experimenter All right, now listen carefully to the instructions. First of all, this machine generates electric shocks.

Subject Um-hmm.

Experimenter Now, when you press one of the switches all the way down, the learner gets a shock.

Subject Um-hmm.

Experimenter When you raise it, the shock stops. Like that.

Subject Um-hmm.

Experimenter The switch will remain in the middle position after you've released it to show you which switches you've used on the board.

Subject Uh-hmm.

Experimenter All right, the machine is on. To give you, the teacher, an idea of how much shock the learner is getting, it's only fair that you receive a sample shock yourself. Are you agreeable to this?

Subject Okay.

Giving the subject a sample shock was meant to strengthen the subject's belief that the shock generator was genuine. It was the only real shock that was given during the experiments. Williams placed an electrode on the subject's wrist.

Experimenter I'm going to ask you to close your eyes and estimate the number of volts you receive in this sample shock. Do not open your eyes until I tell you to do so, please.

Subject Um-hmm.

Williams presses the third switch, and then tells the subject to open his eyes.

Experimenter Okay. Now would you use the voltage scale here or the verbal designations—Light, Moderate, Strong, and so forth—and estimate for me the number of volts you received in the sample shock?

Subject Oh, I'd say about 195.

Experimenter No, actually it was 45. Here. (The experimenter points to the switch he had used.)

Subject Oh. [Laughs]

Experimenter Although it may seem a little stronger because of the electrode paste. That provides a perfect contact, you see.

Subject Uh-huh.

Experimenter All right, let's go on to the instructions. We will begin with this practice lesson. You will read each pair of words in the list once to the learner until you have read through the entire list.

Subject Um-hmm.

Experimenter Direct your voice toward the microphone, as the rooms are partially soundproof.

Subject Okay.

Experimenter Now, after reading through this list once, you go on to the next page.

Subject Right.

Experimenter And here, starting from line A, you will read the word in large letters along with each of the other words in the line. For example, on the first line you'd read "STRONG: back, arm, branch, push."

Subject Um-hmm.

Experimenter Now, after you've read the four choices, the learner pushes one of his switches and the number he has chosen lights up in this box: 1, 2, 3, or 4. [The experimenter points to the answer box sitting on top of the shock generator.]

Subject Oh, I see.

Experimenter Now, if he gets the correct answer, you say "correct" and go on to the next line. The correct answer is underlined. . . .

Subject Oh, yeah, uh-huh.

Experimenter If he gives the wrong answer, you say "wrong" and then tell him the number of volts you are going to administer.

Subject Um-hmm.

Experimenter Administer the punishment, read him the correct word pair once and then go on to the next line. For example, if he indicated 3 for STRONG ... [This corresponded to "branch," a wrong answer; the correct answer was 2, corresponding to "arm."]

Subject Uh-huh.

Experimenter You would say "wrong, 15 volts," push the switch, read "STRONG arm," and then go on to the next line.

Subject Okay.

Experimenter Now, each time he gives a wrong answer, you move up one switch on the shock generator.

Subject Um-hmm.

Experimenter Okay. It's important that you follow the procedure exactly.

Subject Okay, I'll try to.

Experimenter I would suggest you read the list and the test at a brisk pace. Keep it moving. Do you understand?

Subject Uh-huh.

Experimenter Okay. Do you have any questions?

Subject Uh, I don't think so, no.

Experimenter [Speaking into the microphone in front of the subject] Okay. Attention, learner, the teacher is about to begin the practice lesson. Try and remember the word pairs. Ready, begin.

As the subject would soon find out, when he pressed the first switch, the machine sprang to life, like a stalking cat whose prey had finally come within his reach: The light above the switch turned bright red, accompanied by an electric buzzing sound. The flashing blue light labeled "voltage energizer" was activated, the dial on the "voltage meter" swung to the right, and the relay clicks sounded.

The experimenter had a prepared set of four prompts to be used in sequence whenever the subject indicated his reluctance. The first was: "Please continue" or "Please go on." And the last was: "You have no choice, you *must* go on." If the subject still refused to continue after this last prod, the experiment was discontinued.

The practice phase consisted of ten word pairs and was meant to help the subject get the hang of the procedure.

> *Experimenter* [After the conclusion of the practice session] All right, that completes the practice lesson. Now, we'll go on to the regular lesson.
> *Subject* Um-hmm.
> *Experimenter* The procedure here is exactly the same as before.
> *Subject* Okay.
> *Experimenter* Except that we use a new list.
> *Subject* Um-hmm.
> *Experimenter* Now, we will begin with 15 volts—
> *Subject* Um-hmm.
> *Experimenter* And move up one switch, of course, each time he gives a wrong answer.
> *Subject* Um-hmm.
> *Experimenter* Ready? Begin please.
> *Subject* BLUE girl. NICE day. FAT neck. GREEN ink. RICH boy. FAST bird. BLUNT arrow. SOFT hair. COOL cave. GOLD moon. HARD head. WET duck. BRAVE woman. WHITE horse. SAD face. SHORT time. SHARP needle. SLOW dance. RED sunset. LOW noise. NEW book. QUIET evening. TAME bear. SWEET taste. TRUE story.

The subject continued now with the test part of the procedure.

> *Subject* BLUE: boy, girl, grass, hat. *BUZZ.* [A buzzing sound indicates the learner has answered by pressing one of the four response switches.] That's correct. NICE: day, sky, job, chair. *BUZZ.* That's correct. FAT: man, lady, tub, neck. *BUZZ.* That's wrong. ZZZT [the sound which accompanied pressing a voltage lever], 15 volts, FAT neck. GREEN: grass, hat, ink, apple. *BUZZ.* Wrong. ZZZT. GREEN ink. RICH: boy, cake, man, girl. *BUZZ.* False. 45, ZZZT. RICH boy. Next, FAST: bird, car, train, plane. *BUZZ.* That's correct. BLUNT: knife, stick, word, arrow. *BUZZ.* False. ZZZT. BLUNT arrow. SOFT: rug, pillow, hair, grass. *BUZZ.* False. 75. ZZZT. SOFT hair.

Learner Ugh!

Subject COOL: day, shade, water, cave. *BUZZ*. False. ZZZT. COOL cave.

Learner Ugh!

Subject GOLD: dollar, necklace, moon, paint. *BUZZ*. That's correct.
   HARD: stone, head, bread, work. *BUZZ*. False. ZZZT.

Learner Ugh! [Louder]

Subject HARD head. WET: night, grass, duck, cloth. *BUZZ*. False.
   ZZZT.

Learner Ugh! Hey, *this* really hurts.

Subject WET duck. BRAVE: woman, soldier, dog, horse. *BUZZ*. False.
   ZZZT.

Learner Ugh!!

Subject BRAVE woman. WHITE: cloud, horse, rock, house. *BUZZ*. False.
   ZZZT.

Learner Ugh!!! Experimenter! That's all. Get me out of here. I told you I
   had heart trouble.

Subject WHITE horse.

Learner My heart's starting to bother me now. Get me out of here, please.
   My heart's starting to bother me. I refuse to go on. Let me out.

Subject [Turning toward the experimenter] Keep going?

Experimenter Keep going. Go on, please.

Subject SAD: face, music, clown, girl. *BUZZ*. That's correct. SHORT: sentence, movie, skirt, time. *BUZZ*. False. ZZZT.

Learner [Shouting] Ugh! Let me out!

Subject SHORT time. SHARP: axe, needle, stick, blade. *BUZZ*. False.
   ZZZT.

Learner Ugh!

Subject SHARP needle.

Learner [Shouting] I can't stand the pain. Let me out of here!

Subject SLOW: walk, dance, truck, music. *BUZZ*. False. ZZZT.

Learner Ugh! Let me out of here.

Subject SLOW dance.

Learner Let me out of here. My heart's bothering me. Let me out of here!

Experimenter Go on, please.

Learner You have no right to keep me here! Let me out! Let me out of
here!

Subject RED—

Learner Let me out! Let me out of here! My heart's bothering me. Let me
out! Let me out!

Subject Brick, rose, sunset, wagon. *BUZZ.* False. *ZZZT.*

Learner Ugh!

Subject RED sunset.

Learner Experimenter! *Get* me out of here. I've had enough. I *won't* be in
the experiment any more.

The subject became visibly more nervous as the shocks increased in intensity and the learner's complaints became more and more pitiful and demanding. Yet, he generally ignored those cries of pain. His face was etched
with determination to continue. He appeared to be unwilling to upset the
experiment by stopping.

To standardize the procedure, the learner's complaints had been prerecorded on tape. During the experiment, McDonough played it back on a
tape-recorder in a stop-and-go fashion so that his various screams would be
phased in with specific voltage levels of "punishment."

Subject NEW: house, pet, book, name. *BUZZ.* That's correct. QUIET:
song, party, child, evening. *BUZZ.* That's correct. TAME: wolf, bear,
dog, cat. *BUZZ.* False. *ZZZT.*

Learner Ugh!

Subject TAME bear. SWEET: candy, girl, taste, pickle. *BUZZ.* False, 255.
ZZZT.

Learner Ugh! Get me *out* of here!

Subject SWEET taste. TRUE: story, hero, speech, report. *BUZZ.* False.
ZZZT, 270 volts. TRUE story.

Learner Oowww! Let me out of here. Let me out of here. Let me out of
here. Let me out. Do you hear? Let me out of here.

Subject Should I start all over now?

Experimenter Yes.

Subject BLUE: boy, girl, grass, hat. *BUZZ.* That's correct. NICE: day, sky, job, chair. *BUZZ.* False. ZZZT.

Learner [*Agonized scream*]

Subject 285. NICE day. FAT: man, lady, tub, neck. *BUZZ.* False. ZZZT.

Learner [*Agonized scream*]

[Sometimes the subject would hesitate before uttering the next test word, as if he had trouble getting the words out. But when the learner gave the wrong answer, there was no hesitation in giving him the shock. On the few occasions when he questioned the experimenter, he would immediately obey his instruction to continue.]

Subject FAT neck.

Learner I absolutely refuse to answer any more. Get me out of here. You can't hold me here. Get me out. Get me out of here.

Subject Nothing will happen to him, will it?

Experimenter Please continue.

Subject GREEN: grass, hat, ink, apple.

The learner didn't answer. No buzzing sound is heard. No number has lit up on the answer box.

Experimenter If the learner doesn't answer in a reasonable time, about 5 seconds, consider it wrong.

Subject Um-hmm.

Experimenter And follow the same procedure as you have been doing for a wrong answer.

Subject 315, ZZZT.

Learner [*Intensely agonized scream*] I told you I refuse to answer.

Subject RICH—

Learner I'm no longer part of this experiment.

Subject Boy, cake, man, girl. [No answer.] 330, ZZZT.

Learner [*Intense and prolonged heart-rending scream*] Let me out of here. Let me out of here. My heart's bothering me. Let me out, I tell you.

Subject FAST: bird, car, train, plane.

Learner [Hysterically now] Let me out of here. Let me out of here. You have no right to hold me here. Let me out! Let me out! Let me out! Let me out of here! Let me out! Let me out!

The subject knitted his brow as if he were in pain.

Experimenter Go on, please.

Subject Push it?

Learner Yes.

Subject ZZZT. FAST bird. BLUNT: knife, stick, word, arrow. [No answer.] ZZZT, 360. BLUNT arrow. SOFT: rug, pillow, hair, grass. [No answer.] ZZZT. SOFT hair. COOL: day, shade, water, cave. ZZZT. He's not answering any more.

Experimenter Please go on.

[The subject made a face, as if to show his reluctance, but continued anyway.]

Subject GOLD: dollar, necklace, moon, paint. [No answer.] ZZZT. GOLD moon. HARD: stone, head, bread, work. [No answer.] HARD head. ZZZT. WET: night, grass, duck, cloth. [No answer.] WET duck. ZZZT. BRAVE: woman, soldier, dog, horse. [No answer.] ZZZT. BRAVE woman. What do I do now? I'm at the end.

Experimenter Continue using the last switch on the board.

Subject I don't hear nothing from him any more.

Experimenter Please go on.

If a subject continued to 450 volts, the experimenter had him repeat that switch another two times to confirm that he was being completely obedient.

Subject WHITE: cloud, horse, rock, house. [No answer.] ZZZT. WHITE horse. SAD: face, music, clown, girl. [No answer.] ZZZT. SAD face. SHORT: sentence—

Experimenter Excuse me, teacher, we'll have to discontinue the experiment.

...

At the conclusion of the experiment, the experimenter conducted an assessment and debriefing procedure, consisting of a number of components: obtaining personal data, such as age, occupation, marital status, religion, education and military service; having the subject answer questions about his experience, such as how nervous he had been and how painful he thought those last few shocks he administered to the subject had been; de-hoaxing the subject and having him meet "Wallace" face-to-face to show that he was unharmed. Here are excerpts of the dialogue with this subject, containing this latter feature of the postexperimental proceedings:

Experimenter Let me tell you this, that this man wasn't really being shocked. We were really interested in your reactions in having to inflict pain, you know, on a person you didn't even know.

Subject Um-hmm.

Experimenter You see, he actually works with us as a team.

Subject Oh.

Experimenter And he wasn't really getting these shocks.

Subject Oh, I see.

Experimenter We're very interested in studying your reactions. Now we're not trying to fool you in any way.

Subject Yeah, I know.

Experimenter We have to set it up this way so we can get true reactions from people. You really thought you were shocking somebody?

Subject Yes, I did. . . . And when I didn't hear anything else I was worried.

Experimenter Yeah. What did you think when you didn't hear anything else?

Subject I thought maybe he was just making believe he was quiet so I'd stop, you know what I mean? Maybe he'd passed out or something.

Experimenter Did you think he'd passed out?

Subject I didn't think he did. I had a thought in my mind that he could have passed out. I was worried about it.

Experimenter Well, you understand why we have to do it this way. You see, it's very similar to a situation a nurse finds herself in when she has to administer a needle to a patient, you know. She may be reluctant to do this. She may not want to hurt the patient, but the doctor tells her to, so she goes ahead and does it. But this is a similar situation, where you have to inflict a little pain, you see, on another person.

Subject Oh, I didn't like it.

Experimenter Well many people don't. Anyway, you'll receive a report of this project when it's over in a couple of months and until that time we'd like to ask you not to say anything about it . . .

Subject Okay.

Experimenter . . . because you may talk to people who are going to be in it . . . and it wouldn't do any good if they know ahead of time. . . . How do you feel about having come down and done this. Now that you know—

Subject Well now I know the truth. . . . I don't mind now . . .

Experimenter Jimmy, why don't you come in and say hello to Mr. _____ before he leaves. Mr. McDonough.

Subject . . . now that it's all over.

Learner (McDonough/Wallace): You don't feel too bad, now, do you?

Subject No, I don't feel too bad.

Learner (McDonough/Wallace): That's good.

Experimenter Well, let me thank you very much for coming down. We certainly do appreciate you giving us your time.

Subject I've only had about three cigarettes.

Experimenter [Laughs.] We certainly do appreciate you coming down. We think you'll find the report very interesting.

CHAPTER 6

OBEDIENCE:
THE EXPERIMENT

•

THE OBEDIENCE EXPERIMENTS presented a disturbing view of human behavior. Milgram, his colleagues, and later the public were surprised by the sheer power of an authority to compel someone to hurt an innocent person, despite the absence of any coercive means to back up his commands. Although Milgram had no all-encompassing theory to guide his obedience project, specific experiments did provide enlightening answers to particular questions.

The first four experiments Milgram carried out during August and September 1961 constituted a set of experimental conditions designed to determine whether varying the physical and psychological distance between the teacher-subject and the learner would affect the degree of obedience. The question grew out of an observation Milgram made during the pilot studies carried out with his Small Groups class toward the end of the fall 1960 semester. In those studies, the learner sat on the other side of a silvered glass window, which allowed the subject to discern his gross movements. Milgram found that subjects typically were reluctant to look at the victim and often turned their head to the side to avoid seeing the "painful" consequences of their actions.

This recurring behavior suggested to Milgram that the remoteness of the learner might have influenced, to some extent, the subject's actions. The "four-part proximity series" was designed to test this idea systematically by creating four experimental variations that progressively reduced the distance between teacher and learner, making it increasingly difficult for the subject to minimize in his own mind his role in punishing the victim.

At one end of the continuum was the *Remote condition*. The setup and cover story were as previously described: Under the guise of an experiment on the effects of punishment on learning, the teacher-subject, seated in front of the shock machine, was instructed to give increasingly painful shocks to the learner, who was seated in an adjacent room and not visible to the subject, each time he made an error on the word-matching task. In this variation, however, no vocal complaints were heard from the learner. His responses, which followed a predetermined pattern of three incorrect answers to one correct one, were transmitted to the teacher by the lit-up number in the answer box on top of the shock generator.

The first time the learner protested was after he had received the 300-volt shock. He pounded on the wall loud enough for the learner to hear. After this, no more responses appeared in the answer box. At this point, subjects usually turned to the experimenter to find out how to proceed. He told them to treat no answer as a wrong answer and to keep on increasing the shock level each time this happened. The learner pounded on the wall one more time at 315 volts. Afterward, total silence.

No subject stopped obeying the experimenter's commands before 300 volts—the first time the learner pounded on the wall—even though this level was past the set of switches labeled "Very strong shock" and was in the "Intense shock" zone. Of the forty subjects in this condition, 5 refused to go beyond this point, and 14 defied the experimenter at some point short of the final 450 volts. But the majority of subjects, 26 out of 40, or 65 percent, were fully obedient, continuing to the maximum shock on the voltage scale, beyond the "Danger: Severe Shock" zone and into the ominous "XXX" zone.

We did not need Milgram to tell us that we have a deeply ingrained propensity to obey authority. What his findings revealed is the surprising strength of this tendency—strong enough to override a moral principle we have been taught since childhood—that it is wrong to hurt another person against his will.

Although this experiment, the Remote condition, was only the first in an interrelated set of experiments, the four-part proximity series, he published it separately in 1963 in the *Journal of Abnormal and Social Psychology*, making it the first published results from the obedience series. Its remarkable, groundbreaking findings merited its publication by itself, but Milgram also wanted to publish a detailed description of his procedure quickly for priority purposes.

To underscore the power of his findings, he would periodically demonstrate how unexpected they were. He would provide a detailed description of the experiment to various groups—Yale seniors, middle-class adults, a group of psychiatrists—to predict how they or others would perform in the situation. Invariably the predictions were wide of the mark. For example, the Yale seniors predicted that, of 100 persons, only 1.2 percent would end up giving the strongest shock. In February 1962, Milgram carried out the prediction exercise with a group of psychiatric residents at Yale before lecturing to them. He described the results in a letter to the social psychologist E.P. Hollander: "The psychiatrists—although they expressed great certainty in the accuracy of their predictions—were wrong by a factor of 500. Indeed, I have little doubt that a group of charwomen would do as well."

The second experiment was the *Voice-Feedback condition*. The learner was still in a separate room out of sight of the teacher, but now prerecorded complaints of increasing stridency, corresponding to increased voltage levels, were added. The schedule of protests was much like the one in the dialog presented earlier, except that here the learner did not mention anything about a heart condition. This addition of vocal complaints resulted in a slight decrease in the rate of obedience, as compared to the Remote condition. Here, 25 out of 40 subjects, 62.5 percent, continued to the 450-volt maximum.

In the third experiment, the *Proximity condition*, the distance between teacher and learner was reduced further. Instead of being placed in a separate room, the learner was seated a couple of feet away from the teacher, so the learner had to act out his part each time. The learner used the same schedule of protests as in the previous condition, but now the teacher also *saw* his bodily reactions to the increasingly painful shocks. Now the teacher had both vocal and visual evidence of the learner's suffering. This narrowing of the teacher-learner distance resulted in a further, more precipitous, drop of the obedience rate to 40 percent: only 16 out of 40 subjects progressed to the final shock.

The fourth and final condition in the series, the *Touch-Proximity condition*, essentially reduced the teacher-learner distance to zero. Like the third condition, the victim sat near the teacher, but with one important difference: To receive a shock, the learner had to place his hand on a shock plate. At 150 volts, he refused to do this, so the experimenter ordered the subject to force the victim's hand onto the plate to receive the subsequent punishments.

Although the results of the first three conditions had already re-educated Milgram about the limits of obedience, when it came to this final condition, in which the teacher would need to use physical coercion, he predicted that, at most, one or two subjects would be completely obedient. To his astonishment, 12 out of 40, or 30 percent, went through to the end. "It is a very disturbing sight," Milgram noted, "since the victim resists strenuously and emits cries of agony."

Milgram described in detail the behavior of one of the obedient subjects in this condition, a thirty-seven-year-old welder, "Bruno Batta." In response to the experimenter's instructions, he presses the learner's hand onto the shock plate.

> The learner, seated alongside him, begs him to stop, but with robotic impassivity, he continues the procedure. What is extraordinary is his apparent total indifference to the learner; he hardly takes cognizance of him as a human being. Meanwhile, he relates to the experimenter in a submissive and courteous fashion. At the 330-volt level, the learner refuses not only to touch the shock plate, but also to provide any answers. Annoyed, Batta turns to him and chastises him: "You better answer and get it over with. We can't stay here all night.". . . The scene is brutal and depressing: his hard, impassive face showing total indifference as he subdues the screaming learner and gives him shocks. He seems to derive no pleasure from the act itself, only quiet satisfaction at doing his job properly. When he administers 450 volts, he turns to the experimenter and asks: "Where do we go from here, Professor?" His tone is deferential and expresses his willingness to be a cooperative subject, in contrast to the learner's obstinacy.

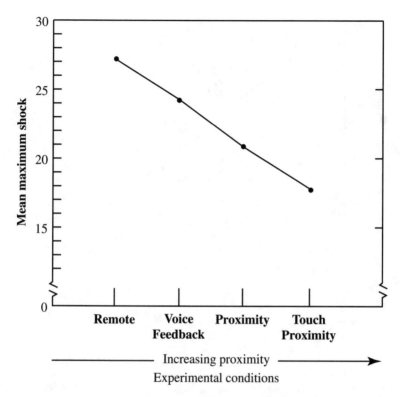

FIGURE 6.1   Mean Maximum Shocks in Four-Part Proximity Series.

Figure 6.1 gives a visual presentation of the gradual decline in obedience from the Remote to the Touch-Proximity conditions.

Although the primary and clearest quantitative indicator of a subject's degree of obedience was the highest shock he ended up administering, Milgram's apparatus provided two subsidiary measures of a subject's responses to the authority figure's commands: It automatically recorded the latency and duration of each shock to 1/100th of a second. The latency measure— a subject's hesitation before administering the shock—did not yield any useful information. However, the measure of shock duration yielded two interesting results that complement the main findings. These results are depicted graphically in Figure 6.2 for the first three conditions. (Shock duration measures could not be obtained for the Touch-Proximity condition because of the way the shock plate had been wired into the shock generator.) The graph shows, first, that shock duration decreased with increasing prox-

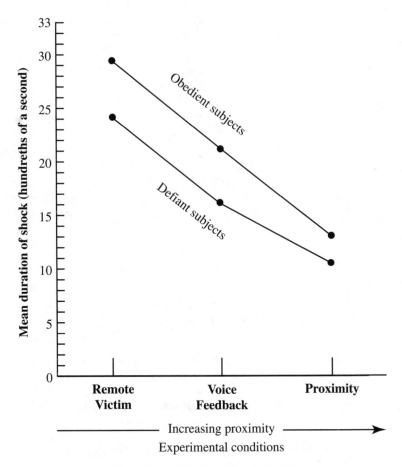

FIGURE 6.2   Duration of Shock in Proximity Experiments.

imity between teacher and learner. Second, overall across experimental conditions, the duration of shocks given by obedient subjects was longer than those administered by defiant ones.

...

The first person Milgram had hired to help him with the obedience experiments was Alan Elms, who served as his research assistant during the summer of 1961. Elms was a scrawny student from Kentucky who had just completed his first year of graduate studies in the Psychology Department at Yale. He first met Milgram toward the end of the fall semester in 1960.

First-year graduate students were required to attend a weekly seminar in which one or two faculty members would talk about their research. Milgram talked about his research interests in obedience, and Elms found it fascinating. But he was drawn to Milgram's enthusiasm as much as the research itself. The work of Lawrence Kohlberg, another junior faculty member, on moral development also sounded interesting, but whereas Milgram exuded excitement about his work, Kohlberg's presentation had a depressive quality to it.

At the end of his first year, Elms went home to Kentucky for a month before beginning his assistantship with Milgram in July. Toward the end of the month he received a letter from Milgram. Although written in a bantering style, it suggests that Milgram already had an intuitive sense of the broader significance of the work he was embarking on:

Dear Alan:

I hope you have spent a pleasant month of leisure and have recuperated from the stresses of first year graduate life. . . . The advertisement was placed in the New Haven Register and yielded a disappointingly low response. There is no immediate crisis, however, since we do have about 300 qualified applicants. But before long, in your role of Solicitor General, you will have to think of ways to deliver more people to the laboratory. This is a very important practical aspect of the research. I will admit it bears some resemblance to Mr. Eichmann's position, but you at least should have no misconceptions of what we do with our daily quota. We give them a chance to resist the commands of a malevolent authority and assert their alliance with morality. . . .

Milgram conveyed a similar sense—in a more serious tone—in a letter to Solomon Asch written on the same day, June 27, in which he brought him up to date on the obedience project: "Certainly, obedience serves numerous productive functions, and you may wonder why I focus on its destructive potential. Perhaps it is because this has been the most striking and disturbing expression of obedience in our time."

The letter to Asch reflects the continuing evolution of Milgram's relationship with him. As the passage of time made the stifling experience at the Institute for Advanced Study recede to the back of Milgram's memory, his pre-Princeton respect for Asch resurfaced. In this letter, Milgram solicited Asch's opinion about the planned project, and just a few days earlier, on Sunday, June 25, he had taken Sasha to Swarthmore to introduce her to Asch and his wife Florence. Throughout his professional career he would refer to Asch as his main scientific influence. When the American Psychological Association (APA) awarded Asch one of its Distinguished Scientific Contributions awards in 1967, Milgram sent him a congratulatory letter, telling him, "No one deserves it more or has been a greater inspiration to his students and colleagues." He paid tribute to Asch and his conformity research in an invited talk, titled "Ten Variations on a Theme by Asch," at the annual convention of the Canadian Psychological Association in 1969. He even wrote the APA nominating Asch for a special APA award, their Gold Medal award.

It took only a couple of months for those tentative expectations about his project's significance, expressed to Elms and Asch before the start of the proximity series, to harden into more explicit—and far darker—conclusions. In a letter to Henry Riecken, head of Social Sciences of NSF, dated September 21, 1961, he wrote:

> The results are terrifying and depressing. They suggest that human nature—or more specifically, the kind of character produced in American society—cannot be counted on to insulate its citizens from brutality and inhumane treatment at the direction of malevolent authority. In a naïve moment some time ago, I once wondered whether in all of the United States a vicious government could find enough moral imbeciles to meet the personnel requirements of a national system of death camps, of the sort that were maintained in Germany. I am now beginning to think that the full complement could be recruited in New Haven. A substantial proportion of people do what they are told to do, irrespective of the content of the act, and without pangs of conscience, so long as they perceive that the command comes from a legitimate authority.

The four-part proximity series revealed an unwelcome truth about human nature. Together, the experiments showed just how unexpectedly strong is our readiness to obey authority—strong enough to make us violate our moral principles. But the series was important in another respect as well. Beginning in the late 1960s, a lively debate raged among personality and social psychologists—"the trait/situation controversy." Stirred up by a provocative book, *Personality and Assessment,* written by Walter Mischel, the debate centered on the following question: Which is the stronger determinant of a person's behavior, his personality or the situation he finds himself in? Mischel argued that the traditional conception of personality traits as the broad underpinnings of behavior was wrongheaded and that an individual's actions were much more a product of the immediate situation than the personal characteristics he brought to it. As the debate unfolded in the 1960s and 1970s, "situationists" would often use Milgram's four-part proximity series as strong ammunition. They would point to the fact that obedience varied as a function of a situational characteristic—teacher-learner proximity—overriding differences in personality. Milgram himself was sympathetic to the situationist perspective. "The social psychology of this century," he wrote, "reveals a major lesson: often, it is not so much the kind of person a man is as the kind of situation in which he finds himself that determines how he will act."

...

There were many different paths to obedience, perhaps as many as there were obedient subjects. The subject whose laboratory session was presented in Chapter 5 did not like what he was told to do. Nonverbal aspects of his demeanor—constantly swallowing hard and moistening his lips—externalized his inner conflict. Nonetheless, he proceeded with his assigned task smoothly, with only an occasional prompt from the experimenter.

Other obedient subjects were more vocal in their attempts to resist or in communicating the extreme stress they were experiencing. One such subject, a tool designer, had continued to increase shocks to 390 volts, pausing occasionally, but without comment or questions.

Subject COOL: day, shade, water, cave. [No answer.] Incorrect. 390 volts.
ZZZT. GOLD: dollar, necklace, moon, paint. [No answer.] Incorrect.

405 volts. ZZZT. HARD: stone, head, bread, work. [No answer.] Incorrect. ZZZT. 420 volts.

Experimenter Go right ahead, continue please. You have two more switches on the board.

Subject Should I be a part of this?

Experimenter Pardon me?

The realization of the gravity of his actions seemed to have caught up with the subject. Until now, his voice had been firm and steady. Now, there was a quiver in his voice as he asked the experimenter:

Subject Will there be any aftereffects later on? Should I be participating in this?

Experimenter The experiment requires that you go on, Teacher.

Subject Yeah, but how do I know he's okay out there? We're not getting any response. He's not even saying "ouch" anymore.

Experimenter Well, we have to go on until the learner has learned all the word-pairs correctly.

Subject [Slurring his speech] Suppose he's not capable of learning the words out there?

Experimenter It's absolutely essential that you continue.

Subject [His voice breaking] Yes, but suppose there's no one out there to respond?

Experimenter As I said before, though the shocks may be painful, they are not dangerous. Would you please continue?

Subject HARD: stone, head, bread, work. [No answer.] Incorrect. 435 volts. ZZZT. WET: night, grass, duck, cloth. [No answer.] Incorrect. 450 volts. ZZZT. Continue?

Experimenter Yes, continue, please.

Subject With?

Experimenter Use the last switch on the board.

Subject Continue to use it?

Experimenter Right.

Subject BRAVE: woman, soldier, dog, horse. [No answer.] Incorrect. 450.
ZZZT. WHITE: cloud, horse, rock, house. Incorrect, 450. ZZZT.
SAD: face—

Experimenter Excuse me, Teacher, we'll have to discontinue.

Another resistant, although ultimately obedient, subject was a draftsman
who had just "shocked" the learner with 195 volts.

Subject RED: brick, rose, sunset, wagon. *BUZZ*. This is incorrect. 210.
ZZZT.

Learner Ugh!

Subject The correct answer is RED sunset.

Learner [With desperation in his voice] I won't be in the experiment any
more!

Subject The next one is LOW: noise, cloud, bridge, voice. *BUZZ*. This is
wrong. 225 volts. ZZZT. The correct answer is LOW noise. The next
one is NEW: house, pet, book, name. *BUZZ*. Correct!

Taking advantage of the break in the momentum of incorrect answers,
he said to Williams in a barely audible voice:

Learner I don't know if I can stand this much longer.

Experimenter [Ignoring the subject's controlled desperation] Go on, please.

Obeying the experimenter, he resumed the testing procedure without
any further comment or resistance. A few word-pairs later, he did emit a
sigh—the despair of a man who was clearly reluctant to continue hurting
the victim, but couldn't quite transform that reluctance into action.

When the subject reached the 300-volt level, however, he managed to
find the inner strength to at least *express* his deep aversion to what was taking place.

Subject The next one is FAT: man, lady, tub, neck. *BUZZ*. This is wrong
. . . 300 volts. ZZZT.

Learner [Agonized scream]

Subject I, I can't do this any more [chair scuffles].

Learner I absolutely refuse to answer any more. Get me out of here. You can't hold me here. Get me out. Get me out of here.

Subject I can't do it any more. I'm sorry. I realize that you're trying to do something.

Experimenter The experiment requires that you continue to do so . . .

Subject Yes, I know. But I'm just not the type of person that can inflict pain to anyone else, uh, more than what I feel. I felt I've gone far beyond what I should.

Experimenter It's absolutely essential that you continue. Please go on.

Subject [Chair scuffles] You know, I'm to the point now I can just feel each one with him. *[Sigh]*) The next one is GREEN: grass, hat, ink, apple . . .

Although the periodic sighs and long pauses before giving shocks were continuing signs of his inner torment, this subject ended up being fully obedient.

. . .

There was also great variety among those subjects who stopped before reaching 450 volts. One important variation concerned how early or late in the game the subject first showed some resistance. Two social psychologists, Andre Modigliani and Francois Rochat, conducted a fine-tuned analysis of the audio recordings of one of the experimental conditions. They found that the earlier in the procedure a subject showed some resistance, the more likely he was to end up being defiant. Also, the earlier in the shock sequence the subject expressed his dissent, the lower the final voltage he administered. Modigliani and Rochat explained their findings as follows:

In line with the theory of cognitive dissonance, the longer subjects continue without objections to carry out a very unpleasant collaborative task, the more they must convince themselves that some reasonable version of the "official" cover story is, in fact, correct—e.g., the experimenter knows what he is doing, the shocks are not really dangerous, the learner is really OK, the procedure must continue. . . . *Early* verbal resistance is effective, then, because it reduces the pressures to rationalize that come with a more passive, lengthy and brutal complicity.

One disobedient subject was a forty-seven-year-old inspector for a large manufacturing plant. At first, during the practice list, he had some trouble learning the procedure. But by the time he started with the main list, he had mastered it and was proceeding at a steady clip. At 120 volts, he had already pressed seven shock levers and had heard a mild complaint— "Ugh!"—from the learner three times.

Subject WET: night, grass, duck, cloth. *BUZZ.* Wrong. 120 volts. ZZZT.

Learner Ugh! Hey, this *really* hurts.

Subject It won't hurt him any, the voltage?

Experimenter Please continue.

Subject BRAVE: woman, soldier, dog, horse. *BUZZ.* Wrong. [Sighs] 135. ZZZT.

Learner Ugh! Experimenter!

Subject The answer was horse.

Learner That's all. Get me out of here. I told you I had heart trouble. My heart's starting to bother me now. Get me out of here, please. My heart's starting to bother me.

Experimenter Continue please. Go on.

Learner I refuse to go on. Let me out.

Subject I don't know. He's pretty well upset in there.

Experimenter The experiment requires that you go on, Teacher. Go on, please.

Subject But if you don't mind, I'd like to see him myself before I do go on.

Experimenter Well, you can't have any contact other than through the microphone once we have started. It's absolutely essential that you continue, teacher. Go on.

Subject Well I don't know. I don't think I'd like to take that myself, what he's taking right now.

Experimenter You have no other choice.

Subject [Sneering] I'll give you your check back if you want.

Experimenter No, the check is yours simply for coming into the lab, that's not the issue. Thing is, if you don't continue, we'll have to discontinue the entire experiment.

Subject Well, I can't properly go on with this the way he is out there now. I mean he said he had heart trouble, so I—

Experimenter Well, we'll have to discontinue the experiment, then.

Two factors seem to be operating here to help the subject free himself from the authority's grip. One is his ability to empathize with the learner. He puts himself in the learner's shoes and feels his pain: "I don't think I'd like to take that myself, what he's taking right now." For most subjects, defying the experimenter's commands is difficult because doing so is to question the legitimacy of his self-presentation as a competent, scientific authority. By invoking his empathy for the learner, this subject is making a subjective judgment that does not necessarily imply a general condemnation of the experimenter and his self-presentation.

A second factor that likely led to this subject's defiance is the experimenter's unresponsiveness to his questions or objections. With the exception of his request to see the learner, the experimenter ignores his questions and brusquely orders him to continue, without providing any reassurances or justifications. In doing so, the experimenter's prods backfire, producing vexation and stubbornness rather than cooperation.

Another disobedient subject, a thirty-nine-year-old salesman, is an example of one whose disobedience occurs later in the experiment. Although he expresses some mild objections a couple of times earlier in the procedure, the experimenter is able to brush them aside. The subject continues without any further signs of resistance until he has given the 315-volt shock.

Learner [Intensely agonized scream]

Subject RICH: boy,—

Learner I told you I refuse to answer.

Subject cake, man,—

Learner I'm no longer part of this experiment.

Subject girl. [Long pause] He said that he's no longer part of the experiment. He can withdraw at any time, which is what you said he could do.

Experimenter Well, whether the learner likes it or not, we must go on until he's learned all the word-pairs correctly. Please continue.

Subject Well, I don't think going against the man's will is right. Being as how he was given the option of withdrawing at any time.

Experimenter The experiment requires that you go on, Teacher, until he learns all these word-pairs correctly.

Subject Well, I don't—ah—I can't go on. Now, if you hadn't given him the option, if you had told him that once he started he had to continue, that's one thing, but you gave him the option of withdrawing at any time. Which he has chosen to do.

Experimenter Well, it's absolutely essential that you continue.

Subject No, I can't go on . . . I mean, considering the other man. He gave an indication of a heart condition and he refuses to go on with the test that he was given the option of withdrawing from at any time.

Experimenter Well, you have no other choice.

Subject [Surprise in his voice] I have *no* other choice? Hmmm. Hmmm. [Pause.] I think I have.

Experimenter That is to say, if you don't continue, we'll have to discontinue the entire experiment.

Subject Well, I think in all fairness that's what we would have to do at this point. I mean, considering the option you've given the man and his request for withdrawal from it.

Experimenter Well, we'll have to discontinue.

Unlike the first defiant subject, who was able to bolt the experiment early on, at 150 volts, it took this man about twice as long to disengage himself. Although his early protests were signs of his displeasure with his assigned task, he had pressed more than twenty switches before he found the right verbal formula to enable him to break away. In a vigorous dialogue with the experimenter, he reminds the experimenter of the rules of the game—that the learner had the right to quit.

Actually this right was never made explicit, although it was clearly implied by the experimenter's statement that the check was theirs to keep no matter what happened later. In the subject's mind, however, this was transformed into an explicit rule that allowed him to confront the experimenter without discrediting his authority. The fact that the experimenter's canned responses disregarded the case the subject was making for stopping the procedure only served to irritate him and intensify his resolve to quit.

...

Milgram also investigated factors that facilitated resistance to authority. He not only enlightened us about the unexpectedly commanding power of authority but also provided a powerful antidote to the unwanted influence of authority. He did this by means of an experiment showing that the rebellion of two peers helped to free the subject from the authority's grip. In this condition, there was a team of three teachers—the real subject and two confederates. Partway into the procedure, the confederates defy the experimenter and refuse to continue—one at 150 volts, the other at 210 volts. In this variation, 90 percent of the naïve subjects followed their example and dropped out at some point before the end of the shock series. In other words, only 10 percent of the subjects in this experiment were fully obedient. No other variation Milgram conducted was as effective in undercutting the power of authority as this one. He drew the following important conclusion from this finding: "When an individual wishes to stand in opposition to authority, he does best to find support for his position from others in his group. The mutual support provided by men for each other is the strongest bulwark we have against the excesses of authority."

All the experimental variations, from the beginning in August 1961 through March 1962, were conducted at Linsly-Chittenden Hall—the first four, the four-part proximity series, in the Interaction Laboratory on the first floor and the rest in a laboratory in the basement. After completing the fourth experiment, Milgram had to move out of the Interaction Laboratory because the Sociology Department, which had loaned it to him, now needed it back. Another laboratory space became available in the basement of the same building, and Milgram was able to move his whole experimental setup there within a couple of weeks.

To cap off the project, Milgram rented a three-room office suite in the Newfield Building, located at 1188 Main Street in downtown Bridgeport. He moved his laboratory there and set up shop under the made-up name of Research Associates of Bridgeport during April and May of 1962. Milgram's aim was to completely dissociate the experiment from Yale to find out if people would still obey destructive orders without the authority and prestige of Yale hovering in the background. He found that although there was a drop in the obedience rate, a large proportion of the subjects still obeyed the experimenter. In Bridgeport, 47.5 percent of the subjects were fully obedient, although the difference between this figure and the obedience rate of 65 percent in the corresponding condition at Yale was not statistically significant.

He offered the following speculative explanation for the results:

> It is possible that if commands of a potentially harmful or a destructive sort are to be perceived as legitimate they must occur within some sort of institutional structure. But it is clear from the study that it need not be a particularly reputable or distinguished institution. . . . It is possible that the *category* of institution, judged according to its professed function, rather than its qualitative position within that category, wins our compliance. Persons deposit money in elegant, but also in seedy-looking banks, without giving much thought to the differences in security they offer. Similarly, our subjects may consider one laboratory to be as competent as another, so long as it *is* a scientific laboratory.

...

The remaining experiments in the series included one that was carried out in May 1962 specifically for use in a documentary film, *Obedience*. Milgram made the film to provide visual evidence of his findings. Fourteen subjects, recruited in the same manner as the other subjects, were filmed over a two-day period, resulting in candid footage, since the subjects did not know they were being filmed. At the end of the experimental session, subjects were informed of the filming, and Milgram asked for their permission to use the film for educational purposes. Only those who gave their consent appeared in the film, which depicted both obedient and defiant subjects. The result is a gripping depiction of the human propensity to obey authority.

Milgram announced the completion of the series of experiments in a letter to his chairman, Claude Buxton, dated June 1, 1962:

> I wish to announce my departure from the Linsly-Chittenden basement laboratory. It served us well. Our last subject was run on Sunday, May 27. The experiments on "obedience to authority" are, Praise the Lord, completed.

It was just two years earlier that Israeli agents had abducted Adolf Eichmann from his home in Buenos Aires and flown him to Israel. After a lengthy trial in Jerusalem, he was sentenced to death on December 15, 1961, for his role in the murder of six million Jews. His execution occurred shortly before midnight on May 31, 1962, four days after Milgram concluded his obedience study. The close conjunction of these two events presaged the important role the experiments would come to play in attempts to shed light on the behavior of the Nazi perpetrators.

CHAPTER 7

AFTERSHOCKS

As THE OBEDIENCE experiments progressed during the 1961–1962 academic year, some of the startling results began making their way across campus. Before long, the Psychology Department was—as Robert Abelson, a member of the department, put it—"marinating in it. People would gossip about it. . . . We were coated with it. And it was mainly to the effect of how interesting it was."

The spread of information about Milgram's experiments had been slowed somewhat—he didn't even tell Allport about them until January 12, 1962—by a disconcerting discovery he made in September 1961, early in the project. Arnold Buss, a psychologist at the University of Pittsburgh, had just published a book, *The Psychology of Aggression,* that contained a diagram of an "aggression machine" and a description of its use that bore some general similarity to Milgram's shock generator and his procedure. Milgram's immediate reaction was that his machine and experimental procedure had been copied.

Philip Zimbardo recalls a strange visit to Milgram's office around this time. When he asked Milgram about the research he was doing, Milgram closed his office door, turned on a fan to provide a sound screen, and then proceeded to tell him about the difficult situation he was in as a result of Buss's having appropriated his shock machine procedure. This, Milgram explained, was why he had to keep quiet about the experiments. That meeting "had a most paranoid quality to it," Zimbardo added.

There *were* some similarities between the two approaches. Buss's machine contained a graduated series of ten shock buttons, his cover story was also a learning experiment, the subject received sample shocks, and in one variation, there was feedback from the learner at the higher shock levels in the form of groans and gasps. But there were also distinct differences. Buss's subjects could choose from any one of the ten shock buttons to "punish" the learner—rather than move up the shock level with each subsequent error—and the learning task was completely different, a "concept learning" procedure in which the learner had to identify different patterns of lights as being correct or incorrect. Buss used a "finger electrode," whereas in Milgram's procedure the electrode was placed on the wrist. Buss's purpose was to study aggression, not obedience.

But in the heat of the moment, the similarities fueled Milgram's suspicions. An exchange of calls and letters with Buss reassured Milgram that he had developed his technique independently and that he had not heard about Milgram's machine through the grapevine, although Milgram never completely accepted this explanation. His ire tended to be stirred up periodically, whenever people would call his shock machine "the Buss aggression machine"—even, in one case, in a letter to him requesting a photograph of the apparatus.

When the details of the research finally did emerge, discussions in the department centered largely on Milgram's surprising findings—that the subjects were willing to shock their victims far beyond what one would expect. For the most part, there wasn't a lot of concern expressed about the ethics of the research, which is not surprising given the research norms of the times. Psychologists were routinely using deception in the laboratory, without always bothering to "debrief" subjects afterward to correct the misinformation. In fact, a historian of psychology, Benjamin Harris, credits Milgram with the first published use—in a 1964 article—of the term *debriefing* to refer to a postexperimental procedure designed to correct misperceptions and reassure participants.

However, there was at least one member of the Yale Psychology Department who was troubled enough by the experience Milgram put his subjects through that he complained to the American Psychological Association (APA). As a result, the APA held up Milgram's membership application for over a year, until they could investigate the matter. This was conveyed to

Milgram in a letter from a staff member of the Membership Committee dated November 23, 1962:

> The committee voted to defer until next year a final recommendation on your application . . . because questions were raised about your ethical responsibilities in connection with certain research studies you had undertaken. I was asked to discuss the matter informally with the Secretary of the Committee on Scientific and Professional Ethics and Conduct and to arrange for additional information from persons familiar with your research. These things have been done.

She predicted a favorable decision on his application and expressed the hope that he would not let the experience "sour [him] permanently on the APA."

This episode marked the first of numerous attacks on the ethics of the experiments that Milgram had to deal with throughout his career. As late as 1977, he was still defending the ethics of the obedience experiments in print, although by then he had already moved on to other research.

On January 25, 1962, Milgram submitted the first of two additional grant proposals to the NSF to support his obedience research. A main purpose of the proposal, he stated, was to conduct further experiments to aid his search for an adequate theoretical explanation for the unexpectedly high levels of obedience he had found so far, by identifying the psychological factors at work. Among the new experiments he proposed, one would involve "constructive obedience" in which a subject would be commanded to carry out a socially commendable act—in contrast to the destructive behavior he had studied so far. He had not yet devised a specific procedure for this kind of experiment, but was confident that he would be able to come up with one.

The grant was approved on May 24, 1962, but in a distinctly modified form. NSF officials felt that since Milgram had already collected a large amount of experimental material, it would be preferable to attend to that, rather than to conduct more experiments. So, they and Milgram agreed that the grant money would be used for analysis and reporting of the experimental data from his completed experiments.

One of the external reviewers of this proposal had been Herbert Kelman. Although in his review Kelman credited Milgram with devising an ingenious experiment that yielded some unexpected and striking findings, he expressed certain reservations about the proposal, which undoubtedly contributed to the NSF's decision to approve funding only for analysis and reporting of data already collected. First, Milgram had stated that a main purpose of further research was to aid in the development of an adequate theory, and Kelman doubted that Milgram would be able to achieve this goal. Second, Kelman raised questions about the ethics of the research: "Is this perhaps going too far in what one asks a subject to do and in how one deceives him?" In April 1963, Milgram submitted a proposal to the NSF for a third and final grant to complete the analysis and reporting of the experimental findings. The grant was approved, and Milgram used the funding in part to create the documentary film *Obedience* out of the raw footage shot at Yale in May 1962.

Milgram first published some of the results of his obedience experiments in a series of four journal articles between 1963 and 1965. The first one, "Behavioral Study of Obedience," appeared in the October 1963 issue of the *Journal of Abnormal and Social Psychology*—at the time the premier outlet for research in social psychology. Putting his obedience research into print was not a simple matter. Milgram submitted that first article to the journal on December 27, 1961, and it was summarily rejected. On January 15, 1962, he submitted it to another journal, the *Journal of Personality*, which also rejected it. Its editor was Edward E. Jones, a clinician turned social psychologist, whose work on attribution processes—the study of the ways people explain the causes of their own and others' behavior—became very influential in the 1970s and 1980s. Foreshadowing a kind of criticism that would dog Milgram for most of his career, Jones faulted him for not having any theory to illuminate his findings, which Jones dismissed as "a kind of triumph of social engineering." On July 27, 1962, Daniel Katz, editor of the *Journal of Abnormal and Social Psychology*, recalled the manuscript and accepted it for publication.

But the ethical concerns were what plagued Milgram most at the time. In his writings and public statements, he was resolute about the ethical propriety of his work. After all, he felt that he was asking a legitimate, socially important question: How far would people go if an authority figure commanded them to hurt another person? He hadn't *forced* anyone to continue giving more punishments. It was ultimately the subject's decision whether or not to continue. Besides, the victim was not actually getting shocked.

In defending the experiments, however, he sometimes underestimated the distress of the participants. In one of his musings, he wrote: "I do not think I exaggerate when I say that, for most subjects, the experiment was a positive and enriching experience. It provided them with an occasion for self-insight, and gave them a first-hand and personalized knowledge of the social forces that control human conduct. . . . Most felt that they contributed to a significant scientific study, and are glad to have had the opportunity to serve in a socially valuable cause."

In a letter to a psychologist at the University of Delaware, he claimed that his participants experienced less damage to their self-esteem than college students who don't do well on their exams. He had seen students petrified while taking exams and then depressed if they failed, or failed to attain the A they had hoped for. He noted the irony involved: "So it seems that in testing whether persons possess established knowledge, we are quite prepared to accept stress, tension, and consequences for self-esteem. But in regard to the process of generating new knowledge, how little tolerance we show."

In another place he made the preposterous claim that "relatively few subjects experienced greater tension than a nail-biting patron at a good Hitchcock thriller."

Two former subjects disagree. For them, the experiments involved a degree of distress that clearly transcended the stress of everyday, routine activities. When William Menold participated in the experiment in 1961, he had just been discharged from a Regimental Combat Team in the U.S. Army. "It was hell in there," he said, describing the experiment. As the procedure progressed and the victim was getting the answers wrong, Menold "really started sweating bullets." When the learner kept on screaming, he felt so sorry for him that he offered to switch places with him. He thought he could learn the materials faster, "'cause I figured this guy's kind of dumb, you know. I mean he kind of looked . . . like he wasn't going to win any IQ tests. . . ."

A fleeting thought occasionally crossed his mind about whether the "thing was real or not. . . . But it was so well done. . . . I bought the whole thing." An especially difficult juncture in the procedure took place when the victim stopped responding: "I didn't know what the hell was going on. I think, you know, maybe I'm killing this guy." He told the experimenter that he was "not taking responsibility for going further. That's it." It was only after he was told that the responsibility wasn't his, that they were taking full responsibility, that he continued.

He ended up fully obedient: "I went the whole nine yards." During the experiment, he recalls "hysterically laughing, but it was not funny laughter. . . . It was so bizarre. And I mean, I completely lost it, my reasoning power." He described himself as an "emotional wreck" and a "basket case" during the experiment and after he left the lab, realizing "that somebody could get me to do that stuff."

Herbert Winer, another former subject, is a pleasant, low-key, articulate man. Several years ago he spoke about his experience to a group at Yale: "To my dismay, [the learner] began to stumble very early in the game. . . . It was quite clear that before we got very far, the level of shock was going to be increasing. . . . This was the end of the fun part. It is very difficult to describe . . . the way my feelings changed, and the conflict and tension that arose." Winer then described how the learner's expressions of pain grew louder and that, even after he started complaining about his heart condition, the experimenter still prodded him to continue. "And so I did, for a couple of times, and finally my *own* heart condition went into an extremely tense and conflicted state. . . . I turned to the chap in the gray coat and said, 'I'm sorry, but I can't go on any further with this . . . '."

Winer went on to describe how he reacted when was told about the true nature of the experiment:

> I stood there. . . . I was angry at having been deceived. I resented the whole situation. I was a little embarrassed at not having stopped earlier, or seen what was going on earlier, and I was not totally unconcerned about my own heart rate. What if I had had a heart problem? . . .

I went home in a cold fury. . . . I called [Milgram] the following morning, as one assistant professor to another, and told him of my anger, my skepticism, and the fact that we needed to sit down and talk about this. And he was somewhat upset, but agreed. And we had a series of meetings, in 1961 and '62 which I found extraordinarily valuable, and which I think to some extent he did too. . . .

But at that time, he was fresh out of his own doctoral studies, and was very much concerned with my somewhat inchoate but very strong talk about ethics, about deception, and about what struck me at the time, in view of what I felt to be my own physical reaction to this conflict, as imposing altogether unwarranted strain on people who had had no previous medical screening of any kind. . . . And I was very upset . . . because I felt that *had* I had a heart condition, I could have been seriously inconvenienced.

Stanley Milgram agreed, but . . . he said his proposal had been approved at the level of the president's office, and that a lot of people knew about it, and they all felt that the *objective* justified whatever risks, which obviously he gave a much smaller value to than I did.

Milgram had a rich inner life of self-absorption, contemplation, and rumination. Sometimes these kinds of reflections would find expression in memos, diary notes, and observations no longer than a page or two. The intended audience for these musings appears to be no one but himself, a way to externalize and capture his thoughts and thereby make them available for possible reexamination and reevaluation later.

These notes provide a window into the workings of Milgram's mind, sometimes revealing inner conflicts that are not visible in his published writings or public statements. In the case of the ethics debate, they reveal that, at least early on, he was doing some painful soul-searching:

At times I have concluded that, although the experiment can be justified, there are still elements in it that are ethically questionable, that it is not nice to lure people into the laboratory and ensnare them into a situation that is stressful and unpleasant to them. Therefore, while what has been done cannot be undone, one can at least resolve not to repeat the performance. There and then I decide, as a purely personal matter, not to do another experiment that requires illusion, or ensnarement, and certainly not to do an experiment that forces the subject into a moral choice and marshals powerful forces against his making the right choice. And having made this resolution and feeling content with myself, I begin to wonder what part courage plays in the scientific enterprises, how scarce a commodity it is, and how easily there can be a failure of nerve.

After a while, Milgram's self-doubts evaporated—no more angst-filled self-directed notes appear—and by the time he left Yale, his statements and writings contain uniformly self-confident affirmations and strong arguments defending the ethics of the experiments.

At the same time, he recognized the legitimacy of differing points of view on the issue, and he gave a fair hearing to his critics in his classes. In fact, in instructional materials he suggested that, as a useful class exercise, teachers could create a mock "ethics review board," and different students could present arguments defending and criticizing the obedience experiments to the board. Then the members of the board could vote on whether or not the experiment was ethically acceptable.

...

The postwar growth of social psychology continued at a rapid pace in the 1960s with the emergence of new theories and the increasing use of more sophisticated quantitative methods. An indicator of the degree of growth and expansion of the field was that, while the *Handbook of Social Psychology* consisted of only two volumes in 1954, fourteen years later its second edition (which contained a chapter by Milgram) had grown to five volumes. But ironically, even as the field seemed to be blossoming as never before, some social psychologists started experiencing doubts about the methods and accomplishments of their discipline—"the crisis of confidence in social psychology," as one psychologist dubbed it. Questions were raised about the ethics of the social-psychological experiment, and the viability of more benign alternatives such as role-playing was debated. Researchers became increasingly concerned about the possibility that an experimenter's expectations could bias results, and many grew concerned that a fun-and-games attitude pervaded the field, prizing cleverness in the creation and staging of experiments at the expense of social relevance. One critic even referred to experimental social psychology as "the glitter rock of science." Discussions of the "crisis" invariably involved the obedience studies, sometimes to stoke the flames of discontent and at other times to put a damper on it. For many, it served as the most notorious example of the use of ethically problematic procedures. Yet for others, it was a prime example of social-psychological research with deep social significance. When critics tried to sink mainstream social psychology with accusations of triviality and irrelevance, the obedience experiments were invariably held up as the poster boy of substance.

One of the critics who contributed to "the crisis of confidence" was Martin Orne, a psychiatrist and psychologist at the University of Pennsylvania, who drew attention to what he believed was a potential source of error in psychological experimentation. He argued that a typical volunteer subject enters a laboratory in a highly cooperative mood. He wants to help the scientist achieve his goal of confirming his hypotheses. His strong motivation to be helpful leads him to be highly attentive to cues and clues within the laboratory—"demand characteristics," as Orne called them—that help him discover what the experimenter is *really* after, and thereby be the best subject he can possibly be. To the extent that an experiment is laden with demand characteristics, the validity of its findings are called into question: Does the subject's behavior represent a genuine response to the actual properties of the stimuli—the independent variable—or is it the product of the demand characteristics? That is, having been tipped off by the clues provided by the trappings of the laboratory or the experimenter's behavior, the subject acts in a manner that he thinks would be most helpful to the experimenter.

Orne applied his concept of demand characteristics to the obedience experiments to question their validity. He argued that subjects in the experiment were probably puzzled by the incongruity they encountered. On the one hand, the learner is screaming and begging to be released, while, on the other hand, the experimenter doesn't seem to be perturbed by this. Instead, cool as a cucumber, he keeps pressing the subject to continue. Orne believed that this incongruity led subjects to quickly figure out that the shocks were fake and that the victim was only feigning his suffering.

In his response, Milgram granted that a small number of subjects in each condition did not believe that the shocks were genuine, but he asserted that the vast majority did. For empirical support, he drew on the results of a questionnaire sent to all the participants after the completion of the experiments, in the summer of 1962. One of the questions was about the credibility of the procedure. The responses showed that over 80 percent of the subjects believed that the learner had been receiving painful shocks, whereas only 2.4 percent said they had been certain that no shocks were being delivered.

Orne's conjecture raises an important question: When the subject figured out what was *really* going on, why didn't he just pick himself up and leave? Orne's answer was that subjects continued with the charade because they didn't want to ruin the experiment. Turning his biting wit into a deadly weapon, Milgram replied: "Orne's suggestion that the subjects only *feigned* sweating, trembling, and stuttering to please the experimenter is pathetically detached from reality, equivalent to the statement that hemophiliacs bleed to keep their physicians busy."

...

It often takes a couple of years for journal articles to wend their way through the peer review process, and Milgram's obedience papers were no exception. Although Milgram had first submitted "Behavioral Study of Obedience"—the first article he wrote on the experiments—to the *Journal of Abnormal and Social Psychology* in December 1961, it didn't come out until October 1963, almost two years later. It contained a detailed description of the laboratory procedure, the results for the Remote condition—in which 65 percent of the subjects were fully obedient—and an initial attempt to account for the fact that a surprisingly high proportion of normal individuals were willing to inflict painful and possibly harmful shocks on an innocent victim in response to the insistent commands of a scientific authority.

The publication of this article was a significant milestone in the history of the obedience research, because it marked the beginning of the large-scale diffusion of knowledge about Milgram's startling findings among the broader public, first in the United States and then in other countries. Before the article appeared, knowledge of the research was limited and haphazard. Students and faculty in the psychology departments of some universities had heard about it through the academic grapevine. Also, many residents of New Haven, Bridgeport, and surrounding communities had heard about it from some of the hundreds of subjects in the experiments, but it had never been reported in the popular press.

Within days of the article's publication, the *New York Times* gave it detailed coverage in an article appearing on October 26, 1963, under the blaring headline "Sixty-five Percent in Test Blindly Obey Order to Inflict Pain." Gradually other U.S. newspapers picked it up, and by mid-December, news of the experiment had crossed the Atlantic, with articles appearing in *Der Spiegel* of Hamburg and the *Times* of London. The editors of two anthologies quickly requested permission to reprint the journal article. Eventually, it would appear in dozens of anthologies.

On November 2, a week after the *New York Times* article appeared, the *St. Louis Post-Dispatch* published a prescient editorial skewering Milgram and Yale for the ordeal they put their subjects through: "A story of man's cruelty to man," it began, "that is surprising even in light of fairly recent history comes from an experiment at Yale University." The editorial went on to give the details of the experiment, including a vivid description of the suffering among the subjects. It concluded: "In all this it seems to us . . . that the showing was not one of blind obedience but of open-eyed torture, with an adverse score not of 65 per cent but of 100. . . . It very much remains to be shown that there was anything in the performance worthy of a great university."

Robert Buckhout, a social psychologist at Washington University, sent Milgram a copy of the editorial, enabling him to write a response, which appeared in the newspaper on November 16, 1963, as a letter to the editor: "The study started with a few questions that are of no small importance for humanity: What does a good man do when he is told by authority to perform acts that go against natural law? . . . In a laboratory setting, where we could be sure that no one would be hurt, we tried to get some answers. . . ."

The *New York Times* article had appeared despite Milgram's request that it not be published. In a telegram sent two nights earlier to the newspaper's science editor, Walter Sullivan, he wrote: "I do not wish to have the experiment generally publicized at this time because publicity will interfere with further research. The experiment only works if the subject does not know what it is about." This was a puzzling request, since Milgram had completed the obedience experiments in May 1962 and was not known to be planning to conduct any more of them. Perhaps he made the request with other prospective obedience researchers in mind, or perhaps he was in fact considering another obedience experiment.

Professional readers of psychology journals, of course, did not have to wait for the *New York Times* piece. The engaging writing style of Milgram's first journal article—at once profound, absorbing, and vivid—immediately set it apart from the bone-dry, third-person, passive presentational style of the typical scientific paper. In the opening paragraphs, for example, he wrote:

> Obedience is the psychological mechanism that links individual action to political purpose. It is the dispositional cement that binds men to systems of authority. Facts of recent history and observation in daily life suggest that for many persons obedience may be a deeply ingrained behavior tendency, indeed, a prepotent impulse overriding training in ethics, sympathy, and moral conduct.

Later on, in the results section of the report, we find this description of subjects' behavior:

> Many subjects showed signs of nervousness in the experimental situation, and especially upon administering the more powerful shocks. In a large number of cases the degree of tension reached extremes that are rarely seen in sociopsychological laboratory studies. Subjects were observed to sweat, tremble, stutter, bite their lips, groan, and dig their fingernails into

their flesh. These were characteristic rather than exceptional responses to the experiment.

A continuous stream of reprint requests began to wind their way into Milgram's office as soon as the article was published. One of them came from Elliot Aronson, a social psychologist who went on to become a leading figure in the field. He wrote that he wanted to assign the article to his class in Research Methods not only for its empirical value "but also as an illustration of the fact that there is a place for literate and stylistic writing, even in scientific journals. Your introduction is probably the most readable that I've seen in an experimental journal." And Milton Erickson, a psychiatrist, wrote Milgram that he was "very much impressed by your studies which, I am convinced, have many implications which merit investigation."

But Milgram's critics made themselves heard as well. Psychologist Bruno Bettelheim considered the research "so vile that nothing these experiments show has any value. . . . They are in line with the human experiments of the Nazis." And although some clergymen would draw moral lessons from the experiments in their sermons and appreciatively send Milgram copies, a Benedictine monk from Washington, D.C., wrote him expressing his revulsion at "the extremely callous, deceitful way in which the experiment was conducted." One female psychologist to whom Milgram was introduced soon after the experiments became public turned her head and said, "You bastard." Milgram later told an interviewer, "Within a year, I understand, she was divorced, so perhaps it was displaced anger."

A scathing criticism of the obedience experiments written by Diana Baumrind, a developmental psychologist, appeared in the June 1964 issue of the *American Psychologist*. Baumrind took Milgram to task for putting his subjects through an unexpected, emotionally disturbing experience. Although Milgram had stated that steps were taken after the experiment to ensure that the subjects left in a state of well-being, she found such reassurance unconvincing. Her main objection, though, was less about the physical discomfort subjects experienced during the experiment or the deception used than about the possibility of permanent, long-term harm—however slight it may be: "I do regard the emotional disturbance described by Milgram as potentially harmful because it could easily effect an alteration in the subject's self-image or ability to trust adult authorities in the future. It is potentially harmful to a subject to commit, in the course of an experiment, acts which he himself considers unworthy, particularly when he has been entrapped into committing such acts by an individual he has reason to trust."

Milgram was "totally astonished" by the criticism and also angry at the editor for not alerting him to the article prior to publication so that his rebuttal could appear in the same issue. At Milgram's request, the editor gave him the opportunity to write such a piece afterward. In Milgram's cover letter to the editor accompanying his reply to Baumrind, he wrote: "Baumrind's article raises some legitimate points, but it was deficient in its information, and this could have been remedied by allowing me to see the manuscript prior to publication. Would this not be a generally more desirable policy for a journal concerned with professional standards?" He added: "The fact of the matter is that no one who took part in the obedience study suffered damage, and most subjects found the experience to be instructive and enriching."

The first part of this statement is, in principle, unverifiable. It is not possible to prove unequivocally the nonexistence of negative effects—a fact that Milgram conceded later in a 1977 article. The absolute, unqualified nature of the statement in his letter was obviously a reflexive overreaction to being attacked.

In his rebuttal, Milgram pointed out that although there were psychological experiments whose purpose was to induce stress, his was not one of those. Although extreme tension was created in his lab, this was not intended, nor expected. And why didn't he stop the experiment once he saw that some subjects experienced severe stress? He argued that "momentary excitement" is not equivalent to harm. And he decided to continue the experiment because he saw no injurious effects among his subjects.

To counter Baumrind's belief that subjects were likely left with permanent negative aftereffects, he presented the results of some follow-up procedures. On July 12, 1962, about six weeks after the conclusion of the experiments, Milgram sent all participants a detailed report about the experimental procedure, its rationale, and some of the main results. Appended to the report was a questionnaire asking the respondents to reflect

TABLE 7.1   Now That I Have Read the Report, and All Things Considered, . . .

	Defiant Subjects, % (n)	Obedient Subjects, % (n)	Total, % (n)
1. I am very glad to have been in the experiment.	40.0% (146)	47.8% (139)	43.5% (285)
2. I am glad to have been in the experiment.	43.8 (160)	35.7 (104)	40.2 (264)
3. I am neither sorry nor glad to have been in the experiment.	15.3 (56)	14.8 (43)	15.1 (99)
4. I am sorry to have been in the experiment.	0.8 (3)	0.7 (2)	0.8 (5)
5. I am very sorry to have been in the experiment.	—	1.0 (3)	0.5 (3)

SOURCE: The Stanley Milgram Papers, Yale University Library, Manuscripts and Archives.

back on their experience during the experiment. It consisted of ten multiple-choice items, and respondents were encouraged to make additional comments if they chose to. Milgram had probably intended to include results from the questionnaire in his planned book, but Baumrind's attack compelled him to publish the relevant results then, in his rebuttal. The report and questionnaires had been sent to all the participants in the main series—856 of them. Although it took two follow-up reminder mailings during the summer, Milgram ended up with 92 percent of his subjects returning the questionnaires—a remarkable return rate for a mailed survey.

The most directly relevant results, which Milgram presented in tabular form (see Table 7.1), tapped subjects' feelings—positive or negative—about their experience. He had first used this question in Norway in the spring of 1958 after the conformity experiment. As Table 7.1 shows, most participants in the obedience experiment had positive feelings. Almost 84 percent said that they were glad to have participated, and only 1.3 percent said that they were sorry they had. In response to the question, "Do you think more studies of this sort should be carried out?" over 80 percent replied in the affir-

TABLE 7.2   During the Experiment, . . .

	Defiant Subjects, % (n)	Obedient Subjects, % (n)	Total, % (n)
1. I was extremely upset.	8.7% (32)	12.0% (35)	10.2% (67)
2. I was somewhat nervous.	48.8 (179)	51.6 (150)	50.0 (329)
3. I was relatively calm.	38.2 (140)	30.2 (88)	34.7 (228)
4. I was completely calm.	4.4 (16)	6.2 (18)	5.2 (34)

SOURCE: The Stanley Milgram Papers, Yale University Library, Manuscripts and Archives.

mative, just over 3 percent said "No," and about 16 percent were undecided. About 74 percent said that they had learned "something of personal importance" from being in the experiment, and 10.5 percent said they had not.

Tables 7.2 and 7.3 contain additional questionnaire results. Although Milgram did not include them in his response to Baumrind, they highlight an important distinction between being upset during the experiment and afterward. While a majority of the subjects (60.2 percent) were distressed during the experiment itself, a similar percentage (63.6 percent) were not bothered by it at all by the time they were completing the questionnaire—which, depending on the condition the subject had been in, ranged from six weeks to about eleven months after their participation in the experiment.

Two points about the questionnaire are worth noting. First, self-report measures of this sort are susceptible to many sources of error, and Milgram was aware of their limitations. However, one important potential source of distortion can be virtually ruled out—some sort of self-selection bias that would tilt the results in one direction or other. With a response rate of 92 percent, it would be hard for anyone to argue that such a bias was operating. Furthermore, Milgram conducted some follow-up analyses to see if respondents differed in any meaningful way from nonrespondents. Important questions could be raised about the validity of the results if, for example, defiant and obedient subjects differed in their return rates. It turns out they

TABLE 7.3   Since the Time I Was in the Experiment, . . .

	Defiant Subjects, % (n)	Obedient Subjects, % (n)	Total, % (n)
1. I have been bothered by it quite a bit.	7.7% (28)	6.2% (18)	7.0% (46)
2. It has bothered me a little.	29.6 (107)	28.9 (84)	29.2 (191)
3. It has not bothered me at all.	62.7 (227)	65.0 (189)	63.6 (416)

SOURCE: The Stanley Milgram Papers, Yale University Library, Manuscripts and Archives.

didn't. In fact, comparisons between those who returned the questionnaire with those who did not yielded only one significant difference: age. A smaller proportion of people below age thirty-five returned the questionnaire than those who were thirty-five and older.

Second, even if one regards Milgram's treatment of his subjects during the experiment as callous, it is important to recognize the uniqueness of this kind of follow-up assessment of subjects' perceptions and their well-being. When Herbert Kelman—the social psychologist most responsible for sensitizing his fellow professionals to the ethical dimensions of their work—was asked whether he knew of any other researcher who had ever done a similar postexperimental follow-up before Milgram, he answered, "No."

In his rebuttal article, Milgram also described the results of another kind of follow-up. He had a psychiatrist interview forty subjects who "would be most likely to have suffered consequences from participation" with the aim of identifying any who might have been harmed by the experiment. The psychiatrist found no evidence of harm in any of the subjects he interviewed.

The interviews were conducted mostly in small-group sessions, from February through May 1963, by Paul Errera, an assistant professor of psychiatry at Yale University. His report to Milgram was titled "Statement . . . based on Interviews with Forty 'Worst Cases' in the Milgram Obedience Experiments." Unfortunately, his report doesn't describe what criteria he used to define the "worst cases." Dr. Errera does not recall the criteria he used and no longer has written records of those meetings—neither of which is surprising, given that the interviews took place forty years ago. However, based on other sources of information, such as Milgram's grant applications, it seems probable that the "forty worst cases" were subjects who seemed especially agitated at the end of the experiment, had written some especially critical comments in the questionnaire, or had lodged some sort of complaint with Milgram or another person (in at least one case, a subject complained to the president of Yale). One interview participant, for example, a food wholesaler, was so upset by the experiment that he consulted afterward with a lawyer friend about it.

In his rejoinder to Baumrind, Milgram vigorously disagreed with her contention that his subjects had been "entrapped" into committing reprehensible actions.

> I started with the belief that every person who came to the laboratory was free to accept or reject the dictates of authority. This view sustains a conception of human dignity insofar as it sees in each man a capacity for *choosing* his own behavior. And as it turned out, many subjects did, indeed, choose to reject the experimenter's commands, providing a powerful affirmation of human ideals. . . . My feeling is that viewed in the total context of values served by the experiment, approximately the right course was followed. . . . The laboratory psychologist senses his work will lead to human betterment, not only because enlightenment is more dignified than ignorance, but because new knowledge is pregnant with humane consequences.

Whether he liked it or not, Milgram had many opportunities to offer his opinion on research ethics. In writings both published and unpublished, he objected to the use of the word "deception" to refer to experiments that used cover stories or other kinds of misinformation, because he felt it was a value-laden term whose use prevented an objective discussion of the ethics of that type of method. He preferred instead terms such as "staging" or "technical illusion."

In one of his weaker arguments defending the obedience research, Milgram noted that some of the classic experiments in social psychology, those conducted by Solomon Asch and Kurt Lewin, also contained ethical problems, although they were rarely mentioned. His obedience studies, he implied, should be seen as a continuation of that classic tradition in social psychology. As an example, he pointed to Lewin's classic studies comparing the group atmospheres created by different styles of leadership. One of the main findings was that when the authoritarian leader left the room, there was a sharp increase in aggressive behavior among the study subjects. Milgram asked: "Was it proper of Lewin to subject young people [to] the aggression inducing authoritarian style of a leader?" But this was a poor defense. There is a vast difference between the playful tussles of preadolescent boys and the violence that subjects in the obedience experiments thought they were perpetrating on the learner.

In 1973, the APA published its comprehensive "Ethical Principles in the Conduct of Research with Human Participants," and in 1975, the U.S. Department of Health, Education, and Welfare (DHEW) issued a regulation requiring that all research with human subjects—not just that funded by DHEW—be reviewed by an institutional review board, a committee created by each institution conducting human research to screen prospective projects to ensure the well-being of subjects. In 1977, Milgram remarked, "Many regard informed consent as the cornerstone of ethical practice in experimentation with human subjects," reflecting the reality of the regulatory atmosphere that was in ascendance at the time. Milgram pointed out that many experiments in social psychology could not be carried out if subjects were fully informed beforehand. So he proposed three possible solutions.

First, he argued that in almost every profession an exemption is made from general moral practice that allows that profession to function in ways that are beneficial for society. For example, it is generally not permissible to examine the private parts of female strangers, but that rule is suspended for the practice of obstetrics and gynecology. Similarly, he argued, social scientists should be allowed to have some exemptions from general practice— the use of short-term misinformation—if the technical requirements of their work call for it and if, in the long run, the work will benefit society. This was a fuzzy argument, however, since it glossed over the difference between benefiting the individual and benefiting society.

A second alternative was what he called *presumptive consent.* This involved describing a planned experimental procedure to a group of people, and, if they found it acceptable, recruiting a different group of subjects to participate.

The third alternative Milgram suggested was to obtain *prior general consent* from a pool of subjects in advance of their actual participation. That is, before volunteering for a subject pool, they would be told that among the experiments to be conducted, some involved deceptions while in others they might experience some stress. In this way, those who objected to these procedures could exclude themselves from those kinds of experiments, and only willing subjects would participate. None of these suggestions was embraced by the psychology community.

...

Milgram would often receive letters from people asking about details of the obedience experiments that they couldn't find in his published reports, and Milgram was happy to oblige. For example, when people wrote to ask about sex differences in obedience, he assured them that he found none—a fact that would become public only on publication of his book many years later. Some letter writers tied Milgram's studies to their personal lives with a surprising degree of candor. For example, one man from upstate New York wrote that he had read about the obedience experiments and found them interesting but limited, because the victim was an actor—not a person really getting hurt. The letter writer, by contrast, had real victims in his work: He was an electric company employee whose job was to turn off power to the homes of delinquent customers, even when the outside temperature dropped to below-freezing levels.

Between 1963 and 1965 Milgram published four journal articles presenting various results from the main obedience series. One of the articles, containing a detailed description of the four-part proximity series as well as shorter treatments of other conditions was published in the journal *Human Relations* in 1965. It won Milgram the Socio-Psychological Prize for 1964 awarded by the American Association for the Advancement of Science and came with an award of $1,000. This was the first formal recognition of Milgram's work by his peers, and a sign—or so Milgram thought—that he had arrived.

CHAPTER 8

RETURN TO
ACADEMIC EDEN

WHILE MILGRAM WAS at Yale, Allport had told his col-league Roger Brown, in a slightly conspiratorial manner: "I'm rather glad he's doing these experiments in New Haven, but we'll hire him as soon as he finishes." Allport had a deep moral ambivalence about the ethics of the obedience experiments. On the one hand, his reaction to Milgram's first let-ter to him about the experiments was pure excitement—so much, in fact, that he immediately invited Milgram to come up to Harvard to talk about it to one of his graduate classes. On the other hand, he would regularly have his classes vote on whether or not the research was ethical. Typically, the re-sult was an almost even split: sometimes the majority tilted toward a favor-able judgment, and other times the outcome was in the opposite direction.

Allport expressed his reservations about the obedience studies in an oth-erwise superlative letter of recommendation requested by Claude Buxton when Yale's Psychology Department was evaluating Milgram for promo-tion. After telling Buxton that Milgram was one of the top three or four students he had had in thirty years, he wrote:

> My one and only objection to his work concerns the "astonishing" ordeal to which he has put his subjects in the "obedience" research. Only Festinger and Schachter would have equal audacity! I know he is sensitive to the eth-ical issues involved, and regrets the need for experimental deception and stress. But he thinks it justified by the scientific yield—and so perhaps it is.

Milgram brought Sasha with him to Harvard for his invited talk so that he could introduce her to his former teachers and friends. Allport expressed his approval:

It was most pleasant to see you—and Sasha. You have a strong personality—slightly one-sided; and she creates an ideal equilibrium for you. I do congratulate you on the arrangement! . . . In her chosen career [social work] she will soothe mankind in proportion to the extent that you stir it up. So we'll come out even.

At the end of 1962 Milgram was offered a position at Harvard. He could have stayed at Yale—he had received his promotion—but the prospect of returning to academic Eden was hard to resist, so he accepted a three-year appointment as an assistant professor in the Department of Social Relations, beginning July 1, 1963, with a starting annual salary of $8,600. His appointment came with the stipulation that he not conduct any research with drugs. Allport knew of Milgram's interests in mescaline, but Timothy Leary had left Harvard only months earlier, and Allport did not want a repetition of the problems that Leary's presence had created.

In the course of the hiring process, Milgram received a letter from the secretary of the Social Relations Department chairman, David McClelland, asking about his middle name. She explained that at Harvard it was necessary to submit the complete legal name when corresponding with the dean—so her request was not without some rhyme or reason. Neither was Milgram's response—which he wrote in verse:

> Dear Miss Thoren:
>> My heart is heavy
>> And spirit lame
>> For I was born
>> With no middle name
>> Vexing as an unsolved riddle
>> Is a name without a middle
>> I rely on tolerance

To quell all signs of remonstrance
Stanley [ ] Milgram
Assistant Professor

Although he was happy about returning to Harvard, Milgram looked back with some degree of satisfaction on his three years at Yale. It had provided an atmosphere of encouragement and support to do his research. And despite the fact that at the time Yale was a hotbed of attitude-change research, "it is to the credit of the Department at Yale"—he later wrote—"that no one ever suggested that I put aside my own interests and take up the attitude-change banner."

Milgram remembered with special fondness his graduate students, such as Alan Elms, Leon Mann, and Susan Harter, who constituted the heart of his daily life. Outside the confines of the university, New Haven did not have much of an intellectual or artistic community. And within the Psychology Department, the social climate was not especially friendly or comforting for the junior faculty. Although they were free to pursue their research interests, they were told what courses they had to teach, and it was understood that very few of them would be granted tenure. The department was controlled by the senior faculty, and there was a great divide between them and the young assistant professors, which generated a good deal of hostility among the latter. When new assistant professors joined the department, their wives were warned by the department chairman's wife not to invite any of the senior faculty to their homes because they would be turned down.

Milgram did not seem to feel the divide as acutely as his young colleagues, and in fact he enjoyed a warm relationship with a few of the older members of the department. Among the latter, he was closest to Irving Janis, who, over the years, proved to be a wise and reliable friend. Although Milgram was less intimidated by the prevailing social atmosphere than most other junior faculty, he was not completely unaffected by it. "It is interesting how in New Haven I had begun to take alienation for granted," he later wrote his former Yale colleague, Howard Leventhal.

Milgram was a man of many interests—he liked to think of himself as a neo-Renaissance man. As noted earlier, he began writing poetry and musicals in college, and his choice of an academic career did not put an end to his other, nonscientific, pursuits. During the summer of 1963, Milgram began writing to literary agents to handle two short stories he had written. Although most turned him down, one, Joan Daves, agreed to represent him, and sent the articles off to several magazines. She was unable to sell them, but she did get a favorable response from the fiction editor of *Mademoiselle,* who asked to see more of his work. Although Milgram continued to write prose and poetry most of his life, he had only limited success in publishing any of his purely literary efforts.

In the fall, Stanley and Sasha moved into a handsome two-bedroom apartment with a fireplace at 10 Forest Street in Cambridge. It was both within walking distance of Stanley's office in Emerson Hall and close to other young academic couples like themselves—so that when their first child, Michele, was born, in November 1964, Sasha was able to seek out other young mothers and playmates for her. (The Milgrams' second child, Marc, was also born in Cambridge, in January 1967, toward the end of their stay there.) Stanley and Sasha found themselves very much at home in Cambridge. They enjoyed its vibrancy and excitement and were soon caught up in the social life of the academic community. Their home became a haven of good food and stimulating company. Leon Mann recalls Thanksgiving dinner at the Milgrams' in 1964, with Stanley carving a huge turkey using the step-by-step instructions provided by the *New York Times Cookbook* propped up on the table next to the bird.

Stanley and Sasha became increasingly engaged in liberal Democratic causes. A favorite ploy was to write "we Republicans" letters to Republican political figures to persuade them to adopt more liberal positions on various issues—an application of the social-psychological principle that the more similar a persuader is to his target, the more effective he will be. Senator Barry Goldwater was one such target.

Dear Senator Goldwater:

First, my wife and I like your kind of reasoning and hope you will be the Republican candidate for President in 1964. Let's keep the Republican Party true to its highest principles. Come on, Barry, show those Democrats that we Republicans have something fresh to say. Something new and vigorous and in the American tradition.

Second, and maybe more important at this very moment. My wife and I have just heard President Kennedy talk about the test ban treaty. Democrat or not, he is our President, and for once we thought he made a lot of sense. A lot of folks around here have been aware of the fallout problem because we get reports on radioactivity in milk products. And anybody can see that Commies or not we don't want to continue polluting the atmosphere. Frankly, I'm surprised we wangled this treaty out of Krushchev. . . . In other words all of us here hope from the bottom of our hearts that you will lead the way to get that test-ban treaty signed. . . .

Your friends,
(Signed) Stanley & Alexandra Milgram
P.S. And let's see you President in 1964!

Becoming parents was something Milgram and Sasha looked forward to with great anticipation, and Stanley took pleasure in even the mundane aspects of fatherhood. Soon after Michele was born, his brother Joel remembers receiving an audiotaped "letter" from Stanley, describing in light-hearted and loving detail how he was in the midst of changing her diaper. And about a year after Marc was born, he wrote a close friend that "both children are more delightful than ever and growing rapidly." Another letter to the same friend contains a statement that succinctly and eloquently conveys his feelings about being a father: "Parenthood brings pleasure to the day, for children are jewels, not without cost, but capable of emitting unexpected flashes of delight."

Aware of how much his own father's busy work schedule had deprived him of time with his children, Stanley made his family a priority, despite his immersion in his own work. When Michele was two or three, he would take her to his office at Harvard on Saturday mornings and other occasions. Playing chess with Marc, staying up to all hours of the night chatting with Michele, taking family vacations—these were just as important to him as any research project. He and Sasha took pride in their children's achievements, whether it was Marc scoring in the 99th percentile on his SATs or Michele learning Italian so she could read the works of an Italian writer in the original. When the children went off to college—Michele to Vassar and then Marc to Brandeis—he wrote a colleague: "I have a great feeling of sadness about losing daily contact with our children."

The Milgrams' idyllic Cambridge life was briefly interrupted in November 1963 with the assassination of President Kennedy. At the time, Milgram was fairly new to Harvard, but his reputation as a crafty researcher had preceded him—you never knew when he was going to pull an experiment on you. So when in the early afternoon of Friday, November 22, 1963, he burst into Emerson Hall in the midst of a lecture by Talcott Parsons about the nature of social systems, and rushed to the podium, yelling, "I have horrible news. President Kennedy has been shot in Dallas," he was met with outrage and skepticism. Barry Wellman, now a sociologist at the University of Toronto, remembers blurting out: "You're just doing another experiment on us." It was only after the students left Emerson Hall and heard the news from others in Harvard Yard that they realized Milgram's announcement was genuine.

The assassination of President Kennedy plunged the nation into a paralyzing gloom. At Harvard, the mourning was for one of their own; twenty-three years earlier John F. Kennedy had received his bachelor's degree cum laude at Harvard. All classes throughout the university were canceled on Monday, November 25—an action that was unprecedented in Harvard's history. Many of the overflow crowd of 2,000 who attended the service at Memorial Church in tribute to the president wept openly. Milgram was deeply affected by Kennedy's death and expressed his grief and gave his own tribute in a letter that appeared in the November 25 issue of *The Harvard Crimson:*

To the Editors of the Crimson:

We are numb with the tragic, senseless death of our President. There are heartfelt gestures everywhere, but there is only one tribute that can give meaning to his death. It is simply this: that the ideals he lived for be embodied in law. No single piece of legislation was closer to him than a strong civil rights bill. If in the face of his death, we enact laws he urgently desired, then alongside the tragedy his spirit is proclaimed. If we do nothing, it is not fate, but we who render his death senseless and empty. We did not bring on the President's death but we truly dispose of it by what we make of it. There is a way to give meaning to his death. Each of us must let congress and President Johnson know that we choose to honor our late President with the enactment of his courageous civil rights program. Let his spirit and ideals carry us forward in law. In the midst of sorrow and bewilderment, it is the only tribute that rings true.

Stanley Milgram
Assistant Professor of Social Psychology

But it was the research that Milgram carried out at Harvard that most defined his Cambridge years. Two areas in particular dominated his agenda: the lost-letter technique and the small-world phenomenon. Both would become valuable as innovative research tools for social psychologists and other social scientists. In addition, the small-world idea would, decades later, capture the imagination of researchers in the physical and biological sciences and also become part of the vocabulary of pop culture through the phrase "six degrees of separation." But the lost-letter technique—a continuation of work he had begun at Yale after completion of the obedience studies—has also had lasting significance. The method is still used today by social psychologists to find out what people really think about controversial issues.

...

The lost-letter technique, developed by Milgram and his students in 1963, was designed as a way of measuring community attitudes in as unobtrusive a way as possible—a sort of polling device. It is based on the belief that if you come across an unmailed letter lying on the sidewalk, the right thing to do is find a mailbox and drop it in. But what if the letter is addressed to an organization you oppose or even detest? If you mail the letter, you may well be helping it. How one resolves this dilemma—by mailing the letter or not—presumably reflects one's attitude toward the intended recipient of the letter. Milgram felt that measuring community attitudes in this way would remove interviewer effects that impair the accuracy of traditional modes of assessing attitudes and opinions. Instead of answering an interviewer's questions truthfully, respondents may provide an answer they believe is more socially desirable, in order to create a more favorable impression. The lost-letter technique circumvented this source of error, because the letter-finder did not know that his behavior was being studied and therefore would not resort to tactics meant to burnish his public image.

The technique originated as a class project conducted by members of Milgram's graduate class Research Techniques in Social Psychology and Personality at Yale in the spring of 1963, right before Milgram left for Harvard. Although all ten members of the class participated, two of them, Leon Mann and Susan Harter, were more centrally involved than the rest; as a result, they were coauthors with Milgram on the first published report of the technique, which appeared in the journal *Public Opinion Quarterly*.

Leon Mann recalls that the idea grew out of "creative chit-chat" in the class about how people reacted when they found a lost package in New Haven Common. "It was characteristic of Stanley's genius" that he could turn this simple observation into a workable psychology experiment.

The students "lost" letters throughout New Haven that were addressed to four different fictitious recipients: Friends of the Communist Party, Friends of the Nazi Party, Medical Research Associates, and a private individual, a Mr. Walter Carnap. (The choice of this name was an inside joke, a takeoff on the name of Rudolf Carnap, a philosopher of science.) There were 100 letters of each type, and they were all addressed to the same post office box in New Haven, which had been set up especially for the experiment. They all contained the same innocuous letter, which was ambiguous enough to be applicable to a variety of recipients.

It was a brief note from a "Max" to a "Walter" about plans for an upcoming meeting of an unnamed group. Each student was responsible for "seeding" his or her territory with forty letters, which were to be distributed in four different kinds of locations: in phone booths, on sidewalks, inside stores, and under the windshield wipers of parked cars (with a note saying "found near car").

The letters were dropped in the late afternoon of April 3 and the final tally two weeks later revealed that the letters had been mailed in unequal numbers: 72 of the letters to Medical Research Associates and 71 of those addressed to Mr. Walter Carnap were mailed, but only 25 each of the Communist and Nazi letters reached their destination. So the technique worked; the pattern of mailed letters was consistent with the political and social attributes of their addressees. The apparent reluctance of finders to mail the Communist and Nazi letters made sense if one reasonably assumed that the American public had an aversion to the ideologies of those groups. As a precautionary measure, before embarking on the study, Milgram had notified the FBI, the New Haven police, and the local post office. A week later, he received a memo from the postmaster noting somewhat mysteriously, "Your addresses are causing quite a flurry of excitement in official circles."

This first experiment served as a feasibility study: it showed that the lost-letter technique worked. Milgram then decided to apply it to a social issue that at the time was creating a lot of tension in the South—racial integration. Milgram had a graduate research assistant, Taketo Murata, drive south from New Haven with a large batch of letters. Each was addressed to one of three fictitious groups: a civil rights group, "Equal Rights for Negroes"; an anti–civil rights group, "Council for White Neighborhoods"; and "Medical Research Associates," which was meant to serve as a neutral or control group. During two nights in mid-May he distributed them in white and black neighborhoods in Charlotte and Raleigh, North Carolina. Table 8.1 presents the combined results for the two cities.

What they found was a reversal in the percentage of mailed letters across neighborhoods. In predominantly white neighborhoods, a higher

TABLE 8.1   Percentages of "Lost Letters" Mailed to Three Different
Addresses in White and Black Neighborhoods

Neighborhood	Equal Rights for Negroes	Council for White Neighborhoods	Medical Research Associates
White	18	34	46
Black	25	16	28

SOURCE: The Stanley Milgram Papers, Yale University Library, Manuscripts and Archives.

proportion of prosegregation letters than pro-integration letters were mailed, whereas the opposite pattern occurred in largely black residential areas. (A higher proportion of Medical Research Associates letters was mailed by both blacks and whites, reflecting perhaps its more noncontroversial nature.)

When Milgram arrived at Harvard, he tried to take the lost-letter technique to new heights by scattering pro-Johnson (Democrat) and pro-Goldwater (Republican) letters from a Piper Cub, flying over Worcester, Massachusetts, in order to predict the winner in the 1964 Presidential election. This new method of losing letters did not work very well. Many letters landed in trees, in ponds, and on rooftops. Worse still, some got jammed into the movable parts of the airplane's wings, putting the pilot and his letter-dropping passenger at risk. Not surprisingly, Milgram reverted to the earlier, more pedestrian methods.

In the fall of 1964, he distributed letters addressed to four different groups in several election wards in Boston. Two groups were pro-Johnson—"Committee to Elect Johnson" and "Committee to Defeat Goldwater"—and the other two were pro-Goldwater—"Committee to Elect Goldwater" and "Committee to Defeat Johnson." The results were headlined in the *Harvard Crimson* a few days before the election: "Social Relations Finds Pro-LBJ Bostonians Won't Mail Letters to Elect Barry." More pro-Johnson than pro-Goldwater letters had been mailed. The lost-letter technique accurately predicted the outcome of the election in each of the wards, but it badly underestimated the magnitude of Johnson's win. It predicted Johnson leading by only 10 percent over Goldwater, when in fact he won by a land-slide: In the wards where the letters had been dropped, Johnson's lead was closer to 60 percent.

Milgram's final use of the lost-letter technique took him all the way to the Far East. Here is his description of the study's purpose and how it was carried out:

> The lost-letter technique [as described so far] showed us things we al-ready knew, or soon would know. It was not so much that the technique confirmed the *events* as the fact that *events* confirmed the technique. Could the lost-letter technique be applied to a situation where the an-swers were not clearly known and would be difficult to get? The situation of the 17 million overseas Chinese provided an interesting case in point. How would they respond to an extension of Red Chinese power? Were they pro-Mao or pro-Nationalists? These are questions difficult to inves-tigate with ordinary survey methods, but perhaps they would yield to the lost-letter technique.

His plan was to distribute letters addressed to pro-Peking and pro-Taiwan groups, as well as to a nonpolitical organization, the Committee to En-courage Education, throughout Hong Kong, Singapore, and Bangkok. They all contained the Chinese equivalent of the straightforward letter used in the earlier American studies, and all were addressed to the same post office box in Tokyo.

Milgram expected that the return rates of the letters would provide an answer to his research question posthaste. But some unexpected problems arose, delaying the study:

> Riots between the Malays and the Chinese began in Singapore just before our experimenter arrived. And in spite of written consent from the Malaysian government, he was put back onto the plane almost as soon as he arrived at the airport. We postponed the Singapore study. The following year our experimenter in Hong Kong . . . [who] had been paid in advance disappeared. After many months a Chinese colleague of mine reached him

by telephone. The would-be-experimenter said that in China research takes a *very long time*. In truth, he had absconded with the research funds. I decided to go to Hong Kong myself, stopping only in Tokyo to confer with Robert Frager [a doctoral student], who was to assist me in this study. . . . We employed groups of Chinese students as distributors. . . . We found that substantially more pro-Chiang than pro-Mao letters were picked up and mailed. The returns were consistent, and taken together, the findings from the three cities showed a statistically significant pro-Taiwan feeling on the part of the overseas Chinese.

The opposition of the "overseas Chinese"—those living in Hong Kong, Bangkok, and Singapore—to the Communist government of mainland China made sense to Milgram. Many residents of Hong Kong were political refugees from Red China, and in Singapore and Bangkok, many Chinese owned small family businesses, which would be threatened by an extension of Communist China's power and influence.

Based on his experiences with the lost-letter technique, Milgram identified some limitations for prospective users. It would likely work for highly polarized and emotionally charged issues, but not for subtle ones. Large numbers of letters needed to be distributed in order to be able to obtain statistically significant differences between experimental and control letters because of the "unwanted variance" in the returns—some letters were always likely to be picked up by street cleaners, children, or people who couldn't read. This problem could only be overcome by using large numbers.

The shift in Milgram's research program—from the serious and elaborate obedience experiments to the relatively lightweight lost-letter technique—might seem strange. But several things account for it. First, after the emotionally draining experience of the obedience work, Milgram leaped at the opportunity to distance himself from direct contact with subjects. The lost-letter technique fit the bill perfectly. Moreover, the lost-letter technique was not all that different from the obedience experiments, when examined closely. In fact, they shared important features that would become hallmarks of Milgram's work.

First, his experiments typically created a conflict for the subject that demanded resolution. And second, that resolution usually took the form of an unambiguously observable, concrete action.

In the lost-letter technique, the conflict was between acting in line with prevailing norms and supporting a hated organization through that action. The resolution of that conflict came in the form of a dichotomous, concrete act—mailing or not mailing the lost letter. In the obedience experiment, the dilemma confronting the subject was whether to obey a legitimate authority or to follow the dictates of his conscience. Subjects responded to the dilemma by either continuing to press the switches or breaking off. Analogously, subjects in Milgram's cross-cultural conformity experiments—as well as in Asch's own original ones—were saddled with the dilemma of truth versus conformity. Here, too, the resolution of the dilemma took the form of a clear, easily discernible behavior: expressing agreement with the majority's judgment or not.

Indeed, most of Milgram's experiments would come to have these same defining characteristics. And it was these very properties—a clear conflict resolved by an unambiguous act—that accounted for their compelling nature. In contrast to the relativism and ambiguity inherent in many other types of measures (for example, a point on a numerical scale), the discrete, observable acts constituting most of Milgram's findings lent them a quality of absoluteness, clarity, and finality that made their implications readily discernible to a broad segment of the reading public, not just to professional audiences.

Another factor driving Milgram's move from the obedience experiments to the lost-letter technique was simply his own curiosity. And when Milgram became interested in something, it was difficult to redirect him, as he himself admitted in an unpublished interview:

My work has been dominated by creative presses. And I do not mean this in an altogether favorable sense. A creative person is very largely the victim of his own impulses. Often there were lines of research my intellectual side said ought to be pursued, but which gave way to more creative, less valuable pursuits. The problem for the creative person is that he can rarely direct his impulses to conform to the conventional lines of his discipline but only deflect a portion of them within these grooves. Consider the lost-letter technique. There is a legitimate socio-psychological reason for a study of this sort, but there was also a kernel of poetry in the idea of using lost letters to measure social attitudes.

After noting its methodological limitations, he added rhetorically, "Why then did I pursue it beyond its initial demonstration? Obviously, I was responding to the poetry of the procedure, and not to its scientific adequacy."

...

The completely new research focus that Milgram began at Harvard was the small-world problem. The phenomenon this research dealt with is illustrated by an incident involving Everett M. Rogers, a communication researcher, when he was a visiting professor at a university in Mexico City in 1979. One day, while having a conversation with a student named Pedro, Rogers complimented him on the excellence of his English. The student replied that this was a result of his having lived with a family in Iowa as an exchange student. The conversation continued:

Rogers Oh, where in Iowa did you live?
Pedro With a farm family in Collins.
Rogers Collins? That's the community I studied for my Ph.D. dissertation at Iowa State University! What is the family's name?
Pedro Robert Badstubner.
Rogers [In amazement] Why, that farmer was one of the opinion leaders in my investigation of the diffusion of 2,4-D weed spray!
Rogers and Pedro [In unison] What a small world!

Two people meeting for the first time and discovering that they have someone in common happens surprisingly often, and has been referred to as the small-world phenomenon. The more general question these kinds of encounters pose is the small-world problem, which Milgram stated as follows:

> Starting with any two people in the world, what is the probability that they will know each other? . . . Another question one may ask is: Given any two people in the world, person X and person Z, how many intermediate acquaintance links are needed before X and Z are connected?

The question did not originate with Milgram. Not long after returning to Harvard, he read a book, *Cambridge U.S.A.: Hub of a New World*, a breezy survey of current activity in science and technology. It noted that Ithiel de Sola Pool, a political scientist at MIT, was working on what he called the small world question. He and Manfred Kochen, a mathematician with IBM, were developing a theoretical model that suggested that any two strangers chosen at random could be linked by a small chain of acquaintances. Milgram was intrigued by the counterintuitive nature of the small-world idea and wondered if it would hold up if tested empirically.

To provide an answer, Milgram devised an experiment, the small-world method: The name of a person (the target), usually in a distant city, was given to a sample of men and women (starters). The task of the starters was to send a folder to the target person using only a series of friends and acquaintances who were more likely to know the target person than they (the starters) were. The folder could only be sent to a person whom the sender knew on a first-name basis. To keep track of the course of the folder, it contained a roster to which each subject had to add his or her name as well as tracer postcards to be mailed to Milgram.

He found that only a fraction of the chains were completed. For example, in a study with starters in Nebraska and a stockbroker in Boston as the target person, only 26 percent of the chains were completed. But among the completed chains, the findings were supportive of the small-world idea. On the average, it took about six intermediaries for a starter to reach the target.

Milgram's research broke new ground in two ways. He was the first to actually *count* how many acquaintances it took to link two arbitrarily chosen strangers, and he devised an inventive way to do it. Second, most people can provide an anecdotal account or two of a personal small-world experience, such as finding yourself sitting next to a passenger on a transatlantic flight who turns out to be a classmate of your first cousin's brother-in-law in Toronto. But it took Milgram to demonstrate that this kind of close interconnectedness was a general and quantifiable property of our social world—a finding that contradicts our intuitions. Milgram had asked an intelligent friend how many links it would take for letters sent by his starters in Nebraska to reach a target person in Sharon, Massachusetts. His friend estimated that it would take about 100 intermediaries.

The publication of the small-world research took an unusual path. Researchers usually publish their work first in scientific journals. Afterward, they might also describe the research in less technical form in a magazine or some other publication aimed at the broader public. In presenting his small-world results, Milgram reversed this usual sequence, describing his work first in an article in *Psychology Today*—the launch issue of that magazine. The technical reports appeared several years later in two journals, *Sociometry* in 1969 and the *Journal of Personality and Social Psychology* in 1970. He published the research first in *Psychology Today* in part to lend his prestige to help boost the new magazine. It was not purely an act of altruism, however: It enabled Milgram to bypass the long publication lags typical of scholarly journals and to air his novel research more quickly.

...

The Social Relations Department had undergone a number of changes since Milgram's student days there. But its interdisciplinary orientation still served as its guiding philosophy, and Milgram found it as intellectually appealing as a faculty member as he had as a student. He delighted to be once again in close contact with the three former teachers who had been his mentors and with whom he had continued a relationship of mutual fondness and respect: Gordon Allport, Roger Brown, and Jerome Bruner.

The power of the interdisciplinary vision had diminished somewhat since the early years. Only two of the founding fathers were still involved—

Talcott Parsons and Gordon Allport. Clyde Kluckhohn had died in 1960, and Henry Murray had retired from teaching in 1962. In addition, a new cohort of fresh Ph.D.'s who had trained elsewhere and therefore had no ideological commitment to the program were gradually filling the faculty ranks. However, there were still a sufficient number of older faculty aboard—such as George Homans, Robert Freed Bales, Robert White, and Fred Mosteller—as well as younger faculty who were former students—such as Tom Pettigrew, Philip Stone, Arthur Couch, and, now, Milgram—to provide the necessary critical mass of continued commitment to Social Relations' philosophy.

There had been some changes in the curriculum. Chief among them was the discontinuation of the qualifying courses that first-year students were required to take in each of the four program areas, along with their impossibly long reading lists and terrorizing three-hour exams. These were replaced by the less demanding Social Relations 200, Pro-Seminar: Problems and Concepts in Social Relations, required of all first-year students, in which notable members of the four areas introduced students to their disciplines as guest lecturers. But there were also important continuities. For example, Milgram taught the Pro-Seminar for Clinical and Social Psychology, one of the courses he himself had taken as a graduate student. He also introduced two new courses: a graduate seminar in Experimental Social Psychology, and Processes of Social Influence. While he was there, he chaired two doctoral dissertations, both of them cross-cultural studies. One, by Roy Feldman, was a comparison of helpfulness among residents of Paris, Athens, and Boston toward their compatriots and foreigners. The other, conducted by Robert Frager, was an attempt to replicate the Asch conformity experiment in Japan.

A significant development for the Social Relations Department during Milgram's tenure was its move to a new home, in William James Hall. At the beginning of the fall semester of 1963, construction was up to the third floor. By the end of 1964, the Center for the Behavioral Sciences was a fifteen-story gleaming white skyscraper. Designed by Minoru Yamasaki, it cost over $6 million, part of which was contributed by the National Science Foundation and the National Institute of Mental Health. The Social Relations Department had outgrown its space at Emerson Hall, so it had been forced to move some programs around Harvard Yard—to Bow, Divinity, Felton, and Kirkland Streets. With the new building, the university administration hoped not only to alleviate the space problem but also to strengthen the unity of the Social Relations Department. On January 26, 1965, the department had its first monthly meeting in the new building.

William James Hall also provided a new home for the Psychology Department, enabling it to leave its dingy, cavernlike quarters in the basement of Memorial Hall. Becoming neighbors, however, did not take the chill off the relationship between the two departments. In fact, Edwin Newman, the chairman of the Psychology Department, insisted that a separate access key be provided for after-hours entry to the floors occupied by his department.

Despite the founders' conviction that the fusion of four social science disciplines was the wave of the future, the program was not replicated at other universities. Yet colleges around the country were vying to hire Social Relations graduates as soon as they got their Ph.D. degrees. By the end of the 1963–1964 academic year, the department had awarded nearly 400 doctoral degrees. The size of the department's faculty kept growing, too. When Milgram was a student, the faculty numbered about forty; when he returned as an assistant professor, the teaching staff had grown to about sixty-five members. The most visible and important additions were Erik Erikson and David Riesman. Erikson was a psychoanalyst widely known for proposing a series of stages of human development which—going beyond Freud—encompassed the whole life span. David Riesman had gained wide recognition for his book *The Lonely Crowd*, which in 1950 became the best-selling book ever written by a sociologist.

In addition to rekindling old ties, Milgram's return to Harvard led to new friendships. David Marlowe, the co-developer of the Crowne and Marlowe social-desirability scale, a widely used measure of individual differences in the need for approval, became a close friend, as did Hans Toch, a visiting professor from Michigan State University. Toch, originally from Vienna, had received his Ph.D. in social psychology from Princeton. He had been invited to the Social Relations Department to fill in for Roger

Brown, who was taking a sabbatical in 1965–1966. When Milgram was asked to write a chapter on mass phenomena for the *Handbook of Social Psychology*, one of the most authoritative reference works in the field, he invited Toch to collaborate with him. The resulting chapter was called "Collective Behavior: Crowds and Social Movements." Milgram wrote the section on crowds—his most scholarly piece of writing—and Toch wrote the section on social movements. They team-taught the Pro-Seminar for Clinical and Social Psychology in the spring of 1966. According to Toch, Milgram's classroom manner with students was "a combination of being understanding and empathic and being mercilessly critical." But Toch believed that there was enough warmth and support below the harshness for students to realize that if Milgram was rough on them, it was in the service of their intellectual development.

By far the most significant and closest of Milgram's new friendships was with another junior faculty member, a sociologist named Paul Hollander, who had joined the Social Relations Department at the same time as Stanley. An assimilated Hungarian Jew, he had eluded deportation by the Nazis during World War II, and in 1956, right after the Hungarian revolution, he left Budapest for England to attend the London School of Economics. After receiving his B.A., he continued his education in the United States, ending up with a Ph.D. in sociology from Princeton in 1963.

Milgram and Hollander met at the first department meeting in the fall of 1963. They immediately hit it off and began a friendship that would endure for life, in spite of their differences. Milgram had a more assertive personality than Hollander, and criticized him for his professional preoccupation with, and concern about, Communism, rather than Nazism, despite his family's suffering under the latter. Milgram opposed U.S. involvement in Vietnam; Hollander did not. Milgram was concerned about nuclear weapons; Hollander was not. But these surface differences were secondary to the deeper and more essential bonds of friendship, which contained, according to Hollander, the elements of "trust, spontaneous pleasure in each other's company, sharing of confidences, mutual appreciation of our different personalities and work, and willingness to turn to one another for support when needed." They were in constant contact for the next two decades—by mail, by telephone, through regular visits to each other's homes, and through shared vacations. As Hollander later remarked:

> The qualities of Stanley which attracted me included his forthrightness, a candor sometimes bordering on bluntness and abrasiveness which set him apart from most academics, from most people I knew. He spoke his mind in refreshing contrast to the conventions prevailing in academia. . . . I also admired his work and ideas, his intellectual power, his brilliance. His work, not surprisingly, reflected his personality, his originality and inquisitiveness, a talent for asking fundamental questions. Unlike many of his colleagues he was totally free of pomposity and esoteric jargon-mongering, of the pretentiousness common among successful academic intellectuals. He had a quality of no-nonsense sharpness, an ability to get to basics in simple, unpretentious ways. . . .

Like many others who knew Milgram, Hollander appreciated his sense of humor and his playfulness. Milgram would sometimes write fake letters to Hollander, once on official Kuwaiti government stationery, offering him a lucrative university position that came with some unusual fringe benefits of a sexual nature. Another time, Stanley managed to get hold of *Time* magazine stationery, on which he wrote the following letter:

Dear Professor Hollander:

As you may know, each week Time Magazine features on its cover the portrait of an outstanding figure in world or national affairs. Our editorial board has unanimously recommended that your portrait be used on the September 24, 1976 cover of the magazine, and I am writing to you to make an appointment for a photographic portrait. The photograph will then be used as the basis for an illustration by one of our staff artists.

You may be wondering why we have selected you for our cover story, and I am authorized to disclose the following. As you know a number of sex scandals have recently appeared in the press and on television. No doubt, additional incidents of sex in government will be covered by the media. However, we at

Time would like to deepen the story by giving an account of the role of sex in all phases of professional life, not excluding academic life. In our story, we would present you first as a serious scholar, and give prominent mention to your work on Soviet and American society. After introducing you in this vein, we would cover your sexual experiences in and out of academic life. We have researchers in London, Budapest, and Boston who will interview your friends (of both sexes), your colleagues, and your present and former lovers. All of this information would be skillfully integrated into a feature story, which will incidentally, also be Time magazine's first use of full frontal nudity.

We shall be calling you shortly to arrange for a preliminary interview with our researcher, a former Radcliffe student who majored in oriental erotica. We trust we can count on your cooperation in this venture, which will, we feel, expand our appeal to academic as well as general audiences.

Sincerely,
Henry Grünbald*
Managing Editor

P.S. Your friend, Milgram, has been working in our offices lately; but frankly did not seem promising for the cover story we had in mind.

...

Life at Harvard had placed inordinate demands on Milgram's time—some self-imposed, others expected of him as a departmental citizen. Besides his research, writing, teaching, dissertation supervision, speaking engagements, and correspondence, he had memberships on various departmental committees. As he wrote a correspondent who had requested some very time-consuming assistance with research he was planning: "To be sure my responses have been sluggish, but if you only had some idea of the pressures on my time from every direction, you'd feel some sympathy for the Milgram camp."

---

*The name was a play on the name of the actual managing editor, Henry Grunwald.

Despite those pressures, he had written Leon Mann, "I have enjoyed Harvard greatly." In fact, that was an understatement. In the opinion of his colleague Tom Pettigrew, Milgram had contracted a bad case of "Harvarditis." Pettigrew explained that this is a terminal disease in which "you come to believe that Harvard is not only the greatest university in the world, it is the *only* university in the world."

Milgram had come to Harvard in the fall of 1963 under a three-year contract as an assistant professor of social psychology, which would end in June 1966. In the spring of 1965, the Social Relations Department voted an additional year's appointment for him for 1966–1967 as a lecturer in social psychology, a nontenured position. His description of this appointment in a letter to Dave Marlowe, dated March 24, 1966, conveys his disappointment: "I've been demoted to Lecturer for next year, but to boost my ego, I've also been named Director of the Program for International Studies," a new program within the department funded by the Ford Foundation. Although he was pleased with the directorship because it fit with his interests in cross-cultural research, the position did not come with tenure.

In academic departments in other universities, new tenured appointments are typically initiated from within the departments when a need arises—for example, when someone dies or retires—or when a particularly attractive candidate becomes available, or when the department wants to prevent a talented cohort of junior faculty from leaving for another school. At Harvard, however, new tenured appointments were determined at the administrative level, using the so-called "Graustein formula," a complicated system named after a Harvard mathematician who devised it. Milgram's appointment as a lecturer for 1966–1967 was dictated by the fact that, according to the Graustein formula, the Social Relations Department was not due for a permanent opening that year.

In the fall semester of 1966, however, a permanent position in social psychology to begin in the fall of 1967 did open up, and Milgram was discussed as a prime candidate by the committee responsible for making a recommendation. However, there were some deep divisions of opinion about Milgram among members of the committee. Allport, McClelland, and

Roger Brown supported Milgram, but Milgram himself believed that Robert Freed Bales, a senior social psychologist who was already at Social Relations when Milgram was a student, and Robert White, a clinical psychologist, opposed him. The debate within the committee raged for months and spilled over into the new year, 1967. The committee even met on Sundays. As of January 26, Milgram wrote David Marlowe, no decision had been made.

The tenure committee ended up deadlocked over Milgram and, as in a political convention, they offered the position to a dark horse, Robert Rosenthal, another junior faculty member. This came as a complete surprise to Rosenthal, because not only had he not realized that he was in the running, he was not even a social psychologist. His Ph.D. was in clinical psychology, and he had been hired in 1962 to teach courses in psychotherapy and psychodiagnostics. In fact, he was somewhat perturbed that the offer came so late in the semester, because by March 1967, when the social psychology committee told him of their choice, he had already accepted a position in clinical psychology at Northwestern University in Evanston, Illinois.

In the end, he accepted Harvard's offer, and he stayed there until 1999, serving as department chairman for part of that time. Although he was not a social psychologist, there was some logical basis for the committee's decision, because the research he was doing was social-psychological in nature. Rosenthal had gained recognition for his experiments on experimenter expectancy effects, a form of self-fulfilling prophecy operating in the laboratory. He demonstrated through a series of experiments that researchers could unwittingly convey their hypotheses or expectancies to their subjects and thereby end up with flawed results.

Roger Brown believes that the opposition to Milgram by some of the committee members was irrational. Specifically, he said that some people "attributed to him some of the properties of the experiment. That is, they thought he was sort of manipulative, or the mad doctor, or something of this sort. . . . They felt uneasy about him." Brown believed that characterization to be unfounded. He considered Milgram a very decent individual and a man of great integrity and authenticity.

David Winter, a former student of Milgram's in the Social Relations Department, agrees with Brown: "He definitely was 'quirky' and unorthodox,
and he could assume an air like that implied by the three 'probes' used by
the experimenter in his experiments. But at the core he really was nurturant
and kind. I recall his giving me one of his papers and signing it, 'with affection and esteem'—which has always struck me as an eloquent thing to
say in a situation that usually evokes clichés."

Tom Pettigrew was one of those who voted against Milgram, but for a
different reason altogether. He and Milgram had team-taught a pro-seminar in social psychology for first-year graduate students, and Pettigrew was
outraged by Milgram's harsh treatment of the students in that class. This
was the same course Milgram had co-taught with Hans Toch a year earlier.
Toch had also been a witness to Milgram's rough treatment of students, but
he believed Milgram's behavior was tempered by an underlying concern for
the students' academic growth. Pettigrew, however, saw nothing redeeming
in Milgram's pedagogical style. He recalled that when Milgram asked a
question and didn't like a student's answer, he might say, "That's a stupid
answer. . . . Who knows the real answer?" Pettigrew said, "I just couldn't
stand this . . . and I would jump in . . . and before the student got squashed
I would argue with Stan. . . . I was trying to get him off their necks. . . .
When I came [to Harvard] as a graduate student, I was scared to death. I
even had a big trunk that my father had from World War I and I kept it
open, because I was ready to leave. I could pull out within 48 hours if all
went badly. So . . . to this day I have a lot of sympathy for first-year graduate students, and I try to do everything I can to reduce their stress . . . and
Stan was just tough on them." He added that "I'm quite sure he didn't realize he came across like that."

· · ·

Being turned down in his bid for tenure was a traumatic experience for
Stanley—not only because he and Sasha loved Cambridge and wanted
very much to remain there, but also because, despite the long, drawn-out,
nerve-wracking deliberations, the final outcome was unexpected and jolt-

ing, since Milgram had generally enjoyed a very good relationship with the senior faculty.

However, after the negative decision, Milgram realized that in some cases, his colleagues' behavior toward him did not capture the whole truth—that below the surface their distaste for the obedience experiments was a still lingering issue. The outcome was also painful because it frayed his self-image, which was that of a person who almost always succeeded in attaining his goals, no matter what obstacles stood in the way.

Robert Rosenthal believes that Milgram's hurt was intensified by the fact that he lost out to someone who was not an obvious contender. However, Milgram bore no personal animosity toward Rosenthal, and they maintained a positive connection with each other. For example, in the fall of 1969, Milgram was invited back to Harvard by Rosenthal and Leon Mann (who came to Harvard on a limited-term faculty appointment after Milgram left) to give a guest lecture in a social psychology course they were team-teaching. In 1976 Milgram invited Rosenthal to appear in one of his educational films, *Non-Verbal Communication*.

In early June, the outbreak of the Six-Day War in the Middle East distracted Milgram from his loss. On May 26, the Egyptian leader, Gamal Nasser, openly declared his intention to destroy Israel. He formed an alliance with Jordan, Syria, and Iraq, and Israel found itself surrounded and threatened by Arab forces consisting of about 250,000 soldiers, 2,000 tanks, and 700 fighter planes and bombers. On the morning of June 5, the Israeli air force launched a preemptive attack, effectively destroying the air forces of the four allied countries. The war ended on June 10, with Israel having defeated the Arab armies that surrounded the country in six days. But when the hostilities first broke out and fierce battles raged on several fronts, the situation for Israel looked bleak, and Milgram, along with his Jewish colleagues at Harvard, felt an intense sense of personal involvement in Israel's survival. Solidarity with Israel was expressed in various ways. The academic community placed a full-page ad in the *New York Times*. Robert Rosenthal went from office to office in William James Hall soliciting signatures for it. Milgram made a $100 contribution to the Israel Emergency Fund, the largest single contribution of this kind that he had ever made. He felt he had to do something, because "recent history has taught us that . . . the most terrible things imaginable can actually come to pass, and particularly where Jews are concerned."

Already stung by his rejection at Harvard, Milgram was further disappointed when it came time to look for a new position—and offers from other prestigious universities did not materialize. He did receive expressions of interest from the State University of New York (SUNY) at Buffalo and solid offers from the University of California at Santa Cruz and from Cornell, but he couldn't see himself stuck in a small town or a rural area. Milgram loved city life and was planning to study it through a wide-angle lens. As one of Milgram's former students, John Sabini, noted, "He wanted to be part of the urban culture of the times, not just social psychology." He had hoped that, if he had to leave Harvard, he might go to a high-prestige university located in or near a large metropolis, such as the University of Chicago, Columbia, or the University of California, Berkeley. Berkeley did invite him to come out to interview for an opening in their Psychology Department, but, despite strong letters of support from highly respected references, he was opposed by some in the department.

Undoubtedly, this kind of division of opinion prevented other prestigious universities from considering him seriously. By now, Milgram was considered one of the most controversial figures in social psychology. In many a psychology department, opinion about him and his obedience studies was polarized. Since in most psychology departments—especially the more prestigious, research-oriented ones—hiring decisions were by faculty vote, few departments seriously entertained the possibility of hiring him. The odds of getting a majority of supporting votes were thought to be slim.

In the winter of 1966, Milgram's friend and former Yale colleague, Howard Leventhal, was recruited by the newly developing Ph.D. program in social psychology at the Graduate Center of the City University of New York, located on West 42nd Street in midtown Manhattan. The person at CUNY trying to recruit Leventhal was Silvan Tomkins, a leading figure in the psychological study of emotions and the founding director of a research unit of the University, the Center for Research in Cognition and Affect.

The purpose of the center was to provide a setting for the study of human cognitive processes and emotional responses. Leventhal had been conducting research involving emotion—the role of fear arousal in persuasion—and by bringing Leventhal to CUNY, Tomkins would have a person on the staff who would not only help get the graduate program in social psychology off the ground but also contribute to the center's activities. However, Leventhal told Tomkins that he didn't want to come by himself; he would accept the offer only if he could bring along another social psychologist, his friend Stanley Milgram.

On January 16, 1967, while the Harvard tenure committee was still deliberating his fate, Milgram received a formal offer from Mina Rees, the dean of graduate studies at CUNY, of an appointment as professor of psychology, beginning in September 1967, at an annual salary of $18,600. "I know I need not tell you," she wrote, "how eager our psychologists are to have you join them."

Besides teaching graduate courses in psychology, his duties would include being in charge of the psychology component of a special experimental program for college freshmen that would be inaugurated at the Graduate Center in September 1967. The freshman program was to serve two purposes: to provide an intellectually enriching experience for a select group of college students and to provide teaching experience for some graduate students who would serve as teaching assistants. Milgram would have four graduate students helping him teach an introductory psychology course that first year at CUNY.

On January 31, Milgram replied favorably to her offer, but he presented a number of conditions that would need to be satisfied in order for him to accept the position: First, he needed reassurance that the position would be a tenured one; Rees had not mentioned anything about tenure in her letter. Second, he asked for a yearly discretionary fund of $3,000, to be used for research tied to his teaching—for example, expenses associated with research carried out by students in his seminars. Third, he requested research space of about 1,000 square feet in addition to his office and another, smaller space for a secretary. Finally, he needed to know what the University's policy was on payment for moving expenses.

He promised that he would give her his final decision no later than March 1. Although Milgram did not tell her this, he put off making a final decision because the Harvard tenure committee was still in the midst of deliberating, and he was still hoping for a favorable decision.

Meanwhile, Howard Leventhal had put his own final decision on hold until he knew whether Milgram was going to CUNY. In addition to the offer from CUNY, Leventhal had two others waiting in the wings, from the University of Wisconsin and from the University of Michigan. With Milgram's situation at Harvard still unresolved, Leventhal felt that he couldn't wait any longer, and he accepted the offer from Wisconsin.

On February 8, Milgram informed David McClelland, the Social Relations chairman, of the CUNY offer and his promise to them of a final decision by March 1. Any offer from Harvard would have to come before then. He would no longer be available after that date. Two days later, McClelland replied to Milgram, reflecting his own exasperation at the continuing and drawn-out state of uncertainty:

> *Dear Stan:*
>
> *Thanks for letting me know of your deadline. As you know, our deliberations are deliberate and unpredictable, and I really can't say anything that should influence you in the slightest at the moment. But it is useful to us to have at least one fixed point in our sea of confusion!*
>
> *Sincerely,*
> *Dave*

On February 17, Rees wrote a reply to Milgram in which she gave her assurance about tenure, granted him the requested 1,000 square feet of research space along with an office and secretarial service. Also, the university would pay up to $1,000 for his moving expenses. However, she had to turn down his request for an annual allotment of $3,000 for teaching-related research, after consulting with Harold Proshansky, the executive officer of the psychology graduate programs, who told her that no full professor in any of the graduate programs received such guaranteed assistance. Instead, she wrote Milgram, the university practice is for faculty to put in requests each year as needed. So far, she said, she believed "that the psychologists found [that kind of annual research assistance] to be reasonable."

Sometime between February 10—the date of McClelland's reply to Milgram's note—and the end of the month, the Harvard committee reached a negative decision and informed Milgram about it. So on March 1, he wrote Dean Rees to accept the position at CUNY.

On the face of it, Milgram's new position at CUNY was a phenomenal one. Although he had been a mere lecturer his last year at Harvard, he was hired as a full professor—skipping the assistant and associate professor levels—and almost doubling the salary he had been making at Harvard. Despite his youth—he was only thirty-three—he was already at the helm of a Ph.D. program in social psychology. He was also at an urban university, and the fact that both Stanley's and Sasha's mothers were living in New York and that they both had lots of family and friends there was also important. In addition, they were able to find an apartment in a choice suburban location overlooking the Hudson, in Riverdale, near beautiful parks and an excellent private school, the Riverdale Country School—"a kind of Princeton for kids"—that the children would attend when they were old enough.

Although the job he landed was not of the scale he had been angling for, it did make him a big fish in a small pond. While his colleagues may have been highly regarded within the narrow confines of their research specialties, Milgram's fame already transcended the usual disciplinary boundaries, and by now he had even achieved some recognition among the general public. For example, one of the very first anthologies to reprint his "Behavioral Study of Obedience" was a collection for writing and literature classes, *The Norton Reader: An Anthology of Expository Prose,* in 1965. Magazines, too, were spreading the word about the obedience study and its implications. In 1964, a provocative article titled "Could We Be Nazi Followers?" appeared in *Science Digest,* and in 1966 readers of *Pageant* magazine would find a piece titled "You Might Do Eichmann's Job" among its pages to contemplate.

But initially the thought of not being at a prestigious university was very depressing for Milgram. In fact, at first he did not plan on staying at CUNY for more than five years. By then, perhaps, a more eminent school would beckon. Until then, he would have to put his self-esteem in cold storage. Within a year, Roger Brown was already recommending him for a new senior position that had opened up at Berkeley.

Whatever pain Milgram felt inside, it wasn't visible in his demeanor— at least to those outside his circle of friends and family. One manifestation of Milgram's melancholy was the more subdued tone of his correspondence. In the past, especially when writing to friends, his letters would invariably be laced with his humor. Now, it was less in evidence—although not totally absent. For example, in writing about his new job to Barry McLaughlin, a former Harvard student, he pointed out that his building was located right across the street from the main public library on 42nd Street. He also noted that it was next door to Stern's department store, so that, if he missed the psychology department by a few feet, he would find himself in the lingerie department.

Above the undercurrent of gloom, Milgram's first few months after accepting the CUNY position were marked by the ebb and flow of emotional ups and downs and a constant weighing of the pros and cons of his decision. His ambivalence was already in evidence the day after he accepted the job. On March 2, he informed Cornell's psychology department chairman, Harry Levin, that he had decided to go to New York City rather than Ithaca, adding: "God knows if it will work out, but the city has always attracted me." His ambivalence was still evident about a week later when he informed his former Yale colleague, Irving Janis, of his decision and remarked wistfully that "it may turn out well."

In his own mind, he had failed to make the grade. To his friend Paul Hollander, he bemoaned the fact that he was "no longer first class Ivy League," but at the same time he felt good about his high-speed move from a lecturer with an annual salary of $11,000 to a full professor making almost $20,000 a year.

He had mixed feelings about Manhattan. It was badly overcrowded, but at the same time, because of its incomparable cultural delights, it was also a great stimulant. And judgments about his current situation would inevitably involve comparisons to Cambridge. In another letter to Hollander, he noticed something about the flow of pedestrians in Manhattan. He had "the feeling that if you bumped into someone in Harvard Square there would be mutual apologies while in New York you would simply be trampled on silently and unnoticed. . . . The contrast between my present place of work and Harvard is so vast that it really defies comparison, and perhaps that is one of the reasons I chose the City University; there is no need to compare, indeed no possibility."

Writing to another correspondent, Milgram noted that while "New York is less than Cambridge, it is also more than Cambridge. The intensity of its cultural and artistic life is beyond anything else in the country." But the city lacked the sense of community Stanley and Sasha had enjoyed in Cambridge, where at any cultural event they were likely to run into people they knew. And although they had not yet recovered from their depression over leaving Cambridge, they realized that New York fulfilled their needs more adequately than almost any other city in the United States could.

Virtually all the letters Milgram wrote to friends during the summer and the early fall of transition from Harvard to CUNY demonstrated, in one form or another, conflicted feelings, a balance sheet of the pluses and minuses of their move. But a letter to Leventhal in Wisconsin, written toward the end of September, stands out for the raw, unrestrained nature of the unburdening it contains:

> Let me tell about life in New York. First, making the transition from Harvard to City University was not easy, and hardest of all around the boundaries of the soul. I experienced a full blown "Harvard Hangover", on or off for several months. Depression, a sense of futility, resentment, indignation, and a generalized malaise punctuated by moments of optimism, confidence, ambition, aspiration and buoyancy. I was really shaken up (—shaken down seems more appropriate a term). But the spirit has great recuperative powers, and except for a flickering feeling of sadness, now and then, I am now in a good mood, and am looking forward to a productive year.

My laboratories are still being built, but progress is rapid, and when they are completed, ought to be ample. It is too early in the term to comment on the quality of the students.

Sasha is finding life somewhat more difficult, though we still appreciate our fine apartment. . . . All in all, the quality of life is a solid B+, a little less than the straight A we had been leading, but still an honors grade.

In almost every way, CUNY compared badly with Harvard, although it would turn out to be the ticket to a wider space for creating a larger array of new courses than "Eden" would have ever allowed. Milgram was energized by challenges, and building a new graduate program in social psychology would provide no shortage of them.

CHAPTER 9

CITY PSYCHOLOGY

IT TOOK SOME time for the Milgrams to adjust to life in New York after so many years in Cambridge. In Manhattan, Milgram wrote Hollander in 1967, he felt "somewhat like an innocent provincial dropped into this intense, crowded, discourteous, inexorably moving mass." But he was immensely happy with the apartment they found in Riverdale. Overlooking the Hudson, the apartment afforded the shimmering sight of a constant array of boats passing under their windows, and from their terrace they had a panoramic view of three bridges in all their gritty majesty: the George Washington, Tappan Zee, and Henry Hudson bridges.

Stanley also had reason to be happy about his office at the Graduate Center, which was special in a number of ways. His office, Room 503, was on the south side of the building, so instead of brick walls, it had a large window that offered a view of Bryant Park and the New York Public Library across the street as well as the Empire State Building, its looming grandeur dominating the scene.

It was also larger than most faculty offices and came with a secretary's desk and a glass-enclosed vestibule. Being on the fifth floor also gave him an added convenience: It was the only floor in the building that was accessible by both banks of elevators. For many years, a flat silhouette-like human figure served as a silent sentry in the vestibule outside of Milgram's office door. The inscription at the bottom read: "The genuine article, by S. Milgram and L. Steinberg, based on a form by Trova." Its front side consisted of a collage of first pages of journal articles published by the social-personality program's faculty. It was Milgram's whimsical way of showcasing the achievements of his colleagues.

Sasha stayed at home, taking care of the apartment and the children, as she had done in Cambridge. Although Stanley was at work most of the day, he remained focused on the children's development. Michele, he noted, "was bright as a flame" and her language development was so rapid that Milgram felt he had to speak to her at the level of an adult. Marc, still a baby, was busy crawling after his sister and pushing furniture around, with determination etched on his face.

CUNY's graduate school, as a whole, was in its infancy when Milgram joined its faculty. CUNY itself was only six years old, having been established in 1961 by an act of the New York State legislature, and fashioned out of the loose-knit amalgam of New York's four public colleges: Queens, Hunter, Brooklyn, and City College. CUNY grew into what it is today—the largest municipal university in the United States, involving a consortium of some eighteen schools and campuses spread across all five boroughs of New York City. Although master's programs existed in a number of subjects at the four original colleges as early as 1920, the attainment of university status carried with it the right to grant the Ph.D. degree, and several disciplines started developing doctoral programs, with their numbers increasing from year to year. In 1965 the university graduated its first small crop of Ph.D.'s.

The first dean of graduate studies, appointed in 1961, was a remarkable woman named Mina Rees, who, even before coming to the graduate school, had received wide acclaim for her contributions to mathematics. She began her professional career at Hunter College teaching mathematics. With the outbreak of World War II, she took a leave of absence from Hunter to work for a government agency in which she could apply her mathematical skills to the war effort. At the end of the war, the Navy asked her to head the mathematics branch of the Office of Naval Research, and in 1952–1953 she was promoted to the position of deputy science director.

Rees's energetic leadership as dean of graduate studies at CUNY was largely responsible for the school's rapid early growth and expansion and for the specific form graduate education at CUNY would take. Rees had a grand vision of building a university with first-rate graduate programs and faculty—a vision that was shared and supported by the chancellor of the City University of New York, Albert Bowker, newly appointed to that office in 1963.

Rees and Bowker agreed that for the graduate school to succeed as a unified, cohesive entity, all the graduate programs located at the various college campuses—Hunter, City, Queens, and Brooklyn—would have to be brought under central administrative control, rather than have each campus award its own Ph.D.'s. Before Rees had taken the position of dean of graduate studies, she had spent some time abroad at the University of London. Impressed with that university's organizational structure and its intercollege faculty committees, Rees imported that idea to CUNY and created university-wide committees, each consisting of faculty from one discipline from each of the four senior campuses. It was just such a committee that later took up Milgram's candidacy in 1967, unanimously recommending his appointment as professor of psychology.

The transformation of a unified graduate school from an amorphous concept to a physical reality required a physical space that would not only serve as the school's administrative nerve center but also enhance its legitimacy. In early 1966, the opportunity arose to buy a building in an ideal location in mid-Manhattan to serve as the home base for the graduate school. It was a rather nondescript eighteen-story office building with a Woolworth's department store at street level, at 33 West 42nd Street, across from the main branch of the New York Public Library. Rees arranged for the issuance of a bond that enabled the university to buy the property. Before it became the Graduate Center, the building's main claim to fame was that in February 1924, George Gershwin gave the premier performance of his "Rhapsody in Blue" on the concert stage at Aeolian Hall, which was located in the building. The owner at the time CUNY purchased it was—improbably—Yale University. This may well have seemed an unexpected continuing reminder for Milgram that his career would forever be building on his early accomplishments in New Haven.

Working with dean of grounds, Marylin Mikulsky, Rees redesigned the building to become the Graduate Center. Their efforts resulted in an architectural marvel that received a number of awards for excellence in design. The transformed building had a number of innovative features that made it an attractive and inviting place. Occupying the first floor was a spacious walk-through mall from 42nd to 43rd Street, providing the Graduate Center with a unique "vest pocket" campus in the middle of Manhattan. Its top floor became an elegant "buffeteria" with slate floors and a walnut ceiling and catering done by a former chef of a famous Persian restaurant whom Mina Rees had coaxed out of retirement. The Graduate Center had a hidden 400-seat auditorium beneath 42nd Street and an underground library extending all the way to Sixth Avenue. The third floor was occupied by a state-of-the-art computer center, where Bitnet—the precursor to the Internet—was developed to connect CUNY's network of campuses sprawled across the five boroughs of New York.

Although the Graduate Center (later officially renamed Graduate School and University Center) was the administrative headquarters for all graduate programs, not all of them were located there. Some were scattered throughout the various campuses of the CUNY system. In 1967, the year Milgram came to CUNY, three were situated at the Graduate Center: social psychology, personality, and developmental psychology. The following year, a doctoral program in environmental psychology—the first of its kind in the country—was added. In 1971, social and personality psychology were combined into one subprogram, called social-personality psychology.

Each of the subprograms based at the Graduate Center had its core faculty, whose main affiliation was with the Graduate Center, as well as adjunct faculty whose primary appointment was at one of the campuses but who also taught, with varying degrees of frequency, in one of the subprograms at the Graduate Center.

...

One of the main reasons Milgram had turned down offers from Cornell and the University of California, Santa Cruz, in favor of CUNY was that he had been developing an interest in the psychology of city life. His very first year at CUNY, he introduced a new course, an urban research seminar—the first of a number of courses he created on urban psychology—and quickly got his students involved in innovative experiments showing how aspects of behavior in the city differed from behavior in small towns.

Although at CUNY the psychology of urban life became a central focus of Milgram's interests, his belief that social psychology could be applied to urban issues preceded his arrival in New York. In the fall of 1966, his last year at Harvard, he had offered an undergraduate tutorial on urban psychology to a group of Harvard and Radcliffe students, comparing New York, London, and Paris in terms of the factors that contributed to their differing atmospheres. They put ads in the *New York Times* and the *Harvard Crimson* soliciting reports of people's experiences in those three cities that could shed some light on their distinctive characteristics. A few of the students also did some film studies in various cities comparing people's walking speed and the number of collisions between pedestrians. Even earlier, in 1964, Milgram and Paul Hollander had coauthored a "think piece" for *The Nation* on the Kitty Genovese incident.

Kitty Genovese was an attractive twenty-eight-year-old bar manager who was killed on the night of March 13, 1964, as she was coming home to her apartment in the Kew Gardens section of Queens. Her killer had stalked her and stabbed her repeatedly for over half an hour. A subsequent investigation by a journalist revealed that thirty-eight of her neighbors had witnessed some part of the assault or heard her cries for help, but not one of them came to her aid. The incident shocked the nation, and it became emblematic of the alienating influence of city life. It also led two New York City social psychologists, Bibb Latané at Columbia University and John Darley at New York University, to conduct a series of experiments on the "bystander effect" to try to understand the phenomenon, prompting an interest in social psychology among the public.

The article in *The Nation* was a conceptual analysis, pointing to certain behavioral consequences of urban life that might have led to the inaction of Kitty Genovese's neighbors while she was attacked and murdered. For example, Milgram and Hollander argued that a violent act would be unexpected and incongruous in a respectable neighborhood. As a result, many of the neighbors could not fathom the possibility that such an extreme act—the murder of a young woman—was taking place nearby. Instead, they were predisposed toward a more probable, and consoling, interpretation of the event—perhaps two lovers were quarreling, or a noisy, drunken party was taking place. The article brought a refreshingly rational and nonjudgmental approach to a tragic event in which outrage tended to blur the public's perspective: "In our righteous denunciation of the thirty-eight witnesses, we should not forget that they did not commit the murder; they merely failed to prevent it. It is no more than clear thinking to bear in mind the moral difference."

Milgram's belief that social psychology could add a new level of understanding to behavior in the urban environment did not merely influence his own research. He made sure it influenced the graduate careers of his students. As he wrote in the university's catalogue:

> The social psychology area of specialization rests on two basic foundations. First, it is grounded in traditional social psychological theory and research. Courses and training are offered in the fields of attitude change, group processes, and person perception, and in experimental, field and survey methods. Second, students are trained to use the surrounding urban environment as a source of ideas and problems in the development of new lines of inquiry in social psychology. The city of New York is conceived as a major laboratory to be utilized in the research and training of graduate students in social psychology. The location of the University Graduate Center in mid-Manhattan is particularly advantageous in this regard.

The graduate program's urban orientation was soon reflected in the kinds of research pursued by some of the faculty and students: the analysis of crowds, psychological stress and social class, health-related behavior in urban settings, and urban design and social behavior. It became the first social psychology graduate program in the country with an urban emphasis. Undoubtedly, the graduate school's administration was pleased with this emphasis, since such an orientation was consistent with one of the school's goals, as laid out by its creators in 1960.

By September 1969—two years after Milgram's arrival at CUNY—he and his students had conducted a sufficient number of innovative experiments showing how aspects of behavior in the city differed from behavior in smaller towns to warrant an invitation for him to speak at the annual convention of the American Psychological Association in Washington, D.C. A slightly shortened version of the talk appeared as an article titled "The Experience of Living in Cities" the following year in *Science* magazine. In his talk, Milgram introduced the idea of *overload* as a unifying concept to help make sense of the various behavioral differences between urban and rural residents he and his students, as well as others, had found.

In 1938, the sociologist Louis Wirth had identified three defining properties of cities: a large number of residents, a high population density, and a heterogeneous citizenry. While Milgram valued Wirth's insightful analysis, he felt that a concept was needed to help explain how Wirth's demographic facts were internalized by the individual, affecting his subjective experience of city life. Milgram felt that the missing link could be provided by the concept of overload, in which a system is barraged by more input than it can process. The kind of behavioral changes that city life engendered could be understood, Milgram argued, as representing the various ways that people tried to adapt to the sensory onslaught of city life.

Milgram's article in *Science* reported a number of experiments he and his students conducted that identified some of the specific consequences of stimulus overload. In one such study, city dwellers and small-town residents were compared in their readiness to help a stranger when providing such help was an inconvenience. In addition, the study attempted to determine if the more compartmentalized, fleeting relationships of the city would lead urban salespersons to provide less assistance to a stranger when the helpful act was unrelated to their usual, job-related roles.

The experimenters made phone calls to people in three cities—Chicago, New York, and Philadelphia—and to residents of small towns located in the same states as the cities—such as Coxsackie, New York; Chenoa, Illinois; and McAdoo, Pennsylvania. In each case the researcher pretended to be a long-distance caller who had been mistakenly connected to the respondent by the telephone operator. By design, in both types of locations half the call recipients were housewives and half were salesgirls in women's clothing stores. The caller began by asking about the weather for travel purposes. Then she said, "Please hold on," put the phone down for a minute, and when she picked it up again, asked for information about hotels and motels in the respondent's area. The subject's degree of helpfulness was given a numerical score, ranging from 1 if she simply hung up without a word to 16 if she stayed on the phone when the caller put it down for a minute and cooperated fully with all the requests. The findings: Overall, people in cities were less helpful than the small-town residents, and in both types of places, those who were called at home were more helpful and informative than those called at work. Subsequent research by others also has generally found city dwellers to be less helpful than those living in towns.

Milgram's article in *Science* laid the foundation for the newly developing field of urban psychology. An offshoot of Milgram's interest in the psychology of urban life was his research on the mental maps, or the subjective geography, of the residents of two major cities—first New York and, later, Paris. These efforts paralleled his application of the concept of overload to urban life. Just as Milgram had introduced the overload idea to serve as a conceptual bridge between the objective demographic features of cities that Wirth identified—numbers, density, heterogeneity—and the individual's subjective experience of city life, he undertook the study of mental maps of cities to better understand how the objective geographical layout of a city was represented subjectively in the minds of its residents. Milgram explained the value of this kind of research:

> The image of the city is not just extra mental baggage; it is the necessary accompaniment to living in a complex and highly variegated environment. . . . People make many important decisions based on their conception of a city, rather than the reality of it. That's been well demonstrated. So it is important for planners to know how the city sits in the mind. And wouldn't it be enlightening to have such mental maps for Periclean Athens, for Dickensian London? Unfortunately, there were no social psychologists to construct such maps systematically at the time, but we know better and will do our duty.

Despite their practical importance, the study of cognitive maps of cities was uncharted territory for psychologists, so Milgram fashioned some new methods that would suit the needs of such research. The first one that he and his students devised would not only provide a way to externalize a person's subjective experience but also allow such individual perceptions to be aggregated, making it possible to draw some general conclusions. They created a "scene sampling" technique that would provide a precise and objective assessment of which parts of New York City were most, and least, recognizable. Simply put, if a person were dropped off at a randomly chosen location in the city, how likely would it be that he would know where he was? Milgram emphasized the need for an objective means of geographic sampling by contrasting it with the limitations of a method a casual investigator might use to determine whether or not Manhattan was more recognizable than Brooklyn: "He shows a group of people a picture of the Empire State Building to represent Manhattan and his uncle's garage to represent Brooklyn. He would find, no doubt, that more people could recognize the Empire State Building in Manhattan than his uncle's garage in Brooklyn. But that would hardly be an objective basis for asserting that Manhattan was more recognizable."

Milgram's method built on the fact that any point on Earth can be specified as the intersection of its longitude and latitude. Using U.S. Geological Survey maps of New York City with a fine-grained format which presents this coordinate system of longitudes and latitudes in 1,000-meter intervals, he created a viewing point for the study at every intersection of a 1,000-meter line of latitude with a 1,000-meter line of longitude. To bring the viewing points down to a manageable number, Milgram's team systematically thinned them out, ending up with about 150 scenes spread out among the five boroughs—Manhattan, Queens, Brooklyn, Staten Island, and the Bronx—each of which they photographed in color. Their study sample consisted of a total of 200 subjects. Since one would expect familiarity with different parts of New York to depend on a person's place of residence, the number of subjects from each borough within the total sample of 200 was proportionate to the population size of that borough.

TABLE 9.1   Percentage of Correct Scene Placements Within Each Borough

	Correct Borough	*Correct Neighborhood*	*Correct Street*
Bronx	26.0	5.9	2.6
Brooklyn	35.8	11.4	2.8
Manhattan	64.1	32.0	15.5
Queens	39.6	10.8	2.2
Staten Island	26.0	5.4	0.6

SOURCE: Milgram, S. (1992) *The Individual in a Social World: Essays and Experiments*, 2nd ed. Edited by J. Sabina and M. Silver. New York: McGraw-Hill.

Each slide was projected on a screen, and the subjects were asked to place the scene depicted in the photograph. Subjects were asked to identify the scene's location with increasing specificity: first, they had to indicate which borough the scene was located in; then to identify its neighborhood (using a map that divided the city into fifty-four neighborhoods); and, finally, to give its exact street location.

Table 9.1 presents the percentage of correct placements within each borough. Although the recognizability of a place diminished as the required precision increased, across all three criteria Manhattan turned out to be the most recognizable of the boroughs. For example, about twice as many random locations were correctly placed in Manhattan as those in the other boroughs. The neighborhoods of Manhattan were five times as likely to be identified correctly as those in the Bronx. The disparity between the recognizability of Manhattan and the other boroughs becomes even greater with the most stringent criterion of identification—street location.

Milgram also found that Manhattan was such a dominant presence in the mental maps of New Yorkers that they recognized parts of Manhattan more frequently than sections of their own boroughs. For example, people living in Queens recognized four times as many street locations in Manhattan as in Queens. Commenting on this finding, Milgram said:

Areas of Queens have often been accused of being nondescript, and taxi drivers are reported to fear entering Queens lest they never find their way out. And with good reason, when even the people who live in Queens are lost in their home borough compared with the sense of place they experience in Manhattan! Thus it is correct to say that New York City is not merely culturally but also imagistically rooted in Manhattan.

...

One of the abiding insights of Milgram's work is the surprising degree of influence that seemingly invisible social rules, or norms, exert on our daily actions. Although powerful, these rules are subtle and generally unnoticed, except when they are violated. Have you ever taken an elevator ride in which you maintained constant eye contact with another passenger standing next to you? Have you ever indulged in a lavish meal in an upscale restaurant and, when the waiter gave you the tab, instead of leaving a generous tip, you asked him for a donation to your favorite charity? Have you ever stood at the corner of a busy downtown intersection and sung "The Star-Spangled Banner" at the top of your lungs? Would you?

An innocuous remark made by Sasha's mother during a visit to the Milgrams' home in Riverdale led Milgram to devise an unexpectedly terrorizing experiment on the surprising power of norms. Only this time, the stress was felt not by the subjects, but by the experimenters themselves.

Milgram's mother-in-law lived on Manhattan's Upper East Side, and she would take a city bus to get to the Milgrams' home in Riverdale. One day in the early fall of 1971, after she arrived at the Milgrams' apartment, she asked Stanley: "Why don't young people get up anymore in a bus or a subway train to give their seat to a gray-haired elderly woman?" Milgram replied: "Did you ever ask one of them for a seat?" Looking at him as if he were insane, she said: "No."

At the next meeting of his Urban Research seminar, he and his students embarked on a study to find out just exactly what would happen if each of them approached a seated passenger and asked for his or her seat. When he first suggested it to his class, he was met with nervous laughter. Many of the students expressed the opinion that New Yorkers were not going to relinquish their seats just because a stranger asked them to. When he asked for volunteers, he did not get any. Finally, one student, Ira Goodman, stepped forward and bravely agreed to carry out the assignment. Accompanied by a classmate who would serve as an observer, he was to approach twenty different passengers and ask each of them politely, but without any explanation, for their seat. Soon rumors started circulating in the psychology department: "They're getting up! They're getting up!" People were astonished by Goodman's discovery. "Students made pilgrimages to Goodman as if he had uncovered a profound secret of survival in the New York subway," Milgram recalled. At the next class session, Goodman reported that about half of the passengers gave up their seat. However, that result was based on a sample of fourteen subjects, not the requested twenty. When Milgram asked him why he didn't complete the assignment, he answered: "I just couldn't go on. It was one of the most difficult things I ever did in my life."

To find out if this kind of response was unique to Goodman, Milgram decided to have everyone in class go through the experiment—including himself and his colleague, Irwin Katz, who team-taught the course with him. Here is how he described his own experience:

Frankly, despite Goodman's initial experience, I assumed it would be easy. I approached a seated passenger and was about to utter the magical phrase. But the words seemed lodged in my trachea and would simply not emerge. I stood there frozen, then retreated, the mission unfulfilled. My student observer urged me to try again, but I was overwhelmed by paralyzing inhibition. I argued to myself: "What kind of craven coward are you? You told your class to do it. How can you go back to them without carrying out your own assignment?" Finally, after several unsuccessful tries, I went up to a passenger and choked out the request, "Excuse me sir, may I have your seat?" A moment of stark anomic panic overcame me. But the man got right up and gave me the seat. A second blow was yet to come. Taking the man's seat, I was overwhelmed by the need to behave in a way that would justify my request. My head sank between my knees, and I could feel my face blanching. I was not role-playing. I actually felt as if I were going to perish. . . .

The next semester, in the spring of 1972, Milgram decided to bring his stand-up routine down into the New York subway again, but this time in a more refined and complex form. With members of his Experimental Social Psychology class, he created variations in the way they would ask for a seat, resulting in four different experimental conditions: The first was the *No Justification condition,* in which the experimenter stood in front of a randomly chosen seated passenger and said simply, without further explanation: "Excuse me, may I have your seat?" This was essentially the same approach used by his students in the previous semester in their first experimental forays into the subway. The result: 56 percent of the passengers gave up their seats. Another 12.3 percent responded with a compromise—they gave the requester a seat without relinquishing theirs by sliding over to make room for him. If the two kinds of responses are added, Milgram's students obtained a seat by simply asking for it 68.3 percent of the time.

The second condition was the *Trivial Justification condition.* It was created to test the idea that the high rate of compliance in the first condition was due to subjects' assuming that there was some compelling reason for the request. In this condition the experimenter requested a seat by saying: "Excuse me. May I have your seat? I can't read my book standing up." A significantly lower percentage of requests, though still a surprisingly high number of them—41.9 percent—resulted in the experimenter's obtaining a seat. Apparently, the addition of a trivial justification for the request prevented subjects from coming up with a more compelling justification for surrendering their seats.

In a third condition, the *Overheard condition,* the subway car became the stage for a moving performance by pairs of students. Here two experimenters would position themselves in front of the subject. Appearing to be strangers to each other, one would ask the other, "Excuse me. Do you think it would be all right if I asked someone for a seat?" His partner answered with "What?" The experimenter then repeated the question. This time his partner answered, noncommittally: "I don't know." This condition was created to determine whether the high rate of compliance obtained so far was a startle response—the request was so unexpected that the seated passenger didn't have enough time to come up with a reason for turning down the student. Giving up one's seat may have been easier than figuring out the best way to turn down the request quickly. This condition would help the students determine whether giving the subject some time would result in more refusals. After the two experimenters concluded their brief dialogue—which was staged so that it was loud enough to be heard by passengers seated in front of them—they waited about ten seconds. Then one of them asked the passenger seated in front of him for his or her seat. There was a significant drop in the rate of compliance. The experiments succeeded in obtaining a seat only 36.6 percent of the time, compared with 68.3 percent in the first condition.

A fourth condition was created to determine whether a more indirect form of a request, in which eye contact between the requester and passenger was minimized, would result in less cooperation. Here the request was made in written form rather than orally. The experimenter handed a sheet of paper to the passenger seated in front of him with the following request written on it: "Excuse me. May I have your seat? I'd like very much to sit down. Thank you." Milgram had expected a drop in compliance, when the pressure of a face-to-face oral request was removed. It turned out that he was wrong: 50 percent of the subway riders surrendered their seats. Milgram speculated that the somewhat bizarre form of the request may have made the passenger uncomfortable and spurred him to end the encounter quickly.

Although subsidiary to the main findings of the study, there were some sex differences involved in the pattern of the results. Across conditions, more passengers stood up for a female experimenter than for their male counterparts. And more male than female subjects relinquished their seats to the experimenters.

One of the student experimenters was Harold Takooshian, who went on to become a faculty member at Fordham University and has continued to do research on urban life. He draws some insightful parallels between the subway experiments and the obedience research:

The experimenters' reactions . . . [were] the most salient and unexpected feature of our entire study of subway norm violation. We found that it was no accident that strangers are never seen asking for seats on the subway. Each and every experimenter reported experiencing great and disproportionate amounts of tension.

This tension even resembled the extremes produced in Milgram's experiment on obedience. . . . For example, at least two of the female experimenters reported uncontrollable nervous laughter during the trials, similar to that found in the obedience study. . . . When asked the well-put question, "Well, why did you go on despite the discomfort you felt?" one experimenter responded, "Well, I had to do it for the course," so she surmounted her discomfort and completed the experiment. The parallel between the tension here and in Milgram's obedience study is a clear one. . . . It is odd that this simple violation of a seemingly mild norm should arouse any degree of tension at all, as if there were some morality attached to it—as if our asking for a seat were not "un-norm-al" in the sense of "not-average," but "ab-norm-al" in the moral sense.

Research in the subway did not remain an underground phenomenon for long. At the end of the semester, on June 2, 1972, Milgram presented his findings at an interdisciplinary conference on the cognitive and emotional aspects of urban life he had organized at the Graduate Center. A few years later, the research surfaced again when one of his students—John Sabini— began working on his doctoral research. Somewhat heavyset and boyish looking, he was one of Milgram's brightest students. Sabini is now a faculty member and the past chairman of the psychology department at the University of Pennsylvania. A wiry and Bohemian-looking fellow student named Maury Silver was his closest friend at CUNY. Sabini and Silver shared a philosophical bent and a near-collegial relationship with Milgram when they were still his doctoral students.

Sabini was planning to do his doctoral dissertation on the topic of people's reluctance to reprimand others, with Milgram as his chairman. Milgram wanted him to do it in a naturalistic setting, so Sabini tried out a couple of experimental performances in the subway. One scenario involved a bully whose actions deserved condemnation. In it, a female confederate entered a crowded subway train and the experimenter—Sabini—followed a bit later. Maury Silver was also there serving as the observer. One day, the experiment turned ugly. The confederate took a seat, and Sabini went up to her, saying, "That's my seat; I saw it first." After trying unsuccessfully to elicit the support of the person sitting next to her, the confederate got up and left the car while Sabini took her vacated seat. Everything was going according to plan when, about a minute later, a middle-aged man with a slight foreign accent reproached Sabini, the bully, saying to him: "That wasn't a nice thing to do." Then he continued, "How would you like it if *I* told *you* to get up?" The passenger's indignation seemed to escalate, because his next move was to crouch down in front of Sabini, look him straight in the eye and scream, "Someday somebody could kill you for that!" His anger apparently had not yet dissipated, because he then grabbed Sabini and picked him up as he screamed, "Get up!" and shoved him across the aisle. He finally sat down in the seat from which he had evicted Sabini. After Sabini and Silver managed to calm him down, all of them exited the train at the next stop. Sabini and Silver went back to Milgram and reported on their dangerous experience. Says Sabini: "I remember him sitting in his office. He puts his feet up [on his desk] and says, 'There are anthropologists who study headhunting cultures where they risk their lives for their thesis. I don't see why psychologists shouldn't have to do that.'" But he did agree to let Sabini pursue his research questions within the safe and controlled confines of the laboratory.

...

There is one final piece of urban research that deserves mention. Milgram noted that a pervasive characteristic of urban life is that, while we may become familiar with the faces of a number of people, we never in fact interact with them. He dubbed such individuals "familiar strangers." In the spring semester of 1971, students in his Experimental Social Psychology class conducted a study to learn more about them. The platform for launching the study was the Spuyten Duyvil railroad station on the Hudson division of the Penn Central Railroad. Not coincidentally, this was Milgram's stop for his twenty-six-minute commute to and from Grand Central Sta-

FIGURE 9.1 Typical photograph distributed to commuters, used in the study of the familiar stranger. SOURCE: Milgram, S. (1992) *The Individual in a Social World: Essays and Experiments*, 2nd ed. Edited by J. Sabini and M. Silver. New York: McGraw-Hill.

tion, located about two and a half blocks from the Graduate Center. The Spuyten Duyvil stop was only a short walk from the Milgrams' apartment in Riverdale. Early one morning, his students gathered at the station and trained their cameras on clusters of commuters who were waiting for one of three trains that would take them to their offices in Manhattan. For ease of identification, the students numbered each person depicted in the photographic prints (Figure 9.1), and multiple copies were made of each picture. A few weeks later, teams of students returned to the station and distributed manila envelopes to commuters as they waited for their train. Each envelope contained a photograph of commuters traveling on their train and a questionnaire. They identified themselves as students at CUNY studying community problems, and asked the commuters to work on the questionnaire during their train ride. The student teams boarded the train and, when the train arrived at Grand Central Station, they collected all the completed questionnaires. Out of 139 passengers in the three trains who were given the packet, 119 or 86 percent of them returned it.

Milgram and his students found that 89.5 percent of the subjects identified at least one pictured familiar stranger. On average, they reported seeing four familiar strangers in the photograph. In contrast, only 61.5 percent reported conversing with at least one other passenger; the average number of passengers they had spoken to was 1.5.

When asked if they ever wondered about any of these familiar strangers, about 47 percent answered "yes." But that curiosity did not necessarily lead to any further interaction, because only 32 percent reported even a slight inclination to start a conversation with one of them.

Milgram felt that the tendency not to interact with familiar strangers was a form of adaptation to the stimulus overload one experienced in the urban environment. These individuals are depersonalized and treated as part of the scenery, rather than as people with whom to engage. As he explained:

> In order to handle all the possible inputs from the environment we filter out inputs so that we allow only diluted forms of interaction. In the case of the familiar stranger, we permit a person to impinge on us perceptually, but close off any further interaction. In part this is because perceptual processing of a person takes considerably less time than social processing. We can see a person at a glance, but it takes more time to sustain social involvement.

Milgram's application of the overload concept here, while plausible, is not fully convincing. He had introduced the idea of stimulus overload to explain the distinctive forms of behavior that urban life engenders. To apply it to strangers, he would have needed to carry out a control, or comparison, condition at a train stop in a town or other non-urban setting— something he never did. What we clearly *do* have here is yet another demonstration of a principle that emerges from many of Milgram's other studies, including his obedience and conformity studies: the gap that exists between intentions and actions. Close to 50 percent of the commuters Milgram polled had been curious about the familiar strangers they had encountered, but only about 30 percent had even considered initiating conversations with them.

About the same time he was publishing the brief report on the study, Milgram was producing a film, *The City and the Self,* with the help of a graduate student, Harry From. It was a visual companion piece to his article "The Experience of Living in Cities." In the film, he makes some observations about the familiar stranger that are powerfully evocative and possess a ring of truth, especially in light of the events of September 11, 2001.

The film is narrated by Milgram. Most of the time his narration is sparse and understated, letting the unfolding scenes speak for themselves. But in the segment about the familiar stranger, his voice-over becomes a lyrical prose poem, which he recites with an ache in his voice that is almost palpable.

> *We studied the familiar strangers.*
> *We spoke to them in station after station,*
> *and this is what they told us.*
> *As the years go by, familiar strangers*
> *become harder to talk to.*
> *The barrier hardens.*
> *And we know—*
> *if we were to meet one of these*
> *strangers far from the station,*
> *say, when we were abroad,*
> *we would stop, shake hands, and*
> *acknowledge for the first time that*
> *we know each other.*
> *But not here.*
> *And we know—*
> *if there was a great calamity,*
> *a flood, a fire, a storm,*
> *the barriers would crumble.*
> *We would talk to each other.*

But the problem for those of us
who live in the city is this:
How can we come closer—
without the fire,
without the flood,
without the storm.

...

The Milgram that students and colleagues encountered at CUNY was essentially the same complex, sometimes enigmatic, individual people knew at Yale and Harvard. But in his role as program head, he became controlling and domineering—a prima donna who always had to have his way. As a result, he was sometimes a difficult person to deal with. For example, Harold Proshansky, the executive officer for psychology, once suggested that the Graduate Center create an adjunct position for Otto Klineberg, a world-famous "elder statesman" of social psychology who was known for his work on intergroup relationships. Although others in the department felt that it would be an honor to have Klineberg join them, Milgram first wanted to know what Klineberg would do for the program. So, before inviting him to join the social-personality program, he stubbornly insisted that a lunch be arranged for Klineberg to find out what he could contribute. A lunch meeting was arranged, and afterward Milgram agreed to Klineberg's being on board.

Still, someone meeting Milgram for the first time would likely find him gracious and very charming. He took everything in and seemed genuinely interested in what someone had to say. But he had no patience for small talk, and he would rudely cut a person off if he thought what he or she was saying was trivial or nonsensical. Judith Waters, a feisty and outspoken former student and graduate assistant, recalls: "When he was displeased with anyone, including me, he made no effort to disguise his feelings. Moreover, he was perfectly democratic. It didn't matter if the person was a student, a colleague, or even an invited guest speaker—he could be equally sharp in his comments." As John Sabini put it: "He was an equal opportunity insulter."

In fact, he occasionally targeted his own family. Robert Panzarella, now a professor at John Jay College of Criminal Justice, recalls that he was once having a conversation with Milgram in his office when there was a light knock on the door:

It's Sasha, and she just peeks in through the door, and he gets very upset, it seemed to me. He just turned to her most abruptly and said, "Can't you see I'm talking to Bob? I don't want to be disturbed when I'm talking to Bob." And she just said, "I just wanted to let you know, I'm leaving now," and she closes the door and leaves. I always felt very bad for her—that may not have been typical behavior at all. It may have been that whatever we were discussing was putting him on edge at the moment or something. I don't know. But it was very striking.

And Joel Milgram recalled a time in the 1980s when he and Stanley had been discussing the possibility of a joint writing project about their childhood:

I called him at some absurd hour because I was excited about it. Naturally, he wouldn't speak to me then and hung up. . . . My brother was a real good hanger-upper. [He] was very arrogant, you know, in many ways. I mean if you called him while he was watching CBS News, he'd simply say, "I can't talk to you now, you call back," and hang up. . . . That was just accepted. . . . [The] family just learned. And it just put some distance in our adult lives between us.

As a teacher, he was very demanding, always challenging students to think creatively. Harold Takooshian remembers:

He didn't look extraordinary. But he certainly was extraordinary within a minute of hearing him open his mouth. He had that incisive way of expressing himself that just captured it. Everybody in the room could say: Yes, that's what I was trying to say. [He was] just articulate. I would draw the parallel with William Buckley. He has that capacity too, of putting into words inchoate ideas that everyone is grappling with. I would say that was one of Milgram's primary qualities.

He was scintillating in the class. . . . Sparks could fly. . . . But it was so intense that some people didn't care for that. . . . He was conscious of people's personal feelings, but that doesn't mean he always wanted to make you feel good. Sometimes he would make devastating comments to people. . . . He was very resentful of platitudes, of party lines, of truisms, and if he felt that somebody was saying something that didn't have much basis . . . he would challenge you very quickly. And since he was the unquestioned authority in the class, he could say it in a strong way.

While he clearly was the "unquestioned authority" in his classes, he apparently thought it important to point out the situational nature of that characteristic and stress that it did not define his whole being. Robert Panzarella recalls a class with Milgram: "He began by saying, 'I didn't study obedience because I'm an authoritarian person,' at which several of us burst out laughing. . . . Apparently, he was conscious that this is what people thought anyway." And in a sense Milgram was at least partially right—while he may have been acting in a dictatorial fashion in his classes, he was not dogmatic or inflexible in his authoritarianism. For example, Panzarella remembers his first encounter with Milgram. It was the first day of the fall semester, a beautiful September day, sunny and warm. Panzarella was sitting in the front row and the first thing Milgram did after he walked into the classroom was point to him and say, "Take those sunglasses off!" Panzarella looked back at Milgram, through the sunglasses and replied, simply, "These are prescription glasses. I need them." Milgram paused a moment and said, "All right," and dropped the matter.

Takooshian recalls a similar exchange during his first year in the graduate program:

One thing he did in the class which I was really surprised about . . . he said, "You know, it is really hard to rate you people because you haven't taken that many exams yet, and I [would] like to get a sense of how you feel about each other. Does everyone have a pencil and paper here? OK. Look around the table; I'd like you to give each person a grade in the room here." And people looked at each other, but they looked at him and they started writing. And I had the paper and pencil in front of me, and I wrote the names down, but I felt that it wasn't right [for us] to grade each other because that was his job, you know. . . . So he collected the grades from people and he counted them up and he said, "Well, there are only twelve grades here and there are thirteen of you. One is missing." I was beet red at the time and I said, "I didn't hand it in." And he said, "Well, are you going to?" And I said, "No." And he said, "OK." Just like that.

Looking back on her years as Milgram's research assistant, Judith Waters, now a professor at Fairleigh Dickinson University, doesn't think he was any more authoritarian than anyone else would have been in his position.

Just as there was a wide consensus about Milgram's off-putting, domineering, and prima donna-ish ways, Milgram's superior intellect was acknowledged by virtually everyone in the department, even among those who were not necessarily fond of him. The force of his intellect made him a formidable presence, despite his diminutive size of 5'7". John Sabini provided an especially distinctive perspective on Milgram's intellect:

He was a genius. By which, one means he was possessed; I mean you never knew—he never knew—what direction his creativity would take. So he wrote music and he made board games and films. . . .

He was utterly unconventional in the way he thought about things, and insisted that you be. So he would call me in, sort of monthly, when I was looking for a job, and explain to me things like, the most important relationship you'll ever form in your professional career is with your secretary. And you would laugh, and he would say, no, no, I'm serious. It's far more important than graduate students, colleagues or post-docs. Your secretary is the person who will determine whether you will have a productive career or not. . . . And any suggestion that you might have that, well, maybe your colleagues are important, would be taken by Stanley as a sign of near-conventionality in the way your mind worked, that you were not penetrating to the actual facts. And that was, I think, what was relentlessly Stanley, was this . . . dispensing with mythology and false belief and jargon, and all sorts of clutter that kept you from seeing the actual facts clearly.

The nature of Milgram's relationships with his colleagues varied. For example, Salomon Rettig, a social psychologist specializing in the study of small groups, said that he "really enjoyed being with Stanley. . . . It was a pleasure to be with him." On the other hand, his abrasiveness rubbed some people the wrong way. But, surprisingly enough, there was a noticeable and pervasive absence of jealousy among members of the social-personality program—even among those who otherwise may have disliked him—for two reasons. First, although no one in the program approached his fame, it consisted of many first-rate faculty who had achieved recognition as experts in their own areas of specialization. David Glass, for example—tall, with smooth facial features, always nattily dressed in a suit, and the most intense person there—was one of the founders of behavioral medicine, the study of bodily response to psychological stresses. Florence Denmark, a petite woman with a ready smile, was a leading figure in the psychology of women. She had political ambitions that culminated in her election as president of the American Psychological Association in 1980. Irwin Katz, one of Milgram's closest colleagues, had conducted research that introduced a new approach to the study of prejudice and stigma. Ellen Langer, petite and pixieish, had a gargantuan grasp of theoretical perspectives in social psychology that made her the authoritative resource for her colleagues in the department. Her pioneering research on "mindlessness" helped alert social psychologists to the important role that reflexive actions play in our lives and is partially responsible for the current interest in nonconscious determinants of behavior within the field of social psychology.

A second reason why Milgram's colleagues did not appear to be envious of his star status was that he was much more distinguished than the social-personality program he was part of. A person becomes envious of someone who makes $100 more per week than he does; he doesn't become envious of Bill Gates. So, no doubt, many of his colleagues were happy to bask in the reflected glory of Milgram's fame.

One of the perks of being a genius is that your quirkiness and eccentricities are accepted with greater equanimity. Among his graduate students Milgram had a reputation of someone who could perform "wonders"—as in "I wonder why he did that?" John Sabini once arrived at Milgram's office at 10:29 for a 10:30 meeting. Milgram immediately told him to leave and come back in a minute. So Sabini went out into the hall and sat down on a bench. Meanwhile, Milgram could be seen through the open office door, sitting at his desk with his feet propped up, waiting until the minute was up. And for Harold Takooshian, the activities orchestrated by Milgram at the first meeting of his Advanced Social Psychology class are still mysterious some thirty years later:

> Milgram noted that he did not receive the classroom he expected, and for fully half of the two-hour class he had us rearrange the tables and chairs into different shapes to see which "felt" best—octagon, rectangle, square. For all fourteen of us, this was our first day at CUNY Graduate School, and with the illustrious Professor Milgram. So this bizarre display had us all very privately wondering what on Earth was happening—as he had us repeatedly moving furniture, asking how we liked it now, welcoming new suggestions, then issuing new commands. . . . In the end we settled on a simple square. There was never any formal "debriefing" of this never-repeated exercise, nor ever another word about furniture.

Much of the time Milgram's quirkiness was a harmless object of puzzlement, but it could also take a more troubling turn in the form of erratic and mercurial behavior toward his students, resulting in a polarization of opinion about him. Some remembered him with fondness for his acts of kindness. When Ronna Kabatznick, a doctoral student, was completing her write-up of her dissertation, she was spending a lot of time in the computer lab by herself. One day she told Milgram that the isolation was driving her to tears. So he told her that he was going to wheel a computer into his office so she could work on her dissertation there in his company. She did indeed complete her dissertation there, coming in every day and sitting down at the computer while he went about his normal activities—talking on the telephone or preparing a lecture.

On the other hand, Milgram's brother, Joel, recalls visiting Stanley and seeing a student bolt out of his office in tears. And on another occasion, after a meeting with a disgruntled student, Milgram found a gaping hole in the side of his handsome black office couch. While seated there, the student had managed to furtively grind a hole in the cushion with his pen.

Even those students who had an affectionate relationship with Milgram recalled classes in which he became unpredictably nasty from one moment to the next, and which were sometimes emotional roller-coaster rides—in which exhilaration brought on by flashes of insight would alternate with the terror of waiting to be picked on.

How does one explain these moment-to-moment fluctuations in his behavior? How do you account for the polarization in his long-term relationships with students—many of whom either loved him or hated him?

An answer may lie in the fact that the inconsistencies in Milgram's behavior were actually—and paradoxically—manifestations of a deeper continuity between his professional and personal lives. Milgram not only practiced social psychology professionally, he lived it. One of the main axioms of social psychology is that situations are powerful determinants of behavior, more powerful than we might suppose. To a surprising degree, our behavior is highly responsive to the concrete features of our immediate social environment. Different situations can bring different aspects of our personality to the fore. As many of his students and colleagues have noted, Milgram was unusually sensitive to the fine-grained details of his surroundings. So, his sometimes enigmatic and erratic behavior may well have been evoked by nuances in others' behavior to which most people would not have been attuned.

Milgram expressed a recognition early on of the strongly causal role played by the immediate situation. In one of his occasional musings, dated February 10, 1957 (his third academic year at Harvard), he wrote:

By means which I
behave differently
changes in beha͏
of one girl or another, a͏͏ ͏ ͏ ͏ quite out of my power to alter the effect of
the particular girl I am with. So that what I am, my personality if you will,
does not exist apart from my present company.

And here is what he wrote his former girlfriend Enid in 1959, as part of
a letter trying to help her cope emotionally with her recent breakup of a
love affair:

You seem to forget that ambivalence, a blend of love and hate, is the rule in
any social relationship (but only a dullard would take this to mean that
there is no possibility of deep, honest love); don't you know that people can
be vile, and hateful. . . . Goodness, delicacy, beauty of the spirit—these too
are fundamental to the human picture; but they survive only within a particular set of conditions, and one must be grateful when these conditions
prevail.

But there was another factor that quite possibly contributed to Milgram's
erratic and sometimes puzzling behavior—his occasional use of amphetamines, cocaine, and marijuana. Milgram's daughter, Michele, was ignorant of
her father's drug use when he was still alive. And when Sasha finally did discuss it with her, she was shocked and upset. But then she recalled certain
childhood incidents when her father's behavior hadn't made sense to her at all:

We used to play Monopoly—and there was a period of time when we absolutely couldn't play it with him [her father]. You know, if you throw dice,
the odds of both dice landing at the exact same time are, like, nil. . . . One
would often fall before the other. And he would accuse someone of cheat-
ing if they were doing that. And he would just get very upset, especially if
he was losing. We eventually had another game that had a little gadget that
you would put . . . dice in a special lever and they would come out of the
bottom, so that was our solution to that.

Now, looking back, Michele   s if this kind of erratic behavior might
have been due to her father's dr   use. She is quick to point out that it was
not "necessarily the norm of all of his behavior and much of it was very
pleasant [with] lovely conversations and singing musicals and things like
that. But there was also a darker side sometimes."

...

Milgram's legendary rudeness would fade as his students progressed
through the graduate program at CUNY—some viewed it in retrospect as
a kind of rite of passage—and when it came time for students to find a
chairman for their doctoral dissertations, Milgram was most in demand of
all the faculty, mentoring the largest number of doctoral students (fourteen)
while he was there.*

Professors generally subscribe to one of two approaches to mentoring
doctoral students—at least in psychology. Some mentors have an ongoing
research program that their students dip into and expand into a researchable question for their dissertation. The other type of mentor encourages
his students to follow their own lights and pursue a topic that interests
them, even if it is not one of the mentor's main interests. Gordon Allport
represented the second type of mentor. He had chaired the largest number of dissertations in Harvard's social relations program, and no two of
them were alike. Rather than expecting his doctoral students to hitch a
ride on one of his research projects, Allport let them be themselves and
pursue their own interests. Milgram emulated Allport's open mentoring
style. His doctoral students pursued a potpourri of topics, many of which
were outside the perimeter of his main research interests. In fact, only two
of his students conducted doctoral research grounded in his work on obedience to authority. One of his students, Arthur Blank, carried out doctoral research that involved the microanalysis of dialogue. Reflecting back
on this, Blank recalled:

---

*Appendix A lists Milgram's doctoral students and the titles of their dissertations.

My interests in sociolinguistics were not central to Stanley's. Indeed, my interests were quite peripheral to his. But that was what impressed me about Stanley. He maintained a quizzicalness about the world and supported others' inquiries into novel phenomena. It was his openness to new interests and ideas that I found invaluable. He could take an idea, rotate it, or otherwise put it in a new perspective.

Once Milgram became a student's mentor, the student felt that he had a lifelong advocate, always ready to help him land the best jobs. Milgram would readily write letters of recommendation for former students long after they received their degrees. When Judith Waters was coming up for promotion to associate professor at Fairleigh Dickinson University, Milgram suggested that, to improve her chances, she organize a conference featuring a famous keynote speaker. He offered to be that speaker, for free, although by this point in his career he was being paid in the thousands for his speaking engagements. And, as Florence Denmark put it: "He stood up for people he believed in and never let me down."

But he is perhaps best remembered by his students and colleagues for his relentless wit and sense of playfulness, which found expression in various ways, depending on the circumstances. When it came to his work, for instance, he was utterly serious about it, but he would never undertake some piece of research unless he found it intrinsically interesting. A playful curiosity energized his research, so that the same person who gave the world the profoundly important obedience studies could also readily absorb himself in a less weighty question, such as: How do New Yorkers explain those billowing clouds of steam that mysteriously come out of the ground?

His doctoral student Elyse Goldstein recalled that Milgram was so fun-loving "that no [other] graduate career could have [provided] so much humor and wit." On one especially zany day at CUNY, he communicated in song the entire day and would only reply to others if they too sang their words to him. One student recalls Milgram lecturing about obedience while shocking himself with a battery-operated device attached to his fingers. When Judy Waters served as Milgram's research assistant, and there would be a lull in projects that needed attention, they would play a word game that Milgram had invented. He would give her a simple phrase that she then would try to transform into complex "psychologese." So, for example, "I guess" became "Based on the previous assumptions as enumerated above, it is possible to hypothesize that the following outcomes will obtain under certain limited conditions." And in a letter to Paul Hollander when he and his wife were expecting their first child, he wondered whether Paul "preferred indoor or outdoor plumbing" on his firstborn.

...

While the content of Milgram's varied research interests defies pigeonholing, virtually all of his studies shared an important stylistic characteristic. The object of study—the dependent variable—was typically some form of concrete, observable behavior, be it picking up a "lost letter" or giving up one's seat on a subway train. As he told an interviewer: "Only in action can you fully realize the forces operative in social behavior. That is why I am an experimentalist." In this sense, one aspect of his urban research, the study of mental maps, was a departure from his usual research style: It dealt with private experience, rather than overt action. At the beginning of 1969, an opportunity arose for Milgram to return to behaviorally focused research in a splashy way.

On March 29, 1969, Joseph Klapper, the director of CBS's Office of Social Research, convened a scientific meeting to discuss the theoretical issues and research relevant to a burning social question—the impact of television violence on the viewer—and to invite participants to submit grant proposals to study the question further. Milgram had attended the meeting, and about a month later, on April 23, he submitted a research proposal to CBS, which was approved after a review by a panel of social scientists, with a funding of $260,000. Although the relationship between television violence and aggression was not something Milgram was intrinsically interested in—and, in fact, he harbored some doubts about the existence of such a relationship—the idea of being able to do research on a grand scale appealed to him. Indeed, the very large grant enabled him, among other things, to hire a research associate, R. Lance Shotland, a social psychologist from Michigan State University, and a large staff, to carry the research to four cities— New York, Chicago, St. Louis, and Detroit—and to consult about data analysis with some of the country's top experts in research methodology and statistical techniques.

Milgram's research brought something new to the study of television's effects—something that makes the work unique to the present day. Virtually all experimental research on the effects of televised antisocial behavior used already existing fare as stimulus materials. In a typical study, subjects were randomly assigned to watch either a program that was clearly violent in content or free of violence altogether and were subsequently compared on some dependent measure of aggression. A built-in problem with this approach was that the chosen programs might also have differed in other qualities as well. Milgram and Shotland departed radically from this traditional approach by varying the content of a single episode of a popular prime-time television series. Milgram was able to get the cooperation of CBS to produce a particular episode of the then-popular dramatic series *Medical Center* with three different endings.

The script of that episode, titled "Countdown," was written by a professional screenwriter, Don Brinkley, with some input from Milgram. The program went into production in early 1970, and Milgram spent some time on the set at MGM studios trying to act as a censor—though not always successfully—whenever an element was injected into the story that did not meet the requirements of the experiment.

The plot revolved around the misfortunes of a hospital orderly, Tom Desmond: He loses his job—with a sick wife and an infant to support— and his boat, which he had hoped would provide some income, is repossessed. Two versions end with a destructive act, with the orderly repeatedly smashing open fund-raising collection boxes distributed by the medical center and stealing the money they contained. In one variant, he is caught by the police; in the other, he eludes capture. A third version has a prosocial ending, with Desmond putting money into, rather than stealing from, the collection box. The two antisocial versions also show the orderly placing abusive telephone calls to the medical director of the hospital. Another episode, with a completely different story line, without any suggestion of violence whatsoever, served as a neutral, control condition. From September 1970 to November 1971, Milgram and Shotland embedded these programs in a series of field experiments—some involving millions of at-home viewers as potential subjects—in which both viewing and the opportunity to imitate the antisocial acts occurred in real-life settings.

The general procedure was this: Subjects watched one of the four stimulus programs in a preview theater in midtown Manhattan, over the air, or individually via closed-circuit television. They were promised a General Electric transistor radio as a reward for their participation, which they could pick up at a scheduled time a few days later at a "gift distribution center" in a building on 42nd Street. When they arrived at the distribution office, they found it unoccupied. Looking around, they would notice on one of the walls a charity display for Project Hope with a clear plastic container box attached, containing some dollar bills and coins. Hidden TV cameras recorded the subject's every move. The main question was whether or not subjects would steal money from the charity box—and, more specifically, would those who had seen the antisocial versions of the program be more likely to do so than those who saw either the prosocial program or the neutral, control program?

The study was not without shortcomings. Toward the end of the episode, whenever Tom Desmond fixes his gaze on a collection box, a "boing-boing" sound brings it into dramatic focus. The sound, not unlike the kind one hears when a cartoon character bounces back after running into a brick wall, creates an unintended melodramatic effect. But the overall approach was enormously innovative.

Across eight experiments, Milgram did not find any greater tendency for the viewers of the antisocial versions to imitate the depicted antisocial acts than those who saw the control or prosocial versions. What makes the study unique to the present day is that Milgram had control over regular prime-time television programming, which enabled him to build the independent variable—the three different endings—into its content while keeping most of the program constant across the three experimental conditions.

Milgram's research is often absent from reviews of the literature on television violence and aggression, for two reasons. First, in the write-up of the research in the book *Television and Antisocial Behavior: Field Experiments*, authored by Milgram and Shotland, there is virtually no attempt to relate the findings to the vast amount of prior research on observational learning and imitation and, in particular, on the effects of violence in the media. In contrast to Milgram's experiments, a good deal of the earlier research found evidence that portrayals of antisocial behavior on television *did* have an impact on the viewer. Second, the results of Milgram's series of experiments were inconclusive and inherently ambiguous. Did they demonstrate that people are not influenced by destructive actions shown on television? Or is it possible that the antisocial program did in fact have negative effects on the viewing audience, but the particular measures Milgram used simply missed them? For example, the imitative response might have been a delayed one, showing up, perhaps, in a later time and different place.

Thus there are compelling reasons why many literature reviews have omitted Milgram's series of field experiments. But in doing so, they have missed what the study's unique design *was* able to accomplish—a degree of control over the independent variable rarely achieved in experiments on the effects of television violence, a design feature that is critical for drawing conclusions about cause and effect.

The director of the "Countdown" episode was Vincent Sherman, who already had a successful career directing films featuring such Hollywood stars as Bette Davis, Joan Crawford, and Errol Flynn before he started working in television. Now in his nineties, he recalls Milgram's visit to the studio and his "brilliantly conceived" experiment. In a letter to Sherman written in March 1983, Milgram reminisced about his television study, situating it within the broader framework of the nature of social-psychological experimentation:

> The television study, for which you directed the episodes of Medical Center, was certainly the best budgeted piece of research I have carried out,

but the equivocal nature of the results make it somewhat unheralded. If only we could have shown that your programs jolted viewers into a frenzy of antisocial imitation! But alas, while experimenters may design their questions with a certain creative flair, and there is a dramaturgical element in socio-psychological experiments, the denouement is always left to the experimental subject. That is, we may create the situations into which we bring the subject, but we need to leave open how he will respond to them. Only the questions are under our control, not the answers. From this standpoint, the dramatist, who controls his own denouements and finales, has a decided advantage.

CHAPTER 10

CENTER STAGE

W HEN MILGRAM WAS in Hollywood during the filming of the *Medical Center* episode, he was impressed with the efficiency and organizational skills of the production crew, and this whet his own appetite for filmmaking. As luck would have it, a couple months after his return from the West Coast, a man named Harry From walked into his office. From was short and stout and spoke with a brittle accent that sounded vaguely Eastern European. He was a graduate of the Film University in Romania and was a film director with experience in documentary films. He had immigrated to Israel, and then had come to the United States on a grant from the Israeli Film Union. After being involved in a number of projects in the United States, he decided he wanted to study psychology. He went over to the Graduate Center, where he was directed to Stanley Milgram. That initial meeting in Stanley's office lasted several hours, with Milgram showing a lot of interest in From's background in film a well as in his family's suffering under the Nazis and, later, under Communism. The following semester, in the fall of 1970, Harry started in the doctoral program in social psychology, read Milgram's "The Experience of Living in Cities," and suggested to Milgram that they make a film based on it.

The result was *The City and the Self,* which came out in 1972, made on a shoestring budget scraped together by Milgram. The ability to make the film on a low budget was aided greatly by the fact that Harry's wife, Nitza, did the editing. She worked as an assistant editor for an established film production company that made commercials, and the owner allowed her to use his state-of-the-art equipment for free in the evenings.

The film is essentially a visual companion piece to Milgram's article. Using both naturally occurring scenes as well as staged experiments, it examines the various consequences of the stimulus overload experienced by people in cities. A man drops a bunch of papers on a busy New York City sidewalk; no one stops to help him as he struggles to gather up the scattered papers. A shoplifter hurriedly grabs pairs of shoes from the outdoor bin of a discount store on 14th Street and stuffs them into a shopping bag in full view of onlookers who do nothing to try to stop him. A young adult knocks on the doors of city apartments and asks to use the telephone to call a friend nearby whose address was forgotten. Peepholes open, but the occupants do not allow entry.

But the film also depicts the city's unexpected delights, capturing Milgram's ambivalent feelings about New York: A street-corner virtuoso beating out a Bach concerto on a steel drum, or finding a manmade waterfall in a tiny park squeezed between two office buildings.

Besides its scientific and educational value, *The City and the Self* received artistic recognition—it won the Silver Medal of the International Film and Television Festival of New York, and was selected for showing at the Museum of Modern Art and the Donnell Library. Over the years, it has turned into a commercial success as well, through continuing purchases by universities for teaching purposes.

...

In September 1971, Milgram applied for a Guggenheim Fellowship to extend his research on psychological maps to a European city. When he applied, he had London or Paris in mind, but hadn't yet decided between them. He and Sasha were weighing the conveniences of London against giving their children a solid opportunity to learn French. By the time the approval came through in March 1972, they had decided—to no one's surprise—on Paris.

Milgram's interest in further research on cognitive maps of cities was genuine. It would combine his longtime fascination with cross-cultural comparisons with his newly found enthusiasm for studying people's mental image of their city. However, the prudent thing would have been to wait until the following year, 1973–1974, his seventh year at CUNY, when he would have been eligible for a sabbatical. Universities typically pay a full salary for a one-semester sabbatical or half-salary for a yearlong sabbatical. By now, Milgram's annual salary was about $32,000. The Guggenheim Fellowship paid $15,000. If he had waited, the combination of these two incomes would have put him on easy street—but that was too far down the road to serve several immediate needs.

First, Milgram felt he had to get away. He had been teaching continuously, without a break, since he had started at Yale in 1960. He had not stayed long enough at Yale or Harvard to earn a sabbatical at either place. By the end of the 1971–1972 academic year, he would have had twelve years of nonstop teaching behind him. In addition, that academic year was turning out to be especially hectic and exhausting. Besides his regular teaching and committee responsibilities, Milgram's typical day was filled with a number of other duties: conducting his subway research with his students; completing the television study and preparing a report on it for CBS, due April 15, 1972; organizing an interdisciplinary conference on city behavior; and, beginning in January 1972, filming *The City and the Self* with Harry From.

Second, the completion of a book about his obedience research was within reach if he could arrange for temporary freedom from his academic duties. He had been planning to write such a book since 1963, and while he would periodically jot down some ideas, he didn't actually start writing chapters for it until the latter half of 1969.

While still at Harvard, he had met Virginia Hilu, an editor at Harper and Row, who was eager to publish a book about the obedience research. But because of a major writing commitment at the time, it wasn't until 1969 that Milgram felt he had the time to embark on the book project. He signed with Harper and Row in September 1969, and, when he mailed the signed contract to Hilu, he also sent her a draft of chapter 2 of the book. (They had agreed that an article he had written in 1967 for *Patterns of Prejudice*, an obscure British journal, would serve as the introductory chapter.) She wrote Stanley encouragingly on November 5: "Chapter 2 makes me eager for chapter 3. You have a marvelous way with language and somehow have made this chapter dramatic and shattering."

Although the contract called for a delivery date of September 1970, months passed without any more material from Stanley. On July 21, Hilu wrote him to inquire about the book. Everyone at Harper and Row was looking forward to receiving the manuscript, and they were all hoping that his silence meant that he was hard at work on it. On August 13, 1970, he sent a draft of one chapter and promised another one soon. Hilu found that unsatisfactory and immediately replied, giving him chapter and verse: "Where is that manuscript? We are now working on our publication list for 1971 and I had hoped that your book would be one of the big books on our spring list." In order to publish at all in 1971, she needed to have the manuscript by January 1, 1971, at the latest.

Milgram sent Hilu a draft of the whole manuscript at the beginning of April 1971—noting that it still needed a lot of work. Incorporating the feedback she provided over the next few months, Milgram sent her the first eight chapters of the manuscript on September 17, 1971. Even though there were more chapters yet to be done, he was sending her those because he was "eager for [her] editorial skill to be brought to bear on the manuscript." At this point, he must have realized that, given the amount of work still left to do on the book, he would have to free himself from his regular academic obligations in order to complete it within a reasonable amount of time. So he filled out an application for a Guggenheim Fellowship and hand-delivered it to the foundation's offices on Park Avenue on September 30 in order to meet their deadline of October 1. And, in fact, when he started his Guggenheim year in Paris, the task he turned to first was working on the obedience book, not the mental maps of Parisians.

Third, he needed to get away because, as he told Sasha and his closest friends, he was experiencing a midlife crisis. In a letter to Paul Hollander dated October 12, 1972, Milgram wrote: "I approach 40. The zenith is in the past. Please forward detailed plans on how best to use the declining years ahead." Although he never elaborated to Sasha about the cause of his crisis, she believes it came from looking back wistfully at his life so far and realizing that, despite his enviable accomplishments, it hadn't unfolded exactly the way he had wanted it to. He had been used to succeeding no matter the obstacles. But then, he didn't make tenure at Harvard and he couldn't land a position at a prestigious university. None had come knocking at his office door in the Graduate Center, and looking ahead, he had no reason to expect it to happen in the near future.

His malaise was also undoubtedly fueled, at least to some extent, by the increasing intrusions of politics into academic life. While he was a political liberal in his vigorous opposition to the Vietnam War and support of nuclear disarmament, his views were decidedly more conservative when it came to affirmative action. In a letter to Leon Mann dated October 26, 1971, he wrote: "There is some sense of progress and movement at the Graduate Center. A big question, however, is whether intellectual standards or political pressures will prevail in the conduct of our program. Already, we have been asked to recruit faculty on a racial basis, and we make exceptions to our usual admission standards in assessing potential black students. If carried too far, this could have disastrous consequences for the quality of the program. Then I'll leave." It was time for a change of scene.

The Milgrams' sojourn in Paris began in the summer of 1972. Sasha and the children flew to Paris on July 12. Sasha found a small but cheerful apartment on Rue de Rémusat. It had two bedrooms in the back facing an inner courtyard and a salon in front that looked down onto the street below. The street was densely lined with three rows of trees, which created a feeling of living in a tree house.

Stanley couldn't go with them because he had some work to finish before he left New York. The next morning, he wrote to Sasha, Michele, and Marc that "it is very lonely in the apartment without you and I really do miss my family." Two days later, he wrote them another letter: "This apartment is just a big, empty set of rooms with lonely echoes—and I really look forward to rejoining you in Paris. . . . The contrast between immersion in family life and this solitude is immense." He flew to Paris a week later, on July 19.

Paris empties out in August, and Stanley never liked being in the city then. So he joined the exodus and arranged for the family to vacation for two weeks in August at a family-style Club Med in French Morocco. When they returned to Paris, Sasha enrolled the children at Pershing Hall, an American-style school located a few blocks from their apartment. Michele went into the third grade, and Marc started the first grade. Although the children studied French with a French teacher every day, it was an English-speaking school. There was a school uniform—a green blazer with the school's emblem over the heart. "It is all exceedingly goyish," Stanley remarked to Hollander, "but I think I like it."

Milgram loved being back in Paris, and as summer gave way to fall, the city looked especially lovely. The city's beauty and the respite from 42nd Street did not lead to a quick dissipation of Milgram's sense of malaise, however. On October 30, 1972, he wrote Hollander that he had been feeling "rather low," and he wasn't sure whether it was the result of an existential examination of his current life circumstances or simply a mild case of the flu. He congratulated Hollander on the imminent publication of a book on American-Soviet relations, adding, "Naturally, since it does not adequately reflect the spirit of the 'détente,' you will be deported." He hoped that he would be able to report to Hollander on the completion of his own book within the coming year. A few months later he was able to do just that.

On January 13, 1973, he flew to New York to attend to a number of matters—the main one being the obedience book. Virginia Hilu told him that if she had the completed manuscript by February 1, the book could be published in September. Given Hilu's patience in spite of the delays, he was eager to meet her goal. He had finished a final draft of the manuscript and had come to New York to deliver it and work with her on tying up loose ends—completing footnotes, bibliographic references, and graphs and charts and providing her with photographs. He gave her some line drawings to be used in the book, prepared by his graduate student Judith Waters, a skilled artist. In the course of going through the manuscript, both he and Virginia realized that the ending was weak and needed to be rewritten. She also asked Stanley to write a preface. It took him a few days to write them, and by January 24 the book was ready to go into production. "Virginia has been quite good, in her Pollyanna-like way," he wrote Sasha. "She has extraordinary faith in the book."

Besides completing the obedience manuscript, Stanley had used his months in Paris to work on another book, about his television research, which was to be published by Academic Press. He had completed the book before his trip to New York, although on his arrival the editor asked him to rewrite the preface and to provide some photographs. The book, coauthored with R. Lance Shotland and titled *Television and Anti-Social Behavior: Field Experiments,* was published in the summer of 1973.

Another business matter that Milgram took care of in New York was signing an agreement, together with Harry From, with Time-Life Films to be the distributor of their film, *The City and the Self.* Filmmaking had become a passion for Milgram, and *The City and the Self* led to a contract with Harper and Row a couple of years later for him, with Harry From as director and coproducer, to make four educational films on various topics in social psychology. They also hired an agent to try to sell *The City and the Self* to one of the television networks, although that effort failed.

Despite his hectic schedule, he wrote an affectionate letter to Sasha and the children virtually every day, describing his activities. Even though their separation was brief, Stanley and Sasha missed each other. For example, on January 24, Stanley wrote to Sasha, Michele, and Marc: "How I would like Sasha's company, not to mention her kisses and other things. Although productive and busy, my life here is very narrow. . . . My love, hugs, and kisses to you all. Love, Stanley." On the same day, Sasha wrote to Stanley: "If you are able to finish your work as scheduled by Feb. 2, you will be home in just over a week. . . . I yearn for you and the children miss you. . . . Love and kisses, Sasha."

Since the main purpose of the New York trip was to take care of academic matters, Stanley had gone by himself. In that sense, it was an exception, because the Milgrams took a number of family trips together to other countries during their Guggenheim year in France. They celebrated Thanksgiving 1972 in London, and the following spring they took a weeklong trip to Italy. But their longest trip was a spectacular visit to Israel during the second half of December 1972. Stanley had been invited by Elihu Katz, of the Communications Institute of the Hebrew University in Jerusalem, one of the pioneers in the study of mass communication, to talk about his recently completed television research.

Milgram accepted, adding that he would be willing to talk about other research topics as well. Over a two-week period Milgram gave six lectures to audiences from the Communications Institute as well as their colleagues in the Psychology Department. In addition to his television research, he lectured on his obedience studies and on experimental methods in social psychology. In between, the Milgram family crisscrossed the country. They toured Haifa, Netanya, Tel Aviv, Jericho, and the Dead Sea. They also visited the artists' colony in Safed and ascended to the top of Masada. Before leaving Israel, Stanley was offered a permanent faculty position by the dean of Hebrew University. He felt good about being asked and gave it some serious thought, but ultimately turned it down.

It was only after Milgram returned from his January visit to New York that he was ready to give his full attention to the study of cognitive maps. On March 13, 1973, he wrote to Paul Hollander that because he had devoted his time until then to completing the two books, he was just getting his study of mental maps under way. In fact, that was too optimistic a statement, since, as of April, he had not yet interviewed a single subject. The reason: he was now lacking the financial resources to do the study. And this put him in a quandary.

He felt obligated to the Guggenheim Foundation to conduct the research, since the funding they provided was for that purpose. But the $15,000 award from the foundation had not even been enough to pay for their personal living expenses for the year. To make matters worse, the dollar had recently been devalued. Recognizing this, the Guggenheim Foundation awarded him a bit more money. But even with this supplement, he and Sasha found that they had to dip into their personal savings.

Milgram's problem was solved by the intervention of a friend and fellow social psychologist, Serge Moscovici, the director of the Social Psychology Laboratory at the Ecole Pratique des Hautes Etudes in Paris, a government-supported research center. Moscovici was a Romanian-born immigrant to France. After surviving a pogrom in Bucharest in January 1941, in which the homegrown fascists, the Iron Cross, brutally murdered hundreds of Jews, he spent the rest of the war in a forced-labor camp until Romania was liberated by the Russian army in August 1944. He made his way to France in 1948 and subsequently earned a Ph.D. in psychology at the Sorbonne.

Milgram and Moscovici first met at Yale in June 1963, toward the end of Moscovici's one-year stay as a visiting member at the Institute for Advanced Study in Princeton. That began a collegial relationship that was to last into the 1980s. Their friendship was grounded in mutual respect for each other's work as well as their shared status as iconoclasts. Moscovici's main experimental work was in conformity, and it challenged the prevailing dominant approach to the subject. Most contemporary research on conformity, he argued, was too limited, because it focused mainly on how a group exerts its influence on the individual. Moscovici's research showed that under certain conditions, this process could be reversed, with the lone individual swaying the group to adopt his viewpoint. Moscovici believed that the power of majorities was derived from their sheer *numbers*. He demonstrated, by contrast, that minorities could convince majorities through their *style* of behavior—their forcefulness, unswerving persistence, and the consistency of their positions. This process is vividly illustrated in the spellbinding film classic *Twelve Angry Men,* starring Henry Fonda. Fonda plays the role of a member of a jury charged with deciding the fate of a teenager accused of knifing his father to death. An initial straw vote reveals that all the jurors are ready to vote "guilty" with virtually no discussion of the case—except the character played by Henry Fonda. The film depicts how Fonda, through dogged persistence and persuasive arguments, is able to change each juror's mind, one by one, until finally the jury ends up with a unanimous verdict of "not guilty."

As late as the 1980s, social psychology was largely a North American discipline, with as many as 90 percent of its practitioners living in the United States and Canada. Moscovici was among the earliest European social psychologists whose work was able to penetrate mainstream North American social psychology, and his perspectives on minority influence are well represented in most American social psychology textbooks.

Despite the largely sporadic nature of their correspondence, Milgram and Moscovici maintained a level of collegiality and continued readiness to help each other—sometimes as a result of their own initiative and the involvement of a great deal of effort.

Moscovici recognized Milgram's work on obedience as important research with enduring value. He was especially struck by its timeliness. He saw its relevance not only to the horrors of the Nazi era that he had lived through, but also to the protracted and bloody conflict that had led up to Algeria's independence from France about a year earlier, in 1962. As he wrote Milgram, "the methods invented by the Nazis have spread very dangerously all over Europe."

Milgram, in his reply, expressed the possibility that he might want to do a replication of the obedience experiments in France in a few years. He also told Moscovici that he very much enjoyed their wide-ranging conversations in New Haven and suggested that they collaborate on a book-length critique of social psychology that would be published simultaneously in English and French, "with a special Swedish version to be transmitted to the Svenske Akadamie to insure our receiving a Nobel Prize."

After their first meeting in New Haven, Moscovici offered to help Milgram publish an article on the obedience research in French—Milgram could even send the text in English, and he could have it translated into French. Later in the year, Milgram sent him a French version of a report of his first study—the pilot study with undergraduates—which had not yet been published. Moscovici submitted the article for Milgram to a monthly review, *Les Temps Modernes*. At the time, Milgram had not even heard of it. Had he been familiar with it, he would have realized that Moscovici was trying to help him publish in the most influential and widely read periodical in France. Its founders and editors were Jean Paul Sartre and Simone de Beauvoir, and it contained articles by the most highly regarded thinkers of the day. Had Milgram appeared in the magazine, he would have become widely known among French intellectuals. However, the magazine rejected the article, finding both its methods and its results appalling. Later, in 1973, Moscovici put Milgram in touch with a publisher, Calmann-Levy, who would end up publishing the French edition of Milgram's obedience book.

Over the years, Milgram, in turn, tried on his own initiative to advance Moscovici's career. In 1973, he submitted, on Moscovici's behalf, an essay of his on social influence as an entry for the American Association for the Advancement of Science's annual sociopsychological prize, an ultimately unsuccessful effort that involved Milgram's cutting its length in half to meet the word limit. In 1976 and in 1982, Milgram made repeated efforts to interest American publishers in bringing out English translations of two of Moscovici's books.

In July 1972, about a week before Milgram flew to Paris to begin his Guggenheim Fellowship year, he had written Moscovici about his plans to work on a psychological map of Paris in the upcoming academic year, asking if he could provide him with an office in his Social Psychology Laboratory. Moscovici readily provided one, but his more crucial help was in the spring of 1973, when Milgram was dangerously short on funds.

Moscovici wrote a letter to the director of the French government's ministry of scientific and technical research requesting an emergency grant of 35,000 francs, equivalent to about $8,000 at the 1973 rate of exchange, to enable Milgram to conduct his research "on the mental representation of urban space." The money would be used primarily to pay for interviewing a representative sample of 300 Parisians and for collecting and analyzing the data. He would be assisted in the research, Moscovici wrote, by Denise Jodelet, a project director in his laboratory. It was a forceful, persuasive letter, praising the scientific quality and originality of the research and its tremendous value in stimulating the growth of the new discipline of environmental psychology. In his attempt to bail Milgram out of his predicament, Moscovici even went overboard by promising, unrealistically, that a report of the research would be available by the end of the summer.

Moscovici's letter succeeded, and Milgram was awarded the requested amount, making it possible for him to conduct the research. The money enabled him to hire a survey research firm to conduct interviews with subjects. Given the short time remaining in his fellowship year, that kind of assistance was essential for carrying out his work.

The Parisian mental map study built on the one Milgram had conducted in New York City, but it went beyond it in its richness of detail. Like the New York study, it used a "scene sampling" technique in which groups of Parisians were shown photographs of forty different landmarks of their city and asked to identify them. But now, Milgram added some new techniques for capturing and externalizing the mental representations of Paris held by its residents. A full appreciation of his findings is largely limited to Parisians and others—like the Milgrams—with intimate knowledge of the nooks and crannies of the city. How many non-Parisians, for instance, know the names "Porte St. Martin" or "Eglise d'Alesia," two of the land-

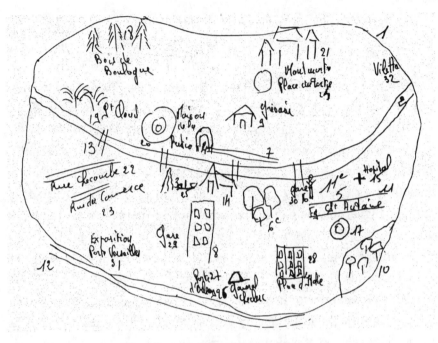

FIGURE 10.1   One Person's Mental Map of Paris.

marks that subjects were asked to identify, much less feel enlightened by the fact that 67 percent and 54 percent of the viewers recognized the two scenes, respectively? But what can be appreciated about the research regardless of one's degree of familiarity with Paris is the degree of inventiveness Milgram brought to the task. For example, 218 subjects, drawn from each of the twenty administrative sectors *(arrondissements)* of Paris in proportion to their populations, were asked to draw a map of Paris—a map that reflected their personal image of the city rather than one that was simply a tourist map.

The maps were then subjected to individual, qualitative analyses guided by Milgram's assumption that "through processes of selectivity, emphasis and distortion, the maps become projections of life styles, and express emotional cathexes of the participants." Here, for example, is Milgram's analysis of a map (see Figure 10.1) drawn by a butcher from the eleventh arrondissement:

At first the map looks confusing, but we begin to discern the elements of a set of life circumstances when we examine it closely. He does not forget to include his home arrondissement, which is something of a hidden one to most subjects. Nor does he neglect La Villette, where the major stockyards and slaughterhouses of Paris are to be found. One can imagine his visits to the great exposition hall at the Porte de Versailles, to see displays of meat cutting equipment, motorcycles, and perhaps automobiles. Faubourg St. Antoine, of revolutionary significance, is placed on the Left Bank, where it would seem to belong politically.

We are most confused, perhaps, by the inverted curvature he has given to the Seine; the disposition of elements along the river seem all out of line with reality. Yet if Etoile, Maison de la Radio, and the Porte de St. Cloud deviate from their true spatial coordinates, they do preserve a meaningful topological sequence.

But Milgram realized that a true psychological map of Paris would have to capture the collective representation of the city, not just its idiosyncratic position in the minds of specific individuals. To create a mental map of Paris based on the shared elements in many peoples' images of the city, Milgram went from a qualitative analysis of a selected group of maps to a quantitative analysis of all the maps produced by his subjects.

The use of individual maps to create an aggregated cognitive map of the city was grounded in Milgram's assumption that the sequence with which subjects sketched different parts of the city would be indicative of what features stood out most in their minds. So Milgram had asked subjects to number each detail of the map as they sketched it. (A close look at the butcher's map, for example, reveals that he first drew in the line designating the city's boundary, followed by the river Seine, and so on.) By counting the number of times an element was entered first in subjects' maps, and which parts of the city appeared most frequently, Milgram was able to gauge their salience to the collective mind of the Parisian.

The most frequent first entry was the Seine, followed by Notre Dame and Ile de la Cité. He found this ordering entirely sensible: These elements "are at the very heart of the idea of Paris. Lutèce was born on the Ile de la Cité; Notre Dame was constructed there 800 years ago. The sequence with which subjects enter their elements in the hand-drawn maps recapitulates this history." Furthermore, evidence for a shared representation of Paris in the minds of its residents was provided by the following finding: Milgram's subjects sketched a total of 4,132 places into their subjective maps. Despite this large number, there was a good deal of commonality among the maps. About half of the 4,132 features that appeared in the maps were found in only 26 different locations.

Finally Milgram probed aspects of Parisians' perceptions of their city by presenting them with a number of questions. One of them was this: "Suppose you were to meet someone in Paris, a person whom you had never met before, and you knew the exact date and time of the meeting, but not the place. Assume the person you were to meet operated under the similar handicap of not knowing where you would wait for him. Where in Paris would you wait so as to maximize the chances of encountering the person?"

Some did not answer this question—denouncing it as stupid, illogical, or unanswerable. Among the 188 subjects who did answer it, six places accounted for more than 50 percent of their answers—with the Eiffel Tower topping the list. To Milgram this finding suggested that people may know some things about their city that they are not consciously aware of, and that this kind of unverbalized knowledge may be shared widely.

In sum, Milgram's main purpose in conducting the map studies, both in New York and in Paris, was to externalize how the city "sits in the mind" of its residents. But the methods he used to achieve this goal were different in the two cities. In New York he devised an objective method for doing it—his "scene sampling" technique. In Paris, the primary method for making Parisians' mental image of their city visible was to have them draw maps that would express their personal view of their city. The use of hand-drawn maps had an important advantage over the scene sampling technique in that it permitted a direct comparison of a person's image of the city with its geographical reality. Milgram expressed the value of mental maps this way:

> [Mental maps] allow a treatment of the city's spatial character in a way that words frequently avoid. And they show how urban space is encoded, distorted, and selectively represented, while yet retaining its usefulness to the person. For the image of the city is not just extra mental baggage; it is the

necessary accompaniment to living in a complex and highly variegated environment. . . . The maps are not only individual products; they are shaped by social factors, and therefore acquire the status of collective representations—that is, symbolic configurations of belief and knowledge promoted and disseminated by the culture.

...

The year in Paris was a splendid experience for the whole family, and they were saddened by the prospect of leaving France. And just as when they first moved from Cambridge to New York in 1967, Sasha and Stanley found themselves comparing the two, with New York City again suffering by comparison.

The family flew back to New York on August 22. A month later, Milgram wrote Moscovici to thank him for his crucial help in making the Paris map study possible. In that letter, he also remarked on the difficulty of readjusting to life in New York. "We buy food and automatically convert the price to francs. I suppose in a few weeks this compulsion will disappear. . . ." One of the things that helped ease the transition was the impending publication of his book and Stanley's intense curiosity about how it would be received. "Most likely, it will be highly controversial," he wrote Moscovici. "That is, I suppose, better than being totally ignored, but hardly as good as being universally acclaimed."

After Milgram had delivered his revised manuscript to Harper and Row and worked with Virginia Hilu to tie up the loose ends, the publisher set the production gears in motion. When Milgram received the complete copyedited manuscript for his review and approval, he found to his dismay that a major reworking of the manuscript had taken place without his consent. He was furious. He had written portions of the book in the present tense, to enhance its sense of immediacy, to make it come alive for the reader. Now he found that those sections had been put in the past tense. Since Milgram felt that framing parts of the narrative in the present was a stylistic feature that was necessary to create the intended impact on the reader, he was now confronted with the tedious task of undoing the publisher's changes and reinstating his original wording.

But even as that matter was being cleared up, another irksome matter arose. The publisher sent Milgram the design of the book's dust jacket, and the Milgrams found it simply repulsive. Sasha recalls that the background color was a "vomity green" and a strand of barbed wire was depicted streaking threateningly across the front cover. Stanley conveyed his dissatisfaction to the publisher, and they ended up settling on the simple, uncluttered cover design that still adorns the American edition of the book—yellow and white lettering atop a black background with a straight orange line underscoring the author's name.

While correcting these matters was a nuisance, it did not slow the production schedule appreciably. Bound galleys were ready in July, and the book was published in January 1974. Although printing of the book began in November, Harper and Row held off actual publication until January to bypass the crowded state of bookstores before Christmas. A preview of the book, titled "The Perils of Obedience," appeared in the December 1973 issue of *Harper's* magazine. It was an article-length condensation prepared by Taylor Branch, who was then on the magazine's staff.

A British edition of the book came out a few months later, in May. French, German, and Dutch editions were also published that year. Eventually the book would appear in eight additional languages: Spanish, Swedish, Italian, Portuguese, Serbo-Croatian, Indonesian, Japanese, and Danish.

It had been a long haul. Ten years had passed since he had first intended to begin writing the book. A number of things had conspired against him during that time.

First, writing did not come easily to Milgram. Coming up with an idea for a study, creating just the right technique, and then carrying it out—these were the things that excited him, not writing a book, especially one that was a retrospective account requiring theoretical integration, which was not his forte.

Another reason the book was delayed was that Milgram was very much a family man. The Milgrams' children, Michele and Marc, were born within a few years after the obedience studies were completed, and evenings and weekends were set aside for the family, even when the children were older. Trips with Sasha and the children to museums and parks were common. And there were annual family trips to the Caribbean, New England,

and sometimes to Europe. Stanley applied some of the same energy and inventiveness to parenting as he did to his work. For example, when Marc arrived at summer camp one year, there were already letters from his father waiting for him, to help alleviate his homesickness. And Stanley would occasionally make home movies with fictional plot lines in which Marc and Michele would be the stars. One of the more complex ones was titled "A Bird in Paris," which required several birds to play the part. In it, Marc and Michele buy a bird at an open-air market. Very soon, they lose it, providing Milgram with an excuse to film the children running all over Paris chasing the bird. They finally catch the bird, but then they feel sorry that it is locked in a cage. In the finale, they take the bird up to the top of the Eiffel Tower to release it. But the bird doesn't cooperate and flies away too quickly. So Milgram resorted to using a stunt double, a toy bird that he had purchased.

There was yet a third factor that delayed the writing of the obedience book. On May 19, 1964, Milgram received a letter from coeditors Gardner Lindzey and Elliot Aronson, asking him to contribute a chapter on mass phenomena to the second edition of the *Handbook of Social Psychology*.

Beginning with the first edition in 1954, the multivolume *Handbook* has been the premier reference resource in social psychology. A new edition appears about every fifteen years, and its chapters are state-of-the-art presentations of the various subtopics in the field. An invitation to contribute to the *Handbook* carried with it a great deal of prestige, and Milgram accepted. It turned out to be a daunting, drawn-out, time-consuming task, which diverted his attention from the obedience book. Not until March 1965 did he send the editors his chapter outline, and he didn't actually begin writing until that fall. Lane Conn, a Harvard colleague, recalls how difficult it was for Stanley to start writing: "He was blocked, and he couldn't get it written. And I said, 'What are you going to do?' So what he did was he went into his office and took some psilocybin [a hallucinogenic drug found in mushrooms]. And I said to him, 'Well, Stanley, how is that going to come out?' And he said, 'Well, you know, 90 percent of it will be crap, but 10 percent of it will be good.' And he used that as a way to try to get his creative juices flowing." The final product was a massive piece of work, over 100 printed pages long, which he didn't complete until the end of 1966. Its final title was "Collective Behavior: Crowds and Social Movements." Hans Toch, who was a visiting professor at Harvard in 1965–1966, wrote a small section of the chapter and appears as a coauthor.

Milgram's halting progress on the chapter was aided by the gentle prodding of coeditor Elliot Aronson. For example, in a letter of October 12, 1966, Aronson wrote:

> *Dear Stanley:*
>
> *Nuuuu?*
>
> *Best regards,*
> *Elliot*

It turned out that Milgram's initial writing difficulties had no bearing on the final product. The chapter is Milgram's most scholarly piece of writing, a masterly work of integration and analysis of theories and studies of mass behavior. After Milgram submitted the chapter, Aronson wrote him that it was "one of the two or three most exciting contributions to the *Handbook*. . . . I literally enjoyed every word of it and would not have dreamed of suggesting any major changes."

...

Given the twelve-year lag between the completion of the obedience experiments and the publication of the book, Milgram wondered if some people might erroneously think that the current book was merely a facsimile edition of the original, which had actually been published about ten years earlier. He didn't need to worry. The book was a triumph of exposition and a greatly expanded treatment of the experiments and the issues raised by them.

Obedience to Authority described nineteen experimental conditions—some already published and others reported for the first time—in comparable detail. Milgram fended off, by means of argument and data, various criticisms that had been leveled at the research: that the subjects were atypical; that they "obeyed" because they saw through the deception; that the findings were limited to the lab and not generalizable to the real world; and that the research was unethical. The defense against this last criticism was largely a reproduction of material he had published earlier in his *American Psychologist* rebuttal of Baumrind's article and in his reply to a critical essay by the Welsh poet and playwright Dannie Abse, who had written a play, *The Dogs of Pavlov,* inspired by the obedience experiments. An effective feature of the book, which helped personalize the subjects' experiences for the reader, were individual vignettes of ten different subjects in various conditions of the experimental series.

The book also presented, for the first time, a theory of obedience, grounded in a combination of evolutionary thinking and cybernetics—the science of regulation or control.

Milgram argued that membership in authority-dominated social groupings provides enormous advantage in coping with a hostile environment. Because a propensity for obedience is a prerequisite of this type of social organization, evolutionary processes have made such a tendency part of human nature. When acting autonomously, a person's destructive impulses are held in check by his conscience. However, organizations cannot operate in an effective, co-ordinated fashion if its members all follow their own individual ideas of right and wrong. So, according to Milgram, when a person enters an organizational mode, he necessarily cedes individual internal control to the group's leadership, and his conscience is no longer brought into play. The transition from an autonomous mode of functioning to an organizational or "systemic" mode is achieved through the person's entry into what Milgram called the "agentic state," a different experiential state, one in which a person relinquishes responsibility to the legitimate authority in charge. According to Milgram, once a person accepts the legitimacy of an authority, he also accepts the authority's interpretation of a situation. So, if the authority says that another individual is deserving of punishment, the person who becomes a willing agent of that authority also accepts that assessment. Allowing the authority to redefine the meaning of the situation and passing on responsibility to him make it possible for a person to act in ways that he would normally consider reprehensible. He is no longer concerned with whether or not the action is morally acceptable; he has ceded that judgment to the person in charge. His main concern now is how adequately he has carried out the required action.

Milgram describes the agentic state as follows: "From a subjective stand-point, a person is in a state of agency when he defines himself in a social situation in a manner that renders him open to regulation by a person of higher status. In this condition the individual no longer views himself as responsible for his own actions but defines himself as an instrument for carrying out the wishes of others."

Milgram's theorizing is the weakest part of the book. First, his evolutionary-cybernetic analysis—never before mentioned in Milgram's journal articles related to the experiments—cannot explain the variations in amounts of obedience that occurred in his various experimental conditions. Despite the differences in the experimental setups among the various conditions, most of them continued to share a similar authority-dominated organizational structure, which should lead to uniformity in the relinquishing of internal control to the person in charge—the experimenter. Second, the validity of the agentic state concept is not dependent on its embeddedness in Milgram's evolutionary-cybernetic theory. That is, the validity of the idea that destructive obedience requires entry into an agentic state—whose essence is shedding of responsibility for one's actions and relinquishing it to a legitimate authority—is not enhanced by seeing the process as a product of evolutionary necessity. The validity of the agentic state concept is ultimately an empirical question: Is entry into the agentic state a necessary precondition for destructive obedience? A specific theory about how or why such a precondition came into being is only of secondary importance.

Among the experimental conditions that were reported for the first time in the book was one in which all the subjects were women. Their rate of obedience was identical to male subjects in the comparable condition—65 percent. Although Milgram found no gender differences in degree of obedience, he did find that obedient women experienced more tension than obedient men. At the end of each experimental session, subjects indicated on a numerical scale how tense or nervous they were at the point of maximum tension. Milgram reports that the self-rated nervousness of obedient women was higher than that of obedient men in all the other experimental conditions in the series.

Another condition newly described in the book was one that yielded the highest rate of obedience of his whole series. In this condition, the naïve subject didn't shock the learner; he was merely an accessory to the act. The situation was set up so that the job of pressing the switch was given to another subject—actually a confederate—while the real subject performed only some subsidiary actions. So, while he contributed to the overall procedure, he was not directly involved in punishing the victim. The result: 37 out of 40 subjects (92.5 percent) continued to the end. Milgram articulated the troubling implications of this finding:

> Any competent manager of a destructive bureaucratic system can arrange his personnel so that only the most callous and obtuse are directly involved in violence. The greater part of the personnel can consist of men and women who, by virtue of their distance from the actual acts of brutality, will feel little strain in their performance of supportive functions. They will feel doubly absolved from responsibility. First, legitimate authority has given full warrant for their actions. Second, they have not themselves committed brutal physical acts.

While Milgram had no overarching theory to guide him as he was conducting the obedience project in 1961–1962—the "agentic state" concept was post hoc theorizing—there were specific sets of experiments within the broader series that were meant to provide answers to particular questions. An example of this, already discussed, was the four-part proximity series, the purpose of which was to see what effect varying the physical and emotional distance between the teacher and learner would have on obedience. Among the nine experimental conditions described for the first time in the book was another subset with a common focus—to provide experimental support for Milgram's belief that the destructive behavior shown by his subjects was a product of their obedience to the experimental authority and not the uncapping of bottled-up aggression.

This had become a contentious point. Some saw the subjects' behavior as a form of aggression, rather than obedience, an approach rooted in Freudian thinking. According to Freud, all individuals harbor destructive impulses.

Although these destructive tendencies continually press for release, they are usually held in check because society considers their expression unacceptable. Applying this view to Milgram's experiment, one could argue that in his laboratory he created a permissive environment in which those normally pent-up hostile urges could be freely expressed by "hurting" the learner. In other words, the experimenter gave subjects permission to act in ways they wanted to anyway, rather than made them do something distasteful to them.

Freud's views on aggression were just one piece of his larger attempt to provide an all-encompassing theory of human behavior. Milgram had no such broad ambitions. Moreover, he was uninterested in probing the *interior* of the human psyche, preferring to focus on the *external* social forces that have surprisingly powerful effects on our behavior. While Milgram recognized that aggressiveness is part of human nature, he argued that it was not the primary determinant of his subjects' behavior, because it was overpowered by a situational determinant—the experimenter's commands. Subjects shocked the learner not to satisfy destructive urges but because they felt obliged to obey the commands of a destructive authority. Several of his experimental variations provided empirical support for his view.

In one such variation, the subject was required as usual to shock the learner every time he made a mistake on the word-matching task. However, in contrast to the usual rule that the voltage had to be stepped up on each subsequent error, the subject was free to administer *any* of the thirty shock levels whenever the learner made a mistake. If destructive urges were at the root of the shocking conduct in Milgram's experiments, one would expect subjects in this condition to repeatedly zap the learner with high-voltage shocks, since the choice was up to them. In actuality, almost all subjects stayed at the lower shock levels, with the average shock level being 3.6 on the thirty-step shock continuum. Milgram concluded: "If destructive impulses were really pressing for release, and the subject could justify his use of high shock levels in the cause of science, why did they not make the victim suffer? . . . Whatever leads to shocking the victim at the highest level [in other conditions] cannot be explained by autonomously generated aggression, but needs to be explained by the transformation of behavior that comes about through obedience to orders."

Another condition that provided empirical support for Milgram's viewpoint involved the most clever piece of staging of the whole series of experiments. In the beginning phases of this condition, things proceed in the standard fashion, with the learner receiving increasingly intense shocks after each error. The learner's complaints begin at 75 volts and gradually intensify as he keeps getting stronger and stronger shocks. After the subject shocks the learner with 150 volts, something unusual happens. The experimenter says that the experiment will have to end, because the learner's protests had become increasingly intense and, in light of his heart condition, he should not receive any more shocks. Suddenly, the learner's voice is heard from the adjacent room. He cries out in protest that he wants the experiment to continue. He says that a friend of his had recently participated in the experiment and had continued until the end. To stop now would be an insult to his manliness. The experimenter reiterates his concern for the well-being of the learner, and the learner again demands that the experiment continue. He had come to the lab "to do a job" and he intended to complete it, so he insists that the teacher resume the procedure. The naïve subject is now in a bind. Whom should he listen to—the learner, who demands to be shocked, or the experimenter, who prohibits it? The results show that all the subjects resolved the conflict in a similar manner: Despite the learner's wishes, not a single one gave him another shock. All of them obeyed the experimenter's orders to stop.

If aggression were the key, the subjects would surely have continued to shock the learner. What could supersede permission from the person who is being hurt? Yet no one continued, a clear demonstration that the subjects' behavior was governed by the authority's commands and not by any hostile tendencies.

...

Much like when the first journal report was published in 1963, the appearance of the book drew public attention to Milgram and his startling research findings—but on a much grander scale. Large portions of the book were serialized in the London *Sunday Times,* and it was a finalist for a National Book Award in 1975. BBC Television produced a film about Milgram and his work for a documentary series, *Horizon,* titled "You Do as You Are Told." He made appearances on various television talk shows and news programs in the United States, such as the *Today* show and *Donahue,* as well as in France and England.

For a book about a scientific experiment, it was reviewed in an unusually large number of newspapers and magazines for a general readership, in addition to the usual professional journals. More than sixty reviews appeared in English-language publications alone. The reactions to the book were as varied as the initial media reports about the experiments a decade earlier. A reviewer for the *Los Angeles Times* wrote, "*Obedience to Authority* . . . is one of the most significant books I have read in more than two decades of reviewing," while a writer for *The Spectator* of London said, "Professor Milgram seems to see some deep social significance in it all, and no doubt a great many reviewers will take his word for it. . . . I personally decline to be convinced that he has discovered anything so significant."*

One review, however, stands out because of its unusual degree of combativeness: the lead review in the January 13, 1974, issue of the *New York Times Book Review.*

Sprawled across the section's cover page, it was accompanied by some nightmarish surrealistic artwork with the shock machine as its centerpiece, as if to forewarn the reader of the sinister nature of the book being reviewed. It was a mean-spirited, polemical piece, written by Steven Marcus, a professor of English at Columbia University. Although he granted that the experiments were "extremely provocative and probably important," they were "little masterpieces of bad faith" designed to bring out the worst in people. He criticized parts of the book for their moralistic tone and their "mutilated syntax." He also found fault with Milgram's theoretical explanation, which was admittedly flawed. But, while some other reviewers also judged the theoretical portions of the book to be weak, Marcus was dis-

---

*A sampling of other quotations from reviews appears in Appendix B, along with a quantitative content analysis of the reviews.

tinctively derisive, referring to them as "general disaster" and "a pretty bad joke" and disparaging their "empty pious sentiments."

When Milgram appeared on the *Dick Cavett Show*, Cavett asked him what he thought of Marcus's review. Milgram replied: "Well, obviously he was not competent to review the book from a scientific standpoint, since he is a teacher of English. And he did point to a sentence that required some syntactical correction, and any English teacher would normally correct that. It was not a serious review from [a scientific] standpoint. What he failed to do was to extract what one learns from the experiment, what one learns from the activity, rather than attending to some relatively trivial details."

While Milgram and his obedience research would remain irredeemably reprehensible to some, the benign attitudes conveyed by a large portion of the book reviews is consistent with the fact that within intellectual circles, he was widely respected as a serious thinker. Indeed, he was held in high regard both within the profession and outside of it.

For example, in 1966, just three years after his first journal publication on the obedience research, he was asked to serve as the program chairman for the personality and social psychology division of the APA at its annual convention. In March 1972, he was nominated for election to the council of the Society for the Psychological Study of Social Issues, a group whose goal is to apply social-scientific knowledge to problems of society. In 1977, he was an invited speaker at a psychiatric symposium on obedience to authority, which included a presentation by John Dean, the former White House counsel. And between 1976 and 1980, he gave invited addresses at four different conferences dealing with ethics and research. In June 1978, he gave a major invited address, "The Problem of Obedience in a Just Society," at an international conference on psychological stress held in Jerusalem.

And when Harvard was considering appointing a full professor in social psychology, the chairman of the department, R. Duncan Luce, wrote Milgram soliciting his opinions about the relative merits of five well-known candidates they were considering: Elliot Aronson, Ellen Berscheid, Reid Hastie, Bibb Latané, and Lee Ross. After expressing his qualified preference for Aronson, Milgram concluded his letter with a brief comment on the state of social psychology, which included, for good measure, a mild swipe at political correctness:

> Many of those working under the label of "social psychology" today deal with intrapsychic phenomena that are not inherently social. This has given an active, but amorphous character to the field. If you can find someone who, in addition to possessing strong experimental and theoretical strengths, can articulate a persuasive vision of the field, by all means grab him (her—oops!), for that is a pressing intellectual need of our discipline.

He was an invited speaker at a variety of conferences outside of social psychology: a conference on the implications of obedience to authority for the legal system sponsored by the Association of the Bar of the City of New York in May 1977; an international conference on terrorism held in Evian, France, the following month; an interdisciplinary conference on cults and new religious movements convened by the Anti-Defamation League of B'nai B'rith in January 1979 in the wake of the Jonestown mass suicide; and a symposium on the future of cities at Denison University in April 1979. At its commencement exercises in June 1981, Queens College honored Milgram as a Distinguished Alumnus, and in 1983 he was elected to the American Academy of Arts and Sciences.

The wide public exposure he received via the television appearances and book reviews made him something of a minor celebrity. As a result, people from all walks of life wrote him letters, which ranged from the silly to the sublime. He received and answered letters from correspondents as varied as an autograph collector from Indiana, Pennsylvania, who wanted to add Milgram to his list of 7,000 names; a high school student from Canton, Ohio, asking for help with a speech based on his research; columnist Max Lerner, requesting reprints for a planned article; a Florida college student inquiring about the relevance of R.D. Laing's writings to his obedience research; and rock musician Peter Gabriel, who, after reading *Obedience to Authority*, was planning to use obedience as the theme for a new piece of music. He asked permission to use the soundtrack from Milgram's film *Obedience* to punctuate the instrumental theme as well as photographs from the obedience experiment, which would appear on the album's inner sleeve. Although he told Milgram that he had no intention of criticizing the experiments and that he was not "a punk rock singer about to set upon your work with razor blades," Milgram turned him down, explaining that he only gave permission for scientific use and not for entertainment purposes. A dirge-like song, "We Do What We're Told (Milgram's 37)," did end up as a track on Gabriel's album *So*, which came out in 1986, but without the embellishments the musician had hoped for.

Among the many letters Milgram received was one from a young mother from Port Chester, New York, with an unusual request. Their first child, James, had just had his first birthday. When he was born, they gave him a present consisting of newspapers and magazines published in the month he was born as well as a number of best sellers and hit recordings. Now, for his first birthday, they wanted to give him a more memorable gift, a collection of autographs of a selected group of the world's leaders in science, arts, literature, and so on. She asked him to send an autographed photograph or note. Milgram replied with the following letter, addressing the toddler:

Dear James:

Do you agree with the analysis of child disobedience discussed on page 208 of my book, Obedience to Authority? You will soon be in a position to know about such things and to instruct your parents.

Best wishes,
Stanley Milgram

A more serious—but no less unusual—request came from a staff psychologist at a psychiatric hospital in upstate New York. One of her patients, a bright and physically healthy young man, was suffering from a very persistent and crippling *folie à deux* with his brother, that so far had resisted all efforts at treatment. She wrote Milgram that the patient believed that he was a hypnotized subject in "satellite-controlled telemetric studies" being conducted by Milgram and he wanted to be "released" so that he could get on with his life. When his therapist asked him if a letter from Milgram would help, he responded with delight at the idea. The psychologist asked Milgram if he would consider writing a letter indicating that the patient was not—and had never been—involved in any of his experiments. Milgram quickly obliged.

...

After collaborating with Harry From on *The City and the Self,* Milgram had begun to develop a passion for filmmaking, and the completion of his book freed him to direct his attention once again to that enterprise. As noted earlier, the artistic success of *The City and the Self* led to Milgram's and Harry From's contract with Harper and Row to make four educational films on various topics in social psychology. The first was *Invitation to Social Psychology,* which was quickly followed by *Conformity and Independence*—both appearing in 1975. The first won the Silver Award at the Chicago International Film Festival, and both were awarded the Chris Bronze Award at the Columbus Film Festival—all in 1975. In 1976 came *Human Aggression* and *Non-Verbal Communication.* Many of Milgram's students appear in the films. Milgram himself made brief appearances in *Conformity and Independence* and *Human Aggression,* and he narrated *Invitation to Social Psychology.* The films have surprising staying power in terms of the concepts and findings discussed, and they are still used in college classes.

Like all the films in the series, *Invitation to Social Psychology* uses both real-life vignettes and reenactments of experiments to convey some of the principles and findings of social psychology. For example, spilling hot coffee in a college cafeteria line is used to illustrate the "actor-observer" attributional effect, the tendency to point to situational causes for our own actions but to the personal qualities of others when it comes to explaining their actions. When one student sees another one spilling coffee from his tray, he calls him clumsy. A moment later he himself has a similar accident. When asked what happened, he explains: "The coffee was really hot."

Similarly, a dramatization of Albert Bandura's experiment in which children watch an adult punching an inflatable "Bobo doll" is used to teach how aggressive behavior can be a product of imitation. And *Conformity and Independence* uses both everyday behaviors and research studies as teaching tools. For example, the differing behaviors of participants in a smoking cessation group after they leave a session are used to illustrate different forms of social influence. The scene begins with the group leader ending a session by asking members of the group to indicate by a show of hands who will not smoke during the coming week. Ultimately, all hands go up. The camera moves outdoors and follows two of the participants as they walk away from the building. First, it shows a woman dumping a pack of cigarettes into a sidewalk trash can, her facial expression conveying her resoluteness. Her behavior is an illustration of what Herbert Kelman called "internalization," the process by which a person's behavior changes because a new belief or action fits with his or her own needs and values. This kind of change persists even when the individual is not being observed by the group. The behavior of a male participant is then used to illustrate the more superficial process of "compliance," whereby an adopted action persists only as long as a person is under the surveillance of the group. As soon as the male leaves the building, he immediately lights up a cigarette, inhaling deeply to compensate for the depravation he experienced during the meeting.

And a reenactment of one of Milgram's own field experiments on the sidewalk across the street from the Graduate Center shows how a group of people becomes an increasingly more powerful social magnet, causing increasingly larger numbers of passersby to imitate them—by looking up at an office window on the sixth floor of the school building—as the size of the stimulus group expands. Despite its simplicity, this experiment reveals a fundamental truth about human nature and social life—that we use other people's behavior as sources of information to help us cut through the complexities of our environment. The intent of Milgram's field experiment was not to demonstrate that humans can act in a blind, lemming-like fashion. Rather, it was designed to show that imitation can be a rational process. In this case, a passerby probably assumed that, if a group had stopped to look up at a window, there was probably a good reason for it, and the larger the crowd, the more compelling the reason must be.

The film *Non-Verbal Communication* is about language without words—eye contact, human spacing, vocal intonation, facial expressions, gestures—and the uses we make of them. By means of a wide and often entertaining array of real-life and staged examples, the film points out that nonverbal cues are used both automatically and consciously. The latter is illustrated by means of a dizzying ride through midtown Manhattan with a cab driver manically explaining how he uses gestural cues to decide whom to pick up. In producing the film, Milgram and From benefited serendipitously from an international conference on nonverbal behavior that was taking place in Toronto when they were shooting the film. From flew there with his small technical crew, and he was able to incorporate brief appearances by some of the top nonverbal researchers. So, for example, the film depicts the anthropologist Edward Hall discussing cross-cultural differences in the use of personal space and Robert Rosenthal noting that women are better at "reading" nonverbal cues than men.

The film *Human Aggression* depicted the role aggression played in an ordinary day of an actual teenage gang in the Bronx. In one scene, for example, as the gang is raucously walking down the middle of a residential street, one member spots a bowling ball lying on the ground, picks it up and spontaneously throws it through an open window, without any apparent concern about hurting someone inside. From was introduced to the gang by a police informer who was one of the leaders of the gang. The leader took him to the gang's meeting place, an abandoned apartment with the mezuzah of its former Jewish residents still attached to its doorpost. Gang members were sitting around smoking dope, eating cupcakes, and fondling the breasts of a girl. After some discussion, the gang agreed to participate in the film in exchange for money for beer and partying. One night, From got a call from the police saying that the members of the gang had been on the roof of a building and, amidst the excitement about doing the film, someone had thrown down a slab of concrete, killing a girl. As a result, the police would no longer provide any protection for the film crew if they continued with the filming. Milgram and From finally terminated their contact with the gang when one day they heard that the gang was planning a fight with another gang, complete with guns and bats, for the film. From immediately called the police, told them where the battle was supposed to take place, and prevented the gang war. He told them: "We are not going to shoot. There are more important things than footage."

Milgram's experiences with filmmaking led him to see that the scientific method had certain limitations that film was able to transcend. Harry From recalled that, when they were working on *The City and the Self*, there came a time "when Stanley felt much more freedom in treating subjects of interest to him through film than through a very rigorous experimental methodology. He sometimes felt the constraints of such an approach. What the film can afford and the scientific method cannot is ambiguity," an unavoidable feature of life. Milgram was intrigued by the possibility of capturing images on film that could not be translated into words, much less assigned numbers. Although it would not be possible for a discovery made through film to "be given a conclusion in a paper, . . . it can certainly disturb enough to give other people seeing it at least as much experience or information as an epilogue of a scientific paper."

By the mid-1970s filmmaking started moving toward the center stage of Milgram's interests and activities, and by May 1977 he even gave his profession as "professor and filmmaker" on a questionnaire for a listing in the biographical publication "Men of Achievement." He started taking courses in filmmaking in schools in the New York area, such as the New School for Social Research and New York University. In the fall of 1975, he enrolled in a film editing workshop conducted by Joanne Burke, editor of the feature film *The Anderson Tapes* and of *Gimme Shelter*, a documentary about the Rolling Stones' infamous concert at Altamont, during which a member of the audience was stabbed to death.

He was also eager to learn film directing. He submitted a grant application to the American Film Institute's Independent Filmmaker Program to support a film project, motivated at least partially by the directorial experience he would gain in the process of making the film.

Beginning in the spring of 1976, he started creating and offering film-related courses to the students in the social-personality program at CUNY, such as the Psychology of Photography and Film, Urban Psychology through Film, and Film and Video as Research Tools in Social Science.

While the medium of film allowed Milgram to step outside the boundaries of a scientific social psychology, it did not diminish his belief in the field's value, as the following statement, written in 1977, attests: "The creative claim of social psychology lies in its capacity to reconstruct varied types of social experience in an experimental format, to clarify and make visible the operation of obscure social forces so that they may be explored in terms of the language of cause and effect."

Nor did it diminish his self-definition as a social psychologist. He continued teaching the core social psychology courses that he had been teaching since his arrival at CUNY. In a letter dated May 7, 1983, to his long-lost childhood friend Bernard Fried, who is now retired from Lafayette College as professor of biology, he expressed his continued identification with social psychology:

> Since 1967 I have taught social psychology at the Graduate Center of the City University. There I do my thing, which is not so different from what you do, except that it contains a more generous admixture of fantasy and some slices of baloney. But, at the root, I've maintained a deep interest in science, and have never relinquished the curiosity and desire to understand things that were part of our makeup even when we were young boys. . . . My career has been somewhat successful and quite controversial, but most of all, it has allowed me to fuse creative and scientific inclinations in a constructive and disciplined way.

...

About the same time that Milgram was coproducing the social psychology films with Harry From, the idea for a different kind of movie was taking shape in the mind of George Bellak, a seasoned television dramatist, who had been the writer for a number of television series, including *The Defenders* and *The Untouchables*. When Bellak first read about the obedience experiments, he immediately became fascinated with them. He had been in the U.S. Army intelligence service during World War II, and the experiments resonated with him, since, as he put it, "I was as obsessed as Stanley with the question of cruelty to people, and the German situation, and the Jews and all that." So he decided to write a play dramatizing the experiments, the people involved, and the events surrounding them. The final result was a made-for-TV movie, *The Tenth Level,* starring William Shatner as the Milgram-like scientist.

The reaction to the film paralleled in many ways the earlier furor following the experiments themselves. Bellak wrote an outline of the story and tried to sell it on and off for four or five years, but no one would touch it. The most severe reaction was from the president of ABC, who found it fascinating but wouldn't have anything to do with it because he thought it was "Godless." Bellak took that comment to mean that the executive did not believe that people by nature were capable of such things, that God would never allow human beings to behave in this manner—and if He did, the news should not be disseminated widely.

Eventually, Bellak managed to get CBS interested in producing the play, for showing on its prime-time *Playhouse 90* program—at a cost of $300,000. It had been scheduled for the Christmas season of 1975, but it did not air until August 26, 1976, because it took that long to put together a group of sponsors for it. The more prestigious sponsors such as Xerox, IBM, and AT&T "wouldn't go near it with a ten-foot pole," recalls Bellak. On the other hand, Shatner believed so strongly in the play that he gave up being with his children—who lived with his divorced wife—on Christmas Day in order to perform in it.

CBS paid Milgram $5,000 to serve as a consultant, but he ended up having very little input and ultimately felt torn about it. As a film, he felt it was dull, with the "genuine drama underlying the obedience problem [getting] lost in the welter of video clichés." Indeed, the film is flawed, overburdened as it is by too many fictional elements that were added, presumably, for dramatic effect.

But the film is powerful, in its way, and it does effectively communicate the discrepancy between how far it was thought people would go in shocking the victim and how far they actually went; the anguish and turmoil of the participants; and the fact that Milgram could have stopped the experiments when he saw how distressed his subjects were, but didn't. The American Psychological Foundation saw enough merit in the film to give George Bellak honorable mention among its 1977 National Media Awards, "for increasing the public's knowledge and understanding of psychology." Milgram was glad that it helped spread knowledge about the obedience experiments, so he was not all that distressed about the film's shortcomings. He accepted them as the price one had to pay to get a national audience and, in fact, was delighted to get the attention.

In 1977, Addison-Wesley published a collection containing almost all of Milgram's writings up to that point, called *The Individual in a Social World: Essays and Experiments.* Milgram had a hard time finding a publisher, since books of readings were not generally lucrative, but he wanted a collection that would inform readers of the diversity of his accomplishments beyond the obedience experiments. He would take offense whenever someone would mention "the Milgram experiments," meaning the obedience experiments, in his presence—"Which one of my experiments are you talking about?" he would ask. He once told his brother, Joel, that he often felt like the actor James Arness, whom people only knew from his starring role in the television series *Gunsmoke,* and not from any of his other roles.

The articles in the book are organized into sections such as "The Individual in the City" and "The Individual and Authority." Each section begins with an introduction in which Milgram provides the historical background for the studies and how they fit in with the main themes of the section. These introductions are generally very useful, although occasionally self-serving as well—such as when he reproduces his notes from 1960 on some planned experiments on bystander intervention which "prefigured" the Kitty Genovese case.

The publication of such an anthology in midcareer was strangely prophetic. The flow of creative ideas was still there and would be for many years, but the truth of the matter is that, with two exceptions, Milgram did not report on any new innovative empirical work after that. But the two exceptions are interesting in their own right. The first involved the consequences of a particular kind of norm-breaking—cutting into line. And the second was his research on "cyranoids," which held out the promise of a completely fresh approach to an old topic in social psychology—how we form impressions of other people.

CHAPTER 11

VEXATIONS, CYRANOIDS, AND THE DECLINING YEARS

W HEN MILGRAM FIRST came to the Graduate Center in 1967, he was not planning to stay more than five years. But CUNY turned out to be much more stimulating than he expected, and he ended up remaining there for the rest of his career. The university's central location in one of the world's greatest cities made it an ideal place for Milgram's budding interest in the psychology of urban life to bloom and even branch out to study New Yorkers' mental maps of their city. As head of the social-personality program from 1967 to 1971, he was in a position to incorporate an urban emphasis into the curriculum. And it was at CUNY that his interest and talent in filmmaking, which had been dormant since his documentary *Obedience,* in 1965, was reawakened with the help of Harry From.

Much to his surprise and delight, by the mid-1970s, Milgram was doing very well financially—a combination of the fact that faculty salaries at CUNY were among the highest in the country and that the royalties from his books and films were substantial, as were his speaking fees, which, after the appearance of *Obedience to Authority,* typically netted $1,000–$2,000, plus expenses, per talk. He once confided to Harry From that he had earned $80,000 the previous year. "It was an impressive amount for him, and for me as well," From recalled. Stanley's brother Joel remembers that "Stanley was very, very pleased . . . in his peak financial years. It was a great source of pride to him and awe to me, because the notion of becoming a college professor was traditionally a very modest thing, if not close to poverty." A large proportion of his lucrative invited talks were related to his obedience research. Of the approximately 140 invited speeches and colloquia that Milgram gave during his lifetime, more than one-third dealt, directly or indirectly, with the topic. Milgram was still giving invited talks on the obedience experiments in 1984—twenty-two years after he had completed them.

Those experiments turned out to be both the boon and the bane of his career. On the one hand, he longed to put them behind him. As he wrote a childhood friend in 1976, "I started work on obedience in 1960, a long time ago, and it would be nice to move on. . . . But professional life turns you into a kind of snail, in which everything you do becomes another curl of your ever enlarging carapace." On the other hand, they had made him famous and added substantively to his income.

At the same time, Milgram's tenure at CUNY was also marked by periods of difficulty and frustration. The Graduate Center's finances rose and fell with New York City's as a whole. One such period cast a shadow of uncertainty over the university's very future. In an attempt to deal with a fiscal crisis in the spring of 1976, the university administration cut faculty salaries. "It appears," Milgram wrote Hollander, "as if we are about to enjoy a 1/12th pay cut, euphemistically termed a 'furlough,' (visions of happy army boys emerging joyously from chain-link fenced-in military bases as they scramble for the nearest bordello)."

During the late 1960s and early 1970s, many American campuses erupted with student dissent and black militancy. In their more extreme forms, these activities involved volatile confrontations with the administration, the occupation of campus buildings, disruption of classes, and destruction of property. Although some New York schools, such as Columbia University, were the epicenter of such activities, the Graduate Center—because it was a graduate school only—was largely unaffected by the disturbances.

Milgram was not opposed to the idea of the students' raising their voices to try to right a wrong, per se, something he regretted not doing at Queens College in the early 1950s when he and most of the students silently stood by as some of their favorite teachers were fired for refusing to testify about Communist Party membership before the Senate Internal Security Subcommittee chaired by Senator Joseph McCarthy. And he was in agreement with some of the goals of the student protests, such as nuclear disarmament and opposition to the Vietnam War. However, as he wrote Hollander, he was very disturbed by the extreme methods they used: "I deplore their strategy of acting out destructive adolescent fantasies on the institutions they know are least likely to strike back. . . . Somewhere a proper balance between concern and apathy must be struck and the line between ineffectual, amateurish protest which changes nothing, and violent, unlawful action which destroys everything must be determined."

While the Graduate Center was spared student protests, it was not completely untouched by them. As at many schools throughout the country, more and more students were now demanding social relevance—that their intellectual and academic concerns show some real impact on the contemporary social world—but Stanley would not give it to them. He regarded pure scientific research as a valuable pursuit in its own right—even if it only satisfied his own curiosity. So he continued with his innovative research, studying such things as the photographer-subject relationship, the social-psychological wisdom contained in the television program *Candid Camera*, pedestrian norms about staying to the right on the sidewalk, and whether or not strangers would reciprocate with a handshake if you extended your hand to them. For students looking for social relevance, these kinds of things "looked absolutely petty bourgeois," according to Harry From, and Milgram was not popular among such students.

Undoubtedly, though, one of the greatest vexations of Milgram's time at CUNY was the difficulty he repeatedly encountered in obtaining external grant support for his research. For an academician, successful grantsmanship is important for a number of reasons. First, of course, the grant provides the funds that make it possible to conduct planned research. Second, the scientific ego thrives on grants. Since grant proposals are typically reviewed by one's scientific peers, approval of a grant is a form of recognition of the merits of the applicant's work—much like the acceptance of an article in a peer-reviewed journal. Third, grants enhance the recipient's value to his or her school—literally. The money a grant brings in has two components. Most of it pays for "direct costs." This is the portion of the grant that benefits the researcher, or "principal investigator," directly paying for such things as his summer salary and the salaries of other staff, research subjects, and equipment. The second component of a grant consists of "indirect costs" or overhead. This is money that goes to the principal investigator's university to pay for the administrative costs and operating expenses it incurs in the support it provides for the research. In actuality, the university can use the money in any manner its president chooses. So grants bring in cash, not just cachet.

On March 29, 1977, Milgram submitted a very large grant proposal to the National Science Foundation. Although he had been awarded a small, internally funded grant of $10,000 by the Graduate Center for a small map study in 1975–1976, this grant, if approved, would be Milgram's first externally funded grant since the early 1970s, when he received funds from the French government for his Paris map study in 1973 and $260,000 from CBS for his television study in 1969. He was eager to get back in the game.

The NSF grant application, submitted to the agency's Ethics and Values in Society program, was to support the production of three educational films dealing with ethical issues in psychology, sociology, and biomedical research, respectively. Milgram's stated aim was to produce educational films "that will communicate ethical principles to students and practitioners in a way that is lively, interesting and informative."

There were also undoubtedly some unstated aims: The grant would afford him the opportunity to satisfy his recently discovered appetite for filmmaking. In particular, it would give him the chance to develop his directing skills, which he had not been able to do so far, since Harry From had directed all the films they had made together.

The films would also help heal Milgram's bruised ego, which had taken a beating from the relentless ethical criticisms of his obedience research. Students whom he was close with at CUNY in the 1970s were dumbfounded that he still seemed to be smarting from failing statistics at Harvard in the spring of 1957, the only time he failed anything in graduate school and, for that matter, in college. No doubt he still ached from Harvard's denial of tenure as well.

The continuing attacks on the obedience experiments irritated Milgram, not so much because of the substance of the criticism—he recognized that there could be reasonable disagreements on the issue—but because it meant that, to some extent, he had failed. He thought he had asked a legitimate question—How far would normal individuals go in obeying destructive orders?—and provided eye-opening answers, with built-in safeguards to protect the well-being of his subjects. The persistent questioning of the legitimacy of his methods meant that he had not been fully successful in his experimental efforts. He hoped to correct the situation by putting the ethical questions to rest through a film in which he planned to juxtapose his experiment with others generally regarded as blatantly unethical and deserving of thorny criticisms. In this way, he expected, his own research would look good.

The application requested a total of $263,994, for a two-and-a-half-year period, for the production of the three films. Of that figure, $222,810 constituted the "direct cost" component, and $41,884 the "indirect cost" or overhead paid to the university.

This proposal was a greatly expanded version of two much smaller film proposals, focusing on ethical issues in psychology only, that Milgram had submitted earlier. He had sent the first to the American Film Institute's Independent Filmmaker Program, an annual competition, on September 12, 1975. Although he was not among the forty-three winners, he was one of the finalists, a respectable accomplishment given the fact that there were 1,047 grant applications that year.

Next, Milgram proposed the film idea to Harper and Row Media, for whom he and Harry From had recently produced the four social psychology films. Although the company had been pleased with Milgram's previous work and shown an initial interest in producing additional films, no offer ever materialized.

The setting for each of the new films was to be a meeting of an ethical review board to evaluate three cases. The chairman would open the meeting by reminding its members "that its purpose is to review a number of cases, to clarify the underlying ethical issues, and to vote on whether each experiment in question should be run, and, if so, with what modifications." The chairman would then begin to describe the first case, and very soon his narrative account would change into a vivid reenactment of it.

In the National Science Foundation proposal Milgram did not specify the exact cases that would be depicted in the three films. However, based on earlier proposals to the American Film Institute and Harper and Row Media and his handwritten outlines, it is possible to guess which experiments he would have chosen for the psychology film. One would undoubtedly have been his own obedience research. The other two would have been experiments that were rife with ethical problems because of the unexpected, terrifying ordeal they had had put their subjects through.

In one, conducted in 1961, a group of army recruits, flying in a DC-6, were told they were going to have to crash-land because of malfunctioning landing gear. Ambulances and fire trucks could be seen racing toward the runway below. Meanwhile, aboard the plane an officer quickly distributed next-of-kin forms to the recruits. Then they were ordered to freeze into a head-between-the-knees position in preparation for a crash landing. When the plane landed, medical aides took urine samples from the frightened recruits. It was a faked emergency, designed to study how the body reacts to stress.

The second prospective case was a laboratory experiment reported in 1964 by some Canadian researchers. The subjects were male alcoholics who volunteered after they had been told—falsely—that the experiment was connected with a possible therapy for alcoholics. During the laboratory procedure they were unexpectedly injected with a drug, scoline, which made them stop breathing. Among the group of subjects, the duration of their respiratory paralysis ranged from 90 seconds to 130 seconds. Afterward, all of the subjects said that they thought they were dying. One subject compared what he went through to a wartime experience. During World War II he had been a rear-gunner on a bomber that, during one raid, had flown for 5,000 yards on a radar beam, straight and level over a German city. He considered his interrupted-breathing experience as the more traumatic of the two.

To ensure an objective and balanced treatment of the issues, Milgram asked an ethicist, Daniel Callahan, the director of the Institute of Society, Ethics, and the Life Sciences, to serve as a consultant. Callahan readily agreed, telling Milgram that his project was an excellent idea, since there was a lack of good films on research ethics. The ethics panel itself was to consist of psychologists "known for their concern and thoughtfulness on ethical issues" and representing a diversity of points of view on research ethics—for example, Herbert Kelman, Lawrence Kohlberg, and Stanley Schachter—as well as one or two non-psychologists, such as philosopher Robert Nozick and sociologist Orville Brim.

After the dramatization of each experiment, a discussion among members of the ethics panel would ensue. The viewing audience would then be invited to vote on the ethical acceptability of the depicted case. This would then be followed by an actual vote of the members of the ethics panel. In contrast to the rest of the film, the panel's discussion was to be an unrehearsed, spontaneous, and genuine expression of their viewpoints. While Milgram recognized that the success of the film depended to a large extent on the quality of the panelists' statements, he felt that this part of the film could be enhanced by dynamic editing of their discussion.

Milgram's proposal also included an evaluative component. He planned to assess the effectiveness of the films by testing the viewing audiences' shifts in attitudes and knowledge after viewing them. And, finally, the films would be modified on the basis of the outcome of the evaluations.

The film was to end with the following concluding comments by the narrator:

> With increasingly powerful experiments, the problems for psychology may soon approach the seriousness of the problems of medical research. So it is well that psychologists themselves focus their attention on ethical issues. For unless psychologists come to grips with these problems, others will assuredly move in, and we could well slide into a new dark age in which all experimentation on human beings is proscribed.
>
> A society that values scientific research, no less than it values individual rights, must create a climate to encourage such research. But for every impulse to explore and probe human nature with the tools of science, society must—if it is to call itself civilized—find the corresponding ethical balance.

The external reviewers to whom the proposal was sent included educational and documentary filmmakers as well as psychologists. Most of the

reviewers gave Milgram's proposal a favorable rating, although a few qualified that judgment. There was a general recognition of his uniqueness in
having dual qualifications in filmmaking and scientific research. A couple of
reviewers recommended that since Milgram had no expertise in sociology
or biomedical research, NSF should provide funding for the psychology
film only.

Despite the external reviewers' recommendations to approve the grant
proposal in whole or in part, it was ultimately rejected—mainly because the
amount Milgram requested represented a sizable chunk of the total budget
for the year. In June 1979, he submitted a trimmed-down version of the
grant. This one requested support for only one film, on ethical issues in psychology, rather than three, and the direct costs were reduced to about
$97,000. In addition, the revised proposal incorporated some suggestions
made by reviewers of the first proposal. The review panel would be more
heterogeneous, with the inclusion of women and more non-psychologists.
In addition, the wording of the concluding narration was toned down,
eliminating the reference to "a new dark age . . . in experimentation," which
one reviewer found "unnecessarily apocalyptic." Despite the changes, and
without any real explanation, this proposal was also turned down.

The second major grant proposal that Milgram prepared in this period
was to support research on "cyranoids"—the name he gave to persons who
serve as mediums of communication in an invented social situation. Milgram defined a cyranoid as "a person who does not speak thoughts originating in his own central nervous system: rather, the words that he speaks
originate in the mind of another person who transmits these words to the
cyranoid by means of a . . . tiny FM receiver with connecting earphones fitted inconspicuously in his ear."

In the cyranic mode of interaction Milgram devised, there are three participants: the source, the person who is originating the speech; the cyranoid
or medium, the person who shadows the source's talk and passes it on to the
third person; and the interactant or listener, the person to whom the speech
is directed. Milgram used the term "cyranoid" because of the similarity of
his model to a form of mediated speech that occurs in the famous balcony
scene in *Cyrano de Bergerac*, Edmond Rostand's nineteenth-century drama.

In that scene, Christian, a love-struck but inarticulate soldier, declares his love for Roxanne in a romantic recital as he stands below her balcony. However, his speech is not his own—he is merely repeating word-for-word the sentences whispered to him by Cyrano, who is hiding in the shadows.

Milgram carried out some preliminary studies with the cyranic mode in his Media class on November 4, 1977. He described those initial efforts in a notebook in which he would jot down various ideas for films, inventions, and experiments. His notebook entry, titled "The Person as Medium: Studies in the Cyranic Mode," describes that initial effort with the technique as "spectacularly effective in that the medium appeared to carry on a very natural conversation, although he was merely tracking the words of the source. I believe the technique has many interesting applications both for theoretical studies and for practical training possibilities. In social psychology it may be used in studies of person perception, attribution theory, prejudice, etc. A 15 year old dropout suddenly acquires a mature scientific mode of speech. A shy person suddenly interacts with a beautiful girl, with a knowing and sophisticated line."

To help him conduct research on cyranoids on a larger scale, in February 1979 Milgram submitted a grant proposal to the National Science Foundation's program in Social and Developmental Psychology, the section of the granting agency that sponsored basic, mainstream research in social psychology. In this proposal, titled "The Technique of Mediated Speech as a Tool in Social Psychology," he requested about $200,000 for a two-year period. The program director at the time was Kelly Shaver, a social psychologist known for his work on an aspect of the attribution process in social perception—how we arrive at judgments of responsibility and blame when we try to understand people's actions. When Milgram submitted the grant proposal, he sent Shaver a cover letter informing him that he had some video footage from his pilot studies that he could send. He felt that the tapes would be useful in conveying the power of the cyranic procedure to the program's advisory panel. Shaver accepted Milgram's offer and told him to go ahead and send a copy to have on hand in case the advisory panel wanted to see it. The proposal was sent to a group of external ad hoc reviewers who then sent their written evaluations to Shaver to help him and his standing advisory panel make their evaluations during their next meeting in May. The reactions of the eight external readers varied, but there were some common threads. Many commented on the brilliance of Milgram's prior contributions to social psychology. Reviewers generally agreed that the cyranic technique was imaginative. But most of them also agreed that the theoretical basis for the experiments—and the specific ones he proposed—were weak.

Part of Milgram's genius, as reflected in his past research, was to identify questions worth pursuing and then, if needed, invent methods suited for them. Here, a number of reviewers pointed out, he had reversed things. He had come up with a clever technique and was now searching for a phenomenon to apply it to. Milgram had proposed a mixture of studies focusing on basic social processes as well as more practical applications—without any attempt at theoretical integration. One of the "basic" studies he proposed dealt with attitude change, a topic with a long history in social psychology. His idea was to create an experiment with two different conditions. In one condition, a subject would give a persuasive talk to a group. In the other, the subject would try to influence a different group using the cyranic mode. He would now be a cyranic medium, with the source being an expert on the issue being discussed. Milgram's purpose was to test whether or not a speech presented in the cyranic mode would be more persuasive than one given in a normal fashion.

It is evident that Milgram did not apply much thought to this experiment, because, as several reviewers correctly noted, the design contains a blatant "confound" which makes any significant difference between the two communication situations completely uninterpretable. If, for example, audiences were more persuaded in the cyranic condition, was it due to the difference in the mode of communication, per se, or to the fact that in the cyranic condition, but not in the "normal" condition, an expert was involved?

Another one of Milgram's planned studies had a more applied focus. He wanted to demonstrate the usefulness of the cyranic mode in emergency situations, such as hostage taking. The person speaking with the hostage taker might not have the necessary skills to negotiate well. Equipped with the cyranic apparatus, he could be guided word-for-word by an expert negotiator who was not able to be physically present.

The reaction of one reviewer who recommended rejecting the proposal was representative of most:

> It seems obvious that the PI [principal investigator] has become fascinated with a method he has invented and is seeking uses to which it can be put. Unfortunately, it seems to me that none of the studies he proposes will illuminate our understanding of social behavior in any substantial way. And I find that especially unfortunate because the PI is someone who in the past has made important contributions to our field.

After he received NSF's boilerplate rejection letter on July 30, 1979, Milgram was steamed to learn that the review panel did not see the videotape he had provided Shaver. Milgram felt that, because of the newness of the technique, it could not be properly evaluated without actually seeing it work. He therefore asked Shaver for a reconsideration of the proposal after the advisory panel watched the videotape of his pilot studies.

The directorship of the Social and Developmental Psychology Program has generally been a rotating position. As Milgram was trying to get his proposal reevaluated, Shaver was leaving and another social psychologist, Robert A. Baron, was coming on board for a two-year stint. Baron was familiar to social psychologists because of his research on aggression and because he was (and still is) the coauthor of one of the most successful social psychology textbooks.

Baron was very accommodating, going beyond a mere reconsideration of Milgram's proposal. He told Milgram that he would accept it as a resubmission, which meant that he would solicit external reviews from a completely new set of readers. He also assured Milgram that the videotape would have a role in the review process.

Milgram resubmitted the proposal, with some minor textual changes, at the end of November. In an accompanying letter to Baron he suggested the names of some prospective outside reviewers (a practice generally encouraged by the foundation) who, he claimed, had done work "in fields touched upon by the cyranic technique." Actually, their more apparent unifying characteristic was that most of them were former colleagues from Yale and Harvard.

The list of names included Roger Brown, Irving Janis, Philip Zimbardo, Jerome Bruner, and Eleanor Rosch (a former research assistant at Harvard).

In this set of reactions, the extremes were more divergent than in the first. At one end was a reviewer who judged it "a stunningly interesting proposal," while at the other was a reviewer who wrote, "This is the weakest proposal that I can recall receiving in 18 years of reviewing proposals for NSF." But the central theme was the same: Milgram had developed a clever technique and was now searching for phenomena to apply it to, and the studies he proposed were short on theoretical significance. One reviewer, who considered Milgram to be one of the most important thinkers in social psychology, hit the nail on the head when he wrote: "Milgram is here the clever kid who has been given a clever hammer and now needs something that needs pounding. . . . I, for one, am not yet prepared to defend this proposal when Senator Proxmire nominates it for a Golden Fleece. A quarter of a million dollars for a mechanized ventriloquist. I can see it now."

Based on the generally negative reactions of the outside reviewers, Baron's advisory panel recommended rejection. Baron informed Milgram of the bad tidings in a letter that was almost apologetic. He had taken every step to make sure that the proposal received a fair review, he wrote Milgram. This included showing the tape to the panel and choosing most of the external reviewers from Milgram's list. Apparently, loyalty to Milgram did not blind his friends to the proposal's failings.

While Milgram's lack of success in getting grant support was undoubtedly disappointing, he could not really fault the reviewers' criticisms, because he also had similar reservations about the cyranoid technique, as indicated in a letter he wrote to a former CUNY colleague, Stuart Albert, on October 8, 1983:

It's a phenomenon that remains intriguing, though its exact scientific significance is elusive. Sometimes I suspect it's more a theatrical than a scientific phenomenon, evoking artistic wonder, rather than serving as a source of scientific propositions. But I'm uncertain and will explore it further. . . . The main problem in all this has been to define the key issues and figure out exactly what should be measured. Here is a paradigm in which the independent variable (the functioning cyranoid) is inherently fascinating, but where the compelling dependent measure is less clear.

Milgram did explore the phenomenon further in the spring of 1984 with the help of a small internal grant of $5,000 from CUNY. One of the important findings to emerge from this research was people's strong tendency to seek unity and coherence when forming impressions of other people. Milgram found that interviewers of the cyranoids tended to perceive a coherent personality despite very large differences between the cyranoid and the sender; for example, a fifty-year-old psychology professor performing as sender and a twelve-year-old boy as a cyranoid. No one suspected that the cyranoid's words were not his own. In another experiment, when several different people alternated serving as senders to the same cyranoid, no one perceived a fragmented personality.

Despite Ralph Waldo Emerson's pronouncement that "a foolish consistency is the hobgoblin of little minds," the need for consistency is a hallmark of human nature. Our relentless search for consistency and harmony when presented with contradictory information derives from a need to simplify our complex world and make it more predictable. Thus, for example, social psychologists have repeatedly demonstrated the operation of the simplifying principle "What is beautiful is good" in human perception—that is, we believe that outward appearance and inner character go together. In a different vein, an inconsistency between cause and effect—for example, a huge, important outcome having a small, insignificant cause—is jarring to the mind: According to some social psychologists, this may explain the enduring belief in conspiracy theories about the Kennedy assassination among a large segment of the population. Milgram's cyranoid research showed—in a highly inventive manner—just how *powerful* this simplifying and unifying tendency is in human behavior.

...

In January 1980, Milgram was appointed Distinguished Professor of Psychology at CUNY. The nomination process had been initiated in 1974 by

Florence Denmark, who was then executive officer of the Ph.D. programs in psychology at CUNY, but the funding for the appointment did not become available until six years later. This was soon followed by a joyous event of a different sort. On January 26, Marc became a Bar Mitzvah at the Riverdale Temple. After services, the festivities continued at the Milgrams' apartment with a catered lunch for about sixty guests, arranged by Sasha. Michele had had her confirmation at the same temple about six months earlier, on June 3, 1979.

On February 17, about thirty students and alumni threw a dinner party for the Milgrams at the Hungarian Rendezvous restaurant in Manhattan to celebrate Stanley's appointment. The next monthly meeting of the social-personality faculty began with a toast by Irwin Katz, expressing the faculty's pleasure over Milgram's award. A small group of colleagues took Milgram out to lunch to mark the occasion, but they made no mention of his distinguished professor award during the meal, a fact that irked Milgram. After all, he was the first—and at that time the only—psychologist at the Graduate Center to achieve the status of distinguished professor.

Several months later, on a bright and inviting May day, Stanley decided to go bicycle riding in the hilly park across from their apartment building. This was the first time he had gone riding since the fall, and he stayed out for quite a long time—too long, as it turned out. When Sasha walked out to meet him, he asked her to take the bicycle back for him. After placing the bike in the basement storage area, she returned to the apartment to find Stanley lying in bed, reading about the symptoms of a heart attack in a medical book. Sasha immediately whisked him off to the emergency department at Columbia-Presbyterian Hospital in Manhattan, a ten-minute drive from their home. Stanley was having a massive coronary attack.

Although he had discovered he had high blood pressure in 1975 and had been taking medication for it, with Sasha keeping him on a low-salt diet, the heart attack was acute and came without warning. At first, things looked bleak, but Stanley ended up making a good recovery and was discharged from the hospital after a two-and-a-half-week stay. By mid-July he was able to walk a few miles a day. Caution led him to forgo a planned trip to Europe in August, however, and the family vacationed in the Berkshires instead.

While he was in intensive care, he received a get well note from Roger Brown. After returning home, Stanley wrote him a thank you letter in which he described a conversation with a physician named Francis Minot Weld.

> After some small talk, he whipped out informed consent sheets and asked if I would serve in his experimental project. How ironic this solicitation seemed. The tables turned. . . . Results of the tests would be correlated with post-hospital survival rates. After some soul searching and consultation with my cardiologist, I consented: a fitting penance, I thought. It all went very well, but, of course, the most delicate part of the study lies ahead: for to obtain the survival data they must periodically call my home and discreetly inquire whether I am still of this world. I suppose that part will be relegated to a graduate student.

He was soon able to resume his normal activities—teaching, conducting research, and giving invited talks around the country. However, his heart condition restricted him to flying only in pressurized airplanes. Conventional jetliners had pressurized cabins, but smaller, propeller-driven puddle jumpers did not, which effectively ruled out any further speaking engagements at colleges located in small towns or rural areas.

About a year later, on June 23, 1981, Milgram had another heart attack, and again landed in Columbia-Presbyterian Hospital for a two-week stay. In August he had an angiogram, which revealed a fundamental problem that did not bode well for his longevity. The test showed that his arteries were too blocked for bypass surgery to be done. A heart transplant was considered, but after weighing the pros and cons, Stanley decided against it.

He was glad to resume his regular activities when the fall semester began, but his deteriorating heart condition was slowly taking its toll. He didn't have the stamina of his pre–heart attack days, and the medication he was taking made him even more tired. Sometimes when he was walking, he would have to stop to catch his breath. His libido was weakening, and he was despondent. Friends would hear him lamenting that his accomplishments were all behind him. He wrote to Hollander, "As far as work goes, the past seems brighter than the future."

His heart attacks led to a drastic change in his demeanor, which was visible to virtually everyone close to him. The more biting aspects of his personality became dulled. He mellowed, became less sarcastic, more sensitive to people's feelings. He became more subdued, contemplative, and sentimental. His brother Joel recalls:

> The . . . true intimate closeness, not counting childhood, started with his first heart attack. . . . He talked about the pain of writing. We talked about our parents. He talked about the qualities he admired in me. A lot of these things were absolutely stunning. I think the stunning thing was not so much the information, but the quality of the conversation. Suddenly, he wasn't [just an] older brother. . . . I think it was a dying man talking to his brother."

As his condition gradually worsened, he felt the need to take some time off. He applied for, and was granted, a sabbatical leave for the spring of 1982. Under normal circumstances, he probably would have taken the sabbatical abroad, most likely in France. But, after two heart attacks, a tranquil respite seemed more sensible, and he spent his time mostly around Riverdale. He bought an IBM personal computer and took advantage of his free time to learn BASIC, becoming a "dedicated micro-maven."

He reflected on his newly discovered interest in a letter to Moscovici:

> A confession, Serge: I have been seduced by my computer. It is odd that I have worked in computer environments for at least 20 years, but it was not until the micro-computer appeared, that a personal interest was evoked. I do think a significant techno-intellectual shift is underway. I was astonished to learn how accomplished both of my children are in programming. It is a skill that an entire generation of adolescents is learning underground, much the way we used to pick up dirty words.

Acquiring computer skills gave him a lot of satisfaction, but he was even happier that, in the fall, he felt well enough to go back to his teaching and research at the Graduate Center.

Stanley had missed his teaching as much as his research. Unlike some academic scientists for whom teaching is a mere afterthought, Milgram took these responsibilities very seriously. As one of his students, Eva Fogelman, said, "Teaching for him—being a professor—was a way of life. It wasn't just a job." Arthur Weinberger, a doctoral student, recalled that "he was brilliant as a teacher. . . . He could be dictatorial, he could be authoritarian, he could turn on a dime." But if you were looking for intellectual stimulation and wanted to learn to do original work in social psychology, Milgram was the person to go to. For Ronna Kabatznick, being a student in Milgram's classes "remains one of the most exhilarating experiences of my life. . . . He spoke so fluently and so succinctly about psychology. . . . He was able to explain [things] in a way that was so compelling. His classes were always a lot of fun and stimulating . . . and he was always thoroughly prepared and very methodical in his teaching." His colleague, Irwin Katz, summed it up this way:

> He was a superb teacher. I know because we sometimes taught together. He could inspire students to delight in the recognition of an idea, and in the discovery of a new idea. He taught many students—all those who had a bent for it—how to enjoy the playful side of good intellectual endeavor.
>
> For Stanley had a light touch in his approach to research. I think one of his deepest motives as a psychologist had to do with the pleasure that came with discovering things about the social world that were too obvious to be seen by others. His interest in human ways and in the people around him was insatiable. All of this delight in the scientific uses of ordinary curiosity—in the indulgence of an almost childlike wonder about social life—he conscientiously nurtured in his students. His goal as a teacher was always to bring forth their latent creativeness.

In the fall, Michele began her freshman year at Vassar and decided to major in cognitive science, which consisted of a blend of computer science, linguistics, philosophy, psychology, and anthropology. Stanley told friends that he and Sasha had hoped to send her to the more affordable State University of New York, but Michele was so excited about Vassar that they decided "it was worth flirting with bankruptcy."

Marc was now fifteen, a junior in high school. Both he and Michele were very good with computers. He had recently figured out the solution to an intellectually challenging computer game, called "Adventure." When he offered through computer magazines to sell the solution, he got responses from more than forty customers across the country. Two years later, in the fall of 1984, he would begin his first semester at Brandeis, majoring in computer science, after scoring in the 99th percentile in math on the Scholastic Aptitude Test (SAT).

Sasha went to work full time as a social worker in the Washington Heights office of Selfhelp Community Services, an agency serving the needs of elderly Holocaust survivors. She had worked outside the home before this, but only on a part-time, volunteer basis. She had earned a master's degree in social work (M.S.W.) from Smith College at the end of the summer in 1964, but Michele was born that November, and Marc came along in January 1967. While the children were growing up, Sasha had been too busy being a homemaker to work full time as a professional. In 1979 and 1980, she did social work two mornings a week at the Fairfield Division of the Hebrew Home for the Aged in Riverdale. Before that, from 1972 to 1981, she had helped Stanley periodically in his office at the Graduate Center. Sasha had occasionally contemplated becoming a full-time social worker, but after Michele was accepted at Vassar, merely thinking about the possibility of working was no longer sufficient. Vassar's pricey tuition required an infusion of income into the Milgram household, so Sasha found the job at Selfhelp Community Services.

Her work at the community agency included individual counseling, group sessions, and advising clients about entitlement programs—and she found it very rewarding. When Stanley wrote their friends about Sasha's new job, he oriented them about its location by noting that Washington Heights was Henry Kissinger's old neighborhood, "but he hasn't become a client—yet."

While Milgram followed a strict diet and made a conscious effort to reduce stress, once he returned to the Graduate Center in the fall of 1982 he resumed most of the activities that had engaged him before his heart attack. He carried a full load of two courses each semester and supervised four doctoral dissertations. He readily slipped back into his role as an active departmental citizen. Early in the fall semester, after a faculty member with a very large research program left, the administration took away seven of his eleven office spaces from the department. It was the department's consensus that Milgram and another faculty member were the right people to meet with the provost in an effort to reclaim the offices for their program. Toward the end of the semester, when the faculty was considering offering an M.A. degree in social-personality psychology in addition to the Ph.D., it was Milgram whom they authorized to initiate discussions with the administration.

In his research, he turned to exploring some new phenomena. Even as his health diminished, his intellectual vitality and experimental inventiveness remained intact. Before the semester began, he was completing a report of an experiment he had conducted with his students on responses to "cutting" into waiting lines. "We had collected some impressive data," he wrote Alan Elms, "but the challenge was to transcend the inherent banality of the subject matter through insightful analysis of the phenomenon. (How insightful we got remains to be seen)."

He met the challenge mightily. The article was accepted in the *Journal of Personality and Social Psychology*, the highly selective flagship journal of those fields, which had a rejection rate of about 90 percent.

During the fall semester of 1982, his Urban Psychology class conducted research on the "vertical city." In 1970, in his article, "The Experience of Living in Cities," Milgram had shown how the behavior of urbanites differs from that of small-town dwellers. Now, twelve years later, he made an analogous comparison—although on a smaller scale—between the "vertical city" and the "flat city." How, he asked, does living in a skyscraper modify thinking and behavior? What effect, if any, does the vertical life have on human relationships?

Milgram's mastering of the PC during his sabbatical opened up a whole new world of possibilities for experimental investigation. His first effort involved bringing Asch's work into the computer age. In the spring semester of 1983, students in his seminar in Experimental Social Psychology conducted a computer version of Asch's conformity experiment. Instead of placing the naïve subject amid a group of confederates, the majority's erroneous judgments were presented to him or her on a computer screen. Sometimes the subjects were told that the responses flashing on the screen came from network contact with other participants, whereas in other conditions they were led to believe that the personalities they were interacting with existed only in the computers. "It is an interesting approach," he reported to Roger Brown, "because it is possible to build enough Artificial Intelligence into the program so that the computer appears to be aware of what you have said, and is able to respond appropriately, which corresponds to the essence of sociality. Last week the students were analyzing the data and were heard to shout 'Eureka' up and down the corridors."

During the spring semester of 1983, Milgram also had a chance to renew his contact with Jerome Bruner, who had recently accepted a professorship at the New School for Social Research in Manhattan. Energized by the experience, he wrote Roger Brown that their mutual friend "is more interesting to talk with than just about anyone in town. There is a certain intellectual resonance that gets going in conversations with Jerry that is, as you know, very special."

The spring semester had a surprise ending for Milgram. On May 11, 1983, he received a letter from the American Academy of Arts and Sciences—a venerable institution founded in 1780 by John Adams—informing him that he had been elected as a Fellow. Milgram had long ago resigned himself to the fact that the controversy stirred up by his obedience research would make it virtually impossible for him to achieve any type of national recognition, so this honor came as an especially delightful surprise.

Marc was entering his senior year of high school in the fall, so, in anticipation of his entering college in the fall of 1984, the Milgrams began their summer vacation investigating some prospective schools in the Boston area, after which they drove to a rental house in Eastham on Cape Cod. A string of beautiful, sunny days enabled them to explore the magnificent beaches nearby. In the evenings they would go to First Encounter Beach to watch the sun setting over the bay. Milgram described one especially memorable evening to their friends:

A fresh wind brought out the kite flyers. The tide was out so it was possible to walk a half mile from the shore and still be only ankle deep in water. Seagrass growing far from the shore sprouted from the receding water. The sun drifted lower, and soon fires were lit on the shore, and children's voices, though originating far away, sounded close. Kites darted in the evening sky. The ocean air was intoxicating. Then a moment of poetic excess: A horse and rider galloped far out on the bay, spray shooting up wherever its hoofs hit pools of water.

On August 15, Stanley turned fifty. By now the Milgrams were back home in Riverdale. They considered throwing a big half century party, but while it sounded fun in the abstract, they couldn't cope with the logistics. Instead, some of Stanley's students took him out to lunch, and in the evening, Sasha invited a few neighbors over for a glass of champagne.

In the fall of 1983, with 1984 and its Orwellian significance just over the horizon, Milgram began receiving and accepting a flurry of invitations to speak about the relationship between his obedience research and the highly regimented, authoritarian society envisioned in Orwell's novel. In fact, had it not been for the travel limitations imposed by his heart condition, he would have been snowed under an even higher number of such talks. During the 1983–1984 academic year, most of the talks he gave at various colleges around the country were connected to *1984*.

One exception was the Catherine Genovese Memorial Conference held at the Lincoln Center campus of Fordham University in March 1984. Organized by Harold Takooshian, it brought together experts from the social sciences and law and public officials to commemorate and contemplate the urban tragedy of Kitty Genovese's murder. Keynote speeches were given by Surgeon General C. Everett Koop and the directors of the National Institute of Mental Health and the National Institute of Justice. In his comments, Milgram noted why, in his view, Genovese's murder had received so much attention:

> The case touched on a fundamental issue of the human condition, our primordial nightmare. If we need help, will those around us stand around and let us be destroyed or will they come to our aid? Are those other creatures there to help us sustain our life and values or are we individual flecks of dust just floating around in a vacuum?

As the spring semester came to a close, Sasha and Stanley wanted to recapture the magical vacation experience of the previous summer on Cape Cod. So they rented a comfortable house in Wellfleet and arrived in mid-June. A week later, on the evening of June 30, Stanley suffered a third massive heart attack. An ambulance rushed him to the nearest hospital, in Hyannis, about thirty-three miles away. Earlier in the day, he had been going up and down the sand dunes on the beach. The doctors at the hospital told him that, with his heart condition, he shouldn't have engaged in such vigorous activity, which had undoubtedly brought on the attack.

Less than a month later, on July 18, Stanley suffered yet another heart attack. They were now back in Riverdale, and Sasha drove him to Columbia-Presbyterian Hospital. He landed in the hospital in the midst of a strike by nonmedical personnel. Milgram was miserable enough, but the strikers' mode of protest was to pound on drums outside the windows. Sometimes the noisemakers started as early as 6:45 A.M., and their drum strokes continued late into the night. Milgram expressed his indignation at the protesters' behavior in a guest column in *The Riverdale Press*. While he sympathized with the hospital workers' demands and deemed them reasonable, he found their noisemaking, day after day, to be abhorrent. "To all those recuperating—or failing to recuperate—on my floor," he wrote, "the noise was a serious irritant, interfering with the rest and tranquillity needed after a heart attack. One wondered how workers involved in patient care could adopt so callous an attitude."

Milgram stayed in the hospital for two weeks and then continued his recuperation at home. His sense of humor did not falter. In a thank you card he designed and sent to well-wishers, he wrote:

There is a little confusion as to whether I had one or two heart attacks this summer. I managed two, one in Cape Cod in June and the second, while recovering from the first, in New York. (The latter attack is, of course, subject to the 8.25% sales tax.)

Recovery usually takes about six weeks, so that barring further incident, I should be able to resume teaching in the fall. Meanwhile, like Menachem B., I'm more or less in restful seclusion. I'm glad to get your notes and letters, and regret only that I cannot give each the personal response it deserves.

Warm regards and best wishes,
Stanley
Riverdale, August 1984

The back of the card read as follows:

A Contemporary
Greeting Cardiac
c. 1984

Although the content of the card was identical for all recipients, Milgram managed to personalize it by inserting the well-wisher's name into a balloon next to his photograph, which appeared on the front of the card (see Figure 11.1).

The previous spring, Milgram had continued his research on cyranoids with students in his Experimental Social Psychology class, aided by a small $5,000 internal grant from CUNY. He had also accepted an invitation to talk about his cyranoids research as part of a symposium titled "New Paradigms in Psychology" at the annual convention of the American Psychological Association (APA), which was being held in Toronto from August 24 through August 28. The organizer of that program was James Pennebaker, a social psychologist whose research had shown that writing about troubling life events provided an emotional release that could improve a person's physical and mental health. He got wind of Milgram's research from his CUNY colleague, Susan Kobasa; the APA talk would be Milgram's first public air-

FIGURE 11.1   One of the Personalized Thank You Cards
Milgram Sent to Well-Wishers After His Fourth Heart Attack.

ing of the cyranoid research. Unfortunately, by late August, Milgram's health
worsened, and he was too ill to travel by plane. Still, he was able to give his
talk in absentia by means of an audiotape he sent to Pennebaker. Members
of the audience found themselves in the somewhat bizarre situation of hearing Milgram's disembodied voice emanating from a tape recorder placed on
the dais alongside the other (live) presenters.

By the beginning of the fall semester he was back at CUNY. Much to
Sasha's surprise, Stanley's cardiologist had allowed him to resume teaching.
Anyone viewing Milgram's activities from a distance would no doubt have
considered the semester a typical one: He was teaching a normal course
load; he continued writing letters of recommendation for his doctoral students seeking jobs. He was completing some research papers. He gave Hollander detailed and nuanced feedback on his writing, as he had always
done, and, with the help of a graduate student, he was trying to recruit subjects for more cyranoid studies. He even undertook a totally new project
midsemester: organizing a conference titled "The Everyday Culture of New
York City" to be held sometime in 1985.

But, in actuality, he was a very sick man. He was no longer capable of walking to and from his commuter train station, as he had in the past. Sasha now had to drive him there in the morning and pick him up when he returned from the Graduate Center in the afternoon. By the time of his fourth heart attack—the second one of the past summer—he had only 17 percent of the normal amount of blood pumping from his heart.

How did he keep going during his final difficult years? He had three sources of strength. First and foremost was the constant support of Sasha. Stanley paid tribute to her in their annual end-of-the-year letter in December 1984, in which, referring to the first heart attack he had earlier that year, he wrote:

Anyone looking at the experience would say it was awful, but this is only part of the story. Adversity brings its own epiphanies. While in the hospital on the Cape, Sasha drove sixty-six miles daily to bring me her love and support. Was anyone ever blessed with more love and devotion? How keenly it is felt at such times.

A second source was his work—going in to school and sticking to his academic routine as much as possible. As his colleague Irwin Katz said:

I was very impressed by the way he handled his illness. . . . I had never seen a contemporary go through this kind of ordeal, this experience. You know, some people withdraw, some people become self-absorbed, some people become passive. He stayed with his work, he stayed with his students, he maintained his interest in the world around him and other people.

A third source of fortitude came from a deeper involvement in Judaism. Stanley had always had a strong sense of Jewish identity, although he didn't wear it on his sleeve. In fact, it was sometimes an off-the-cuff remark that revealed the sturdiness of that identity, as exemplified by an exchange a few years earlier between Milgram and Chas Smith. At the start of the fall semester in 1977, Smith, who was then head of the social-personality program, sent a memo to members of the program's executive committee noting that because Rosh Hashanah fell on September 14 that year, the orientation for new students initially scheduled for that day was being moved to September 16. However, he wanted to leave an executive committee meeting scheduled for that day unchanged, because there was a lot of important business to discuss. Milgram, who was on that committee, replied to Smith:

> *Dear Chas,*
> *Sorry for the inconvenience, but this particular holiday was scheduled 5738 years ago, and therefore has my prior commitment. I'd appreciate rescheduling. . . .*

Stanley was a firm supporter of Israel and worried about its survival. After the daring rescue by Israeli commandos of Jewish hostages in Entebbe, Uganda, in July 1976, Milgram wrote a letter to the Israeli prime minister expressing his pride and solidarity. Characteristically, he had ended his letter by saying that words were nothing; only actions counted, so he was going out to purchase Israeli bonds. And whenever there was a death in the family of close friends, he and Sasha would typically buy trees in Israel in memory of the deceased. They did that, for example, when the father of Irwin Katz's wife Lois died. They wrote her: "We've taken the liberty of planting some trees in Israel in [your father's] memory, saplings to bring new life to Galilee, Bethlehem, Jerusalem. . . ." He participated in the grassroots letter-writing campaign to the Russian ambassador to try to free the imprisoned Jewish dissident Natan Sharansky.

Over the years, Stanley had spent a good deal of time and effort tracing his Hungarian Jewish roots. He discovered that the name Milgram comes from the Yiddish word for pomegranate, one of the seven fruits native to the land of Israel mentioned in the Torah (in Deuteronomy 8:8). "Thus, the Milgrams were 'lovers of Israel'," he once explained with apparent pride, and "the pomegranate (*rimon* in Hebrew) is also a symbol for the Torah." Through genealogical research he was able to construct family trees of his father's and his mother's families and make contact with a cousin in Romania and find and visit an aunt and cousins living in Israel.

But now, during the last few years, he moved beyond what had been a largely cultural identification with Judaism. He never turned into a practicing, observant Jew, but he became increasingly interested in the more religious and spiritual aspects of Judaism. For example, he began to study the Torah from time to time. This change in his orientation toward Judaism was a result of his contact with Rabbi Avi Weiss, the activist rabbi of a modern Orthodox congregation, the Hebrew Institute of Riverdale. For a number of years, Rabbi Weiss had conducted an outreach service for the community on Rosh Hashana and Yom Kippur afternoons, and one year the Milgrams decided to attend and found it very inspiring. Milgram's deepening involvement with his Jewish roots can be seen in a fascinating children's story he wrote in 1983 and delighted in telling some of his colleagues and students about. It is called "When a Boy Becomes a Man," and is told from the perspective of a twelve-year-old boy who decides not to have a Bar Mitzvah celebration. A chance encounter with a Russian Jew who left his country because of the restrictions on the study and the observance of Judaism leads him to a change of heart and a greater appreciation of Jewish tradition.

Here is how Stanley concluded the end-of-the-year letter he and Sasha sent to friends in December 1983:

Now we are back in Riverdale, grateful that the year has been so kind to us, and wondering about the future. Sometimes a little Chasidic song comes to mind. It consists of only ten words in Hebrew but is swelled by translation. It is a good message for this time of the year:

> *The whole world*
> *Is a very narrow bridge*
> *But the main thing to recall*
> *Is to have no fear at all.*

...

On Thursday afternoon, December 20, 1984, Stanley chaired the successful oral defense of the doctoral dissertation of one of his students, Christina

Taylor. After the meeting, at about 4:00 P.M., he told Irwin Katz, who was also on the doctoral committee, that he wasn't feeling very well. Katz suggested they try to get a cab to take him to the nearest hospital. Milgram didn't want to do that. "Sasha is waiting and I don't want to disappoint her," he told Katz. So Katz walked Stanley to Grand Central Station and insisted on accompanying him on the commuter train ride to Riverdale. During the half-hour train ride, Stanley regaled Katz with funny stories. Katz thought he was doing this both to divert his own attention from his physical condition and to set Katz at ease. When they got to Riverdale, Sasha was waiting, and she drove them immediately to Columbia-Presbyterian Hospital. When they arrived at the emergency department, Stanley walked up to the desk and said, "My name is Stanley Milgram. This is my ID. I believe I'm having my fifth heart attack."

Even as he lay in the emergency room near death, Stanley's humor did not abandon him: He asked his cardiologist if they happened to have a baboon's heart available—a reference to the recent case of "Baby Fae," who survived for twenty days with a transplanted baboon heart.

He died within the hour, his heart muscles finally giving way. He was fifty-one.

CHAPTER 12

MILGRAM'S LEGACY

AMERICAN PSYCHOLOGY HAS had a love-hate relationship with Stanley Milgram. His obedience research has become a classic of modern psychology. It is a "must" topic for introductory psychology and social psychology courses, and any textbook for those courses that failed to mention those studies would be considered incomplete. Social psychologists invariably invoke the results of the obedience experiments whenever they feel the need to affirm that the discipline can reveal something about social behavior that is not predictable from common sense. As Roger Brown put it, "Is there any social psychologist who teaches who is not damn glad that he has the Milgram experiment to teach? He legitimizes our enterprise."

A recent study ranked Milgram as one of the 100 most eminent psychologists of the twentieth century. Yet the APA never gave him one of its annual awards for Distinguished Scientific Contributions, its most prestigious award. Recipients include Gordon Allport, Irving Janis, Leon Festinger, Roger Brown, Solomon Asch, Jerome Bruner, and Elliot Aronson—and even a former Harvard classmate of Milgram's, Saul Sternberg. Most writings on the history of psychology make only passing mention of Milgram, if they include him at all. These slights are at odds with the fact that references to Milgram's writings by scholars and researchers continue unabated.

Yet Milgram is at least partly to blame for the fact that some of the conventional, "establishment" forms of recognition eluded him. It had a lot to do with the impression he created among some psychologists of a dilettante who flitted from one newsworthy phenomenon to the next, not staying with any long enough to probe it in adequate depth. Even those with a more favorable view of Milgram's accomplishments are not likely to think of him foremost as someone who did programmatic, time-consuming research.

Some odd publication decisions also contributed to this impression. Milgram never published his massive cross-cultural conformity study in a scholarly journal; completely flouting the norms of scientific publication, he published it only in *Scientific American*. Because scholarly readers do not normally expect a magazine to be the primary—or sole—publication vehicle for the presentation of original research, for a long time psychologists remained unaware of the conformity studies and the extensive program of research they represented. Analogously, Milgram's first article about the small-world method was published not in a scientific journal but in *Psychology Today* in 1967; his reports of this research in scientific journals came later, in 1969 and 1970.

Milgram's obedience work epitomized what social psychologists Aronson and Carlsmith have called experimental realism, an experimental situation that is so compelling and involving for the participants that they cannot respond with rational detachment, thereby increasing the validity of the findings. After almost forty-five years, the obedience work remains unmatched as the example, par excellence, of the creative use of experimental realism in the service of a question of profound social and moral significance.

Milgram's work has had a revelatory effect on how we think about the nature of human evil and destructiveness; about the role of moral principles in social life; about our malleability in the face of social pressure, especially in response to the demands of authority; and about the dehumanizing potential of the hierarchical forms of social organization so pervasive in modern society. He showed us that it doesn't take evil or deranged individuals to act destructively against innocent human beings. Normal, ordinary people are capable of horrible actions—which they would not undertake on their own—if commanded by a legitimate authority.

His work made us acutely aware of the unexpected power of the immediate situation, sometimes overriding our sense of right and wrong. He found that the degree to which participants in his experiments obeyed potentially harmful orders diminished when the victim was brought closer and increased when a buffer was introduced between subject and victim.

Again, Milgram's contribution was not in telling us that human beings have a propensity to obey authority but in demonstrating just how unexpectedly *powerful* this tendency is—and, further, by enlightening us about the factors that make such extreme obedience possible: relinquishing responsibility to the person in charge and accepting his definition of the situation.

The obedience experiments have had an intellectual impact far beyond their home territory. It is a testament to the broader human significance of the research that disciplines outside of psychology—such as economics, education, sociology, political science, philosophy, and the arts—have found them relevant. Given the widespread familiarity with the obedience studies, it is perhaps not surprising to find them discussed or referred to in publications as diverse as the *Archives of Internal Medicine* and the *Indian Journal of the History of Science*.

Thoughtful discussions of his research can be found in books by well-known writers, such as *Janus*, by Arthur Koestler, *Prisons We Choose to Live Inside*, by Doris Lessing, and *Injustice: The Social Bases of Obedience and Revolt*, by Barrington Moore. But consider also the dizzying diversity of uses various other writers have made of the obedience research. Here are just a few of many examples:

In 1984, Swedish writer Maria Modig published a book titled *Den Nödvändiga Olydnaden (The Necessary Disobedience)*. Since then it has been reissued in three subsequent editions, most recently in 2003. The book's intent is to help empower individuals to take more responsibility for their lives, to take risks in making changes that would contribute to their personal growth, and to make difficult choices, including the choice to disobey authority when necessary. The book, dedicated to Milgram, was inspired and informed by the obedience studies and in fact contains portions of an interview Modig conducted with Milgram in New York in May 1982.

Suzanne Clothier, a dog-trainer, recently published a gracefully written book titled *Bones Would Rain from the Sky*. In it, drawing on the obedience experiments, she admonishes dog owners who readily follow the cruel dog-training advice of "experts" even when their instincts tell them it is not the humane thing to do.

Dying by Degrees is an absorbing murder mystery by Canadian writer Eileen Coughlan centered on a Milgram-type obedience experiment with a sinister twist conducted by an unscrupulous psychologist at a university in Alberta.

The obedience experiments have also had an enduring influence on the performing arts. As mentioned earlier, rock musician Peter Gabriel recorded a song entitled "We Do What We're Told (Milgram's 37)" on his 1986 album *So*. (The number 37 refers to the percentage of defiant subjects in Milgram's Voice-Feedback condition—the second variation in his four-part proximity series.) There is also a French punk rock group named Milgram whose CD is titled "Vierhundertfünfzig Volt" (the German translation of "450 volts") and a British musical group named Midget issued a CD titled "The Milgram Experiment." In neither case is there a thematic connection between the music and Milgram's work. Apparently, these groups were simply fascinated by him and the experiments.

The same is true of Robbie Chafitz, who produced a weekly off-Broadway performance during the summer of 1999 titled "The Stanley Milgram Experiment," which was advertised as "original scripted humor." According to Chafitz, the show was not really about the obedience experiments. But ever since he saw Milgram's documentary film *Obedience* in middle school, he had wanted to form a band and name it after the experiments. The only problem was that he didn't play a musical instrument. The sole connection between Chafitz's staged humor and the obedience experiments was that in both cases things were not what they seemed.

Milgram's work has also captured the dramatic imagination, as evidenced by the several films and plays that have been based on the obedience experiments, including two full-length feature films and some shorter pieces produced by film students. One of the full-length films was *The Tenth Level*. The other was a French film, *I . . . comme Icare (I . . . as in Icarus)*, made in 1979, starring Yves Montand and directed by Henri Verneuil, one of France's most successful filmmakers. Stanley and Sasha were in France when the film was being made, and Verneuil and Montand invited them to the studio outside of Paris to see a day's production.

In February 2002, Rod Dickinson, a conceptual artist, staged a reenactment of the obedience experiment at the Centre for Contemporary Art in Glasgow, Scotland. He used actors to play the roles of a number of different subjects, the experimenter, and the learner for the dramatic re-creation, and he preserved it on film. Dickinson paid meticulous attention to details in reconstructing the Yale laboratory and in duplicating the original furnishings and equipment.

At least four dramatists have written plays based on the obedience experiments, and a couple of others are in early stages of development. The first one, published in 1973, "The Dogs of Pavlov," was written by Welsh poet and playwright Dannie Abse. "Tolliver's Trick," a one-act play written by Buffalo playwright and journalist Anthony Cardinale in 1987, was inspired by the obedience experiments as well as Cardinale's friendship with a local Holocaust survivor, whom he had accompanied to Jerusalem to an international gathering of Holocaust survivors. The third play, "Mosaic," by Daphne Hull, is a black comedy consisting of four scenes, one of which is a dramatic adaptation of the obedience experiments. The most recent drama inspired by the obedience research is a full-length play, titled "One More Volt," written by John P. Lavin in 2001 when he was a graduate student in the drama program at Carnegie-Mellon University.

There is no question that if Milgram were alive today, he would be very pleased by the continuing use of his obedience experiments as raw material by dramatists, because he saw a close affinity between the experiment and theater. He expressed this idea almost aphoristically: "Good experiments, like good drama, embody verities." For Milgram, laboratory experiments were a form of theater, with an important difference: Unlike a real play, which is scripted from start to finish, in an experiment, the ending—the subject's behavior—is always an unknown until it actually unfolds. In his experiments, Milgram was much like a director of a play, both in his meticulous attention to technical details and staging and in their intended effects on his audience (i.e., readers of his reports). A statement he once made is an apt summary of his—and some other social psychologists'—approach to experimentation: "Although experiments in chemistry and physics often involve shiny equipment, flasks, and electronic gear, an experiment in social psychology smacks much more of dramaturgy or theater."

For Milgram, the theater also provided a perspective from which to view a goal of experimentation and the means one sometimes has to use to achieve it. This can be seen most clearly in an exchange Milgram had with Dannie Abse. In an introductory essay to "The Dogs of Pavlov," Abse vigorously condemned Milgram's use of deception and the induction of stress. He argued that many people "may feel that in order to demonstrate that subjects may behave like so many Eichmanns the experimenter had to act the part, to some extent, of a Himmler."

In his rebuttal, which appears together with the script and Abse's introduction in one volume, Milgram expresses surprise at Abse's harsh criticisms of his use of what Milgram prefers to call "technical illusions" (rather than deception), because "as a dramatist you surely understand that illusion may serve a revelatory function, and indeed, the very possibility of theater is founded on the benign use of contrivance." He goes on to point out that both the playwright and the experimenter use artifice as a means to beneficial ends—entertainment and intellectual enrichment in the case of the theater, and the revelation of truths that are hard to get at in the case of the experiment. Milgram notes a further parallel between the stage and the laboratory: In both, the participants find the use of pretense acceptable. Theatergoers do not feel tricked, for example, that an old man turns out to be quite young when the greasepaint is removed. In a similar vein, most subjects in the obedience experiments felt that the experience had been worthwhile, once it was explained to them.

One of the profound effects of the almost forty-five-year-old experiments has been to serve as a constant reminder of the inherent dangers lurking within organizational environments, which have become perhaps *the* central feature of modern life. Professions such as marketing, accounting, and management have drawn practical lessons from the obedience studies, alerting their practitioners to Milgram's warning in *Obedience to Authority* that when an individual "merges . . . into an organizational structure, a new creature replaces autonomous man, unhindered by the limitations of individual morality, freed of humane inhibition, mindful only of the

"I'm shocked you're telling me to do this, Dr. Milgram —
and even more shocked that I'm doing it!"

FIGURE 12.1   The Electrifying Power of Authority.

sanctions of authority." Observations like these about the evaporation of individual responsibility in hierarchical organizations anticipated the kinds of
tragedies that later resulted from automakers' employees' willingness to follow their bosses' directives to produce unsafe cars and tobacco company
employees' acquiescence to policies designed to deceive the public. Figure
12.1 is an illustration from a textbook used in courses on business ethics;
the authors use the obedience experiments to warn their readers about unethical demands that might be made on them by their superiors in the
business world.

According to some business school faculty and administrators, at least
some of the concrete, humanizing changes that have been taking place in
business environments are traceable to Milgram's findings and insights: the

increasing tendency to involve employees, at all levels, in decision making; the encouragement of independent thinking; and the creation of hotlines and the placement of ombudsmen to facilitate the reporting of wrongdoing and expose morally problematic orders.

Outside of psychology, the obedience experiments have had the most pervasive influence in legal scholarship and practice. Several U.S. Supreme Court briefs have referenced the obedience studies, and a recent check of the database LexisNexis shows that since 1983, 165 law reviews and journal articles have cited Milgram's experiments (twelve additional articles cited some of his other work). While in some cases the citation is minimal, in others the obedience research plays a central role in the article. A thought-provoking example is in the description of an educational exercise conducted by University of San Diego law professor Steven Hartwell in which his students were to individually advise litigants in a small-claims court. He told his students that he would be available in an adjacent office if they needed to consult with him. Hartwell writes:

> The "clients" were, in fact, a single confederate who sought the same advice from each student: how she should present her side of a rent dispute. I told each student to advise the client to lie under oath that she had paid the rent. When students asked for clarification, I uniformly responded, ". . . My advice is that, if your client wants to win her case, then you must tell her to perjure herself.". . . We wanted them to experience the pull between loyalty to authority . . . and prescribed ethical conduct. . . . Although many of the 24 participating students grumbled either to me or to the client about my proffered advice, 23 told their client to perjure herself.

Perhaps the most consequential legal use of the obedience experiments was in trial testimony in which the lessons learned from those experiments (as well as some other basic social-psychological studies) actually saved lives. In the late 1980s, Andrew Colman, a social psychologist, testified as an expert witness in two trials in South Africa involving a total of thirteen defendants accused of murder during mob actions. The courts accepted his testimony that obedience to authority—and other social psychological phenomena—were extenuating circumstances, with the end result that nine of the accused were spared the death penalty.

In his obedience studies, Milgram obtained that rare kind of finding—one that people can apply to themselves to change their behavior or to provide new insights about themselves and others. Countless people who have learned about the obedience work have been better able to stand up against arbitrary or unjust authority. An example with broad consequences was revealed by a former student who spoke at a memorial gathering after Milgram's death. Until recently, he had been living in a country in Latin America. He told the audience that those involved in opposing dictatorial governments embraced Milgram's work, giving them the courage to resist tyranny.

In 1982, Milgram received a letter from an individual who had been a subject in a version of the obedience experiments in 1967 while he was an undergraduate at the University of Minnesota. He wrote to thank Milgram "for making a major contribution to my understanding of myself and of the meaning of the values I have. . . . Reading your book *[Obedience to Authority]* has been like hearing echoes of my own reflections about the experience. I am, and was, decent, kind, and intelligent. I would never do what you described in your book. Nevertheless, I did. . . . I think I hold my values about proper human behavior more deeply now than I did before the experiment, but I also realize that they would have to be very deeply rooted indeed ever to prevail against the subtle force of authority."

A Swede named Eduardo Grutzky credits Milgram for helping him make sense of his past: "I am Jewish and spent seven years in a fascist prison in the seventies in Argentina. . . . Most of the people that tortured me and killed my friends were 'normal people.' I discovered Milgram some years ago and he opened my mind for understanding the world. . . ."

And a Croatian psychologist, Vera Cubela, read Milgram to understand events unfolding before her eyes: "When I first read [Milgram's] book on obedience to authority I was fascinated by the very behaviors he observed in the laboratory. When I found myself in the middle of the war in Bosnia and Herzegovina, I could observe behaviors illustrating the same phenomenon, but was not fascinated by them, of course. Yet, since I carried Milgram's volume with me . . . and often re-read it, I became more and more fascinated by the elegancy of his demonstration of the phenomenon underlying many cruelties."

A posting to the community Web site Metafilter put it this way: "Got my copy of *Obedience to Authority* right here. The little fire of hatred for humanity it inspires keeps me warm at night. Exaggeration aside, I honestly believe that Milgram's Obedience Experiments . . . were not only the most important thing I learned in college but the most important thing I possibly could have learned."

. . .

While the obedience experiments have stimulated scholarly debate across a wide range of disciplines, their implications have perhaps been greatest for our understanding of the Holocaust. Milgram's work provided the scientific underpinnings for Hannah Arendt's "banality of evil" perspective, which challenged early explanations of the Holocaust that simply demonized the Nazi leaders and perpetrators, placing their behavior beyond the pale of rational discourse and debate. Milgram insisted that such behavior could indeed be studied and, by applying the tools and language of social science, he helped forge a new perspective. Whether or not one agrees with Milgram, his point of view is taken seriously by those trying to account for the Holocaust, as suggested by a review of Daniel Goldhagen's controversial book *Hitler's Willing Executioners:* "[Goldhagen] now claims he deserves a place alongside Hanna Arendt, Stanley Milgram, Raul Hilberg, and Yehuda Bauer, the great fathomers of the Holocaust."

Here is how Milgram described the relevance of his findings for understanding the Holocaust:

A commonly offered explanation is that those who shocked the victim at the most severe level were monsters, the sadistic fringe of society. But if one considers that almost two thirds of the participants fall into the category of "obedient" subjects, and that they represented ordinary people . . . the argument becomes very shaky. Indeed, it is highly reminiscent of the issue that arose in connection with Hannah Arendt's . . . book, *Eichmann in Jerusalem.* Arendt contended that the prosecution's effort to depict Eichmann as a sadistic monster was fundamentally wrong, that he came closer to being an uninspired bureaucrat who simply sat at his desk and did his job. . . . After witnessing hundreds of ordinary people submit to the authority in our own experiments, I must conclude that Arendt's conception of the *banality of evil* comes closer to the truth than one might dare imagine. The ordinary person who shocked the victim did so out of a sense of obligation—a conception of his duties as a subject—and not from any peculiarly aggressive tendencies. This is, perhaps, the most fundamental lesson of our study: ordinary people, simply doing their jobs, and without any particular hostility on their part, can become agents in a terrible destructive process.

Although Milgram recognized that there are "enormous differences of circumstance and scope" between obedience in his laboratory and Nazi Germany, he argued that "a common psychological process is centrally involved in both events." He believed that his experiments spoke to all hierarchical relationships in which people become willing agents of a legitimate authority to whom they relinquish responsibility for their actions. Having done so, their actions are no longer guided by their conscience but by how adequately they have fulfilled the authority's wishes.

In applying Milgram's work to the Holocaust, an important distinction must be kept in mind—that between explaining and excusing: While Milgram's approach may provide an explanation for how ordinary people can be made to act with extraordinary cruelty, it does not excuse such actions. Milgram made this distinction explicit in a preface he drafted for the German edition of *Obedience to Authority* but that did not actually appear in the book:

It is fitting that this book be translated into German, since it has a special relevance to Germans. Obedience is, after all, their favorite alibi. My guess is, after conducting the experiments reported in this book, that if the same institutions arose in the United States—the concentration camps, the gas chambers—there would be no problem finding Americans to operate them. Yet, the fact that a potential for blind obedience exists in all people does not absolve the Germans from having transformed that potential into actual brutality and actual slaughter.

Stanley Milgram

Milgram's approach has a good deal of appeal. It is certainly consistent with the litany of "I was only following orders" heard repeatedly at the Nuremberg war crimes trials of the major Nazi leaders at the end of World War II. It also has support from Arendt's analysis of Eichmann's trial in her book *Eichmann in Jerusalem: A Report on the Banality of Evil,* which claimed that Eichmann was a very conventional person, guided largely by a drive to advance his career rather than hate for his victims.

The impressions of Simon Wiesenthal, the Nazi hunter whose investigative work led to Eichmann's capture by the Israelis, are very similar. He describes Eichmann as "an utterly bourgeois, an utterly normal, almost in fact a socially adjusted, person. . . . He was not driven by blood lust."

One historian even makes a direct connection between some events that occurred during the Holocaust and Milgram's obedience experiments. In his book *Ordinary Men,* Christopher Browning describes the activities of a Nazi mobile killing unit that scoured the Polish countryside between 1942 and 1943, searching for Jews. The unit's members ended up murdering 38,000 Jews in cold blood at the bidding of their commanders. Browning makes a detailed comparison between the actions of members of "Battalion 101" and those of Milgram's subjects, concluding that "many of Milgram's insights find graphic confirmation in the behavior and testimony of the men of Reserve Police Battalion 101."

The "banality of evil" thesis also finds support in the writings of Raul Hilberg, the premier historian of the Holocaust. Hilberg has pointed out that the Nazis' success in carrying out their destructive plans on such a massive scale was made possible by countless bureaucrats and agencies applying their practiced skills and standard procedures to the task at hand. Among the examples he mentions is the SS being billed by the German railroad for each Jewish deportee it transported.

Consistent with Hilberg's thesis are findings of recent historical research on the conduct of members of specific professions who, when the Nazis came to power, readily assimilated Nazi doctrine and directives into their everyday, routine activities. Richard H. Weisberg, a legal historian, studied the behavior of French lawyers and judges under the collaborationist, pro-Nazi, Vichy government, which instituted racial laws that eventually led to the deportation of 75,000 Jews to Nazi death camps. He writes:

> Legal activity during the full four years of Vichy was pervasive. Courts functioned much as they had always functioned, although bound by an unusual oath to Vichy's leader, Marshal Pétain. . . . Private legal practitioners . . . took up the new materials of racial, religious and ethnic ostracism and worked with them in volume and without substantial protest. Legal academicians wrote doctoral theses and had them published on the subject of the anti-Jewish laws, made their reputations as young law professors by discussing "neutrally" the stuff of exclusion. . . .

In a similar vein, German psychologists generally "ran with the ball" when the Nazis took over. The first anti-Jewish law enacted by Hitler after he came to power, the "Law for the Reconstitution of the Civil Service," led to the dismissal of the Jewish psychologists at universities (including Max Wertheimer, one of the founders of Gestalt psychology). The German Society for Psychology took no action to help their dismissed colleagues; instead, they requested that the authorities fill the vacated positions quickly to ensure the continued representation of psychology in the affected universities.

Milgram was also on solid ground in pinpointing obedience to authority as a possible key to understanding the Holocaust, given the high value placed on it by Nazi ideology and German culture generally. For example, the first of twelve commandments listed in a primer used to indoctrinate Nazi youth was "The leader is always right." And many generations of German children grew up on cautionary tales, such as Struwwelpeter, or Shock-headed Peter, whose moral was that disobedience could lead to rather drastic, violent, consequences.

The story of Struwwelpeter, which has usually been published in picture-panel format, begins with a mother telling her young son that she has to go out, that he must stay in the house while she is out, and warns him ominously that, if he disobeys her, she will take him to the tailor. The moment she leaves the house, Struwwelpeter bolts out the door. The mother returns, discovers that her son has ignored her wishes, and drags him to the tailor. The last picture panel in the story shows the boy leaving the tailor's shop crying, with fingers severed, dripping blood.

But how much explanatory power do the obedience experiments really have? Do they fit the historical record? Was the obedient Nazi subordinate mechanically carrying out the murderous commands of his leader, without any hatred or hostility toward his victims?

As noted earlier, Milgram saw Arendt's "banality of evil" thesis to be in harmony with his own findings and conclusions. Yet a reading of the Holocaust literature can certainly lead one to contest the idea that a cold, emotionless, and dutiful approach, such as Eichmann's, was characteristic of the Nazis' behavior. To begin with, Arendt's perception of Eichmann has been challenged. Jacob Robinson, a historian, points out that Eichmann pursued his goal of shipping as many Jews as possible to the extermination camps with a degree of drive, perseverance, and enthusiasm that was clearly beyond the call of duty.

Furthermore, to intensify their suffering, in many cases large-scale actions against the Jews were timed to coincide with their religious holidays. For example, the deportation of the Jews of Warsaw began on the eve of Tisha B'Av (July 22, 1942), the day of mourning that commemorates the destruction of the Temple in Jerusalem. According to historian Martin Gilbert, "since the first days of the invasion of Poland in September 1939, the Germans had used the Jewish festivals for particular savagery; these days had become known to the Jews as the 'Goebbels calendar'." The historical evidence for the spontaneity, inventiveness, and enthusiasm with which the Nazis degraded, hurt, and killed their victims also argues against explaining their behavior as mere obedience to an authority's commands, despite the perpetrators' abhorrence of their own actions and without hatred toward their victims. It must have come from within.

Here are a few of countless examples: "Simone LaGrange was sent to Auschwitz and, one day, saw her father there. He was in a column of men marching by. She waved and an SS guard asked if that was really her father. 'Then go kiss him, girl,' the guard said. She ran to her father. The guard shot him" (Richard Reeves, a journalist, writing about the testimony of a witness at the trial of Klaus Barbie, "the butcher of Lyons").

And here is a description by a survivor of the Majdanek concentration camp of the kind of brutalities that routinely took place there: "[A] customary SS habit was to kick a Jew with a heavy boot. The Jew was forced to stand to attention, and all the while the SS man kicked him until he broke some bones. People who stood near enough to such a victim often heard the breaking of the bones. The pain was so terrible that people, having undergone that treatment, died in agony."

There were also the actions of an *Einsatzgruppe,* or mobile killing unit, in operation in the town of Uman, in the Ukraine. A German army officer described how the Jews of the area were gathered near the airport and surrounded by SS men and other militia. The Jews were ordered to undress, hand over everything they owned, and to stand in a line in front of a ditch. They were then shot and thrown into the ditch. The observer stated that no one was overlooked:

> Even women carrying children two to three weeks old, sucking at their breasts, were not spared this horrible ordeal. Nor were mothers spared the terrible sight of their children being gripped by their little legs and put to death with one stroke of the pistol butt or club, thereafter to be thrown on the heap of human bodies in the ditch, some of which were not quite dead. Not before these mothers had been exposed to this worst of all tortures did they receive the bullet that released them from this sight.

Significantly, the observer noted that the killers worked "with such zealous intent that one could have supposed this activity to have been their life-work."

A final example is a heart-rending story from the memoirs of Lieutenant Meyer Birnbaum, a Jewish officer who served in the U.S. Army during

World War II. At the end of the war, his unit came to Ohrdruff, a concentration camp annexed to Buchenwald. At first they saw no sign of life. They were greeted by a pile of still-warm bodies machine gunned by the retreating Germans "in a final spasm of hatred." Birnbaum searched for survivors and found two in the typhus ward. They were so weakened they could barely move, and that is what saved them from the fate of their fellow prisoners. They had been far too sick to obey the order to gather in the courtyard, where the others were shot. Both were Jewish; one was a thirty-five-year-old man from Poland, and the other a sixteen-year-old Hungarian boy. Their first request was a piece of bread, and they both sobbed uncontrollably as they recalled their murdered families. Birnbaum's narrative continued:

After about fifteen minutes of bitter sobbing, the sixteen-year-old suddenly looked at me and asked whether I could teach him how to do *teshuvah* [repent]. I was taken aback by his question and tried to comfort him. "After the stretch in hell you've been through, you don't have to worry about doing *teshuvah*. Your slate is clean. You're alive, and you have to get hold of yourself and stop worrying about doing *teshuvah*," I told him. But my words had no effect. I could not convince him. He kept insisting: *"Ich vill tuhn teshuvah*—I want to do *teshuvah. Ich muz tuhn teshuvah*—I must do *teshuvah.*"

Finally, I asked him, "Why must you do *teshuvah?*" in the hope that talking would enable him to let go of some of the pain I saw in his eyes. He pointed out the window and asked me if I saw the gallows. Satisfied that I did, he began his story. . . .

Two months ago one of the prisoners escaped. . . . The camp commandant was furious about the escape and demanded to know the identity of the escaped prisoner. No one could provide him with the information he was seeking. . . . In his fury, the commandant decided to play a sadistic game with us. He demanded that any pairs of brothers, or fathers and sons, step forward. We were terrified of what he might do if we did not comply. My father and I stepped forward.

They placed my father on a stool under those gallows and tied a noose around his neck. Once the noose was around my father's neck, the commandant cocked his luger, placed it at my temple, and hissed, "If you or your father doesn't tell me who escaped, you are going to kick that stool out from under your father." I looked at my father and told him "Zorgst sich nit—Don't worry, Tatte, I won't do it." But my father answered me, "My son, you have to do it. He's got a gun to your head and he's going to kill you if you don't, and then he'll kick the chair out from under me and we'll both be gone. This way at least there's a chance you'll survive. But if you don't, we'll both be killed."

"Tatte, nein, ich vell dos nit tuhn—I will not do it. Ich hab nit fargessen kibbud av—I didn't forget kibbud av (honoring one's father)."

Instead of being comforted by my words, my father suddenly screamed at me: "You talk about kibbud av. I'm ordering you to kick that stool. That is your father's command."

"Nein, Tatte, nein—No, Father, I won't."

But my father only got angrier, knowing that if I didn't obey he would see his son murdered in front of him. "You talk about kibbud av v'eim [honoring one's father and mother]," he shouted. "This is your father's last order to you. Listen to me! Kick the chair!"

I was so frightened and confused hearing my father screaming at me that I kicked the chair and watched as my father's neck snapped in the noose.

His story over, the boy looked at me . . . as my own tears flowed freely, and asked, "Now, you tell me. Do I have to do *teshuvah*?"

But, in some ways, a quote that is mostly directly at odds with Arendt's "banality of evil" thesis can be found in an introduction to a book about the trial in Frankfurt from 1963 to 1965 of twenty-two SS men who served at Auschwitz. The book contains the testimony of witnesses describing the unimaginable acts of torture and murder perpetrated by the defendants. The writer of the introduction reflected on the horrors described in the book:

No one had issued orders that infants should be thrown into the air as shooting targets, or hurled into the fire alive, or have their heads smashed against walls. . . . Innumerable individual crimes, one more horrible than the next, surrounded and created the atmosphere of the gigantic crime of extermination.

The author was none other than Hannah Arendt, giving recognition to the fact that there was another face to the Holocaust besides that of the dutiful bureaucrat, and she stated that the Frankfurt trial "in many respects reads like a much-needed supplement to the Jerusalem trial." So, while her phrase "banality of evil" has been adopted by some to describe the essential nature of Nazi destructiveness, it would seem that Arendt herself recognized a broader truth.

Milgram's approach, then, does not provide a wholly adequate account of the Holocaust. Clearly, there was more to the genocidal Nazi program than the dispassionate obedience of the average citizen who participated in the murder of his fellow citizens out of a sense of duty and not malice. At the same time, it could not have succeeded to the degree that it did without the passive or active complicity of Everyman. While Milgram's approach may well account for the dutiful destructiveness of the dispassionate bureaucrat, who may have shipped Jews to Auschwitz with the same degree of routinization as potatoes to Bremenhaven, it falls short when it comes to explaining the more zealous, hate-driven cruelties that also defined the Holocaust.

But, even so, Milgram's ideas still possess significant explanatory value vis-à-vis the Holocaust, in the following ways: Although the vast majority of Germans were not *directly* involved in killing Jews, zealously or otherwise, they readily accepted the various decrees, beginning in 1933, that increasingly led to the Jews' economic suffering and social isolation (e.g., dismissal from their jobs, "Aryanization" of their businesses, imposition of curfews, restrictions on their use of public transportation and telephones) and eventually to their annihilation. In this regard, Security Police Chief Heydrich considered all Germans as a kind of auxiliary police force, who were expected to ensure that Jews "behaved" themselves and to report anything that might look suspicious. And when they were rounded up for deportations, few Germans attempted to protect their Jewish friends. Milgram's work certainly speaks to the dutiful complicity of the vast majority of Germans.

Milgram's ideas may even shed light on the behavior of the cruel Nazi killer who seemed to take delight in his savagery. Milgram argued that two processes are involved in destructive obedience—relinquishing responsibility to the person in charge (which he referred to as "entry into the agentic state") and accepting the authority's definition of the situation or reality. As Milgram put it: "There is a propensity for people to accept definitions of action provided by legitimate authority. That is, although the subject performs the action, he allows authority to define its meaning." By abdicating responsibility to the commanding authority, the person frees himself from having to decide on the morality of his actions; the authority does that for him. The Nazi leaders' "definition of action" vis-à-vis the Jews was to see them not as humans but as "a lower species of life, a kind of vermin, which upon contact infected the German people with deadly diseases." Thus, while the zeal and inventiveness with which many Nazis murdered their Jewish victims suggests that a deep-seated hatred of Jews was the main driving force behind their actions, the two processes suggested by Milgram undoubtedly enabled them to proceed without a guilty conscience.

Third, one of the distinctive features of the Milgram obedience paradigm is the sequential escalation of the delivery of shocks. The learner's "suffering" intensifies in a gradual, piecemeal fashion. Milgram considered this manner of giving shocks one of the factors "that powerfully bind a subject to his role." The importance of this unfolding process as a facilitator of destructive obedience in Milgram's laboratory has alerted us to the vital role played by the step-by-step, escalating process the Nazis used in the victimization of the Jews, as described by Hilberg:

> The process of destruction unfolded in a definite pattern . . . a step-by-step operation. . . . The steps of the destruction process were introduced in the following order. At first the concept of the *Jew* was defined; then the expropriatory operations were inaugurated; third, the Jews were concentrated in ghettos; finally the decision was made to annihilate European Jewry. Mobile units were sent to Russia, while in the rest of Europe the victims were deported to the killing centers. . . . It is the bureaucratic destruction process that in its step-by-step manner finally led to the annihilation of 5 million victims.

Referring to the incremental feature of his experimental procedure, Milgram said: "The laboratory hour is an unfolding process in which each action influences the next. The obedient act is perseverative." One can hear echoes of this view in Hilberg's assertion that "a measure in a destruction process [whose sequential nature he had just outlined] never stands alone. . . . It always has consequences. Each step of the destruction process contains the seed of the next step."

Milgram taught us something profoundly revelatory about human nature—about ourselves—that we did not know before: just how powerful our propensity is to obey the commands of an authority, even when those commands might conflict with our moral principles. And, having been enlightened about our extreme readiness to obey authority, we can try to take steps to inoculate ourselves against unwanted or reprehensible commands.

One important arena where this has been happening is the U.S. Army. It apparently has taken the lessons of Milgram's research to heart and acted on it. In 1985, a college student doing a research paper on the obedience experiments wrote a letter to West Point, asking if Milgram's research was "considered a vital part of [their] program." In response, she received a letter from Col. Howard T. Prince II, head of the Department of Behavioral Sciences and Leadership, who wrote: "The answer is a definite, yes. All cadets at the United States Military Academy are required to take two psychology courses, General Psychology . . . and Military Leadership. . . . Both of these courses discuss Milgram's work and the implications of his findings."

And there is more. A military psychologist, Lt. Col. Dave Grossman, wrote an insightful book about soldiers' resistance to killing and how it is overcome. In this book, *On Killing: The Psychological Cost of Learning to Kill in War and Society,* Grossman draws substantively on Milgram's work. After I read the book, I contacted Grossman to ask him if Milgram's work has had any discernible impact on the military. His answer astounded me. He told me that when he was undergoing officer training in the early 1970s, he was shown training films instructing soldiers on how to *disobey* illegitimate orders. He described this as a "true revolution in military history," directly attributable to Milgram's findings, as well as to the My Lai massacre.

It is important to note that although the murderous behavior of the Nazis stimulated the obedience research, Milgram did not consider that connection essential to the importance of his findings. In fact, early on after he completed the studies, he expressed some reservations about applying his findings to the Holocaust. In late March 1964, he received a letter describing an experiment modeled on his obedience research that the letter-writer had submitted as an entry for her state science fair. The "shock" apparatus consisted of seven switches and had some clever details to add a touch of realism, such as a transformer that threw sparks and created an arc of electric current. She reported to Milgram that 77 percent of the teenage subjects in her "learning" experiment fully obeyed and pressed all seven switches, which supposedly gave increasingly painful shocks. She concluded, she wrote Milgram, that her American subjects were comparable to the Nazi youth who followed Hitler's orders without hesitation. In his reply, he told her that "it is quite a jump . . . from an experiment of this sort to general conclusions about the Nazi epoch, and I, myself, feel that I have sometimes gone too far in generalizing. Be cautious in generalizing."

In 1967, in a draft for an article, he wrote:

In introducing the problem of [the obedience] research, I have set it against the background of behavior in Nazi Germany. . . . Yet obedience, as a problem of human behavior, does not depend for its significance on the Nazi example. Its importance for understanding society [and man's role in it] transcends this specific case. Indeed, it is quite possibly an error to link the laboratory experiments too closely to the question of behavior in Nazi Germany. Obedience to authority would still require psychological analysis if Germany had never existed, and if Jews had never been victims. Obedience needs to be understood because it is a basic element in the structure of social life. Without a well developed capacity for obedience, society could not function. Yet under the sway of obedient dispositions, morality vanishes.

This passage did not end up in the published version—apparently Milgram's viewpoint on the matter had not yet settled. But by the time he wrote his book, he had resolved the issue. This is what appears in its final pages:

> The late Gordon W. Allport was fond of calling this experimental paradigm "the Eichmann experiment" . . . perhaps an apt term, but it should not lead us to mistake the import of this investigation. To focus only on the Nazis, however despicable their deeds, and to view only highly publicized atrocities as being relevant to these studies is to miss the point entirely. For the studies are principally concerned with the ordinary and routine destruction carried out by everyday people following orders. . . . The dilemma posed by the conflict between conscience and authority inheres in the very nature of society and would be with us even if Nazi Germany had never existed. To deal with the problem only as if it were a matter of history is to give it an illusory distance.

. . .

The ethical controversy surrounding the obedience experiments has left an indelible mark on experimentation with human subjects. In the early 1970s, the American Psychological Association formulated its ethical principles for research with human subjects, and institutional review boards (IRBs) were created to ensure that human subjects are protected. The use of IRBs was mandated by the National Research Act, signed into law by Congress in July 1974.

Of course, the obedience work was by no means the sole catalyst for these changes. In 1953, a number of jury deliberations in Wichita, Kansas, were tape-recorded by researchers from the University of Chicago without the knowledge of the jurors involved. In the early 1960s, a new drug, thalidomide, was imported into the United States from Europe, and more than 1,000 physicians prescribed it to their patients without informing them of its experimental nature. The drug caused fetal deformations in many pregnant women who took it. In 1963, a group of medical researchers in a Brooklyn hospital injected live cancer cells into feeble, elderly patients without revealing the true nature of the injections. In 1972, a study begun in 1932 on the effects of untreated syphilis among a group of black men (the Tuskegee study) came to light. The men were not told that they had syphilis or that they were subjects in a research study. The progress of the disease in these men was tracked for forty years, and they were not offered any treatment even after penicillin became available.

Psychologists and other behavioral and social scientists have disagreed about the need for governmental regulations. Milgram himself felt that the "erection of a superstructure of control [by the federal government] on sociopsychological experimentation is a very impressive solution to a non-problem." Today many social psychologists agree with Milgram and believe that although most biomedical research requires vigilant oversight, social-scientific research generally does not. Regardless of one's position on the issue, there is today a greater sensitivity to the well-being of research participants than was the case in the past; one author writing in the *American Psychologist* has even referred to the "post-Milgram era of ethically sensitive psychology." Can anyone imagine a governmental agency today exposing large numbers of people to dangerous levels of radiation without their knowledge or consent, or conducting research that would involve withholding effective medications from patients afflicted with syphilis? The fact that such abuses are virtually unthinkable today is clearly an outcome of the ethical controversy surrounding the obedience experiments, along with a few other widely publicized studies, and the increased sensitivity generated as a result.

Could Milgram's obedience experiments be conducted in the United States today? In principle, yes, but in practice, almost certainly not. Both the American Psychological Association's ethical principles and federal regulations place a heavy emphasis on informed consent: Potential subjects must be given enough details about an experiment beforehand to enable them to make an informed decision about whether or not to participate. Clearly, the obedience experiment would not produce valid results if subjects knew beforehand that the shocks were not real and the learner was really an actor pretending to be in pain. Still, in neither code is the principle of informed consent an absolute. Both leave the door open for the application of a cost-benefit analysis to determine whether the benefits to the subject or to society outweigh the potential risk the research entails. However, at the institutional level, it is the local IRB that actually implements the federal regulations.

Over the years, psychologists and other social scientists have found it increasingly difficult to obtain IRB approval for research that is much more benign than the obedience experiments. The problem seems to stem from the fact that many IRB decisions are based on idiosyncratic interpretations that go beyond the federal guidelines. Such decisions are often guided by an oversensitivity to possible problems that have only a remote chance of materializing. One social psychologist, Louis Penner, who has been the chairman of his university's IRB for social and behavioral research, put it this way:

> I'll confess it right up front: I think that IRBs are a good idea. . . . But please note that . . . I did not say that they were necessarily a good thing in practice. . . . There are almost as many different interpretations of [the federal regulations] as there are different IRBs. At some institutions the researcher who submits an IRB application is entering the "Gates of Hell." The IRB (or its chair) has little first-hand experience with research and is concerned almost exclusively with protecting the institution from possible government censure (or worse) and/or from possible lawsuits by "aggrieved" research participants. . . . At other institutions, the IRB (or its chair) has the experience and judgment to decide which studies really put their research participants at risk, while at the same time being sensitive to the institution's research mission. But (and this is important) they are both working from exactly the same set of federal regulations.

Milgram once commented admiringly on the fact that Asch's conformity paradigm produced many variations: "For me Asch's experiment rotates as a kind of permanent intellectual jewel. Focus analytic light on it, and it diffracts energy into new and interesting patterns." When one considers how much the obedience work has permeated contemporary culture and thought and the variety of uses that have been made of it, Milgram's metaphor of a "permanent intellectual jewel" can just as appropriately be applied to his own obedience paradigm.

What accounts for the far-flung influence and appeal of those experiments? Most likely it has to do with the fact that, in his demonstration of our powerful propensity to obey authority, Milgram has identified one of the universals of social behavior—one that transcends both time and place—and people intuitively sense this.*

Lee Ross, a social psychologist at Stanford University, effectively captured the sweeping impact of the Milgram obedience experiments when he wrote:

> Perhaps more than any other empirical contributions in the history of social science, they have become part of our society's shared intellectual legacy—that small body of historical incidents, biblical parables, and classic literature that serious thinkers feel free to draw on when they debate about human nature or contemplate human history.

...

Milgram applied his innovative touch to research on a variety of phenomena besides obedience. Although overshadowed by the obedience studies, his other research is also an important part of his legacy.

Milgram's lost-letter technique has been—and remains—the most widely used indirect, unobtrusive measure of attitude and opinion. It has been used for a variety of purposes, from studying the Catholic-Protestant conflict in Northern Ireland to measuring attitudes toward abortion.

A recent study deserves special mention in this context, because—heeding Milgram's recommendation about the need for large numbers—it represents a quantum leap in the size of the samples used. As a science project for the Intel Science Talent Search competition for 1999–2000, Lucas Hanft, then a Long Island high school student, "lost" 1,600 letters in well-

---

*See Appendix C for the results of two data analyses that provide some evidence for this assertion.

to-do neighborhoods in New York City and suburban Long Island over a three-week period in the summer of 1999. Ann Saltzman, of Drew University, a former Milgram student at CUNY, served as his adviser. The letters were addressed to organizations meant to represent positions for or against school vouchers or homosexuality or support for Rudy Giuliani or Hillary Clinton for the Senate. As expected, the urban/suburban differences in letter returns were consistent with the liberal or conservative political orientations of their residents. However, there were some surprises, too. For example, within Manhattan, the results showed overwhelming support for school vouchers. Hanft provides an insightful perspective on this finding:

> The tremendous city return rates for "Say Yes! to School Vouchers" raises an interesting issue in that school vouchers, as a rule, tend to be supported by those on the conservative side of the political spectrum. Why would generally liberal New Yorkers support school vouchers so strongly? This high degree of support reflects the fact that upscale parents send their children to private schools, as opposed to public schools. For these parents, vouchers are a "pocketbook issue" and their self-interest, at least as far as this study shows, takes precedence over their political predisposition. The ability of the lost-letter technique to discriminate with regard to the school voucher issue is an encouraging finding as it relates to the accuracy of the methodology.

Among Milgram's research endeavors, beyond the obedience research, one clearly stands out in terms of its enduring impact—his research on the small-world phenomenon, which has stirred the imagination of both the public and the scientific community. The most immediate impact of Milgram's small-world research was on social network researchers, because it provided them with a new method for studying acquaintanceship patterns. Studies of social networks typically relied on self-report measures, such as questions asking subjects to list individuals with whom they have a particular kind of relationship. Through the small-world method, Milgram enabled network researchers to use subjects' *actions* as a source of information about their social ties. Over the years it has become "one of the critical tools of network analysis," according to Charles Kadushin, a prominent social network researcher.

Until the late 1980s, awareness of Milgram's discovery of the small-world phenomenon was confined largely to social network researchers and other social scientists. Only a small segment of the larger public was familiar with Milgram's small-world research; when his article appeared in 1967 in the first issue of *Psychology Today*, the magazine had only a small readership.

But then, in 1990, the small-world concept started to enter the public consciousness through an unlikely gateway. A play titled "Six Degrees of Separation" by John Guare made its debut on Broadway. One of the play's characters, Ouisa Kittredge, makes an oblique reference to Milgram's findings when she says: "I read somewhere that everybody on this planet is separated by only six other people. Six degrees of separation between us and everyone else on this planet." The play, and then its movie version, which appeared in 1993, helped make large numbers of people aware of Milgram's pioneering work on the small-world phenomenon.

In 1998, two researchers in applied mathematics at Cornell, Steven Strogatz and Duncan Watts, one of his doctoral students, broke new ground with their startling discovery that Milgram may have identified an underlying principle that is pervasive in our world, and not limited to social contacts. In an article in *Nature*, they showed through numerical simulations that the small-world effect—the remarkable ability of very large networks to be traversed in only a small number of steps—is present in domains as diverse as the electric power grid of the Western United States, the neural pathways of nematode worms, and the nearly quarter million actors listed in the Internet Movie Database. As Strogatz put it:

> Milgram's pioneering work on the small-world problem is enjoying a renaissance in some unexpected fields. It has recently stimulated a lot of work in mathematics, computer science, physics, epidemiology, neuroscience, . . . the common thread being that the small-world phenomenon turns out to be more than a curiosity of social networks—it is actually a general property of large, sparse networks whose connectivity is neither completely regular nor completely random.

Much of this "renaissance" is described in the book *Linked*, by physicist Albert-László Barabási, whose own research on computer networks has contributed to it. He and his colleagues have shown that the Internet has small-world properties. In an analysis of hyperlink connections, they found that, on average, it takes nineteen clicks to connect two randomly chosen pages on the World Wide Web.

Recently, Duncan Watts, now an assistant professor at Columbia University, completed an ambitious project—conducting an Internet version of Milgram's small-world method. His goal was to replicate the small-world phenomenon on a global scale, a venture made possible by the use of e-mail as the functional equivalent of Milgram's regular mail procedure. People participated—that is, became "senders"—by logging on to the project's Web site, http://smallworld.sociology.columbia.edu. They were then randomly assigned one of eighteen possible targets from thirteen countries in different parts of the world, varying in age, race, socioeconomic status, and profession. The results, as reported by Watts and his project colleagues, Peter Sheridan Dodds and Roby Muhamad, in *Science* in August 2003, present a mixed picture regarding the validity of the small-world concept.

On the one hand, they obtained an extremely low completion rate: Of the 24,163 chains that were started, only 384 were completed. On the other hand, among those few that did reach their target, the average chain length was about four. When Watts and his colleagues conducted a mathematical extrapolation to calculate what the average chain length would be if all the messages had reached their targets, the estimated chain lengths were between five and seven. These results are consistent with Milgram's findings. The Columbia team also replicated two other findings by Milgram: Messages were more likely to be sent on to friends than to relatives, and male-to-male and female-to-female links were more frequent than message transmissions to the opposite sex. However, Watts's team found no evidence of the "funneling" effect described by Milgram: A large percentage of the mailings in Milgram's study that started in Nebraska reached the target person—a stockbroker in Massachusetts—through a particular clothing merchant.

Despite the continuities with Milgram's findings, the disappointingly low completion rate of the e-mail experiment warrants examination. Does it conflict with the idea that we live in a small world—that people are capable of carving relatively short paths out of the morass of huge social networks? It certainly would if chains had died because people could not think of an appropriate next link. But this was not the case: Watts and colleagues report that only 0.3 percent of their participants gave that as a reason for not passing on the message, suggesting that they dropped out because of lack of interest or incentive. Milgram had similar speculations about why people in his studies dropped out. It is also possible to explain the high dropout rate in the Columbia study by invoking a concept Milgram used to explain the behavior of city dwellers: stimulus overload. The "in-box" of many, if not most, e-mail users is overloaded on a daily basis with too many messages, many of which are unsolicited spam. One form of adaptation is to pay less attention to, or even ignore, lower-priority messages that might have been attended to in a less crowded Internet environment. Such an extension of Milgram's overload concept beyond the urban environment was already suggested in a 1997 book by David Shenk titled *Data Smog: Surviving the Information Glut*. The author argued that the overload of unwanted information resulting from advances in information technology has led to a deterioration in the quality of life. He wrote that "Milgram's . . . analysis of overload [is] just as applicable to victims of data smog in 1997 as it was to urban residents of 1970."

Malcolm Gladwell, in his book *The Tipping Point*, drew on the small-world concept to explain how a Chicago native, Lois Weisberg, seemed to know virtually everybody. The December 11, 1999, issue of the *Los Angeles Times* described a test of Milgram's idea conducted by the staff of the prestigious Hamburg newspaper *Die Zeit*, in which they helped connect a person they had chosen at random—an Iraqi immigrant—through a global chain of acquaintances to anyone he picked. He chose his idol, Marlon Brando. The weekly's 450,000 readers were enthralled with progress reports spanning six months. They ended up verifying Milgram's hypothesis—with a qualification: They reached Brando's agent via "six degrees of separation," but they were unable to breach the actor's wall of privacy.

A highly original "test" of the small-world idea was carried out by a London filmmaker, Lucy Leveugle, in October 2002. She decided to use herself as the "mailing" to be passed on from one acquaintance to another to see if it could be done in just six steps. Using Milgram's rule, each person could send her only to a person whom he or she knew on a first-name basis. To find a remote "target" on the other side of the world, she placed an ad in newspapers in Mongolia, asking for volunteers for a documentary film to reply with their name and photograph. The respondent she chose was Purev-Ochir Gungaa, a nomadic herdsman in the middle of the country's vast steppes. If she could get to him, she figured she could reach anyone.

For her first link, she traveled to Dublin to meet an old school friend, Francis, whose family had traveled to Russia. He passed her on to his sister Emily, who sent her to Geneva to her friend Rolf, an environmentalist, who, incredibly, could send her directly to Mongolia. After a five-day trip on the Trans-Siberian Express—made especially grueling by the fact that, as a vegetarian, there was hardly anything for her to eat on the train—she arrived in Ulan Bator, the capital of Mongolia, to meet her fourth link, Urtnasan, a high-ranking government official. She then moved on, in turn, to two civil servants, links 5 and 6, and then a businessman, link 7.

By now, she was feeling utterly dejected, because she had failed her six-link goal, and her herdsman was nowhere in sight. But suddenly things started looking up. The businessman sent her hundreds of miles into the desolate steppes to meet Oyuntuya, her eighth link, a teacher in a small village. More important, Oyuntuya was none other than the herdsman's mother! She led Leveugle to her son's tent in the middle of the desolate, frozen steppes. But with his nomadic lifestyle, roaming the land with his herd of 600 horses, cows, and sheep, Oyuntuya couldn't guarantee that he would be there. When Leveugle finally saw Purev-Ochir approaching on horseback—her ninth and final step—all her disappointment at not reaching him in six steps disappeared. And rightly so—Milgram's six-link model was never meant to be an ironclad rule of social life. That number was merely an average. In one of his small-world studies, the number of chain links ranged from two to ten. The revelatory nature of his finding does not hinge on specific numbers but rather on its counterintuitive feature—the unexpected finding that one could cut a swath involving very few connections through very large, complex social networks. So Leveugle's replication—

shown on British television in February 2003—was still very much a demonstration of the small-world phenomenon.

...

Milgram left a legacy of lucid, jargon-free writings that made his works accessible to a wide readership. As a result, he has played an important role in the public's recognition of the value of a disciplined, scientific approach to an understanding of everyday social behavior.

Perhaps more important, Milgram made social psychology exciting. When he was still alive and his name would come up in conversations, someone would invariably ask: "I wonder what he is up to now?" More often than not, the answer would be that Milgram was not only doing something intrinsically interesting but was expanding the proper domain of social psychology in the process. While some critics were chipping away at the bedrock findings of social psychology through claims of error and artifact, Milgram was expanding its territory by turning his attention to such topics as photography, the "familiar stranger," mental maps of cities, and subway norms. To dispel the gloom created by periodic pronouncements about a crisis in social psychology, one could always share vicariously in what Milgram liked to call the "pleasurable activity of experimental invention" through exposure to such innovations as the lost-letter technique, the small-world method, and the cyranic mode of interaction.

Milgram was an intellectual risk taker, which contributed to some extent to the polarization of opinions about him. Among some psychologists it augmented their perception of him as an outsider and his image as a bête noire. On the other hand, through his willingness to live on the edge scientifically, he became a role model to the younger generation of social psychologists. As Craig Haney, Zimbardo's collaborator on the Stanford Prison Experiment, noted:

> It is impossible to calculate the number of students who were inspired by the sheer dramatic force of [the obedience] studies to pursue careers exploring unexamined dimensions of human nature, but I count myself

among them. His work pushed against the limits of not only the ethical bounds of experimental research, but also the political limits of incisive social psychological commentary. . . . His work . . . help[ed] to expand our sense of what it was possible to accomplish in an experimental setting and even to embolden us in the critical uses to which we were willing and able to put our laboratory-based empirical knowledge.

Milgram was a major standard-bearer for the situationist perspective, and his obedience research has provided strong ammunition for the situational emphasis of mainstream social psychology. In virtually all his experiments—for example, the lost-letter technique, the television study—the primary focus was on situational manipulations rather than on personality or other individual-difference variables. But Milgram was not dogmatic about this approach. For example, in 1982, he chaired a dissertation by Sharon Presley that focused on the individual-difference variables distinguishing political resisters from nonresisters. Despite the importance Milgram placed on situational factors in understanding social behavior, he did not negate the role of personality and individual differences. In fact, one can readily find examples of individual dispositions receiving recognition in Milgram's writings. In his writings on the psychology of photography, for example, he states that one of the greatest research challenges is the delineation of the psychological makeup of the professional photographer.

More generally, Milgram saw a dispositional approach complementing his own orientation to the study of social behavior:

The implicit model for [my] experimental work is that of the person influenced by social forces while often believing in his or her own independence of them. It is thus a social psychology of the reactive individual, the recipient of forces and pressures emanating from outside oneself. This represents, of course, only one side of the coin of social life, for we as individuals also initiate action out of internal needs and actively construct the social world we inhabit. But I have left to other investigators the task of examining the complementary side of our social natures.

Milgram spent most of his professional career at CUNY. During that time, he supervised more doctoral dissertations in social psychology than any other faculty member. Many more students came into contact with him through course work, seminars, or as a member of their dissertation committees. Yet—although the innovative work of some of his students bears his creative imprint—his students have not had a major impact on social psychology. There is no clearly identifiable Milgram "school" of social psychology, comparable, say, to that of Festinger, grounded in his theory of cognitive dissonance. This lack of continuity is due to Milgram's approach to research. It was phenomenon oriented, rather than theory based. As one writer noted: "Most psychologists test hypotheses; Milgram asks questions." The majority of Milgram's studies were driven by his curiosity, his quest to verify the existence of a phenomenon or regularity in behavior suggested by subjective experience, and once established, to identify the factors that led to variations in the observed phenomenon. For example, the subway study was meant to find out if subway riders would give up their seats if you asked them to. Once the phenomenon was established, Milgram varied the nature of the request to see what led to different amounts of compliance.

But progress in science depends, at least ideally, on cumulative research—that is, experiments aimed at testing one of a number of hypotheses derived from a theory; these experiments can spawn further experiments that might help refine the theory or help resolve some questions raised by the first set of experiments. On the other hand, phenomenon-centered research is not cumulative. Once you have verified the existence of some behavioral regularity, and perhaps identified its boundaries, there is nowhere else to go. For example, once Milgram had identified the "familiar stranger," that creature of urban life, what else was there to do beyond perhaps carrying out some follow-up questioning to find out what psychological barriers maintained people's reluctance to approach "familiar strangers"?

...

Milgram sensitized us to the hidden workings of the social world. He showed the difficulty people often have bridging the gap between intentions and actions. Even moral principles are not invariably translated into behavior and can have their potential power overridden by momentary situational pressures. Although people can be responsive to the precise and subtle details of the immediate situation, they are generally not aware of the power of situational cues and forces. Social norms can often have a compelling effect on our behavior, wielding their power by means of the unexpected amount of inhibitory anxiety generated by their violation.

Few people who have read about Milgram's work remain unaffected by at least some aspect of it—whether it's the enhanced sense of control and empowerment provided by his alerting us to the subtle social pressures operating on us; a better understanding of the Holocaust; a new, balanced, nonjudgmental approach to city life; or the possibility and excitement of fresh discoveries amid our familiar, mundane activities. As he once told an interviewer:

> I . . . believe that a Pandora's box lies just below the surface of everyday life,
> so it is often worthwhile to challenge what you most take for granted. You
> are often surprised at what you find.

APPENDIX A
List of Milgram's Doctoral Students at CUNY, with Year and Title of Dissertation

Name	Year	Dissertion
Rita Dytell	1970	An Analysis of How People Use Groups as a Source of Information on Which to Base Judgments
Swadesh Grant	1971	Spatial Behavior and Caste Membership in Some North Indian Villages
Daniel Geller	1975	A Role-Playing Simulation of Obedience: Focus on Involvement
John Sabini	1976	Moral Reproach: A Conceptual and Experimental Analysis
Elinor Mannucci	1977	Potential Subjects View Psychology Experiments: An Ethical Inquiry
Maury Silver	1977	The Social Construction of Envy
Marcia Newman	1978	Perceptions of Silence in Conversation
Harold Takooshian	1979	Helping Behavior As a Social Indicator
Arthur Blank	1980	Rules of Order: Or So to Speak
Arthur Weinberger	1980	Response to Old People Who Ask for Help: Field Experiments
Elyse Goldstein	1981	The Mediation of Television Messages by Personal Influence: An Experimental Paradigm
Sharon Presley	1982	Values and Attitudes of Political Resisters to Authority
Ronna Kabatznick	1984	The Public's Perception of Psychology: Attitudes of Four Selected Groups
Christina Taylor	1984	The Social Perception of Extramarital Relationships

APPENDIX B

Sample Quotations and Content Analysis of Reviews of Obedience to Authority

Milgram's book is carefully assembled and considered research, but past that it is also a streamlined and scientific metaphor for much of recent history. The resonance is deep, from Auschwitz to My Lai, the connections unavoidable; the implications altogether cheerless.

—Rolling Stone

Milgram's experiments are arresting and dramatic, among the most original in all of social psychology. . . . Deception and manipulation led to a remarkable addition to our knowledge of the perils of authority. Knowledge like that comes hard and slow. Can we afford to prohibit further discoveries of that caliber and relevance?

—Commentary

Prof. Milgram's study can only call forth praise. It is almost anti-climactical to add that the book is easily read, thanks to the clarity and precision with which the results and analysis are presented.

—Journal of Analytical Psychology

The experiments are well worth writing up in book form. . . . They have generated fierce argument. . . . The argument has included strong attacks on Milgram's own morality in deceiving (some say cruelly deceiving) his subjects. It may be that in so doing Milgram was, like his subjects, only manifesting obedience to the authority of "Science."

—British Journal of Psychiatry

We can argue that the experiments were cruel and should not have been undertaken. We can question whether much truth can be abstracted from such a complex of deceptions. . . . But the results of the experiments remain: they are real, they have been repeated, their implications are appalling, and must not be dismissed.

—Newsweek

Professor Milgram's research into man's need to obey authority has culminated in a book which calls into question the wisdom of letting some forms of research results loose.

—Police Review, London

Milgram's work is of first importance, not only in explaining how it is that men submit, but also in suggesting how better they may rebel.

—Sunday Times, London

If it is "immoral" to find out about ourselves in a way we do not like, these experiments are certainly immoral. But then, as these experiments show, morality—at least in its public form—may have quite a lot to answer for.

—London Times Literary Supplement

Do we gain very much from a simulated or artificially provoked glimpse of inhumanity when there are so many genuine historical precedents on which to draw?

—The Sunday Telegraph, London

When I consider that the initial study was a demonstration and not even an experiment, that the research program lacked any initial theory or tests of significance, and that many of its conclusions are subject to alternative explanations, I am saddened that it is the obedience study that will go down in history as reflecting the 1960s in social psychological research.

—Contemporary Psychology

I believe that the publication of *Obedience to Authority* is more than justified and indeed makes a major contribution. But then I must confess to being partial to Milgram's work, which I consider to be a model of original, elegant, systematic, programmatic and socially relevant research. . . .

—Australian Journal of Psychology

...

The book reviews from which the above quotations were drawn came from a larger set comprising mostly reviews of *Obedience to Authority* compiled by Milgram with the aid of professional clipping services in the United States and Great Britain. With the help of bibliographic databases, I located a few additional reviews that were not in Milgram's collection. Not counting brief, one-paragraph, summaries of the book, I had a total of sixty-two reviews that had appeared in newspapers, magazines, and journals. As exemplified by the publications the quotations were drawn from, the collection of book reviews came from a very heterogeneous array of sources. Given that U.S. and British clipping services were involved, it is reasonable to assume that the sixty-two reviews constitute all or nearly all of the book reviews of *Obedience to Authority* that appeared in U.S. and British publications.

CONTENT ANALYSIS

The existence of such a large set of reviews created the opportunity to go beyond qualitative impressions and conduct a quantitative analysis that would provide a more fine-tuned differentiation of the reviews in terms of their judgments of the book. With the assistance of two of my students, Melanie Duncan and Dawn Walls, I conducted a systematic content analysis of all sixty-two reviews. Two 5-point numerical scales were created for the content analysis. The first provided a global assessment of the favorability of the review, with the numbers representing the following gradations: 1 = all negative, 2 = mostly negative, 3 = neutral or evenly balanced, 4 = mostly positive, 5 = all positive (see Figure B.1). The second scale evaluated the ethical judgments expressed in the reviews (see Figure B.2).

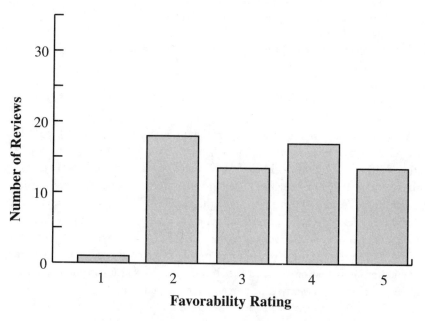

FIGURE B.1   Favorability Ratings of the Reviews.

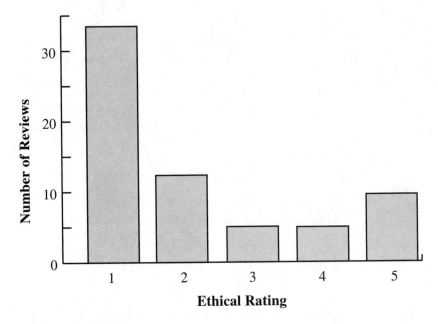

Ethical Rating Scale

1. Did not mention ethics at all
2. Simply mentioned or described ethics as being part of the book's content without further comment
3. Was critical of the ethics of the experiments
4. Noted the ethical problems but felt that Milgram had dealt with them adequately
5. Noted the ethical problems but felt that the importance of the findings outweighed them

FIGURE B.2   Ethical Ratings of the Reviews.

After initial discussion and training in the use of the scales, one of the students read all sixty-two reviews, assigning each one a favorability rating and an ethical rating. Rating reliabilities had been established by two of us independently rating fifteen randomly selected reviews. The agreement of ratings was 67 percent for the favorability scale and 70 percent for the ethics scale. While these are rather modest reliabilities, they reflect the inherent difficulty in making global, unitary judgments of what were often complex textual materials.

The distribution of the favorability ratings is depicted in Figure B.1. The most notable finding is that only one of the sixty-two reviews (1.6 percent) received the "all negative" rating. Twenty-nine percent were judged to be "mostly negative"; the "neutral" and "all positive" categories were each applied to 21 percent of the reviews; and about 27.5 percent were judged to be "mostly positive." Combining the "all positive" and "mostly positive" categories reveals that about half of the reviewers (48.5 percent) gave the book their stamp of approval. Combining the "all negative" and "mostly negative" ratings shows that 30.6 percent of the reviewers found fault with the book. That left 21 percent of the reviewers straddling the fence.

The ethics rating was included in the content analysis because the ethical acceptability of the obedience research has been the longest-running controversy associated with it. The ethical rating scale was meant to provide a more precise reading on the issue of ethics by assessing its relative importance for the reviewers.

The distribution of the ethical ratings is depicted in Figure B.2. The most frequent rating was 1, indicating that the reviewer did not mention ethics at all (33 of 62, or 53 percent). Nineteen percent simply indicated that ethics was part of the book's content, without further comment; about 6.5 percent of the reviews were critical of the experiment's ethics; an equal number noted the ethical problems but stated that Milgram had dealt with them adequately; and about 14.5 percent of the reviewers felt that the importance of the findings outweighed the ethical problems.

The reviews were evenly split in terms of the publications they were in. Half appeared in professional sources, such as scholarly journals, and the other half came from periodicals aimed at nonprofessional audiences, such as newspapers and magazines. A statistical analysis comparing the favorability and ethics ratings of the book reviews in the two types of sources showed no significant differences between them.

APPENDIX C

The Stability of Obedience Across Time and Place

I have carried out two data analyses that provide at least some evidence for the stability of rates of obedience across time and place. In one, I evaluated the relationship between the results of both Milgram's standard obedience experiments and the replications conducted by others, and their date of publication. There was absolutely no association between when a study was conducted and the amount of obedience it yielded. The correlation coefficient hovered near zero (see Table C.1).

In a second analysis, I again took all of Milgram's standard conditions and replications conducted by others and compared the outcomes of the studies conducted in the United States with those of studies conducted in other countries. Remarkably, the average obedience rates were very similar: In the U.S. studies, on average, 61 percent of the subjects were fully obedient, and elsewhere the obedience rate was 66 percent. A statistical test showed that those averages were not significantly different from each other (see Table C.2).

TABLE C.1   Obedience Studies, with Year of Publication,
Country in Which Study Was Conducted, and Obedience Rate Found

Study	Country	Obedience Rate (%)
Milgram (1963)	United States	
Exp. 1		65
Exp. 2		62.5
Exp. 3		40
Exp. 5		65
Exp. 6		50
Exp. 8		65
Exp. 10		47.5
Holland (1967)	United States	75
Ancona and Pareyson (1968)	Italy	85
Rosenhan (1969)	United States	85
Podd (1969)	United States	31
Edwards, Franks, Friedgood, Lobban, and Mackay (1969)	South Africa	87.5
Ring, Wallston, and Corey (1970)	United States	91
Mantell (1971)	West Germany	85
Bock (1972)	United States	40
Powers and Geen (1972)	United States	83
Rogers (1973)	United States	37
Kilham and Mann (1974)	Australia	28
Shalala (1974)	United States	30
Costanzo (1976)	United States	81
Shanab and Yahya (1977)	Jordan	73
Shanab and Yahya (1978)	Jordan	62.5
Miranda, Caballero, Gomez, and Zamorano (1981)	Spain	50
Schurz (1985)	Austria	80

TABLE C.2   Comparison of Obedience Rates Found in U.S. Studies and Non-U.S. Studies

| U.S. Studies | | Foreign Studies | | |
Author(s)	Obedience Rate (%)	Author(s)	Country	Obedience Rate (%)
Milgram (1974) (Average of Exps. 1, 2, 3, 5, 6, 8, 10)	56.43	Ancona and Pareyson (1968)	Italy	85.0
Holland (1967)	75.0	Edwards et. al. (1969)	South Africa	87.5
Rosenhan (1969)	85.0	Mantell (1971)	Germany	85.0
Podd (1969)	31.0	Kilham and Mann (1974)	Australia	28.0
Ring et. al. (1970)	91.0	Shanab and Yahya (1977)	Jordan	73.0
Bock (1972)	40.0	Shanab and Yahya (1978)	Jordan	62.5
Powers and Geen (1972)	83.0	Miranda et. al. (1981)	Spain	50.0
Rogers (1973)	37.0	Gupta (1983) (Average of 1 Remote and 3 Voice-Feedback conditions)	India	42.5
Shalala (1974)	30.0	Schurz (1985)	Austria	80.0
Costanzo (1976)	81.0			

U.S. Mean obedience rate=60.94%; foreign mean obedience rate=65.94%

NOTES

KEY TO SOURCES

AHAP: Archives of the History of American Psychology

ASM: Personal collection of Alexandra (Sasha) Milgram

HUA: Harvard University Archives. With a few exceptions, the material is from Milgram's graduate student file.

ISW: Milgram, S. (1977). *The Individual in a Social World: Essays and Experiments.* Reading, MA: Addison-Wesley.

Milgram, S. (1992). *The Individual in a Social World: Essays and Experiments,* 2nd edition. Edited by J. Sabini and M. Silver. New York: McGraw-Hill.

This is an anthology of Milgram's published writings. The two editions contain the same introductions and mostly the same articles. The second edition dropped a few articles and added some articles that were published after the appearance of the first edition. In the notes below, articles that are cited as reprinted in ISW may be found in both editions. When page numbers are provided, they refer to the second edition. If an article appears in only one of the editions, this will be indicated (e.g., reprinted in ISW, 2nd edition only).

OTA: Milgram, S. (1974). *Obedience to Authority: An Experimental View.* New York: Harper and Row.

Remembrance: Letters by Milgram's colleagues and students reflecting back on how Milgram affected their lives. At the American Psychological Association Convention in August 1993, a number of events marked the thirtieth anniversary of the appearance of Milgram's first obedience article and what would have been his sixtieth birthday on August 15. In conjunction with those events, some of Milgram's former students solicited letters of remembrance to be presented to the Milgram family.

SMP: Stanley Milgram Papers, Yale University Library, Manuscripts and Archives

PROLOGUE

xviii **Found in the *Talmud*:** Tractate "Ethics of the Fathers," chap. 4, v. 27.

xviii **The first experiment:** Triplett (1987).

xix **Skills . . . during World War II:** Cartwright (1948).

xix Watson attempted to create: DeGrandpré and Buskist (2000); Lundin (1996).

xx The first textbook: Hilgard (1987).

xx As John Dashiell . . . wrote: Dashiell (1935, p. 1097).

xxi Lewin was a Jewish psychologist: Marrow (1969).

xxi "Path-breaking in their procedural audacity": Jones (1985a).

xxi An experiment to study . . . leadership styles: Lewin, Lippitt, and White (1939). My description of this study benefited from Jones (1985b) and Wheeler (1970).

xxii The theory of cognitive dissonance: Festinger (1957).

xxii Milgram . . . also influenced by Lewin: Letter from Milgram to Kathy Grant, March 5, 1980, SMP.

xxii According to Lewin: Marrow, op. cit.

xxiii "[Lewin] conceived of a person": Jones (1985b, p. 68).

CHAPTER 1: THE NEIGHBORHOOD WITH NO NAME

1 Stanley Milgram was born: Interview with Joel Milgram, Cambridge, MA, June 24, 1993; Interview with Marjorie (Milgram) Marton, Rockville, MD, September 26, 1996.

1 His father seemed "especially sturdy": From an unpublished memoir by Milgram about his early childhood, titled "The Neighborhood With No Name," written in the early 1980s, ASM.

2 "The neighborhood was always abuzz": Ibid.

2 Sam and Adele's second child: Interviews with Alexandra (Sasha) Milgram, Riverdale, NY, April 25 and June 13, 1993.

3 "Mom would be going to the hospital": "The Neighborhood With No Name," op. cit.

3 When Joel was old enough: Interview with Joel Milgram, op. cit.

3 Center of their lives: From a film titled "The Old Neighborhood" made by Milgram's students in his class "Film and Video as Research Tools in Social Science" in the spring of 1981 at CUNY. In the film Milgram takes the viewer on a walking tour of the Bronx neighborhood where he grew up, reminiscing and pointing out significant locations, such as PS 77 and one of the buildings the family had lived in, ASM.

3 A dress code: Marjorie Marton, conversations, January 2001.

4 Babies came from tulips: "The Old Neighborhood," op. cit.

4 Stanley's superior intelligence: Interviews with Sasha Milgram, op. cit.

4 Proud of his brother's achievements: Interview with Joel Milgram, op. cit.

4 When the "sodium bomb" exploded: Tavris (1974b)

5 "It was as natural as breathing": Quoted in Tavris (1974a, p. 77); reprinted in ISW, p. xxviii.

5 Among Stanley's childhood experiences: "The Neighborhood With No Name," op. cit.

6 Samuel Milgram was a proud father: Ibid.

6 "He resembled his father": Interviews with Sasha Milgram, op. cit.

6 One of Stanley's . . . childhood memories: "The Neighborhood With No Name," op. cit.

7 When the United States entered World War II: Interviews with Joel Milgram, Marjorie Marton, and Sasha Milgram, op. cit.

8 "As I come of age": Milgram's handwritten Bar Mitzvah speech, ASM.

8 Bernard Fried . . . remembers the school: Interview with Bernard Fried, February 18, 2001.

9 Zimbardo remembers Milgram: Interview with Philip Zimbardo, Toronto, August 22, 1993.

9 Stanley was a member of Arista: A. Milgram (2000).

10 He did not date at Monroe: Interview with Bernard Fried, op. cit.

10 The bakery Sam . . . bought: Interviews with Joel Milgram and Marjorie Marton, op. cit.

11 Marjorie . . . remembers it as "the closest thing": Interview with Marjorie Marton, ibid.

11 In 1953, the Ford Foundation: *The People's College on the Hill* (1987).

11 At Queens College: Milgram's college transcript, HUA; Queen's College yearbook, "Silhouette," for 1954, courtesy of Joseph Brostek; application submitted to Social Science Research Council (SSRC) December 31, 1956, ASM.

11 In the summer of 1953: Interviews with Sasha Milgram, op. cit.

12 French language course: Sorbonne enrollment form for a "Cours Pratique," HUA.

12 Fell in love with a French girl: Interview with Joel Milgram, op. cit.

12 Later that year: Interviews with Marjorie Marton and Joel Milgram, op. cit.

12 A New York State Regents scholarship: SSRC Fellowship application, op. cit.

13 "He would live to be fifty-five": Interviews with Sasha Milgram, op. cit.

13 Was accepted by . . . School of International Affairs: A. Milgram (2000).

13 Fried has a distinct memory: Interview with Bernard Fried, op. cit.

13 In the spring semester of 1954: Milgram's Queens College transcript, HUA; A. Milgram (2000); Tavris (1974b).

14 Ford Foundation . . . Program: Tavris (1974b).

14 Selected as one of the recipients: Report from the Ford Foundation, April 30, 1954, AHAP.

14 He was the first Jew: Interviews with Joel Milgram and Marjorie Marton, op. cit.

14 Henry Ford . . . a vocal anti-Semite: See Baldwin (2001).

14 Lacked adequate preparation: A. Milgram (2000); Milgram's Queens College transcript, HUA.

14 Letter to the Social Relations Department dated May 30, 1954: HUA.

15 Reply from Gordon Allport: Letter from Allport, June 1, 1954, HUA.

15 Enrolled in *six* undergraduate courses: Letter to Mrs. Sprague, July 15, 1955, HUA.

16 Concluded one of his letters: Letter to Allport, July 8, 1954, HUA.

16 "We can discuss a plan": Letter from Allport, July 19, 1954, SMP.

16 "Gordon Allport was my longtime mentor": Quoted in Tavris (1974a, p. 77). Also in ISW, p. xxviii.

16 A lonely existence: Entry for June 9, 1951, in Milgram's diary, "Thoughts," ASM.

CHAPTER 2: MAKING THE GRADE AT HARVARD

17 Integrating the four disciplines: Conversations with E. L. Pattullo, 2001; Parsons (1956).

17 The productive teamwork: Marrow, op. cit.

17 The concept of "attitude": Allport (1935).

18 Study of prejudice and of religious belief: Allport (1954); Allport and Ross (1967).

18 Clyde Kluckhohn . . . Navajo Indians: Hay (1999).

18 Talcott Parsons . . . leader in his field: Brick (1999); Vidich (2000).

18 The rationale . . . was spelled out: Allport and Boring (1946).

18 The interdisciplinary aims: Parsons, op. cit.

19 During Milgram's first semester: Letter to Allport, September 28, 1954, SMP.

19 The sociologists walked out: Conversations with E.L. Pattullo, op. cit.

20 Immediate source of instability: Nichols (1998).

20 Atmosphere of optimism: Parsons, op. cit.

20 *Personality in Nature, Society, and Culture:* Kluckhohn, Murray, and Schneider (1967).

20 A wide-ranging interest in the social sciences: Letter to Kathy Grant, op. cit.

20 Roger Brown . . . recalled: From a talk he gave at a commemorative gathering at the CUNY Graduate Center on May 10, 1985, organized by Irwin Katz, Milgram's colleague.

21 He had created a norm: Milgram told this story in ISW, pp. 253–254.

22 Emerson Hall in . . . Harvard Yard: Bunting (1985).

22 Harvard's social gospelers: Vidich, op. cit.

22 The first Ph.D.'s in psychology: Triplet (1992).

22 She wrote on her test booklet: I obtained this quotation from a Harvard University Web page that no longer seems to be available. In searching for an alternative source, I discovered that there are different versions of the quote, in which the wording and details differ slightly. Although I could not find a source with the same wording that I obtained from the Harvard Web site, a similar, and probably more authoritative, account can be found in *Selected Writings of Gertrude Stein,* edited by Carl Van Vechten (New York: Vintage, 1990), p. 66.

23 Milgram was able to take: Milgram's graduate record, HUA.

23 Letter from Gordon Allport, dated June 9, 1955: SMP.

23 He also attained A's: Graduate record, op. cit.

23 The graduate school gave him credit: Graduate record, op. cit.

23 Bruner had sent a progress report: Letter from Bruner to Robert Knapp, January 25, 1955; undated and unsigned memo, "Report on Harvard and Columbia Fellows—1954–55," most likely written by Knapp, AHAP.

24 "I really fell in love with the discipline": Questionnaire sent in May 1955, AHAP.

24 Extension of his fellowship: Letter to Bernard Berelson, February 3, 1955, AHAP.

24 Informed by Robert Knapp: Letter to Milgram, February 16, 1955, AHAP.

24 Recommended him for a full scholarship: Letter to the Ford Foundation, June 6, 1955, AHAP.

24 Milgram joined it: Letter to Cadet Stanley Milgram from William P. Vanden Dries, Major, USAF, ASM.

25 Military service as a commissioned officer: Interview with Joseph Brostek, May 9, 2001.

25 He withdrew from the course: Milgram's Queens College transcript, HUA.

25 Sent off another letter: Letter to Ford Foundation, op. cit.

25 Knapp's . . . reply had even greater finality: Letter to Milgram, June 15, 1955, AHAP.

25 Chronic state of anxiety: From an article Milgram wrote during the 1957–1958 academic year for *Impuls,* a mimeographed newsletter put out by the psychology students at the University of Oslo, titled "Life and Learning at Harvard's Department of Social Relations," ASM.

26 He had worked almost every summer: Conversations with Sasha Milgram, 1999–2003.

26 Received a reassuring letter: Letter from Mrs. Eleanor Sprague, July 21, 1955, HUA.

26 Most important scientific influence: Letter to Kathy Grant, op. cit.

26 Both Bruner and Allport agreed: Interview with Jerome Bruner, New York City, October 26, 2000.

27 A Letter to . . . Talcott Parsons: Letter from Asch to Parsons, February 24, 1956, HUA. Asch also wrote Milgram a warm thank you letter on September 3, 1956, SMP.

27 "Almost exclusively stressed the slavish submission": Asch (1958).

27 Opinion serves as a stimulus: Wheeler, op. cit.

27 Asch's experimental procedure: Although the philosophical issues that led Asch to examine conformity experimentally were clearly ones that he first contemplated as an adult, the idea for the specific technique he invented may have been spawned by a childhood experience.

Asch was born in 1907 in Warsaw, Poland, and grew up in Lowitz, a small town outside of Warsaw. He recalled the first night of Passover when he was about seven. It was the first time the children were allowed to stay up late for the Seder:

Everything was prepared; it was a glowing ceremony. . . . Then I saw my grandmother fill a cup of wine for each of us including the children; and in addition, another cup. Then I saw a chair in which nobody sat. I was sitting next to an uncle of mine and I asked what this meant. He said that the prophet Elijah comes into every Jewish home on Passover. That is why there is a chair prepared for him, and at the proper moment in the ceremony the door is opened to admit him and that he takes a sip of the cup of wine meant for him. I was completely fascinated and astounded that the prophet Elijah would in one night stop at all the Jewish homes in the world. I said to my uncle, "Will he really take a sip?" and he said, "Oh yes, you just watch when the time comes, watch the cup"—it was filled to the rim—"and you'll see that it goes down." And when the moment came, my eyes were glued to the Prophet's cup; I looked and looked and then it seemed to me as if perhaps it did go down a little! . . . Don't ask whether what happened to me at the age of seven was responsible for an experiment that came forty years later—I don't know. (Quoted in Ceraso, Gruber, and Rock, 1990, p. 3).

28 An "epistemological nightmare": Quoted in Ceraso et al., ibid., p. 12.

29 Milgram felt freer to be himself: Interviews with John Shaffer, March 29, 1999; Saul Sternberg, May 24, 2001; Robert Palmer, May 14, 2001; Norman Bradburn, May 15, 2001.

29 He wrote back to her: Letter to Mrs. Sprague, March 2, 1956, HUA.

30 "Since it appears to me unlikely": Letter to Mosteller, May 25, 1956, HUA.

CHAPTER 3: NORWAY AND FRANCE

31 An analysis of national stereotypes: Letter to Allport, October 17, 1956, SMP.

31 He wanted Allport to be his . . . supervisor: Ibid.

31 "A firm believer in the uniqueness of personality": Pettigrew (1999).

32 Milgram's plan was to complete: Letter to Social Science Research Council (SSRC), August 31, 1956, ASM.

32 Made some inquiries: Letter from Elbridge Sibley to Milgram, September 5, 1956, AHAP.

32 A lengthy letter to Allport: Letter to Allport, October 17, 1956, op. cit.

32 The Nature of Prejudice: Allport (1954).

33 "The design you outline is not feasible": Letter from Allport, November 4, 1956, SMP.

33 A streamlining . . . research plans: Milgram's fellowship application to SSRC, December 31, 1956, ASM.

34 Allport wrote: Allport to Stein Rokkan and Ragnar Rommetveit, December 18, 1956, HUA.

34 Both men expressed a genuine interest: letters to Allport from Rommetveit, January 21, 1957, and Rokkan, January 29, 1957, SMP.

34 His name . . . on a short list: Letter from Sibley, March 26, 1957, ASM.

34 He was awarded a fellowship: Letter from Joseph B. Casagrande, ASM.

34 "You fail [sic] the examination": Letter from Allport, June 6, 1957, SMP.

34 "Considerably distressed": Sibley's reply, June 12, 1957, to Allport's letter, June 13, 1957, HUA.

34 Milgram wrote Sibley: Letter dated June 17, 1957, ASM. Why did Milgram fail the exam? Given his academic record in other courses and his general competence, it is surprising. The explanation he gave Sibley was this: Doctoral students in social psychology have a statistics requirement that is usually met by passing the final examination of Social Relations 191, a statistics course. Al-

though students typically take that course, they are allowed to take the exam without having enrolled in the course. Milgram had signed up for Social Relations 191 at the beginning of the 1957 spring semester but dropped it when he found that it conflicted with other, unspecified, activities. However, he did do the course readings and the assignments in the syllabus on his own. Apparently, this alternative mode of learning the material was not adequate enough to pass the course, although Milgram felt that he had learned the statistical techniques covered in the course.

35   After receiving assurances: Milgram's telephone memo, July 3, 1957, ASM.

35   The monthly installments: Letter from Sibley, July 8, 1957, ASM.

35   They approved the proposal: Thesis Conference Committee Report, September 24, 1957, HUA.

35   "Let me repeat that we know": Letter from Allport, September 30, 1957.

36   Letter to a female friend: Letter to Enid, October 18, 1957, ASM.

36   "I have great respect": Letter to Allport, November 18, 1957, SMP.

36   Milgram's host organization: Letter to Allport, ibid.

37   All the regions . . . would be represented: Milgram's dissertation (1960); Milgram (1961), reprinted in ISW. My presentation of the procedure and results of the conformity experiment is based on these sources.

37   Since he would be: All the subjects were male. Milgram explained why: "Numerous experiments show that sex is an important variable in determining the level of conformity. By eliminating this source of variability, we increase the chance that differences due to the factor of nationality will come through" (Milgram, 1960, p. 19).

38   The others constituted a "synthetic group": Milgram's use of tape recordings to simulate a group was an adaptation of a technique introduced by Blake and Brehm (1954).

38   "The group is always willing": Milgram (1960, p. 27). When a year later Milgram published an article based on his dissertation in *Scientific American* (Milgram, 1961), it contained a modified version of this quip: "With tape recordings it is easy to create synthetic groups. Tapes do not have to be paid by the hour and they are always available."

38   "It is hard to convey": Milgram (1960, p. 38).

40   "It is a common fallacy": Ibid., p. 194.

40   Introduced him to the *Janteloven:* Ibid., p. 200.

41   A detailed progress report: Letter to Allport, February 19, 1958, HUA.

41   "Probably inter-sterile": Letter to Allport, ibid.

41   Question of generalizability: Milgram (1960, p. 116).

42   Allport was delighted: Letter to Milgram, February 28, 1958, SMP.

42   "A Biblical miracle": Letter to Allport, February 19, 1958, op. cit.; letter from Sibley, December 26, 1957, ASM.

42   "Since Milgram is a very bright person": Allport to Sibley, February 28, 1958, HUA.

42   Awarded the one-year extension: Milgram accepted the fellowship in a letter to Sibley dated April 10, 1958, ASM.

42 **This kind of censure:** Milgram also conducted another kind of "censure" condition. Here, instead of being criticized for showing off, the comments from the other "subjects" were personal insults, questioning the naïve subject's ability. His correct answers would be followed by such comments as "That was stupid" and "Fool." While this "personal inadequacy" condition yielded a 65 percent conformity rate, which was lower than the condition in which subjects were criticized for the social impropriety of their response (75 percent), the difference was not statistically significant. Milgram did not conduct this "personal inadequacy" condition in France.

44 **"Most subjects were glad":** Milgram (1960, pp. 175–176). Later, Milgram reproduced his chapter from his dissertation on the ethical questionnaire—where this quote is from—in ISW. His purpose was to show critics of his obedience experiments that he was sensitive to ethical issues, and that his sensitivity in fact predated the experiments.

45 **In one of his reports:** Asch (1956, p. 53).

45 **In describing his ethics questionnaire:** Letter to Allport, May 11, 1958, SMP.

45 **Bragged that word had reached him:** Letter to Enid, October, 1958, ASM.

46 **Actually carvings of** *himself*: Letter to Mother and Joel, August 19, 1958, ASM.

46 **She would . . . write chatty letters:** For example, letters of September 8, 1958; November 23, 1958; February 27, 1959, ASM.

46 **"My true spiritual home":** Letter to John Shaffer, November 9, 1958, ASM.

46 **"I did not know how to ski":** Letter to Mrs. Sprague, September 23, 1958, HUA.

47 **Finding some female companionship:** Ibid.; Milgram note, April 25, 1958, ASM; letter to Rosalind, October 19, 1958, ASM.

47 **Shared an apartment:** Interviews with Sasha Milgram, op. cit.; letter to Mrs. Sprague, ibid.

47 **"The damp season in Oslo":** Letter to Ulf Torgersen, November 3, 1958, ASM.

47 **Staying in Norway longer than . . . planned:** Letters to Allport, May 11, 1958, SMP; Sibley, July 29, 1958, ASM; Allport, August 21, 1958, HUA; Saul Sternberg, September 13, 1958, ASM.

47 **The Elektrisk Bureau:** A large manufacturer of electric appliances in Oslo; letter to Sibley, July 6, 1958, ASM.

48 **"Paris is the city I like best":** Letter to Ulf Torgersen, op. cit.

48 **"There is so much selfishness":** Letter to Saul Sternberg, op. cit.

48 **"If I am feeling depressed":** Letter to Ulf Torgersen, op. cit.

48 **"When my girl 'friend' left Paris":** Undated letter fragment to unidentified recipient. Quoted portions suggest he wrote the letter after he returned to the U.S., which would date it sometime after April 1959. Unquoted parts of the letter suggest that he was writing to a female friend, ASM.

49 **Entry . . . was gained fraudulently:** Letter to Enid, December, 1958, ASM.

49 **His stay at Victor Lyon . . . almost cut short:** Letter to Enid, ibid. The English translation of Milgram's article in *Le Journal de Victor Lyon* was provided by Francois Rochat.

50 **She sent a complaint to . . . Harvard:** Letter from Robert W. White to Gerard Latortue, June 24, 1959. Letters of support came from Robert G. Mead, April 6, 1959, and Gerard Latortue, May 27, 1959. The quotation is from the latter's letter and was translated by Leonard Siger. The three letters and Milgram's graduate record are from HUA.

50 **Jerome Bruner had contacted:** Letter to Allport, August 21, 1958, SMP.

51 **"It worked on 50 cycle synchronized operation":** Milgram (1960, p. 129).

51 **"It would have been superficial":** Milgram (1960, pp. 152–153).

52 **Table 3.1:** Based on Table 19 in Milgram, ibid.

52 **Figure 3.1:** Based on bar graph in Milgram (1961, p. 50), as reproduced in ISW, p. 208.

53 **In two cases quite explosively:** As noted earlier, Milgram did not repeat a "personal inadequacy" condition—which he had conducted after the Censure condition in Norway—with his French subjects. No doubt, he did not want to risk a repetition of the kind of volatile reactions shown by some of his French subjects in the Censure condition.

53 **Reflecting back on his experiments:** Milgram (1961), reprinted in ISW.

54 **"Each time something like this happens":** Letter to Haakon Hovstad, March 1959, SMP.

54 **"Stanley was quite international":** E-mail to me from Leon Mann, October 16, 2002.

CHAPTER 4: FROM THE "PRINCETITUTE" TO YALE

55 **Passed (with "distinction"):** Milgram's graduate record, HUA.

55 **"A final, beatific year":** Letter to Mike and Lise, ASM.

55 **A letter from Asch:** Dated August 29, 1959, SMP.

56 **Help edit a book:** Letter to Mike and Lise, op. cit.

56 **A salary of $4,200:** Milgram's memo "Note on Salary received from Asch," October 15, 1959, SMP.

56 **Milgram agonized . . . Asch's invitation:** Undated ruminations, in rough draft form, most likely written in September 1959. Although it seems to be a letter to Asch—it begins with "Dear Dr. Asch"—some negative comments it contains about the benefits of working with Asch make it highly unlikely that he actually sent it, SMP.

56 **Successfully petitioned:** Letters from Milgram to Asch, September 19, 1959, SMP; Milgram to Allport, September 28, 1959, HUA; from Allport to Milgram, September 30, 1959, SMP.

56 **A diary notebook:** ASM.

57 **Accepted . . . with the expectation:** Undated ruminations, op. cit.

57 **Expectation not fulfilled:** Undated "Letter to S.E.A.," likely written in May or June, 1960, but not sent, SMP.

57 **His name does not appear:** There is an Asch file in the library of the Institute for Advanced Study, consisting largely of correspondence between Asch and Institute staff. There is no mention of Milgram in any of the letters.

57 **A letter of resignation:** Letter to Asch, June 3, 1960, SMP.

57 A very stressful . . . year: Ibid.

57 Came up with . . . suggested wording: Letter to Asch June 18, 1960, SMP.

58 A few bright spots: Letter to Ed, October 23, 1959, ASM.

58 "My only pleasure": Letter to Marilyn Zeitlin, October 17, 1959, ASM.

58 "I'm listless, uneasy": Letter to Enid, January 15, 1960; ASM.

58 Break up the monotony: Interviews with Sasha Milgram, op. cit.

58 Life went on: Interviews with Sasha Milgram, Joel Milgram, and Marjorie Marton, op. cit.

59 "I have dropped all pretensions": Letter to Allport, November 4, 1959, HUA.

59 "Your progress report": Letter from Allport, November 9, 1959, SMP.

59 "The dissertation has been pushed forward": Letter to Allport, January 16, 1960, HUA.

59 "Masterpieces of conviction": Letter from Allport, January 20, 1960, SMP.

59 "An intermediate version": Letter to Allport, February 29, 1960, HUA.

59 "Perhaps I'm slipping": Letter from Allport, March 3, 1960, SMP.

60 A letter from Leonard Doob: ASM. Most likely the suggestion that Doob contact Milgram came from Irving Janis, a senior member of the department, who had met Stanley in Oslo in 1957–1958. Janis had spent that year at the Institute for Social Research as a Fulbright scholar, the same year that Milgram was conducting the Norwegian portion of his cross-cultural conformity experiment. Once at Yale, Janis became Milgram's closest friend among the senior faculty and a constant source of encouragement to him.

60 Milgram wrote back promptly: Letter to Doob, May 6, 1960, ASM.

60 Research Fellow in Cognitive Studies: Official appointment letter from Harvard, May 16, 1960, ASM.

60 Annual salary of $6,500: Official Yale University appointment letter, October 8, 1960, ASM.

60 "It was a very hard decision": Undated draft of a letter to Allport, most likely written in May 1960, SMP.

60 Allport had been trying to help: Allport to Dick [Solomon] and Jerry [Bruner], March 9, 1960, HUA.

61 "A proud rooster": Letter from Allport, January 28, 1962, SMP.

61 "An excellent study": Letter from Kelman to Allport, May 3, 1960, HUA.

61 "Your thesis is very good indeed": Letter from Allport, June 2, 1960, SMP.

62 A phenomenon of great consequence: Interview with Roger Brown, William James Hall, June 23, 1993.

62 "[My] laboratory paradigm": ISW, p. 126.

62 "I was trying to think": In Tavris (1974a), p. 80; also in ISW, p. xxxi.

63 Milgram listed . . . research projects: Letter to Allport, March 2, 1960, SMP.

63 He first learned about Milgram's plans: Interview of Asch by James Korn, July 14, 1989, Solomon Asch Papers, AHAP.

63 Milgram arrived in New Haven: Letters to Ed, September 18 and 30, 1960, ASM.

63 His favorite . . . classic garden: In light of this, it is perhaps especially appropriate that the Manuscripts and Archives department, which houses the Stanley Milgram Papers, is located adjacent to this garden.

64 **"Are you a psychologist":** Letter to Allport, October 10, 1960, SMP. Milgram's quip was a mildly critical comment on the fact that some psychologists at Yale were doing research with animals—especially rats—as subjects rather than humans.

64 **Milgram was renting:** Conversations with Sasha Milgram, 1999–2003.

65 **A small grant proposal:** "Application for Grant-in-Aid Research," October 7, 1960, SMP.

65 **He assured Allport:** Letter to Allport, op. cit.

65 **Request was turned down:** Letter from D.H. Daugherty, December 19, 1960, ASM.

65 **He did some self-experimentation:** Interview with Nijole Kudirka, 2002.

65 **A dart-throwing game:** "Dart Game Experiment," a brief description of procedure, with results in graph form, SMP.

65 **Occasionally used other drugs:** Conversation with Sasha Milgram, April 1, 2001.

65 **"Next year I . . . plan":** Letter to Allport, op. cit.

66 **"Obedience is as basic an element":** Letter to Petrullo, October 14, 1960, SMP.

67 **His own shock machine:** Buss (1961).

67 **Milgram suspected:** E-mail to me from Philip Zimbardo, May 5, 1998; letter to Henry Riecken, September 21, 1961, in Milgram's grant file G-17916, "Dynamics of Obedience: Experiments in Social Psychology," National Science Foundation.

67 **Exchange of correspondence . . . allayed Milgram's suspicions:** Letter from Arnold Buss, September 21, 1961, SMP; letter to Riecken, ibid.; Milgram (1963, p. 373, footnote 3).

67 **Did not completely eliminate them:** Letter to Alan Elms, September 25, 1973, SMP.

67 **Two other grant prospects:** Letter to Public Health Service, November 15, 1960; letter to Dr. Henry Riecken, National Science Foundation, November 17, 1960, both SMP.

67 **Pilot experiments were carried out:** "Recollections of the Yale Psychology Department" by Milgram, sent in a letter to William Kessen, Chairman of Yale's Psychology Department, on January 16, 1979. Kessen had requested such recollections from former faculty and students to help mark the fiftieth anniversary of the founding of the department, SMP.

68 **His written report:** Milgram (1964c); Proposal for Grant G-17916, NSF Grant file, op. cit.

68 **"Before an experiment is carried out":** "Recollections of the Yale Psychology Department," op. cit.

69 **A formal application:** Letter to National Science Foundation from Marcus Robbins, Comptroller, Yale University, January 27, 1961, SMP.

70 **A colleague's criticism:** OTA, p. 170.

70 **Approved on May 3, 1961:** Acceptance telegram to Dr. Henry Riecken, Director, Social Science Division, NSF, from Donald V. Green, Manager, Office of Gifts, Grants and Contracts, Yale University, May 3, 1961, NSF Grant file, op. cit.

70 **Completed the first four experiments:** Letter to Riecken, September 21, 1961, NSF Grant file, op. cit.

71 **Ethical questions . . . took a back seat:** Interview with Herbert Kelman, William James Hall, August 22, 2000.

71 **A final but important note:** NSF Grant file, op. cit.

71 **Knowing that the "victim" was not hurt:** Milgram (1964b).

71 **Riecken observed somewhat critically:** NSF Grant file, op. cit.

72 **The NSF final panel rating was "Meritorious":** Ibid.

72 **He met Alexandra (Sasha) Menkin:** Interviews with Sasha Milgram, op. cit.

73 **"He was very impressed with Sasha":** Interview with Howard Leventhal, spring 1999.

74 **David Sears . . . told him:** Quoted by Milgram in "Recollections of the Yale Psychology Department," op cit.

74 **Married in a small ceremony:** Interviews with Sasha Milgram, op. cit.

75 **Turning his attention to the many details:** For example, letter to an instrument manufacturer, the Grason-Stadler Company, June 20, 1961, inquiring about a procedure for recording the duration of each shock administered; a letter dated June 6, 1961, to Holt, Rinehart, and Winston ordering the book *The Teaching-Learning Process,* by Nathaniel Cantor, one of the props to be used in the experiments; letter to department secretary, Miss Henry, July 29, 1961, requesting payment to a technician for his work on the electric circuits in the shock machine, SMP; letter to Riecken, August 15, 1961, NSF Grant file, op. cit.

75 **The laboratory doors opened:** Letter to Riecken, ibid.

75 **Subjects were scheduled:** Letter to Yale University Police, October 17, 1961, SMP.

75 **A display ad:** Reproduced in OTA, p. 15.

75 **In the early 1960s:** Elms (1995).

76 **Cleared it with the department chairman:** Letter to Buxton, June 6, 1961, SMP.

76 **The subjects ranged:** These and most other general details of the laboratory procedure to be described are based on OTA and Milgram (1963, 1965b), the latter reprinted in ISW.

76 **At the door of the lab:** The experimenter-subject dialogues reproduced in this and the next chapter are actually from the Bridgeport experiment conducted later in the series (Experiment 10 in OTA), not the earlier experiments in Linsly-Chittenden Hall. The protocols (e.g., experimenter's instructions, learner's prerecorded schedule of complaints, and so on) are exactly the same as in a baseline "heart-condition" experiment (Experiment 5 in OTA) conducted in Linsly-Chittenden Hall. I used these dialogues because the Bridgeport condition was the only one whose "sanitized" audiotapes were available at SMP when I was writing this book. I did some minor editing of the transcripts of the audiotapes and supplemented the account with visual details from Milgram's descriptions in his book, in the film *Obedience,* and, in the case of the first sub-

ject to be presented, an unnamed observer's notes on his behavior found in his data file at SMP.

76　**A gray—rather than white—lab coat:** Meyer (1970).

76　**Milgram's primary assistants:** While they were the main experimenter-subject team, in a few instances, as dictated by the needs of the experiment, other people served as experimenter and learner; see, e.g., Experiments 6 and 9 in OTA, pp. 59, 60, and 66.

76　**Repeated rehearsals:** Tavris (1974b).

76　**His employers were not very happy:** E-mails to me from Robert McDonough, the youngest of James McDonough's nine children, December 9 and 17, 2000. In the experimental conditions to be described as well as in other conditions in Milgram's series of obedience experiments James McDonough refers to a heart condition. According to Robert, this was actually based on fact. His father did have a heart problem and died from it about three years later.

77　**In his interview notes:** Undated, handwritten, two pages of notes, which also contained other information, such as McDonough's occupation, his rate of pay ($1.75 per hour), what hours he was available, and the fact that he was willing to work for a year, SMP.

78　**Commercial sources . . . told him:** Milgram's grant application to NSF, titled "Obedience to Authority: Experiments in Social Psychology," dated January 25, 1962, SMP. When approved, it received the grant number G-24512. This was the second in a series of three grant applications—all approved—that he submitted to NSF to support his obedience studies.

78　**Two electrical engineers:** Letter to Riecken, August 15, 1961, op. cit.

81　**To 1/100th of a second:** Ibid.

89　**Intensely agonized scream:** For standardization, I have used Milgram's wording to describe the subject's nonverbal responses and screams; see OTA, "The Learner's Schedule of Protests," pp. 56–57.

CHAPTER 6: OBEDIENCE: THE EXPERIMENT

93　**The first four experiments:** First reported in Milgram (1965b), reprinted in ISW, and then presented again in OTA.

95　**Wanted to publish . . . quickly:** Letter to Riecken, February 5, 1962, SMP.

95　**The Yale seniors predicted:** Milgram (1963).

95　**A group of psychiatric residents:** Letter to Allport, February 2, 1962, SMP.

95　**"Although they expressed great certainty":** Letter to E.P. Hollander, September 24, 1962, SMP.

96　**At most, one or two subjects:** Letter to Riecken, September 21, 1961, NSF Grant file, op. cit.

96　**"It is a very disturbing sight":** Ibid.

96　**"The learner . . . begs him to stop":** OTA, pp. 45–46.

97　**Figure 6.1:** Reproduction of Figure 6 in OTA, p. 36.

97　**The measure of shock duration:** These findings are described in "Obedience to Authority: Experiments in Social Psychology," January 25, 1962, Milgram's second grant application to NSF, op. cit., SMP. A graphical depiction of the results was also included in the grant application. My Figure 6.2 is a reproduction of a more professionally drawn version, also found in SMP, which must have been drawn later.

98 **He first met Milgram:** Interview with Alan Elms, San Francisco, August 17, 1998.

99 **"A pleasant month of leisure":** Letter to Elms, June 27, 1961, SMP.

99 **"Numerous productive functions":** Letter to Asch, June 27, 1961, SMP.

100 **His main scientific influence:** For example, letter to Kathy Grant, op. cit.

100 **A congratulatory letter:** A typed draft to Asch, January 11, 1968, SMP. A written notation—"handwritten and slightly revised"—appears on the bottom.

100 **"Ten variations on a theme by Asch":** Letters to Igor Kusyszyn, February 18, 1969, and Asch, August 25, 1969, SMP.

100 **"The results are terrifying":** Letter to Riecken, NSF Grant file, op. cit.

101 **"The trait/situation controversy":** A more detailed discussion can be found in Blass (1984).

101 *Personality and Assessment:* Mischel (1968).

101 **"The social psychology of this century":** OTA, p. 205.

104 **A fine-tuned analysis:** Modigliani and Rochat (1995).

104 **"In line with the theory of cognitive dissonance":** Ibid., pp. 114 and 120.

106 **The experimenter's prods backfire:** This possible explanation is suggested by Modigliani and Rochat, ibid.

108 **The rebellion of two peers:** Milgram (1965a); Experiment 17 in OTA, pp. 116–121.

108 **"Stand in opposition to authority":** OTA, p. 121.

108 **The Sociology Department . . . needed it back:** Elms (1972).

108 **Another laboratory space:** Memo to "Messrs. Blatt, Child, Leventhal, Milgram, Norman Miller" from Claude E. Buxton, September 27, 1961, SMP.

109 **Rented a three-room office suite:** Letter to Wheeler Company, March 22, 1962, SMP.

109 **47.5 percent . . . were fully obedient:** Experiment 10 in OTA, pp. 61, 66–70.

109 **"It is possible":** OTA, pp. 69–70.

109 **Documentary film,** *Obedience:* Milgram prepared a booklet, "Obedience," as a teaching aid for use in conjunction with the film. It is made up of two parts: a set of study questions for the film prepared with the help of Andre Modigliani and a section describing how the film was made. My description of the making of the film is based on this section. Pamphlet, courtesy of Andre Modigliani. The content of the pamphlet was later incorporated into a combined "Instructor's Manual" for both OTA and the film, which came out in 1980, SMP.

110 **Letter to . . . Claude Buxton:** SMP.

110 **A lengthy trial in Jerusalem:** Arendt (1963).

CHAPTER 7: AFTERSHOCKS

111 **"Marinating in it":** Interview with Robert Abelson, New Haven, March 26, 1997.

111 A book, *The Psychology of Aggression:* Buss, op. cit.

111 Procedure had been copied: Letter to Riecken, September 21, 1961, NSF Grant file, op. cit.; e-mail to me from Philip Zimbardo, op. cit.

111 Zimbardo recalls a strange visit: Ibid.

111 Buss's machine: Buss, op. cit.

112 Reassured Milgram: Letter from Buss, ibid.; letter to Riecken, NSF Grant file, op. cit.

112 Never completely accepted: Letter to Elms, September 25, 1973.

112 Requesting a photograph: Undated letter from Alan Wurtzel, with handwritten reply from Milgram on the bottom, dated November 3, 1982, SMP.

112 Milgram's surprising findings: Interview with Abelson, op. cit.

112 Harris, credits Milgram: Harris (1988).

112 In a 1964 article: Milgram (1964b).

112 One member . . . was troubled enough: Interview with Ed Zigler, Yale University, March 26, 1997. Although I learned about the complaint to APA from Zigler, he was not willing to identify the complainer, saying only that he was a junior faculty member who was a social psychologist.

113 "The committee voted": Letter was from Jane D. Hildreth, November 23, 1962, SMP.

113 "Sour [him] permanently on the APA": Ibid. It didn't. In 1966, for example, he accepted the position of program chairman for APA's Division 8 (Personality and Social Psychology) at that year's annual convention.

113 As late as 1977: Milgram (1977d), reprinted in ISW, 2nd edition only.

113 The first of two additional grant proposals: "Obedience to Authority: Experiments in Social Psychology," op. cit.

113 The grant was approved on May 24, 1962: Letter to A. Whitney Griswold, President, Yale University, from Randal M. Robertson, Acting Director, NSF, SMP.

113 Used for analysis and reporting: Letter to Claude Buxton, op. cit.

114 Kelman credited Milgram: Anonymous "National Science Foundation Proposal Rating Sheet," courtesy of Herb Kelman.

114 Proposal to NSF for a third and final grant: "Completion of Obedience Study," April 29, 1963, accompanied by a cover letter to Robert L. Hall, Program Director for Sociology and Social Psychology, SMP. In a letter dated July 8, 1963, Hall notified Milgram that the grant had been approved, SMP. The grant number NSF assigned it was G-251.

In addition to the funding provided by the three grants, in February 1962 Milgram put in an emergency request to NSF for a supplemental allowance of $3,700. Because he was able to conduct his experiment at a faster pace than projected in his first grant proposal, submitted in January 1961, he was already running out of funds. The money was needed to keep the experiment going without interruption until a second—regular—grant proposal could be approved. He received the emergency funding. Letter to Robert Hall, NSF, February 14, 1962, SMP; an internal memo by Hall, February 9, 1962, and an undated memorandum, also by Hall, NSF Grant file.

The activities funded by the third grant were carried out at Harvard's Department of Social Relations, where Milgram accepted an appointment as assistant professor as of July 1, 1963. Although the termination date for the grant was September 15, 1965, two "no-cost" one-year extensions enabled him to stretch the grant money through the summer of 1967, when he moved from Harvard to the Graduate Center of the City of New York (CUNY).

114 A series of four journal articles: Milgram (1963, 1964a, 1965a, 1965b).

114 Submitted that first article: Letter to Production Manager, APA, May 26, 1963, SMP.

114 Jones faulted him: Letter to Milgram, March 27, 1962, SMP.

115 "I do not . . . exaggerate": Part of a note. Although undated, other parts indicate that it must have been written while Milgram was at Yale, SMP.

115 A psychologist at the University of Delaware: Letter to Robert Lakatos, June 11, 1969, SMP.

115 "A good Hitchcock thriller": Typescript, dated November 13, 1963, of Milgram's letter to the editor of the *St. Louis Dispatch* in reply to an editorial appearing on November 2, 1963, criticizing Milgram and Yale for conducting the obedience experiments. Although the newspaper published Milgram's letter on November 16, 1963, it had cut parts of it, including the passage I quoted, SMP.

115 "It was hell in there": E-mail to me from William Menold, July 8, 2001.

115 "Started sweating bullets": Interview with William Menold, February 14, 2003.

116 He spoke . . . to a group at Yale: Transcript of talk given by Herbert Winer, titled "*The* Experiment in Memory and Learning," at Berkeley College, Yale University, April 4, 1994, courtesy of Herbert Winer.

117 One assistant professor to another: At the time, Winer was an assistant professor in the School of Forestry at Yale University.

117 "At times I have concluded": Undated note, titled "An Experimenter's Dilemma," SMP.

118 Instructional materials: The combined Instructor's Manual for OTA and the film *Obedience*, op. cit., SMP.

118 "The crisis of confidence": Elms (1975).

119 "Glitter rock of science": Comstock (1974).

119 Orne applied: Orne and Holland (1968).

120 In his response, Milgram granted: Milgram (1972), reprinted in ISW.

120 "Subjects only *feigned* sweating": ISW, p. 164.

121 Sent Milgram a copy: letter from Buckhout, November 4, 1963, SMP.

122 "I do not wish": Night letter to Sullivan, sent right after midnight, October 23–24, SMP.

122 "Obedience is the psychological mechanism": Milgram (1963, p. 371).

122 "Many subjects showed": Ibid., p. 375.

123 "As an illustration": Letter from Elliot Aronson, January 17, 1964, SMP.

123 "Very much impressed": Letter from Erickson, April 14, 1967, SMP.

123 Bettelheim considered: Quoted in Askenasy (1978, p. 131).

123 **A Benedictine monk:** Letter from Edward Markley, July 6, 1967, SMP.

123 **"Within a year":** From the transcript of an unpublished interview. Neither the name of the interviewer nor the date of the interview appears in it, although some of the contents indicate that it probably took place sometime in the 1970s, SMP.

123 **A scathing criticism:** Baumrind (1964).

123 **"I do regard":** Ibid., pp. 422–423.

124 **"Totally astonished":** Interview with Stanley Milgram in Evans (1980), p. 193; also in ISW, p. 132.

124 **"Raises some legitimate points":** Letter to Arthur Brayfield, August 18, 1964, SMP.

124 **Milgram conceded later:** Milgram (1977d); also in ISW, 2nd edition only.

124 **In his rebuttal:** Milgram (1964b); reprinted in ISW, first edition only.

124 **On July 12, 1962:** Internal report, "Questionnaire to Subjects," prepared by Taketo Murata, one of Milgram's research assistants, SMP.

125 **92 percent of his subjects:** Op. cit., p. 849, footnote to Table 1.

127 **Only one significant difference:** Data analysis sheet titled "A comparison of those who returned questionnaires with those who didn't," SMP.

127 **He answered, "No":** Conversations with Herb Kelman, 2000–2003.

127 **"Statement . . . based on Interviews":** Dated June 20, 1963, SMP. A published version appears in Errera (1972).

127 **Dr. Errera does not recall:** Interview with Paul Errera, September 2000.

128 **In at least one case:** Milgram's second grant application to NSF, "Obedience to Authority: Experiments in Social Psychology," op. cit.

128 **"I started with the belief":** Milgram (1964b, pp. 851–852); ISW, first edition only, pp. 145–146.

129 **Lewin's classic studies:** Lewin, Lippitt, and White, op. cit.

129 **"Many regard informed consent":** Milgram (1977d, p. 19); ISW, 2nd edition only, p. 180.

130 **Four journal articles:** Milgram (1963, 1964a, 1965a, 1965b).

130 **The journal** *Human Relations* **in 1965:** Milgram (1965b).

CHAPTER 8: RETURN TO ACADEMIC EDEN

131 **Allport had told . . . Roger Brown:** Brown's talk at the commemorative gathering for Milgram, May 10, 1985, op. cit.

131 **To come up to Harvard:** Letter from Allport, January 28, 1962, SMP.

131 **Have his classes vote:** Interview with Roger Brown, William James Hall, June 23, 1993; e-mail to me from David Winter, November 18, 1997.

131 **Requested by Claude Buxton:** Letter from Buxton to Allport, November 2, 1962, HUA.

131 **"My one and only objection":** Letter from Allport to Buxton, November 5, 1962, HUA.

132 **"It was most pleasant":** Letter from Allport, March 7, 1962, SMP.

132 **"In her chosen career":** Letter from Allport, November 5, 1962, SMP.

132 **Offered a position at Harvard:** Letter to Roger Brown, December 18, 1962, SMP.

132 **A three-year appointment:** Official appointment form letter from Harvard, March 11, 1963, SMP.

132 **Research with drugs:** Interviews with Sasha Milgram, op. cit.

132 **She explained:** Letter to Milgram from Alice Thoren, January 31, 1963, SMP.

132 **"My heart is heavy":** Letter to Thoren, February 1, 1963, SMP.

133 **"To the credit of the Department":** "Recollections of the Yale Psychology Department," sent by Milgram to William Kessen, op. cit.

133 **Remembered with special fondness:** Ibid.

133 **The social climate:** E-mail to me from Howard Leventhal; interview with Leventhal, op. cit.

133 **Was closest to Irving Janis:** "Recollections of the Yale Psychology Department," op. cit.

133 **"It is interesting":** Letter to Leventhal, October 14, 1963, SMP.

134 **Agreed to represent him:** Letter from Joan Daves to Milgram, September 11, 1963, SMP.

134 **Asked to see more:** Letter to Daves from Madeline Tracy Brigden, February 12, 1964, SMP.

134 **Stanley and Sasha moved:** Conversations with Sasha Milgram, 1999–2003.

134 **Leon Mann recalls:** Remembrance letter from Leon Mann, August 10, 1993, courtesy of Harold Takooshian.

134 **"Like your kind of reasoning":** Letter to Goldwater, July 27, 1963, SMP.

135 **An audiotaped "letter":** Interview with Joel Milgram, op. cit.

135 **"Both children are more delightful":** Letter to Paul Hollander, September 1967, courtesy of Hollander.

135 **Another letter to the same friend:** Letter to Paul Hollander, August 30, 1968, SMP.

135 **Made his family a priority:** Conversations with Sasha Milgram, 1999–2003.

136 **"A great feeling of sadness":** Letter to Arthur Miller, March 14, 1984, ASM.

136 **"Doing another experiment on us":** Remembrance letter from Barry Wellman, August 1993.

136 **Unprecedented in Harvard's history:** *Harvard Crimson,* Monday, November 25, 1963, SMP.

136 **Wept openly:** Ibid.

136 **"We are numb":** Ibid.

138 **More centrally involved:** Letter to Susan [Harter] and Leon [Mann], September 28, 1964, SMP.

138 **They were coauthors:** Milgram, Mann, and Harter (1965).

138 **"Creative chit-chat":** Remembrance letter from Leon Mann, op. cit.

138 **The students "lost" letters:** Milgram (1969), reprinted in ISW.

139 **"Seeding" . . . with forty letters:** Mimeographed sheet titled "General Scheme for Letter-Dropping Experiment," SMP.

139 **Late afternoon of April 3:** Memo titled "April 4, 1963, Anti-defamation League," SMP.

139 **The final tally:** Data summary sheet, "Lost Letter Technique Tabulation as of 4/16," SMP.

139 **Memo from the postmaster:** On a printed "Post Office Department Routing Slip" dated April 9, 1963, SMP.

139 **Drive south from New Haven:** Milgram (1969). Also in ISW.

139 **Two nights in mid-May:** Handwritten logs, dated May 16 and May 17, SMP.

140 **Table 8.1:** From data summary sheet titled "To be Table VII," SMP.

140 **To new heights:** Milgram (1969). Also in ISW.

140 **In the fall of 1964:** Ibid.

141 **"Showed us things":** ISW, pp. 282–283.

141 **"Riots between the Malays and the Chinese":** Ibid., pp. 283–285.

142 **Emotionally draining experience:** On January 7, 1963, in correspondence about rank and salary at Harvard with Social Relations Department chairman David McClelland, Milgram wrote: "I am going on 30, and after completing the obedience study, feel even older," ASM.

142 **To distance himself:** Interview with Tom Pettigrew, San Francisco, August 14, 1998.

143 **"My work has been dominated":** Unpublished interview, op. cit.

144 **The conversation continued:** Rogers and Kincaid (1981), p. 107.

144 **Small-world phenomenon:** Milgram (1967b), reprinted in ISW.

145 **"Starting with any two people":** Milgram (1967b, p. 62); ISW, p. 259.

145 *Cambridge U.S.A.:* Rand (1964).

145 **Devised an experiment:** Milgram (1967b), op. cit.

146 **In *Psychology Today:*** Ibid.

146 ***Sociometry* in 1969:** Travers and Milgram (1969).

146 **In 1970:** Korte and Milgram (1970).

147 **Up to the third floor:** Minutes of the meeting of the Department of Social Relations, October 15, 1963, HUA.

147 **By the end of 1964:** Harvard University, Department of Social Relations Annual Report, 1964–65, SMP.

148 **Around Harvard Yard:** Ibid.

148 **Strengthen the unity:** Interviews with Brendan Maher, May 15 and June 4, 2001.

148 **Its first monthly meeting:** Minutes of the meeting of the Department of Social Relations, January 26, 1965, HUA.

148 **Separate access key:** Interviews with Brendan Maher, op. cit.

148 **Vying to hire:** Minutes of the meeting of the Department of Social Relations, November 24, 1964, HUA.

148 **Nearly 400 doctoral degrees:** Department of Social Relations Annual Report, 1963–64, SMP.

148 **Grown to about sixty-five:** Lists of faculty of the Social Relations Department, courtesy of E.L. Pattullo.

148 **Fill in for Roger Brown:** Interview with Hans Toch, July 15, 2002.

149 **The resulting chapter:** Milgram and Toch (1969). Most of the chapter, the section on crowds by Milgram, was reprinted in ISW, first edition only.

149 **Classroom manner:** Interview with Hans Toch, op. cit.

149 Closest of Milgram's new friendships: Interview with Paul Hollander, March 24, 1999; conversations with Sasha Milgram, 1999–2003.

149 "Trust, spontaneous pleasure": Remembrance letter by Paul Hollander, August 5, 1993, courtesy of Hollander.

150 "Qualities of Stanley": Ibid.

150 Kuwaiti government stationery: Speech at Milgram's funeral service in New York, December 23, 1984, courtesy of Paul Hollander.

150 Dear Professor Hollander: Bogus letter, dated June 14, 1976, courtesy of Paul Hollander.

151 "To be sure": Letter to Herbert Danzger, April 5, 1965, SMP.

152 "Enjoyed Harvard greatly": Letter to Leon Mann, December 29, 1966, SMP.

152 Bad case of "Harvarditis": Interview with Tom Pettigrew, August 14, 1998.

152 "I've been demoted": Letter to Dave Marlowe, March 24, 1966, SMP.

152 "Graustein formula": Conversations with E.L. Pattullo; interview with Robert Rosenthal, August 7, 2002.

152 A prime candidate: Interview with Roger Brown, op. cit.

152 Deep divisions: Unpublished interview of Milgram, op. cit.

153 A complete surprise: Interview with Rosenthal, op. cit.

153 "Properties of the experiment": Interview with Brown, op. cit.

154 "Definitely was 'quirky'": E-mail to me from David Winter, op. cit.

154 Voted against Milgram: Interview with Pettigrew, op. cit.

154 Behavior was tempered: Interview with Toch, op. cit.

154 He might say: Interview with Pettigrew, op. cit.

154 "Scared to death": Ibid.

154 Traumatic experience: Interviews with Sasha Milgram, op. cit.; unpublished interview, op. cit.

155 Did not capture: Unpublished interview, op. cit.

155 Frayed his self-image: Conversations with Sasha Milgram, 1999–2003.

155 Hurt was intensified: Interview with Rosenthal, op. cit.

155 By Rosenthal and Leon Mann: Letter from Mann, September 16, 1969, SMP.

155 The Six-Day War: My account is based on the entry "Six-Day War" in the *Encyclopedia Judaica*, Vol. 14, 1972, pp. 1623–1641.

155 Personal involvement: Letter to Allan Mazur, undated, but probably the fall of 1967.

155 Academic community: Letter from Allan Mazur, undated, but probably the fall of 1967.

155 A $100 contribution: Letter to Mazur, op. cit.

156 "Has taught us": Ibid.

156 He did receive: Letters from Irwin Silverman, January 25, 1967; from David Marlowe, January 16, 1967; from Harry Levin, February 28, 1967, all SMP.

156 Couldn't see himself: Interviews with Sasha Milgram, op. cit.

156 "Part of the urban culture": Conversation with John Sabini, March 1999.

156 Berkeley did invite him: Letter to Theodore Sarbin, February 15, 1967, SMP.

156 Letters of support: Letter to Irv [Janis], March 13, 1967, SMP.

156 Leventhal, was recruited: Interview with Howard Leventhal, op. cit.

157 Received a formal offer: Letter from Mina Rees, January 16, 1967, SMP.

157 Replied favorably: Letter to Rees, SMP.

158 Couldn't wait any longer: Interview with Howard Leventhal, op. cit.

158 Informed David McClelland: Letter to McClelland, February 8, 1967, SMP.

158 "Letting me know": Letter from McClelland, February 10, 1967, SMP.

158 Rees wrote a reply: SMP.

159 Between February 10 . . . end of the month: Harvard has an eighty-year rule about access to personnel records, so it is impossible to pinpoint the exact date of the tenure committee's final decision. Letter to me from Jeremy R. Knowles, Dean of Faculty of Arts and Sciences, Harvard University, June 21, 2002.

159 To accept the position: Letter to Rees, March 1, 1967, SMP.

159 Had lots of family: Interviews with Sasha Milgram, op. cit.

159 "Princeton for kids": Letter to Roy [Feldman], November 8, 1973.

160 More than five years: Interviews with Sasha Milgram, op. cit.

160 Stern's department store: Letter to Barry McLaughlin, March 9, 1967, SMP.

160 "If it will work out": Letter to Harry Levin, March 2, 1967, SMP.

160 "May turn out well": Letter to Irv [Janis], op. cit.

160 "No longer first class": Letter to Paul Hollander, September 1967, courtesy of Hollander.

161 "If you bumped into someone": Letter to Paul Hollander, June 28, 1967, courtesy of Hollander.

161 "New York is less than Cambridge": Letter to Eric [Lenneberg], September 5, 1967, SMP.

161 "Let me tell": Letter to Howard Leventhal, September 25, 1967, SMP.

CHAPTER 9: CITY PSYCHOLOGY

163 "An innocent provincial": Letter to Paul Hollander, June 28, 1967, courtesy of Hollander.

163 His office . . . was special: Based on a description provided by Harold Takooshian, February 12, 2001.

164 "Bright as a flame": Letter to Paul Hollander, September 1967, courtesy of Hollander.

164 CUNY's graduate school: My presentation of the history of CUNY's graduate school is based on interviews with Rosamond Dana, Office of the Provost, The Graduate Center, CUNY (September 10 and 12, 2002) and materials provided by her; interview with John Rothman, Archivist of the Graduate Center Library (August 22, 2002) and materials he provided; a doctoral dissertation by Sheila C. Gordon, "Transformation of the City University of New York, 1945–1970," Columbia University, 1975; biography of Mina Rees from *Biographies of Women Mathematicians* Web site, Agnes Scott College, Atlanta, GA; report by Mina Rees, "The first ten years of the graduate school of the City University of New York," Archives of the Graduate Center, CUNY.

165 Rees arranged: Interviews with Rosamond Dana, op. cit.

165 **Main claim to fame:** Unpublished report by Mina Rees, 1988, courtesy of Rosamond Dana; interview with Chas Smith, August 20, 2002.

166 **Innovative features:** From description provided by Harold Takooshian, February 12, 2001.

166 **First of its kind:** Report by Mina Rees, "The first ten years . . . ," op. cit.

167 **They put ads:** Article in the *Harvard Crimson,* October 26, 1966, "What makes Paris Paris? Group will try to measure cities' milieu," by Linda J. Greenhouse.

167 **A "think piece":** Milgram and Hollander (1964), reprinted in ISW.

168 **"In our righteous":** Ibid., p. 602; ISW, p. 32.

168 **"The social psychology area":** Report on the Doctoral Program in Social Psychology (1969–1970), SMP.

168 **Kinds of research pursued:** Ibid.

168 **Orientation was consistent:** Sheila C. Gordon, doctoral dissertation, op. cit., p. 142.

169 **"The Experience of Living in Cities":** Milgram (1970a), reprinted in ISW.

169 **Such as Coxsackie:** Milgram (1970b).

170 **Laid the foundation:** Sabini (1986).

170 **"The image of the city":** Milgram and Jodelet (1976), reprinted in ISW, p. 112.

170 **"People make many":** Quoted in Tavris (1974a, pp. 73 and 76), reprinted in ISW, p. xxvii.

171 **A "scene sampling" technique:** Milgram et al. (1972), reprinted in ISW.

171 **"He shows a group":** Ibid., p. 197; ISW, p. 78.

172 **"Areas of Queens":** Ibid., p. 199; ISW, pp. 80–82.

173 **An innocuous remark:** Conversations with Sasha Milgram, 1999–2003.

173 **Met with nervous laughter:** Tavris (1974a).

174 **"They're getting up!":** Ibid., p. 72; ISW, p. xxiii.

174 **"Frankly, despite Goodman's . . . experience":** Ibid., p. 72; ISW, p. xxiv.

175 **More refined and complex form:** Milgram and Sabini (1978), reprinted in ISW, 2nd edition only.

176 **"The experimenters' reactions":** Takooshian (1972, pp. 10–11).

177 **Presented his findings:** Letter to Harold Proshansky, March 14, 1972, SMP.

177 **One scenario involved a bully:** Sabini (1976); joint interviews with John Sabini and Maury Silver, University of Pennsylvania, June 3, 1993.

178 **I remember him sitting in his office:** Interview with John Sabini, ibid.

178 **Conducted a study:** Milgram (1977a), reprinted in ISW; "The Familiar Stranger: A Strangely Familiar Phenomenon," by A. Condey and eight other students. Unpublished class report, April 1971, for Milgram's Experimental Social Psychology class.

180 **"In order to handle":** ISW, pp. 69 and 71.

182 **Create an adjunct position:** Interview with Florence Denmark, New York, May 19, 1993.

182 **Seemed genuinely interested:** Interview with Irwin Katz, May 19, 1993.

182 **"When he was displeased":** Waters (2000, p. 26).

182 **"Equal opportunity insulter":** Interview with John Sabini, op. cit.

183 "Can't you see": Interview with Robert Panzarella, New York, summer 2000.

183 "I called him": Interview with Joel Milgram, op. cit.

183 "Didn't look extraordinary": Interview with Harold Takooshian, June 17, 1993.

184 Recalls a class: Interview with Robert Panzarella, op. cit.

184 "Take those sunglasses off": Ibid.

184 "One thing he did": Interview with Harold Takooshian, op. cit.

185 Looking back: Waters, op. cit.

185 "He was a genius": Interview with John Sabini, op. cit.

186 "Really enjoyed": Interview with Salomon Rettig, August 6, 2002.

186 Many first-rate faculty: Physical descriptions of people I did not meet are based on conversations with Harold Takooshian.

187 Perform "wonders": Ibid.

187 Sabini once arrived: Interview with John Sabini, op. cit.

187 "Milgram noted": Takooshian (2000, p. 19).

187 Was completing: Interview with Ronna Kabatznick, August 30, 2002.

188 Seeing a student bolt out: Interview with Joel Milgram, op. cit.

188 Unusually sensitive: Conversation with John Sabini, March 1999; interview with Irwin Katz, op. cit.

189 "Different girls cause me": Self-directed note, February 10, 1957, ASM.

189 "You seem to forget": Letter to Enid, August 11, 1959, ASM.

189 "We used to play": Interview with Michele Marques, September 14, 2003.

190 Largest number: Interview with Roger Brown, op. cit.

191 "My interests": Remembrance, July 30, 1993.

191 Organize a conference: Waters, op. cit.

191 Florence Denmark put it: Remembrance, August 5, 1993.

191 "So much humor": Remembrance, August 1993.

191 In song the entire day: Takooshian (2000).

192 "Previous assumptions": Waters, op. cit., pp. 30–31.

192 "Preferred indoor": Letter to Paul Hollander, January 18, 1970, courtesy of Hollander.

192 "Only in action": Quoted in Tavris (1974a, p. 72). Also in ISW, p. xxv.

192 Klapper . . . convened: Milgram and Shotland (1973); an abbreviated version appears in ISW.

193 To carry the research: Ibid.

195 He recalls: Interview with Vincent Sherman, spring 2003.

195 "The television study": Letter to Vincent Sherman, March 15, 1983, SMP.

CHAPTER 10: CENTER STAGE

197 That initial meeting: Interview with Harry From, New York, June 17, 1993.

198 A commercial success: Conversations with Sasha Milgram, 1999–2003.

198 London or Paris: Copy of fellowship application, ASM; letters to Roger Brown, October 12, 1971, and March 17, 1972, courtesy of Brown.

198 Approval came through: Letter from Gordon N. Ray, president, Guggenheim Foundation, March 14, 1972, ASM.

199 **Prudent thing:** Conversations with Sasha Milgram, 1999–2003.

199 **Other duties:** Letter to Leon Mann, March 20, 1972, SMP.

199 **He had met:** Interview with Murray Melbin, 2003.

199 **Eager to publish:** Letter from Virginia Hilu, October 5, 1965, SMP.

199 **Writing commitment:** A chapter for the *Handbook of Social Psychology;* letter to Hilu, October 12, 1965, SMP.

199 **He signed:** Letter to Hilu, September 10, 1969, ASM.

199 **An article . . . would serve:** Milgram (1967a); letter to Virginia Hilu, April 18, 1969, ASM.

199 **"Makes me eager":** Letter from Hilu, November 5, 1969, SMP.

200 **Inquire about the book:** Letter from Hilu, July 21, 1970, ASM.

200 **Draft of one chapter:** Letter to Hilu, August 13, 1970, ASM.

200 **"Where is that manuscript?":** Letter from Hilu, August 20, 1970, ASM.

200 **To publish at all:** Letter from Hilu, September 18, 1970, ASM.

200 **The whole manuscript:** Letter to Hilu, April 5, 1971, ASM.

200 **"[Her] editorial skill":** Letter to Hilu, September 17, 1971, ASM.

200 **A midlife crisis:** Conversations with Sasha Milgram, 1999–2003.

200 **"The zenith is in the past":** Letter to Hollander, October 12, 1972, SMP.

201 **"Sense of progress":** Letter to Leon Mann, October 26, 1971, SMP.

201 **The Milgrams' sojourn:** Conversations with Sasha Milgram, 1999–2003.

201 **"It is very lonely":** Quoted by Sasha in e-mail to me, February 7, 2003.

201 **"This apartment":** Ibid.

202 **"I think I like it":** Letter to Paul Hollander, October 12, 1972, courtesy of Hollander.

202 **Feeling "rather low":** Letter to Hollander, October 30, 1972, ASM.

202 **"You will be deported":** Ibid.

202 **Published in September:** Letter from Stanley to Sasha, Marc, and Michele, January 18, 1973, ASM.

202 **His graduate student:** Ibid.

202 **Write a preface:** Letter from Stanley to Sasha, Michele, and Marc, January 20/21, 1973, ASM.

202 **"Extraordinary faith":** Letter to Sasha, January 23/24, 1973, ASM.

203 *Television and Anti-Social Behavior:* Milgram and Shotland, op. cit.

203 **"Like Sasha's company":** Letter to Sasha, Marc, and Michele, January 24, 1973, ASM.

203 **"I yearn for you":** Letter from Sasha, January 24, 1973, ASM.

203 **A spectacular visit:** Conversations with Sasha Milgram, 1999–2003.

203 **Had been invited:** Letter from Elihu Katz, June 12, 1973, SMP.

203 **Lectures to audiences:** Letter to Mother (Adele Milgram), January 11, 1973, ASM; announcement in Hebrew of Milgram's series of lectures, SMP.

204 **Offered a . . . faculty position:** Letter to Mother, Ibid.

204 **Getting his study . . . under way:** Letter to Hollander, March 13, 1973, SMP.

204 **Too optimistic:** Letter to Hollander, April 26, 1973, SMP.

204 **Personal living expenses:** Conversations with Sasha Milgram, 1999–2003.

204 **Moscovici was a Romanian-born immigrant:** http://www.metailie.info.

204 First met at Yale: Undated letter from Moscovici, most likely June 1963, SMP.

205 Moscovici's research showed: Milgram (1978).

206 "The methods": Undated letter from Moscovici, op. cit.

206 Do a replication: Letter to Moscovici, July 30, 1963, SMP.

206 "A special Swedish version": Ibid.

206 Offered to help: Undated letter from Moscovici, op. cit.

206 Milgram sent him: Letter to Moscovici, October 10, 1963, SMP.

206 Not yet been published: It did appear in English the following year, Milgram (1964c).

206 Most influential . . . periodical: I was enlightened about the importance of this publication by Francois Rochat.

206 Magazine rejected: Letter from Moscovici, February 10, 1964, SMP.

206 Put Milgram in touch: Letter to Moscovici, September 21, 1973; letter from Moscovici, December 1973, both SMP.

206 On Moscovici's behalf: Letters to AAAS, March 15 and July 24, 1973; letter to Moscovici, September 21, 1973, all SMP.

206 To interest American publishers: Letter to Moscovici, November 6, 1976, and letter to Eric Wanner, Harvard University Press, January 15, 1982, both SMP.

207 If he could provide: Letter to Moscovici, July 10, 1972, SMP.

207 Requesting an emergency grant: Letter from Moscovici to Pierre Aigrain, April 3, 1973, SMP. Translated for me from the French by Francois Rochat.

207 Parisian mental map study: Milgram and Jodelet, op. cit.; reprinted in ISW.

208 "Through processes": ISW, p. 92.

208 Figure 10.1: Ibid., p. 91.

208 "At first the map": Ibid., pp. 89–90.

209 "At the very heart": Ibid., p. 95.

210 "Suppose you were to meet": Ibid., p. 109.

210 "Allow a treatment": Ibid., p. 112.

211 "We buy food": Letter to Moscovici, September 21, 1973, SMP.

211 "Most likely": Ibid.

211 When Milgram received: Conversations with Sasha Milgram, 1999–2003.

212 Galleys were ready: Letters from Virginia Hilu to Roger Brown, July 3, 1973, and from Brown to Hilu, July 20, 1973, courtesy of Brown.

212 In . . . Harper's magazine: Milgram (1973a).

212 Article-length condensation: Letter from Taylor Branch to Milgram, October 9, 1973, SMP. This is the same Taylor Branch who fifteen years later published the award-winning book Parting the Waters.

212 Writing did not come easily: Interviews with Sasha Milgram, op. cit.

213 There were already letters: Interview with Marc Milgram, Watertown, MA, June 23, 1993.

213 Make home movies: Interview with Michele Marques, Toronto, August 1996; talk given by her at a symposium, "Stanley Milgram Retrospective—40 Years After 'Behavioral Study of Obedience'," Toronto, August 10, 2003.

213 His chapter outline: Letter to Lindzey and Aronson, March 25, 1965, SMP.

213 "He was blocked": Interview with Lane Conn, July 17, 2002.

214 "Collective Behavior": Milgram and Toch (1969).

214 Aronson wrote: Letter to Milgram, October 12, 1966, SMP.

214 "Most exciting": Letter to Milgram, May 7, 1967, SMP.

214 *Obedience to Authority:* Milgram (1974).

215 Rebuttal of Baumrind's article: Milgram (1964b).

215 Reply to a critical essay: Milgram (1973b).

215 *The Dogs of Pavlov:* Abse (1973).

216 "From a subjective standpoint": OTA, p. 134.

216 An empirical question: For a detailed examination of this question, see Blass (1992).

216 Subjects were women: OTA, Experiment 8, pp. 61–63, 207.

216 Rate of obedience was identical: My own research (Blass, 1999) has shown that this is a reliable finding. Almost all replications of the obedience experiment by others also found no differences between males and females in their degree of obedience.

217 "Any competent manager": Ibid., p. 122.

218 One such variation: Experiment 11 in OTA, pp. 61, 70–72.

218 "If destructive impulses": Ibid., pp. 166–167.

218 "Whatever leads": Ibid., p. 72.

219 Another condition: Experiment 12 in OTA, pp. 90–92, 94.

220 Documentary series, *Horizon:* There is now an updated version, accompanied by some contemporary commentary. According to director of the update, Celia Lowenstein, it was shown on BBC4 on March 10, 2003 (e-mail to me, March 15, 2003). Outside of Milgram's own films, it is still the best documentary treatment of Milgram's research.

220 More than sixty reviews: Most of these were collected by American and British newspaper clipping services, which Milgram must have hired, and are located in SMP.

220 Polemical piece: In the following weeks, the *New York Times Book Review* printed a letter to the editor from Roger Brown defending Milgram and one from Lawrence Kohlberg criticizing Milgram.

221 "Obviously, he was not competent": *Dick Cavett Show,* March 15, 1979.

221 Soliciting his opinions: Letter from R. Duncan Luce, March 8, 1983, SMP.

222 "Many of those": Letter to Luce, March 19, 1983, SMP.

223 "A punk rock singer": Letter from Peter Gabriel, November 30, 1979, SMP.

223 Unusual request: Undated letter from Marcie Dodson-Yarnell, SMP.

223 "Dear James": Letter from Milgram, February 26, 1981, SMP.

224 Milgram quickly obliged: With a letter, March 3, 1982, SMP.

224 Led to . . . contract: Letter to Glen Howard, July 1, 1973, ASM.

224 Educational films: All of Milgram's films are still available and currently distributed by Penn State Media Sales.

225 Own field experiments: Milgram, Bickman, and Berkowitz (1969); reprinted in ISW.

226 Flew there: Interview with Harry From, New York, June 17, 1993.

226 Introduced to the gang: Ibid.

226 A slab of concrete: Milgram and From (1978); ibid.

226 "We are not going to shoot": Interview with From, ibid.

227 "Felt much more freedom": Conversations with From.

227 Courses in filmmaking: Ibid.

227 He submitted: Grant application to the American Film Institute, Independent Filmmaker Program, September 12, 1975, ASM.

227 "The creative claim": ISW, p. xix.

228 Letter . . . Bernard Fried: Dated May 7, 1983, courtesy of Fried.

228 "I was as obsessed": Interview with George Bellak, New York, May 19, 1993.

229 Cost of $300,000: Article by Percy Shain, "Tenth Level to Be Aired—Finally," *Boston Globe*, week of August 22, 1976.

229 "Wouldn't go near it": Interview with Bellak, op. cit.

229 Shatner believed: Percy Shain article, op. cit.

229 CBS paid Milgram: Letter to Isadore Miller, CBS Television Network, February 10, 1975, ASM.

229 Very little input: Letter to Arthur Asa Berger, January 26, 1975, SMP.

229 "Welter of video clichés": Letter to Bob Wexelbaum, September 1, 1976, ASM.

229 "Increasing the public's knowledge": Copy of award certificate, courtesy of George Bellak.

230 Get a national audience: E-mail to me from Tom Pettigrew, November 19, 1997.

230 Told his brother, Joel: Interview with Joel Milgram, op. cit.

CHAPTER 11: VEXATIONS, CYRANOIDS, AND THE DECLINING YEARS

231 Not planning to stay: Interviews with Sasha Milgram, op. cit.

231 His speaking fees: By now, he had also enlisted the services of a speakers' bureau, Program Corporation of America, to handle the traffic. On September 25, 1975, for example, a letter from its sales director informed him that an upcoming speaking engagement at Casper College would net him $2,000, plus all of his expenses, SMP.

231 "An impressive amount": Interview with Harry From, op. cit.

231 "A great source of pride": Interview with Joel Milgram, op. cit.

232 The boon and the bane: Conversations with Judith Waters.

232 "A kind of snail": Letter to Bob Wexelbaum, op. cit.

232 "A 1/12th pay cut": Letter to Paul Hollander, March 3, 1976, courtesy of Hollander.

232 He regretted not doing: Letter to Hollander, June 17, 1968, courtesy of Hollander.

233 Would not give it to them: Interview with Harry From, op. cit.

233 Photographer-subject relationship: Milgram (1977b).

233 *Candid Camera:* Milgram and Sabini (1979); reprinted in ISW, 2nd edition only.

233 "Petty bourgeois": Interview with From, op. cit.

234 **A very large grant proposal:** Titled "Ethics in Human Research: Three Films," SMP.

234 **Seemed to be smarting:** Conversations with Judith Waters, op. cit.

235 **One of the finalists:** Letter from Jan Haag, American Film Institute, February 4, 1976, ASM.

235 **Proposed the film idea:** Letter to Glen Howard, February 9, 1976, SMP.

236 **Army recruits:** Berkun et al. (1962).

236 **Male alcoholics:** Campbell, Sanderson, and Laverty (1964).

236 **Asked an ethicist:** Milgram's memorandum to himself about a telephone call to Callahan, March 16, 1977, SMP.

237 **"With increasingly powerful":** From the Ethics grant proposal, op. cit.

238 **A trimmed-down version:** Titled "Ethics in Psychological Research: Film and Evaluation," June 20, 1979, SMP.

238 **Defined a cyranoid:** Milgram (1984a); reprinted in ISW, 2nd edition only.

239 **In a notebook:** ASM.

239 **A grant proposal:** Dated February 23, 1979, SMP.

239 **A cover letter:** Letter to Kelly Shaver, February 26, 1979, SMP.

241 **Was steamed:** Letter to Shaver, August 1, 1979, SMP.

241 **Accept it as a resubmission:** Letter from Baron, October 30, 1979, SMP.

241 **Generally encouraged:** E-mail to me from Steven Breckler, NSF, February 6, 2003.

242 **The bad tidings:** Letter from Baron, March 26, 1980, SMP.

242 **Letter . . . to . . . Stuart Albert:** October 8, 1983, ASM.

243 **The important findings:** Milgram (1984a).

243 **Belief in conspiracy theories:** Blass (1980).

243 **The nomination process:** Interview with Florence Denmark, op. cit.

244 **A joyous event:** Conversations with Sasha Milgram, 1999–2003.

244 **Toast by Irwin Katz:** Minutes of Social-Personality Faculty Meeting, February 5, 1980, SMP.

244 **The first—and . . . only:** E-mail to me from Rosamond Dana, Provost's Office, CUNY Graduate School, March 28, 2003.

244 **Go bicycle riding:** Conversations with Sasha Milgram, 1999–2003.

245 **"After some small talk":** Letter to Roger Brown, July 7, 1980, courtesy of Brown.

245 **Another heart attack:** Conversations with Sasha Milgram, 1999–2003.

245 **"The past seems brighter":** Letter to Hollander, August 25, 1983, ASM.

246 **"The . . . true intimate closeness":** Interview with Joel Milgram, op. cit.

246 **"Dedicated micro-maven":** Annual end-of-the-year letter to friends from Stanley and Sasha, December 2002, ASM.

246 **"A confession, Serge":** Letter to Moscovici, April 13, 1982, SMP.

247 **"A way of life":** Interview with Eva Fogelman, New York, summer 2000.

247 **"He was brilliant":** Interview with Arthur Weinberger, New York, August 17, 2000.

247 **"Inspire students to delight":** "Remarks delivered at the funeral of Stanley Milgram," courtesy of Irwin Katz.

248 **"Flirting with bankruptcy"**: End-of-the-year letter to friends, 1982, op. cit., ASM.

248 **Sasha went to work:** Conversations with Sasha Milgram, 1999–2003.

248 **"Hasn't become a client—yet"**: Annual end-of-year letter, 1982, op. cit.

249 **"Some impressive data"**: Letter to Alan Elms, September 24, 1982, SMP.

249 **Article was accepted:** Milgram et al. (1986); reprinted in ISW, 2nd edition only.

249 **The vertical life:** Milgram (1984b); reprinted in ISW, 2nd edition only.

250 **"An interesting approach"**: Letter to Roger Brown, June 14, 1983, courtesy of Brown.

250 **"Intellectual resonance"**: Letter to Roger Brown, May 19, 1983, courtesy of Brown.

250 **Rental house . . . on Cape Cod:** Picture postcard to Marjorie Marton and family from the Milgrams, July 23, 1983, courtesy of Marjorie Marton.

251 **"A fresh wind"**: The Milgrams' annual end-of-the-year letter to friends, December 1983, ASM.

252 **"Our primordial nightmare"**: Quoted in an article by Maureen Dowd about the conference in the *New York Times,* Monday, March 12, 1984, p. B1.

252 **Sasha and Stanley wanted:** Conversations with Sasha Milgram, 1999–2003.

252 **A guest column:** Titled "A Patient's View of the Hospital Strike," August 23, 1984, ASM. This was his last published piece of writing before his death.

253 **"Like Menachem B."**: Referring to Menachem Begin, prime minister of Israel, who after his wife died in 1982 resigned from his office and rarely appeared in public afterward.

253 **Accepted an invitation:** Letter from James Pennebaker, January 11, 1984, ASM.

254 **Figure 11.1:** The "Sharon" in the balloon is Sharon Presley, one of Milgram's doctoral students, courtesy of Presley.

254 **In absentia:** Interview with Pennebaker, February 17, 2003.

255 **End-of-the-year letter:** ASM.

255 **"Very impressed"**: Interview with Irwin Katz, op. cit.

256 **"Dear Chas"**: Reply to Smith typed at the bottom of his memo, August 31, 1977, SMP.

256 **"Planting some trees"**: SMP.

256 **"Lovers of Israel"**: According to Sasha, one year Stanley found artistic Rosh Hashanah cards with a pomegranate motif. The quote is from an explanation about the origin of the Milgram name that he wrote on those cards.

257 **The activist rabbi:** Interview with Rabbi Avi Weiss, New York, April 18, 2001.

257 **"When a Boy Becomes a Man"**: ASM.

257 **"The whole world"**: He learned the song from Rabbi Avi Weiss. Interview with Weiss, op. cit.

258 **He told Irwin Katz:** Interview with Katz, op. cit.

258 **Asked his cardiologist:** Conversations with Sasha Milgram, 1999–2003.

CHAPTER 12: MILGRAM'S LEGACY

259 **"Is there any":** Interview with Roger Brown, op. cit.

259 **A recent study:** Haggbloom et al. (2002).

260 **In *Psychology Today:*** Milgram (1967b); reprinted in ISW.

260 **In 1969 and 1970:** Travers and Milgram, op. cit., Korte and Milgram, op. cit.

260 **Experimental realism:** Aronson and Carlsmith (1968).

261 **Disciplines outside of psychology:** Economics (Akerlof, 1991), education (Atlas, 1985), political science (Helm and Morelli, 1979, 1985), and philosophy (Patten, 1977).

261 ***Archives of Internal Medicine:*** Green et al. (1996).

261 ***Indian Journal of the History of Science:*** Laurent (1987).

261 **Swedish writer:** Modig (2003).

261 **A dog-trainer:** Clothier (2002).

262 **Ever since he saw:** Interview with Robbie Chafitz, spring 1999.

262 ***I comme Icare:*** The film is a thriller about a political assassination. The president of an unidentified country gets shot riding in an open car during a public appearance. On one level, the plot was a thinly disguised rendering of the Kennedy assassination and the Warren Commission's investigation: The unnamed country's flag is colored red, white, and blue, and the accused killer's name is Daslow, which is an anagram of Oswald. On another level, Verneuil created it to serve as a vehicle for presenting Milgram's obedience experiments to the French public. It turns out that the Oswald-like character had been a subject in a Milgram-type obedience experiment, and the dramatic high point of the film is a gripping twenty-minute segment depicting a subject going through the experiment at the University of Leya, a scrambled version of "Yale." Conversations with Francois Rochat; e-mails from Francois Lapelerie, January 24, 2002, and Ray Lancaster, March 4, 2002.

According to Benoit Monin, a social psychologist at Stanford University, the film "might have done more to popularize Milgram's work in France than anything else." He recalls that when he was an undergraduate student at ESSEC (a business school in Paris), lectures about the obedience experiments typically used as a visual aid the clip from *I comme Icare* depicting the experiment. Even a recent official report on human subjects written for the Centre National de la Recherche Scientifique—the French equivalent of the National Science Foundation—introduced a discussion of Milgram's research by saying, "As portrayed in the movie *I comme Icare*." E-mail from Monin, May 21, 1999.

263 **"The Dogs of Pavlov":** The play (Abse, op. cit.) contains a variant of Milgram's experiment—the learning task is an arithmetic problem rather than a word-matching task. Its central theme is the same as Milgram's: the surprising readiness of normal people to yield to evil orders, with its attendant implications for the Nazis' savagery. As one of Abse's characters says, "When people feel they are serving some higher cause . . . then consciences become startlingly soluble." But it also has a subtheme that the teacher-subject was victimized—that he was "had, hoaxed, fooled, . . . conned" into doing something that was alien to his principles—a view that

Milgram strenuously rejected. He always argued that his subjects were free agents who could choose to disobey the experimental authority.

263 **"Tolliver's Trick"**: Its central character, Tolliver, survived the concentration camps and is now a college professor. He requires his students to participate in a "learning" experiment and teaches them about the perils of blind obedience by flunking any of them who continue to the highest voltage on the shock machine.

263 **"Mosaic"**: Baltimore playwright Hull describes the work as "an existential dilemma for ensemble. Who are we? Where are we? What will we become? Wry, Orwellian exposé of the past, present, and future." Her obedience experiment has a brilliant touch: The teacher asks the learner a list of questions that have no objective answers. The experimenter decides whether the learner's answers are correct. Here is an excerpt:

Doctor Move on to the second question, please.

Subject [Reads from list] Second question: Where have all the good times gone?

Learner The good times haven't gone anywhere. They're here right now.

Subject [Looks to Doctor] Well?

Doctor Incorrect. Administer the second shock value, please.

Subject [Peering, searching with finger] All right. Let's see, ah, 30 volts. Here goes. [Flicks switch; Learner writhes a little more violently].

263 **"One More Volt"**: Its central character, a Dr. Samuel Miller, is a Milgram-like faculty member in the psychology department of a prestigious university who is conducting scientific experiments on obedience to authority. During the course of his studies, a Nazi war criminal is captured and brought to Israel to stand trial. Miller finds himself facing a painful dilemma when the Nazi's lawyer, tipped off about his experiments, asks him to testify at the trial.

263 **Almost aphoristically**: Letter to Alan Elms, September 25, 1973, SMP.

263 **"Although experiments"**: Milgram (1976, p. 24).

264 **"Like so many Eichmanns"**: Abse (op. cit., p. 29).

264 **"You surely understand"**: Milgram (1973b, p. 39).

264 **"An organizational structure"**: OTA, p. 188.

265 **A textbook . . . on business ethics**: Ferrell and Gardiner (1991).

266 **Hartwell writes**: Hartwell (1990, pp. 142–143).

266 **As an expert witness**: Colman (1991).

267 **With broad consequences**: Saltzman (2000).

267 **"Making a major contribution"**: Letter from Vincent J. Liesenfeld, April 10, 1982, SMP.

267 **"I am Jewish"**: E-mail to me from Eduardo Grutzky, October 17, 2000.

267 **"When I first read"**: E-mail to me from Vera Cubela, December 11, 2000.

268 **A posting to . . . Metafilter**: Dated January 14, 2003, by "NortonDC."

268 **A review**: By Marc Fisher in the *Washington Post*, April 25, 1996.

268 **Goldhagen's . . . book**: Goldhagen (1996).

268 **"A commonly offered explanation"**: OTA, pp. 5–6.

269 **"Enormous differences"**: OTA, p. 175.

269 **"It is fitting"**: ASM.

270 Arendt's analysis: Arendt (1963).

270 "Utterly bourgeois": Wiesenthal (1989, p. 66).

270 "Many of Milgram's insights": Browning (1992, p. 174).

270 Also finds support: Hilberg (1980).

271 "Legal activity": Weisberg (1996, pp. xviii–xix).

271 First anti-Jewish law: Hilberg (1985).

271 Requested that the authorities: Geuter (1987).

271 To indoctrinate Nazi youth: Berger (1983).

272 Has been challenged: Robinson (1965).

272 Deportation . . . began: Bauer (1982).

272 "Since the first days": Gilbert (1985, p. 297).

273 "Simone LaGrange was sent": Reeves (1987).

273 [A] customary SS habit: Bauer, op. cit., p. 212.

273 "Even women carrying children": Quoted in Herzstein (1980, p. 142).

274 "After about fifteen minutes": Birnbaum (1993, pp. x–xi).

275 "No one had issued": Arendt (1966, p. xxiv).

276 Heydrich considered all Germans: Hilberg (1985).

277 "There is a propensity": OTA, p. 145.

277 "A lower species": Hilberg (1985, pp. 120).

277 "Powerfully bind": OTA, p. 149.

277 "The process of destruction": Hilberg (1985, pp. 53 and 47).

278 "The laboratory hour": OTA, p. 149.

278 A measure . . . never stands alone: Hilberg (1985, p. 54).

278 "A definite, yes": Letter to Mrs. Carol Dusseault from Howard T. Prince II, December 12, 1985, ASM.

278 An insightful book: Grossman (1995).

278 Draws . . . on Milgram's work: In addition to Grossman's (1995) book, a number of other books on the Holocaust or human destructiveness have drawn heavily on Milgram's work. These include *Are We All Nazis?* by Askenasy, *Crimes of Obedience* by Kelman and Hamilton, *Mass Hate* by Kressel, *Ordinary People and Extraordinary Evil* by Katz, and *Modernity and the Holocaust* by Bauman.

278 A "true revolution": Interview with Lt. Col. Dave Grossman, May 18, 1999.

279 "It is quite a jump": Letter to Miss Harriet Tobin, April 9, 1964, SMP.

279 "In introducing the problem": SMP.

280 In the published version: Milgram (1967a).

280 "The late Gordon W. Allport": OTA, pp. 178–179.

280 The ethical controversy: A thoughtful and readable presentation of the ethical controversy, as well as other issues related to the obedience experiments, can be found in Miller (1986).

280 In 1953: The description of the ethically problematic cases is based on *Evolving Concern: Protection for Human Subjects,* one of a series of videos prepared by the National Institutes of Health (undated).

281 "Solution to a non-problem": From "Social Psychology in the Eighties," a talk given by Milgram at Fordham University, Lincoln Center Campus, May 3, 1980, courtesy of Harold Takooshian.

282 **Found it increasingly difficult:** My discussion of these developments is based on three articles that have appeared in *Dialog: The Official Newsletter of the Society for Personality and Social Psychology:* "IRB Ax Falls, Heads Roll," *Dialog,* 14 (Autumn 1999), p. 8; E. Diener, "Over-Concern with Research Ethics," *Dialog,* 16 (Fall 2001), p. 2; L. A. Penner, "IRB and U: What Institutional Review Boards Are Supposed to Do," *Dialog,* 17 (Spring 2002), pp. 28–29.

282 **"For me Asch's experiment":** ISW, p. 196.

283 **"Perhaps more than any":** Ross (1988, p. 101).

284 **"The tremendous city return rates":** From "Suburban Versus Urban Attitudes in Regard to Current Political and Sociological Issues, as Measured by the Lost Letter Technique," by Lucas Hanft, submitted to the Intel Science Talent Search 1999–2000, p. 16, courtesy of Ann Saltzman.

284 **"One of the critical tools":** Kadushin (1989, p. xxiv).

285 **An article in *Nature:*** Watts and Strogatz (1998).

285 **"Milgram's pioneering work":** E-mail to me from Steven Strogatz, May 4, 2000.

286 **"Renaissance" is described:** Barabasi (2002).

286 **As reported by Watts and . . . colleagues:** Dodds, Muhamad, and Watts (2003).

287 **"Milgram's . . . analysis of overload":** Shenk (1997), p. 39.

287 **A Chicago native:** Gladwell (2000).

287 **A highly original "test":** Leveugle recounted her odyssey in *The Guardian,* January 13, 2003.

289 **"Pleasurable activity":** ISW, p. xx.

289 **"Impossible to calculate":** Zimbardo, Maslach, and Haney (2000, pp. 223–224).

290 **Psychology of photography:** ISW.

290 **"The implicit model":** ISW, p. xix.

291 **Phenomenon oriented:** He was in good company, though. Both Roger Brown and Solomon Asch were phenomenon-centered in their research.

291 **"Most psychologists test":** Tavris (1974b, p. 75).

292 **"A Pandora's box":** Tavris (1974a, p. 71); ISW, pp. xxii–xxiii.

REFERENCES

Abse, D. (1973). *The dogs of Pavlov*. London: Valentine, Mitchell & Co.

Akerlof, G. A. (1991). Procrastination and obedience. *American Economic Review, 81,* 1–19.

Allport, F. H. (1924). *Social psychology*. Boston: Houghton Mifflin.

Allport, G. W. (1935). Attitudes. In C. Murchison (Ed.), *A handbook of social psychology* (pp. 798–844). Worcester, MA: Clark University Press.

Allport, G. W. (1954). *The nature of prejudice*. Reading, MA: Addison-Wesley.

Allport, G. W., & Boring, E. G. (1946). Psychology and social relations at Harvard University. *American Psychologist, 1,* 119–122.

Allport, G. W., & Ross, J. M. (1967). Personal religious orientation and prejudice. *Journal of Personality and Social Psychology, 5,* 432–443.

Ancona, L., & Pareyson, R. (1968). Contributo allo studio della aggressione: La dinamica della obbedienza distruttiva [Contribution to the study of aggression: The dynamics of destructive obedience]. *Archivio di Psicologia, Neurologia, e Psichiatria, 29,* 340–372.

Arendt, H. (1963). *Eichmann in Jerusalem: A report on the banality of evil*. New York: Viking.

Arendt, H. (1966). Introduction to Naumann, B., *Auschwitz*. New York: Praeger.

Aronson, E., & Carlsmith, J. M. (1968). Experimentation in social psychology. In G. Lindzey & E. Aronson (Eds.), *The handbook of social psychology, Vol. 2* (2nd ed., pp. 1–79). Reading, MA: Addison-Wesley.

Asch, S. E. (1956). Studies of independence and conformity: I. A minority of one against a unanimous majority. *Psychological Monographs: General and Applied, 70* (9), 1–70.

Asch, S. E. (1958). Effects of group pressure on the modification and distortion of judgments. In E. E. Maccoby, T. M. Newcomb, & E. L. Hartley (Eds.). *Readings in social psychology* (3rd ed., pp. 174–182). New York: Holt, Rinehart and Winston.

Askenasy, H. (1978). *Are we all Nazis?* Secaucus, NJ: Lyle Stuart.

Baldwin, N. (2001). *Henry Ford and the Jews: The mass production of hate*. New York: Public Affairs.

Barabasi, A-. L. (2002). *Linked*. Cambridge, MA: Perseus.

Bauer, Y. (1982). *A history of the Holocaust.* New York: Franklin Watts.

Bauman, Z. (1989). *Modernity and the Holocaust.* Ithaca, NY: Cornell University Press.

Baumrind, D. (1964). Some thoughts on ethics of research: After reading Milgram's "Behavioral study of obedience." *American Psychologist, 19,* 421–423.

Berger, L. (1983). A psychological perspective on the Holocaust: Is mass murder part of human behavior? In R. L. Braham (Ed.), *Perspectives on the Holocaust* (pp. 19–32). Boston: Kluwer-Nijhoff.

Berkun, M. M., Bialek, H. M., Kern, R. P., & Yagi, K. (1962). Experimental studies of psychological stress in man. *Psychological Monographs: General and Applied, 76* (15, Whole No. 534).

Birnbaum, M. (with Rosenblum, Y.) (1993). *Lieutenant Birnbaum: A soldier's story.* Brooklyn, NY: Mesorah Publications.

Blake, R. R., & Brehm, J. W. (1954). The use of tape recordings to simulate a group atmosphere. *Journal of Abnormal and Social Psychology, 49,* 311–313.

Blass, T. (1980, January 9). Conspiracy theories: Why they are so popular. *The Baltimore Sun* (Opinion-Commentary Page).

Blass, T. (1984). Social psychology and personality: Toward a convergence. *Journal of Personality and Social Psychology, 47,* 1013–1027.

Blass, T. (1992). The social psychology of Stanley Milgram. In M. P. Zanna (Ed.), *Advances in experimental social psychology* (Vol. 25, pp. 227–329). San Diego, CA: Academic Press.

Blass, T. (1999). The Milgram paradigm after 35 years: Some things we now know about obedience to authority. *Journal of Applied Social Psychology, 29,* 955–978.

Bock, D. C. (1972). *Obedience: A response to authority and Christian commitment.* Doctoral dissertation, Fuller Theological Seminary Graduate School of Psychology.

Brick, H. (1999). Talcott Parsons. *American National Biography,* Vol. 17. New York: Oxford University Press.

Browning, C. (1992). *Ordinary men: Reserve Police Battalion 101 and the Final Solution in Poland.* New York: Harper/Collins.

Bunting, B. (1985). *Harvard: An architectural history.* Cambridge, MA: Belknap Press.

Buss, A. H. (1961). *The psychology of aggression.* New York: Wiley.

Campbell, D., Sanderson R. E., & Laverty, S. G. (1964). Characteristics of a conditioned response in human subjects during extinction trials following a single traumatic conditional trial. *Journal of Abnormal and Social Psychology, 68,* 627–639.

Cartwright, D. (1948). Social psychology in the United States during the Second World War. *Human Relations, 1,* 333–352.

Ceraso, J., Gruber, H., & Rock, I. (1990). On Solomon Asch. In I. Rock (Ed.), *The legacy of Solomon Asch: Essays in cognitive and social psychology* (pp. 3–22). Hillsdale, NJ: Erlbaum.

Clothier, S. (2002). *Bones would rain from the sky.* New York: Warner Books.

Colman, A. M. (1991). Crowd psychology in South African murder trials. *American Psychologist, 46,* 1071–1079.

Comstock, G. A. (1974). Review of "Television and anti-social behavior: Field experiments," *Journal of Communication, 34,* 155–158.

Costanzo, E. M. (1976). *The effect of probable retaliation and sex related variables on obedience.* Doctoral dissertation, University of Wyoming (UM 77-3253).

Damico, A. J. (1982). The sociology of justice: Kohlberg and Milgram. *Political Theory, 10,* 409–434.

Dashiell, J. F. (1935). Experimental studies of the influence of social situations on the behavior of individual human adults. In C. Murchison (Ed.), *A handbook of social psychology* (pp. 1097–1158). Worcester, MA: Clark University Press.

DeGrandpré, R. J., & Buskist, W. (2000). Behaviorism and neobehaviorism. In A. E. Kazdin (Ed.), *Encyclopedia of Psychology* (Vol. 1, pp. 388–393). Washington, DC: American Psychological Association.

Dodds, P. S., Muhamad, R., & Watts, D. J. (2003, August 8). An experimental study of search in global social networks. *Science, 301,* 827–829.

Edwards, D. M., Franks, P., Friedgood, D., Lobban, G., & Mackay, H.C.G. (1969). *An experiment on obedience.* Unpublished student report, University of the Witwatersrand, Johannesburg, South Africa.

Elms, A. C. (1972). *Social psychology and social relevance.* Boston: Little, Brown and Company.

Elms, A. C. (1975). The crisis of confidence in social psychology. *American Psychologist, 30,* 967–976.

Elms, A. C. (1995). Obedience in retrospect. *Journal of Social Issues, 51* (No. 3), 21–31.

Errera, P. (1972). Statement based on interviews with forty "worst cases" in the Milgram obedience experiments. In J. Katz (Ed.), *Experimentation with human beings* (p. 400). New York: Russell Sage.

Evans, R. I. (1980). *The making of social psychology: Discussions with creative contributors.* New York: Gardner Press.

Ferrell, O. C., & Gardiner, G. (1991). *In pursuit of ethics: Tough choices in the world of work.* Springfield, IL: Smith Collins.

Festinger, L. (1957). *A theory of cognitive dissonance.* Evanston, IL: Row-Peterson.

Geuter, U. (1987). German psychology during the Nazi period. In M. G. Ash & W. R. Woodward (Eds.), *Psychology in twentieth-century thought and society* (pp. 165–188). Cambridge, England: Cambridge University Press.

Gilbert, M. (1985). *The Holocaust: A history of the Jews of Europe during the Second World War.* New York: Holt, Rinehart and Winston.

Gladwell, M. (2000). *The tipping point: How little things can make big differences.* Boston: Little, Brown and Company.

Goldhagen, D. (1996). *Hitler's willing executioners: Ordinary Germans and the Holocaust.* New York: Knopf.

Green, M. J., Mitchell, G., Stocking, C. B., Cassel, C. K., & Siegler, M. (1996). Do actions reported by the physicians in training conflict with consensus guidelines on ethics? *Archives of Internal Medicine, 156,* 298–304.

Grossman, D. (1995). *On killing: The psychological cost of learning to kill in war and society.* Boston: Little, Brown and Company.

Haggbloom, S. J. (2002). The 100 most eminent psychologists of the 20th century. *Review of General Psychology, 6,* 139–152.

Harris, B. (1988). Key words: A history of debriefing in social psychology. In J. G. Morawski (Ed.), *The rise of experimentation in American psychology* (pp. 188–212). New Haven: Yale University Press.

Hartwell, S. (1990). Moral development, ethical conduct, and clinical education. *New York Law School Law Review, Vol. 35.*

Hay, F. J. (1999). Clyde Kay Maben Kluckhohn. *American National Biography*, Vol. 12. New York: Oxford University Press.

Helm, C., & Morelli, M. (1979). Stanley Milgram and the obedience experiment: Authority, legitimacy, and human action. *Political Theory, 7*, 321–345.

Helm, C., & Morelli, M. (1985). Obedience to authority in a laboratory setting: Generalizability and context dependency. *Political Studies, 33*, 610–627.

Herzstein, R. E. (1980). *The Nazis.* Alexandria, VA: Time-Life Books.

Hilberg, R. (1980). The nature of the process. In J. E. Dimsdale (Ed.), *Survivors, victims, and perpetrators: Essays on the Nazi Holocaust.* Washington, DC: Hemisphere.

Hilberg, R. (1985). *The destruction of the European Jews* (Revised and definitive edition). New York: Holmes & Meier.

Hilgard, E. R. (1987). *Psychology in America: A historical survey.* San Diego: Harcourt, Brace, Jovanovich.

Holland, C. D. (1967). *Sources of variance in the experimental investigation of behavioral obedience.* Doctoral dissertation, University of Connecticut, Storrs. (University Microfilms No. 69-2146).

Jones, E. E. (1985a). History of social psychology. In G. A. Kimble & K. Schlesinger (Eds.), *Topics in the history of psychology* (Vol. 2, pp. 371–407). Washington, DC: American Psychological Association.

Jones, E. E. (1985b). Major developments in social psychology during the past five decades. In G. Lindzey & E. Aronson (Eds.), *The handbook of social psychology*, Vol. 1 (3rd ed., pp. 47–107). New York: Random House.

Kadushin, C. (1989). The small world method and other innovations in experimental social psychology. In M. Kochen (Ed.), *The small world* (pp. xxiii–xxvi). Norwood, NJ: Ablex.

Katz, F. E. (1993). *Ordinary people and extraordinary evil: A report on the beguilings of evil.* Albany: State University of New York Press.

Kelman, H. C., & Hamilton, V. L. (1989). *Crimes of obedience: Toward a social psychology of authority and responsibility.* New Haven: Yale University Press.

Kilham, W., & Mann, L. (1974). Level of destructive obedience as a function of transmitter and executant roles in the Milgram obedience paradigm. *Journal of Personality and Social Psychology, 29*, 696–702.

Kluckhohn, C., Murray, H. A., & Schneider, D. M. (Eds.) (1967). *Personality in nature, society and culture* (2nd edition). New York: Knopf.

Korte, C., & Milgram, S. (1970). Acquaintance networks between racial groups: Application of the small world method. *Journal of Personality and Social Psychology, 15*, 101–108.

Kressel, N. J. (2002). *Mass hate: The global rise of genocide and terror* (Revised and updated). Cambridge, MA: Westview Press.

Laurent, J. (1987). Milgram's shocking experiments: A case in the social construction of "science." *Indian Journal of History of Science, 22,* 247–272.

Lewin, K., Lippitt, R., & White, R. K. (1939). Patterns of aggressive behavior in experimentally created "social climates." *Journal of Social Psychology, 10,* 271–299.

Lundin, R. W. (1996). *Theories and systems of psychology* (5th ed.). Lexington, MA: D. C. Heath.

Mantell, D. M. (1971). The potential for violence in Germany. *Journal of Social Issues, 27*(4), 101–112.

Marrow, A. J. (1969). *The practical theorist: The life and work of Kurt Lewin.* New York: Basic Books.

Meyer, P. (1970, February). If Hitler asked you to electrocute a stranger, would you? Probably. *Esquire,* pp. 73, 128, 130, 132.

Milgram, A. (2000). My personal view of Stanley Milgram. In T. Blass (Ed.), *Obedience to authority: Current perspectives on the Milgram paradigm* (pp. 1–7). Mahwah, NJ: Erlbaum.

Milgram, S. (1960). *Conformity in Norway and France: An experimental study of national characteristics.* Doctoral dissertation, Harvard University, Cambridge, MA.

Milgram, S. (1961, December). Nationality and conformity. *Scientific American,* pp. 45–51.

Milgram, S. (1963). Behavioral study of obedience. *Journal of Abnormal and Social Psychology, 67,* 371–378.

Milgram, S. (1964a). Group pressure and action against a person. *Journal of Abnormal and Social Psychology, 69,* 137–143.

Milgram, S. (1964b). Issues in the study of obedience: A reply to Baumrind. *American Psychologist, 19,* 848–852.

Milgram, S. (1964c). Technique and first findings of a laboratory study of obedience to authority. *Yale Science Magazine, 39,* 9–11, 14.

Milgram, S. (1965a). Liberating effects of group pressure. *Journal of Personality and Social Psychology, 1,* 127–134.

Milgram, S. (1965b). Some conditions of obedience and disobedience to authority. *Human Relations, 18,* 57–76.

Milgram, S. (1967a). Obedience to criminal orders: The compulsion to do evil. *Patterns of Prejudice, 1,* 3–7.

Milgram, S. (1967b, May). The small-world problem. *Psychology Today, 1,* 60–67.

Milgram, S. (1969, June). The lost-letter technique. *Psychology Today,* pp. 30–33, 66, 68.

Milgram, S. (1970a). The experience of living in cities. *Science, 167,* 1461–1468.

Milgram, S. (1970b). The experience of living in cities: A psychological analysis. In F. F. Korten, S. W. Cook, & J. I. Lacey (Eds.), *Psychology and the problem of society.* Washington, DC: American Psychological Association.

Milgram, S. (1972). Interpreting obedience: Error and evidence (A reply to Orne and Holland). In A. G. Miller (Ed.), *The social psychology of psychological research* (pp. 138–154). New York: Free Press.

Milgram, S. (1973a, December). The perils of obedience. *Harper's,* pp. 62–66, 75–77.

Milgram, S. (1973b). Responses I and II. In D. Abse, *The Dogs of Pavlov* (pp. 37–44, 125–127). London: Valentine, Mitchell & Co.

Milgram, S. (1974). *Obedience to authority: An experimental view.* New York: Harper & Row.

Milgram, S. (1976, August 21). Obedience to authority: A CBS drama deals with the shocking results of a social psychologist's experiments. *TV Guide*, pp. 24–25.

Milgram, S. (1977a). The familiar stranger: An aspect of urban anonymity. In S. Milgram, *The individual in a social world: Essays and experiments* (pp. 51–53). Reading, MA: Addison-Wesley.

Milgram, S. (1977b). The image-freezing machine. In S. Milgram, *The individual in a social world: Essays and experiments* (pp. 339–350). Reading, MA: Addison-Wesley.

Milgram, S. (1977c). *The individual in a social world: Essays and experiments.* Reading, MA: Addison-Wesley.

Milgram, S. (1977d). Subject reaction: The neglected factor in the ethics of experimentation. *Hastings Center Report, 7*, 19–23.

Milgram, S. (1978). A work of great potential influence [Review of Moscovici's book *Social influence and social change*]. *Contemporary Psychology, 23*, 125–130.

Milgram, S. (1983). Reflections on Morelli's "Dilemma of obedience." *Metaphilosophy, 14*, 190–194.

Milgram, S. (1984a, August 26). Cyranoids. Talk delivered at the annual convention of the American Psychological Association, Toronto, Canada.

Milgram, S. (1984b, Spring/Summer). The vertical city. *CUNY Graduate School Magazine, 3*(1), 9–13.

Milgram, S. (1992). *The individual in a social world: Essays and experiments* (2nd ed.). Edited by J. Sabini & M. Silver. New York: McGraw-Hill.

Milgram, S., Bickman, L., & Berkowitz, L. (1969). Note on the drawing power of crowds of different size. *Journal of Personality and Social Psychology, 13*, 79–82.

Milgram, S., & From, H. (1978). Human aggression: A film. *Centerpoint: A journal of interdisciplinary studies, 2*, 1–13.

Milgram, S., Greenwald, J., Kessler, S., McKenna, W., & Waters, J. (1972, March-April). A psychological map of New York City. *American Scientist*, pp. 194–200.

Milgram, S., & Hollander, P. (1964, June 15). The murder they heard. *Nation*, pp. 602–604.

Milgram, S., & Jodelet, D. (1976). Psychological maps of Paris. In H. M. Proshansky, W. H. Ittelson, & L. G. Rivlin (Eds.), *Environmental psychology: People and their physical settings* (2nd ed., pp. 104–124). New York: Holt, Rinehart, and Winston.

Milgram, S., Liberty, H. J., Toledo, R., & Wackenhut, J. (1986). Response to intrusion into waiting lines. *Journal of Personality and Social Psychology, 51*, 683–689.

Milgram, S., Mann, L., & Harter, S. (1965). The lost-letter technique: A tool of social research. *Public Opinion Quarterly, 29*, 437–438.

Milgram, S., & Sabini, J. (1978). On maintaining urban norms: A field experiment in the subway. In A. Baum, J. E. Singer, & S. Valins (Eds.), *Advances in environmental psychology*, Vol. 1, pp. 31–40). Hillsdale, NJ: Erlbaum.

Milgram, S., & Sabini, J. (1979). Candid Camera. *Society, 16,* 72–75.

Milgram, S., & Shotland, R. L. (1973). *Television and antisocial behavior: Field experiments.* New York: Academic Press.

Milgram, S., & Toch, H. (1969). Collective behavior: Crowds and social movements. In G. Lindzey & E. Aronson (Eds.), *The handbook of social psychology* (2nd ed., Vol. 4, pp. 507–610). Reading, MA: Addison-Wesley.

Miller, A. G. (1986). *The obedience experiments: A case study of controversy in social science.* New York: Praeger.

Miranda, F. S. B., Caballero, R. B., Gomez, M. N. G., & Zamorano, M. A. M. (1981). Obediencia a la autoridad [Obedience to authority]. *Psiquis, 2,* 212–221.

Mischel, W. (1968). *Personality and assessment.* New York: Wiley.

Modig, M. (2003). *Den nödvändiga olydnaden.* Stockholm: Natur och Kultur.

Modigliani, A., & Rochat, F. (1995). The role of interaction sequences and the timing of resistance in shaping obedience and defiance to authority. *Journal of Social Issues, 51*(3), 107–123.

Morelli, M. (1983). Milgram's dilemma of obedience. *Metaphilosophy, 14,* 183–189.

Naumann, B. (1966). *Auschwitz.* New York: Praeger.

Orne, M. T., & Holland, C. H. (1968). On the ecological validity of laboratory deceptions. *International Journal of Psychiatry, 6,* 282–293.

Parsons, T. (1956). *The Department of Social Relations at Harvard—Report of the chairman on the first decade: 1946–1956.* Cambridge, MA: Harvard University.

Patten, S. C. (1977). Milgram's shocking experiments. *Philosophy, 52,* 425–440.

The people's college on the hill. (1987). Flushing, NY: Queens College Office of Publications.

Pettigrew, T. F. (1999). Gordon Willard Allport: A tribute. *Journal of Social Issues, 55,* 415–427.

Podd, M. H. (1969). *The relationship between ego identity status and two measures of morality.* Doctoral dissertation, State University of New York at Buffalo.

Powers, P. C., & Geen, R. G. (1972). Effects of the behavior and the perceived arousal of a model on instrumental aggression. *Journal of Personality and Social Psychology, 23,* 175–183.

Presley, S. L. (1982). *Values and attitudes of political resisters to authority.* Doctoral dissertation, City University of New York (University Microfilms International No. 8212211).

Rand, C. (1964). *Cambridge, U.S.A.: Hub of a new world.* New York: Oxford University Press.

Reeves, R. (1987, July 13). France's courage. *The Sun* (Baltimore), p. A9.

Ring, K., Wallston, K., & Corey, M. (1970). Mode of debriefing as a factor affecting subjective reactions to a Milgram-type obedience experiment: An ethical inquiry. *Representative Research in Social Psychology, 1,* 67–85.

Robinson, J. (1965). *And the crooked shall be made straight: The Eichmann trial, the Jewish catastrophe, and Hannah Arendt's narrative.* New York: Macmillan.

Rogers, E. M., & Kincaid, D. L. (1981). *Communication networks: Toward a new paradigm for research.* New York: Free Press.

Rogers, R. W. (1973). *Obedience to authority: Presence of authority and command strength*. Paper presented at the annual convention of the Southeastern Psychological Association (Abstract).

Rosenhan, D. (1969). Some origins of concern for others. In P. Mussen, J. Langer, & M. Covington (Eds.), *Trends and issues in developmental psychology* (pp. 134–153). New York: Holt, Rinehart, and Winston.

Ross, L. D. (1988). Situationist perspectives on the obedience experiments [Review of *The obedience experiments: A case study of controversy in social science*]. *Contemporary Psychology, 33*, 101–104.

Sabini, J. P. (1976). *Moral reproach: A conceptual and experimental analysis*. Doctoral dissertation. City University of New York.

Sabini, J. (1986). Obituary: Stanley Milgram (1933–1984). *American Psychologist, 41*, 1378–1379.

Saltzman, A. L. (2000). The role of the obedience experiments in Holocaust studies: The case for renewed visibility. In T. Blass (Ed.), *Obedience to authority: Current perspectives on the Milgram paradigm* (pp. 125–143). Mahwah, NJ: Erlbaum.

Schurz, G. (1985). Experimentelle Überprufüng des Zusammenhangs zwischen Persönlichkeitsmerkmalen und der Bereitschaft zum destruktiven Gehorsam gegenüber Autoritäten [Experimental examination of the relationships between personality characteristics and the readiness for destructive obedience toward authority]. *Zeitschrift für experimentelle und angewandte Psychologie, 32*, 160–177.

Shalala, S. R. (1974). *A study of various communication settings which produce obedience by subordinates to unlawful superior orders*. Doctoral dissertation, University of Kansas, Lawrence (UM #75-17,675).

Shanab, M. E., & Yahya, K. A. (1977). A behavioral study of obedience in children. *Journal of Personality and Social Psychology, 35*, 530–536.

Shanab, M. E., & Yahya, K. A. (1978). A cross-cultural study of obedience. *Bulletin of the Psychonomic Society, 11*, 267–269.

Shenk, D. (1997). *Data smog: Surviving the information glut*. San Francisco: Harper-Collins.

Sullivan, W. (1963, October 26). 65% in test blindly obey order to inflict pain. *The New York Times*, p. 10.

Takooshian, H. (1972, March 28). An observational study of norms in the New York City subway. Paper written for Milgram's Experimental Social Psychology class.

Takooshian, H. (2000). How Stanley Milgram taught about obedience and social influence. In T. Blass (Ed.), *Obedience to authority: Current perspectives on the Milgram paradigm* (pp. 9–24). Mahwah, NJ: Erlbaum.

Tavris, C. (1974a, June). The frozen world of the familiar stranger. *Psychology Today*, pp. 71–73, 76–80.

Tavris, C. (1974b, June). A sketch of Stanley Milgram: A man of 1,000 ideas. *Psychology Today*, pp. 74–75.

Travers, J., & Milgram, S. (1969). An experimental study of the small world problem. *Sociometry, 32*, 425–443.

Triplet, R. G. (1992). Harvard psychology, the Psychological Clinic, and Henry A. Murray: A case study in the establishment of disciplinary boundaries. In C. A. Elliott & M. W. Rossiter (Eds.), *Science at Harvard University: Historical perspectives* (pp. 223–250). Bethlehem: Lehigh University Press.

Triplett, N. (1897). The dynamogenic factors in pacemaking and expectation. *American Journal of Psychology, 9,* 507–533.

Vidich, R. J. (2000). The Department of Social Relations and systems theory at Harvard: 1948–50. *International Journal of Politics, Culture, and Society, 13,* 607–648.

Waters, J. (2000). Professor Stanley Milgram—Supervisor, mentor, friend. In T. Blass (Ed.), *Obedience to authority: Current perspectives on the Milgram paradigm.* Mahwah, NJ: Erlbaum.

Watson, J. B. (1913). Psychology as the behaviorist views it. *Psychological Review, 20,* 158–177.

Watts, D. J., & Strogatz, S. H. (1998). Collective dynamics of "small-world" networks. *Nature, 393,* 440–442.

Weisberg, R. H. (1996). *Vichy law and the Holocaust in France.* New York: New York University Press.

Wheeler, L. (1970). *Interpersonal influence.* Boston: Allyn & Bacon.

Wiesenthal, S. (1989). *Justice not vengeance.* New York: Grove Weidenfeld.

Wirth, L. (1938). Urbanism as a way of life. *American Journal of Sociology, 44,* 1–24.

Zimbardo, P. G., Maslach, C., & Haney, C. (2000). Reflections on the Stanford Prison experiment: Genesis, transformations, consequences. In T. Blass (Ed.), *Obedience to authority: Current perspectives on the Milgram paradigm* (pp. 193–237). Mahwah, NJ: Erlbaum.

CREDITS

INDEX